ROS Robotics By Example
Second Edition

Learning to control wheeled, limbed, and flying robots using ROS Kinetic Kame

Carol Fairchild

Dr. Thomas L. Harman

BIRMINGHAM - MUMBAI

ROS Robotics By Example
Second Edition

First published: June 2016

Second edition: November 2017

Production reference: 1301117

Published by Packt Publishing Ltd.
Livery Place
35 Livery Street
Birmingham B3 2PB, UK.

ISBN 978-1-78847-959-2

www.packtpub.com

Credits

Authors
Carol Fairchild
Dr. Thomas L. Harman

Reviewer
Lentin Joseph

Acquisition Editor
Frank Pohlmann

Project Editor
Alish Firasta

Content Development Editor
Venugopal Commuri

Technical Editor
Bhagyashree Rai

Copy Editor
Safis Editing

Proofreader
Safis Editing

Indexer
Aishwarya Gangawane

Graphics
Kirk D'Penha

Production Coordinator
Nilesh Mohite

About the Authors

Carol Fairchild is the owner and principal engineer of Fairchild Robotics, a robotics development and integration company. She is a researcher at Baxter's Lab at the University of Houston–Clear Lake (UHCL) and a member of the adjunct faculty. Her research involves the use of Baxter for expanded applications. Ms. Fairchild has been involved in many aspects of robotics from her earliest days of building her first robot, a Heathkit Hero. She has an MS in computer engineering from UHCL and a BS in engineering technology from Texas A&M. Ms. Fairchild has taught middle-school robotics, coached FLL, and volunteered for FIRST Robotics in Houston.

Dr. Thomas L. Harman is the chair of the engineering division at UHCL. His research interests are control systems and applications of robotics and microprocessors. Several of his research papers with colleagues involve robotic and laser applications in medicine. In 2005, he was selected as the UHCL Distinguished Professor. He has been a judge and safety advisor for the FIRST robotic contests in Houston. Dr. Harman has authored or coauthored 18 books on subjects including microprocessors, MATLAB and Simulink applications, and the National Electrical Code. His laboratory at UHCL has a Baxter two-armed robot and several TurtleBots as well as other robots.

About the Reviewer

Lentin Joseph is an author, entrepreneur, electronics engineer, robotics enthusiast, machine vision expert, embedded programmer, and the founder and CEO of Qbotics Labs from India.

Lentin completed his bachelor's degree in electronics and communication engineering at the Federal Institute of Science and Technology (FISAT), Kerala. For his final year engineering project, he made a social robot that can interact with people. The project was a huge success and was mentioned in many forms of visual and print media. The main features of this robot were that it could communicate with people and reply intelligently, and it had some image processing capabilities such as face, motion, and color detection. The entire project was implemented using the Python programming language. His interest in robotics, image processing, and Python started with that project.

After his graduation, Lentin worked for 3 years at a start-up company focusing on robotics and image processing. In the meantime, he learned to work with famous robotics software platforms, such as Robot Operating System (ROS), V-REP, and Actin (a robotic simulation tool), and image processing libraries such as OpenCV, OpenNI, and PCL. He also knows about 3D robot design and embedded programming on Arduino and Tiva Launchpad.

After 3 years of work experience, Lentin started a new company called Qbotics Labs, which mainly focuses on research into building some great products in domains such as robotics and machine vision. He maintains a personal website and a technology blog called TechnoLabsz. Lentin publishes his works on his tech blog. He was also a speaker at PyCon2013, India, on the topic *Learning Robotics Using Python*.

Lentin is the author of the books *Learning Robotics Using Python* (`learn-robotics.com`), *Mastering ROS for Robotics Programming* (`mastering-ros.com`), and *ROS Robotics Project* (`http://rosrobots.com`)—all books were published by Packt Publishing. The first book was about building an autonomous mobile robot using ROS and OpenCV. This book was launched at ICRA 2015 and was featured on the ROS blog, Robohub, OpenCV, the Python website, and various other such forums. The second book is on mastering Robot Operating System, which was also launched at ICRA 2016, and is one of the bestselling books on ROS. The third book is ROS Robotics Project, which was launched in ICRA 2017 and it is also one of the bestselling books on ROS. Along with writing, he reviewed books such as Effective Robotics Programming using ROS, Raspberry Pi Image Processing Programming, and Raspberry Pi Supercomputing and Scientific Programming. He started a new platform called Robocademy.com exclusively for learning robotics using ROS.

Lentin and his team were also winners of the HRATC 2016 challenge conducted as a part of ICRA 2016. He was also a finalist in the ICRA 2015 challenge, HRATC.

www.PacktPub.com

eBooks, discount offers, and more

Did you know that Packt offers eBook versions of every book published, with PDF and ePub files available? You can upgrade to the eBook version at www.PacktPub.com and as a print book customer, you are entitled to a discount on the eBook copy. Get in touch with us at customercare@packtpub.com for more details.

At www.PacktPub.com, you can also read a collection of free technical articles, sign up for a range of free newsletters and receive exclusive discounts and offers on Packt books and eBooks.

https://www.packtpub.com/mapt

Get the most in-demand software skills with Mapt. Mapt gives you full access to all Packt books and video courses, as well as industry-leading tools to help you plan your personal development and advance your career.

Why subscribe?

- Fully searchable across every book published by Packt
- Copy and paste, print, and bookmark content
- On demand and accessible via a web browser

Customer Feedback

Thanks for purchasing this Packt book. At Packt, quality is at the heart of our editorial process. To help us improve, please leave us an honest review on this book's Amazon page at https://www.amazon.com/dp/1788479599.

If you'd like to join our team of regular reviewers, you can email us at customerreviews@packtpub.com. We award our regular reviewers with free eBooks and videos in exchange for their valuable feedback. Help us be relentless in improving our products!

Table of Contents

Preface

Being excited about learning ROS and working with ROS robots such as Baxter and TurtleBot is the beginning of a big adventure. The features and benefits of ROS are substantial, but the learning curve is steep. Through trial and error, we have foraged a path through many of the ROS applications trying everything. In this book, we hope to present to you the best of our knowledge of ROS and provide you with detailed step-by-step instructions for your journey. Our approach centers on using the ROS robots that are featured, namely TurtleBot, Baxter, Crazyflie, and Bebop, as well as simulated robots—Turtlesim and Hector.

This book provides introductory information as well as advanced applications featuring these ROS robots. The chapters begin with the basics of setting up your computer and loading ROS and the packages for ROS robots and tools. Straightforward instructions are provided with troubleshooting steps for when the desired results are not achieved. The building blocks of ROS are described first in the simulation Turtlesim, then on each of the featured robots. Starting with basic ROS commands, the ROS packages, nodes, topics, and messages are explored to gain an overall knowledge of these ROS robotic systems. Technical information on these example robots is provided to describe the robot's full capabilities.

ROS encompasses a full spectrum of software concepts, implementation, and tools that attempt to provide a homogeneous view of the complex systems and software integration required in robotics. Extensive libraries of sensor and actuator drivers and interfaces are already in place, as well as the latest and most efficient algorithms. What ROS doesn't provide directly is imported from other prevailing open source projects such as OpenCV. ROS also possesses a spectrum of time-saving tools to control, monitor, and debug robot applications: rqt, rviz, Gazebo, dynamic reconfigure, and MoveIt, to name a few.

In the pages that follow, each of these areas will be incrementally introduced to the reader as part of the robot examples. With TurtleBot, the subjects of navigation and mapping are explored. Using Baxter, joint control and path planning are described for your understanding. Simple Python scripts are included to provide examples of implementing ROS elements for many of these robots. These robots are all available in simulation to accomplish the exercises in this book. Furthermore, instructions are provided for you to build and control your own robot models in simulation.

The power of ROS, the variety of robots using ROS, and the diversity and support of the widespread ROS community make this adventure worthwhile. Extensive online tutorials, wiki instructions, forums, and tips and tricks are available for ROS. So dive into the pages of this book to begin your adventure with ROS robotics!

What this book covers

Chapter 1, Getting Started with ROS, explains to you the advantages of learning ROS and highlights the spectrum of robots currently using ROS. Instructions for installing and launching ROS on a computer running an Ubuntu operating system are provided. An overview of the ROS architecture is given and its components are described. The Turtlesim simulation is introduced, and used to provide a deeper understanding of how the components of ROS work and a familiarity with ROS commands.

Chapter 2, Creating Your First Two-Wheeled ROS Robot (in Simulation), introduces you to the ROS simulation environment of Gazebo. We will lead you through the steps to create your first robot simulation (a two-wheeled differential-drive base) and teach the structure of the Universal Robotic Description Format. The use of the ROS tool rviz and Gazebo are detailed to enable you to display your robot and interact with it.

Chapter 3, Driving Around with TurtleBot, introduces you to real ROS robots, TurtleBot2 and the recently available TurtleBot 3. These mobile base robots can be used in the simulation environment of Gazebo if you do not own one. ROS commands and Python scripts are used to control TurtleBot through a variety of methods. The ROS tool rqt is introduced, and subsets of its plugins are used to control TurtleBot and monitor its sensor data.

Chapter 4, Navigating the World with TurtleBot, explores visual sensors and the ability for a robot to map its environment. The 3D sensor options for TurtleBot's vision system are described and their setup and operation using ROS enables TurtleBot to navigate autonomously. The knowledge of the Simultaneous Localization and Mapping techniques is applied in combination with TurtleBot's navigation stack to move about in the mapped environment.

Chapter 5, Creating Your First Robot Arm (in Simulation), provides a gentle introduction into the complexity of robotic arms. A simulated robot arm is designed and built using the macro language of Xacro. Controllers for the arm are created to operate the arm in Gazebo. Through developing the controllers for this arm, an insight into the mechanics and physics of a simple robot arm is offered.

Chapter 6, Wobbling Robot Arms Using Joint Control, takes a deeper look at the intricacies of controlling robotic arms. Baxter has two 7 degree-of-freedom arms and a number of other sensors. Baxter Simulator is available as open source software to use for the instructions in this chapter. Examples are provided for control of Baxter's arms using position, velocity, and torque modes with control for both forward and inverse kinematics. The ROS tool MoveIt is introduced for motion planning in simulation and execution on either a real or simulated Baxter.

Chapter 7, Making a Robot Fly, describes a growing area of ROS robotics — unmanned air vehicles. This chapter focuses on quadrotors, and an understanding of quadrotor hardware and flight control is provided. Instructions for downloading and controlling the simulated quadrotor Hector are supplied. With skills from flying a simulated quadrotor, you can move on to control a real Bitcraze Crazyflie or Parrot Bebop. Quadrotor control is via teleoperation or ROS topic/message commands.

Chapter 8, Controlling Your Robots with External Devices, presents a number of peripheral devices you can use for controlling a ROS robot. Joystick controllers, controller boards (Arduino and Raspberry Pi), and mobile devices have ROS interfaces that can be integrated with your robot to provide external control.

Chapter 9, Flying a Mission with Crazyflie, incorporates many of the ROS components and concepts presented in this book into a challenging mission of autonomous flight. The mission involves the Crazyflie quadrotor flying to a "remote" target all mapped through a Kinect 3D sensor. This mission uses ROS message communication and co-ordinate transforms to employ the Kinect's view of the quadrotor and target to orchestrate the flight. Flight control software for Crazyflie using PID control is described and provided as part of the mission software.

Chapter 10, Controlling Baxter with MATLAB©, delves into a new realm of communicating with and controlling ROS robots through MATLAB and its Robotics System Toolbox. Baxter, the two-armed robot introduced in *Chapter 6, Wobbling Robot Arms Using Joint Control*, will be used to show how to set up a ROS robot in MATLAB by adding custom messages into the Robotics System Toolbox. Communication and control of Baxter and his arms will be accomplished using MATLAB scripts and ROS commands.

What you need for this book

The format of this book is intended for the reader to follow along and perform the instructions as the information is provided. The reader will need a computer ideally with Ubuntu 16.04 (Xenial Xerus) installed. Other Ubuntu versions and Linux distributions may work, as well as macOS, Android, and Windows, but documentation for those versions will need to reference the ROS wiki (`http://wiki.ros.org/kinetic/Installation`).

The version of ROS that this book was written around is Kinetic Kame, which is the current release recommended for stability. Its end of life is targeted for April 2021.

All software used in this book is open source and freely available for download and use. Instructions for downloading the software are found in the chapter where the software is introduced. In *Chapter 1, Getting Started with ROS,* instructions are given for downloading and setting up the ROS software environment.

Our preferred method to download software is the use of Debian packages. Where no Debian packages exist, we refer to downloading the software from repositories such as GitHub.

Gazebo simulation performs intensive graphics processing, and the use of a dedicated graphics card is advised but not required.

Peripheral devices, such as 3D sensors, Xbox or PS3 controllers, Arduino or Raspberry Pi controller boards, and Android mobile devices are optional equipment.

Who this book is for

If you are a robotics developer, whether a hobbyist, researcher, or professional, and are interested in learning about ROS through a hands-on approach, then this book is for you. You are encouraged to have a working knowledge of GNU/Linux systems and Python.

Conventions

In this book, you will find a number of text styles that distinguish between different kinds of information. Here are some examples of these styles and an explanation of their meaning.

Code words in text, directory names, filenames, file extensions, and pathnames are shown as follows: "The Terminal commands `rostopic` and `rosnode` have a number of options…"

A block of code is set as follows:

```
<?xml version='1.0'?>
<robot name="dd_robot">
  <!-- Base Link -->
  <link name="base_link">
    <visual>
      <origin xyz="0 0 0" rpy="0 0 0" />
      <geometry>
          <box size="0.5 0.5 0.25"/>
      </geometry>
    </visual>
  </link>
</robot>
```

To avoid repeating previous code blocks, but provide with placement of new code blocks, previous code left for reference is abbreviated and grayed-out as follows:

```
<?xml version='1.0'?>
<robot name="dd_robot">
  <!-- Base Link -->
  <link name="base_link">
  …
  </link>

  <!-- Right Wheel -->
  <link name="right_wheel">
```

Any command-line input is written as follows:

```
$ rosrun rqt_reconfigure rqt_reconfigure
```

Output from command is written as:

[INFO] [1427212356.117628994]: Starting turtlesim with node name /turtlesim

New terms and **key words** are shown in bold.

Words that you see on the screen, for example, in menus or dialog boxes, appear in the text like this: "By clicking on the **Add** button on the **Displays** panel…"

URL references are shown as: http://www.ros.org/about-ros/

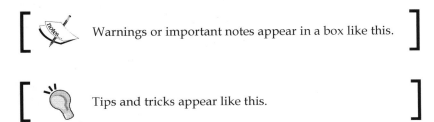

[Warnings or important notes appear in a box like this.]

[Tips and tricks appear like this.]

Reader feedback

Feedback from our readers is always welcome. Let us know what you think about this book—what you liked or disliked. Reader feedback is important for us as it helps us develop titles that you will really find useful and enjoyable.

To send us general feedback, simply email feedback@packtpub.com, and mention the book's title in the subject of your message.

If there is a topic that you have expertise in and you are interested in either writing or contributing to a book, see our author guide at www.packtpub.com/authors.

Customer support

Now that you are the proud owner of a Packt book, we have a number of things to help you to get the most from your purchase.

Downloading the example code

You can download the example code files for this book from your account at http://www.packtpub.com. If you purchased this book elsewhere, you can visit http://www.packtpub.com/support and register to have the files emailed directly to you.

You can download the code files by following these steps:

1. Log in or register to our website using your e-mail address and password.
2. Hover the mouse pointer on the **SUPPORT** tab at the top.
3. Click on **Code Downloads & Errata**.
4. Enter the name of the book in the **Search** box.

5. Select the book for which you're looking to download the code files.
6. Choose from the drop-down menu where you purchased this book from.
7. Click on **Code Download**.

Once the file is downloaded, please make sure that you unzip or extract the folder using the latest version of:

- WinRAR / 7-Zip for Windows
- Zipeg / iZip / UnRarX for Mac
- 7-Zip / PeaZip for Linux

The code bundle for the book is also hosted on GitHub at `https://github.com/ PacktPublishing/ROS-Robotics-By-Example-Second-Edition`. We also have other code bundles from our rich catalog of books and videos available at `https://github.com/PacktPublishing/`. Check them out!

Downloading the color images of this book

We also provide you with a PDF file that has color images of the screenshots/ diagrams used in this book. The color images will help you better understand the changes in the output. You can download this file from `http://www.packtpub. com/sites/default/files/downloads/ROSRoboticsByExampleSecondEdition_ ColorImages.pdf`.

Errata

Although we have taken every care to ensure the accuracy of our content, mistakes do happen. If you find a mistake in one of our books—maybe a mistake in the text or the code—we would be grateful if you could report this to us. By doing so, you can save other readers from frustration and help us improve subsequent versions of this book. If you find any errata, please report them by visiting `http://www.packtpub. com/submit-errata`, selecting your book, clicking on the **Errata Submission Form** link, and entering the details of your errata. Once your errata are verified, your submission will be accepted and the errata will be uploaded to our website or added to any list of existing errata under the Errata section of that title.

To view the previously submitted errata, go to `https://www.packtpub.com/books/ content/support` and enter the name of the book in the search field. The required information will appear under the **Errata** section.

Piracy

Piracy of copyrighted material on the Internet is an ongoing problem across all media. At Packt, we take the protection of our copyright and licenses very seriously. If you come across any illegal copies of our works in any form on the Internet, please provide us with the location address or website name immediately so that we can pursue a remedy.

Please contact us at `copyright@packtpub.com` with a link to the suspected pirated material.

We appreciate your help in protecting our authors and our ability to bring you valuable content.

Questions

If you have a problem with any aspect of this book, you can contact us at `questions@packtpub.com`, and we will do our best to address the problem.

1
Getting Started with ROS

In this chapter, we will introduce the **Robot Operating System (ROS)**, which is a collection of software packages to aid researchers and developers using robotic systems. After we discuss the instructions to install ROS on your computer system using the Ubuntu operating system, the ROS architecture and many of its components are discussed. This will aid you in understanding the use of ROS to develop software for robotic applications.

ROS will be introduced in terms of its elements and their functions. An understanding of the ROS vocabulary is necessary to become proficient in using ROS to create programs for the control of real or simulated robots as well as devices, such as cameras.

To make the discussion more concrete, the **turtlesim simulator** will be presented with various examples of the ROS command usage. This simulator is part of ROS and it provides an excellent introduction to the capabilities of ROS.

In this chapter, we will cover the following topics:

- What ROS is and which robots use ROS
- How to install and launch ROS on your computer
- How to navigate the ROS directories
- An introduction to ROS packages, nodes, and topics
- Examples of useful ROS commands
- How to use ROS commands with the turtlesim simulator

What does ROS do and what are the benefits of learning ROS?

ROS is sometimes called a meta operating system because it performs many functions of an operating system, but it requires a computer's operating system such as Linux. One of its main purposes is to provide communication between the user, the computer's operating system, and equipment external to the computer. This equipment can include sensors, cameras, as well as robots. As with any operating system, the benefit of ROS is the hardware abstraction and its ability to control a robot without the user having to know all of the details of the robot.

For example, to move a robot's arms, a ROS command is issued or scripts in Python or C++ written by the robot designers cause the robot to respond as commanded. The scripts can, in turn, call various control programs that cause the actual motion of the robot's arms. It is also possible to design and simulate your own robot using ROS. These subjects and many others will be considered in this book.

In this book, you will learn a set of concepts, software, and tools that apply to an ever-increasing and diverse army of robots. For example, the navigation software of one mobile robot can be used, with a few changes, to work in another mobile robot. The flight navigation of an aerial robot is similar to that of the ground robot and so on. All across the broad spectrum of robotics, system interfaces are standardized or upgraded to support increased complexity. There are readily available libraries for commonly used robotics functions. ROS not only applies to the central processing of robotics but also to sensors and other subsystems. ROS hardware abstraction combined with low-level device control speeds the upgrade toward the latest technology.

ROS is an open source robotic software system that can be used without licensing fees by universities, government agencies, and commercial companies. The advantages of open source software are that the source code for the system is available and can be modified according to a user's needs. More importantly for some users, the software can be used in a commercial product as long as the appropriate licenses are cited. The software can be improved and modules can be added by users and companies.

ROS is used by many thousands of users worldwide and knowledge can be shared between users. The users range from hobbyists to professional developers of commercial robots. In addition to the large group of ROS researchers, there is a ROS-Industrial group dedicated to applying ROS software to robots for manufacturing. Other versions of ROS currently under development include:

- ROS-M for military robotic systems
- H-ROS is Hardware ROS for interoperable robot components
- ROS 2.0 to upgrade ROS with the latest technology and software

Who controls ROS?

A ROS distribution is a set of ROS software packages that can be downloaded to your computer. These packages are supported by the **Open Source Robotics Foundation (OSRF)**, a nonprofit organization. The distributions are updated periodically and given different names by the ROS organization. More details about the ROS organization are available at: http://www.ros.org/about-ros/

Which robots are using ROS?

There is a long list of robots on the ROS wiki website, http://wiki.ros.org/ Robots, which use ROS. For example, we are using four different robots in this book to provide you with an experience of a wide range of ROS capabilities. These robots are as follows:

- TurtleBot, a mobile robot
- Baxter, a friendly two-armed robot
- Crazyflie and Bebop, flying robots

The images of these robots are in the following figures:

TurtleBot 2 and 3

Of course, not everyone has the opportunity to use real robots such as Baxter (shown in the following image):

Baxter in the authors' laboratory

However, there is good news! Using the ROS Gazebo software, you can simulate Baxter as well as many other robots whose models are provided for Gazebo. We will simulate TurtleBot using Gazebo and actually design our own mobile robot in the upcoming chapters of this book.

Bebop and Crazyflie

Installing and launching ROS

For this book, we assume the reader has a computer with Ubuntu Wily 15.10 or Xenial 16.04 installed. The examples in this book have been developed using ROS Kinetic and this version of ROS is only supported by these two versions of Ubuntu. The instructions for ROS installation provided in this section are for installing Debian (binary) packages. This is the most efficient and preferred way to install ROS.

If you wish to install the ROS Kinetic source code and build the software, refer to the instructions at http://wiki.ros.org/kinetic/Installation/Source. The instructions presented here to install ROS Kinetic with Debian packages can also be found at http://wiki.ros.org/kinetic/Installation/Ubuntu.

If you have any problems while installing ROS, refer to this site and the ROS forum at http://answers.ros.org.

> This book is written using Ubuntu16.04 as the operating system and **ROS Kinetic Kame** as the version of the ROS distribution. Always make sure that you check for any updates for the Ubuntu or ROS versions you are using.

Configuring your Ubuntu repositories

To configure your Ubuntu repositories to allow restricted, universe and multiverse, perform the following steps:

1. Click on the Ubuntu **System Settings** icon in the menu on the left side of your desktop.

2. Click on the **Software & Updates** icon. On the **Software & Updates** screen, select the appropriate checkboxes to match the following screenshot:

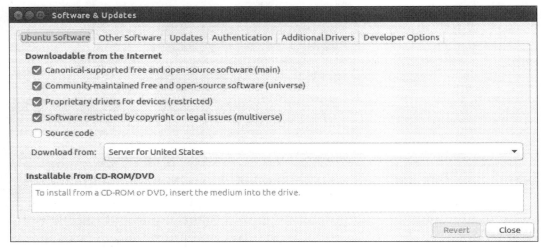

Ubuntu Software & Updates screen

Setting up your sources.list file

Open a terminal window to set up the `sources.list` file on your computer to accept software from the ROS software repository at `http://packages.ros.org` which is the authorized site for the ROS software.

At the $ command prompt, type the following command as one long command:

```
$ sudo sh -c 'echo "deb http://packages.ros.org/ros/ubuntu
$(lsb_release -sc) main" > /etc/apt/sources.list.d/ros-latest.list'
```

 In copying such two line commands from the electronic version of this book, be sure to delete the Carriage Return at the end of the first line.

This step allows the operating system to know where to download programs that need to be installed on your system. When updates are made to ROS Kinetic, your operating system will be made aware of these updates.

Setting up your keys

Keys confirm the origin of the code and verify that unauthorized modifications to the code have not been made without the knowledge of the owner. A repository and the keys of that repository are added to the operating system's trusted software list. Type the following command:

```
$ sudo apt-key adv --keyserver hkp://ha.pool.sks-keyservers.net:80
--recv-key 421C365BD9FF1F717815A3895523BAEEB01FA116
```

Installing ROS Kinetic

Before you begin with the installation, the current system software must be up to date to avoid problems with libraries and wrong versions of software. To make sure your Debian package index is up-to-date, type the following command:

```
$ sudo apt-get update
```

Install the **desktop-full** configuration of ROS. Desktop-full includes ROS, rqt, rviz, robot-generic libraries, 2D/3D simulators, navigation, and 2D/3D perception. In this book, we will be using rqt and rviz for visualization and also the Gazebo 3D simulator, as well as the ROS navigation and perception packages. To install, type the following command:

```
$ sudo apt-get install ros-kinetic-desktop-full
```

ROS Kinetic is installed on your computer system when the installation process is complete!

Initialize rosdep

The ROS system may depend on software packages that are not loaded initially. These software packages external to ROS are provided by the operating system. The ROS environment command `rosdep` is used to download and install these external packages. Type the following commands:

```
$ sudo rosdep init
$ rosdep update
```

Environment setup

Your terminal session must now be made aware of these ROS files so that it knows what to do when you attempt to execute ROS command-line commands. Running this script will set up the ROS environment variables:

```
$ source /opt/ros/kinetic/setup.bash
```

Alternatively, it is convenient if the ROS environment variables are automatically added to your terminal session every time a new shell is launched. If you are using bash for your terminal shell, do this by typing the following commands:

```
$ echo "source /opt/ros/kinetic/setup.bash" >> ~/.bashrc
$ source ~/.bashrc
```

Now when a new terminal session is launched, the bash shell is automatically aware of the ROS environment variables.

Getting rosinstall

The rosinstall command is a command-line tool in ROS that allows you to download ROS packages with one command.

To install this tool on Ubuntu, type the following command:

```
$ sudo apt-get install python-rosinstall
```

Troubleshooting – examining your ROS environment

The ROS environment is set up through a number of variables that tell the system where to find ROS packages. Two main variables are ROS_ROOT and ROS_PACKAGE_PATH that enable ROS to locate packages in the filesystem.

To check whether the ROS environment variables are set correctly, use the env command in the following form that lists the ROS environment variables:

```
$ env | grep ROS
```

The output of the preceding command is as follows:

```
ROS_ROOT=/opt/ros/kinetic/share/ros
ROS_PACKAGE_PATH=/opt/ros/kinetic/share
ROS_MASTER_URI=http://localhost:11311
ROSLISP_PACKAGE_DIRECTORIES=
ROS_DISTRO=kinetic
ROS_ETC_DIR=/opt/ros/kinetic/etc/ros
```

If the variables are not set correctly, you will need to source your `setup.bash` file, as described in the *Environment setup* section of this chapter. Check whether the `ROS_DISTRO=` `"kinetic"` and `ROS_PACKAGE_PATH` variables are correct, as shown previously.

The tutorial that discusses the ROS environment can be found at: `http://wiki.ros.org/ROS/Tutorials/InstallingandConfiguringROSEnvironment`

Creating a catkin workspace

The next step is to create a catkin workspace. A catkin workspace is a directory (folder) in which you can create or modify existing catkin packages. The catkin structure simplifies the build and installation process for your ROS packages. The ROS wiki website is `http://wiki.ros.org/catkin/Tutorials/create_a_workspace`.

A catkin workspace can contain up to three or more different subdirectories (`/build`, `/devel`, and `/src`), each of which serve a different role in the software development process.

We will label our catkin workspace `catkin_ws`. To create the catkin workspace, type the following commands:

```
$ mkdir -p ~/catkin_ws/src
$ cd ~/catkin_ws/src
$ catkin_init_workspace
```

Even though the workspace is empty (there are no packages in the `src` folder, just a single `CMakeLists.txt` link), you can still build the workspace by typing the following commands:

```
$ cd ~/catkin_ws/
$ catkin_make
```

The `catkin_make` command creates the catkin workspace. If you view your current directory contents, you should now have the `build` and `devel` folders. Inside the `devel` folder there are now several `setup.*sh` files. We will source the `setup.bash` file to overlay this workspace on top of your ROS environment:

```
$ source ~/catkin_ws/devel/setup.bash
```

Remember to add this source command to your `.bashrc` file by typing the following command:

```
$ echo "source ~/catkin_ws/devel/setup.bash" >> ~/.bashrc
```

To make sure your workspace is properly overlaid by the setup script, make sure the `ROS_PACKAGE_PATH` environment variable includes the directory you're in by typing the following command:

```
$ echo $ROS_PACKAGE_PATH
```

The output of the preceding command should be as follows:

```
/home/<username>/catkin_ws/src:/opt/ros/kinetic/share
```

Here, `<username>` is the name you chose for the user when Ubuntu was installed.

ROS packages and manifest

The ROS software is divided into **packages** that can contain various types of programs, images, data, and even tutorials. The specific contents depend on the application for the package. The site `http://wiki.ros.org/Packages` discusses ROS packages.

A package can contain programs written in Python or C++ to control a robot or another device. For the `turtlesim` simulator package, for example, the package contains the executable code used to change the background color or move a turtle around on the screen. This package also contains images of a turtle for display and files used to create the simulator.

There is another class of packages in ROS called **metapackages** that are specialized packages that only contain a `package.xml` manifest. Their purpose is to reference one or more related packages, which are loosely grouped together.

ROS manifest

Each package contains a manifest named `package.xml` that describes the package in the **Extensible Markup Language (XML)** format. In addition to providing a minimal specification describing the package, the manifest defines properties about the package such as the package name, version numbers, authors, maintainers, and any dependencies on other packages.

Exploring the ROS packages

Occasionally, we would like to find packages that we wish to use and display the files involved. This section introduces several useful ROS commands:

- `rospack` used for information about a package
- `roscd` used to navigate the ROS directories
- `rosls` used to list directories and files in a package directory

The `rospack` command can be used to list ROS packages, locate packages by name, and determine if a package depends on another package, among other uses. For more information use the following command with the `help` or `-h` option in the form:

```
$ rospack help | less
```

We will use the `turtlesim` package for the examples here. To change directories to the location of `turtlesim`, use the following command:

```
$ roscd turtlesim
```

This changes the location on one of the author's workstations as follows:

```
linux@D158-45929:/opt/ros/kinetic/share/turtlesim$
```

On your computer, the `$` command prompt will be preceded by the information about your computer. Generally, that information for our computers will be deleted in our examples using ROS commands. Once you are in the `turtlesim` directory, the standard Linux commands can be used with the subdirectories or files, or the ROS commands can be used. To determine the directories and files in the `turtlesim` directory but without changing to the `turtlesim` directory, use the following command:

```
$ rosls turtlesim
```

Here is the result from the home directory of the author's workstation with ROS installed:

```
cmake images  msg package.xml srv
```

To see the filenames of the images loaded with `turtlesim`, specify the `images` directory in the package as follows:

```
$ rosls turtlesim/images
```

The output of the preceding command is as follows:

```
box-turtle.png     groovy.png    indigo.svg    palette.png
diamondback.png    hydro.png     jade.png      robot-turtle.png
electric.png       hydro.svg     kinetic.png   sea-turtle.png
fuerte.png         indigo.png    kinetic.svg   turtle.png
```

There are various turtle images that can be used. The `rosls turtlesim` command will also work to show the contents of the `turtlesim` subdirectories: /msg for messages and /srv for services. These files will be discussed later. To see the manifest, type the following commands:

```
$ roscd turtlesim
$ cat package.xml
```

This will also show the dependencies, such as `roscpp` for C++ programs.

rospack find packages

The `rospack find <package name>` command returns the path to the package named `<package name>`. For example, type the following command:

```
$ rospack find turtlesim
```

The preceding command displays the path to the `turtlesim` directory.

rospack list

Execute the following command:

```
$ rospack list
```

This lists the ROS package names and their directories on the computer. In the case of the workstation mentioned earlier, there are 195 ROS packages listed!

> If you really want to see all the ROS packages and their locations, use the following command form:
>
> ```
> $ rospack list | less
> ```
>
> This form allows paging of the long list of names and directories for the packages. Press *Q* to quit.
>
> 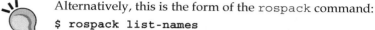 Alternatively, this is the form of the `rospack` command:
>
> ```
> $ rospack list-names
> ```
>
> This lists only the names of the packages without the directories. After such a long list, it is a good idea to open a new terminal window or clear the window with the `clear` command.
>
> This is the form of the `rospack` command:
>
> ```
> $ rospack list-names | grep turtle
> ```
>
> This lists the packages with `turtle` in the name.

More information on commands that are useful to navigate the ROS filesystem is available at the ROS website `http://wiki.ros.org/ROS/Tutorials/NavigatingTheFilesystem`

ROS nodes, topics, and messages

Here we will explore some of the main components of ROS. One of the primary purposes of ROS is to facilitate communication between the ROS **nodes**. These nodes represent the executable code. The code can reside entirely on one computer, or nodes can be distributed between computers or between computers and robots. The advantage of this distributed structure is that each node can control one aspect of a system.

For example, one node can capture the images from a camera and send the images to another node for processing. After processing the image, the second node can send a control signal to a third node for controlling a robotic manipulator in response to the camera view.

The main mechanism used by ROS nodes to communicate is by sending and receiving **messages**. The messages are organized into specific categories called **topics**. Nodes may **publish** messages on a particular topic or **subscribe** to a topic to receive information.

ROS nodes

Basically, nodes are processes that perform some computation or task. The nodes themselves are really software processes but with the capability to register with the ROS Master node and communicate with other nodes in the system. The ROS design idea is that each node is independent and interacts with other nodes using the ROS communication capability. The Master node is described in the *ROS Master* section to follow.

One of the strengths of ROS is that a particular task, such as controlling a wheeled mobile robot, can be separated into a series of simpler tasks. The tasks can include the perception of the environment using a camera or laser scanner, map making, planning a route, monitoring the battery level of the robot's battery, and controlling the motors driving the wheels of the robot. Each of these actions might consist of a ROS node or a series of nodes to accomplish the specific tasks.

A node can independently execute code to perform its task but can also communicate with other nodes by sending or receiving messages. The messages can consist of data, commands, or other information necessary for the application.

ROS topics

Some nodes provide information for other nodes, as a camera feed would do, for example. Such a node is said to publish information that can be received by other nodes. The information in ROS is called a **topic**. A topic defines the types of messages that will be sent concerning that topic.

The nodes that transmit data publish the topic name and the type of message to be sent. The actual data is published by the node. A node can subscribe to a topic and transmitted messages on that topic are received by the node subscribing.

Continuing with the camera example, the camera node can publish the image on the `camera/image_raw` topic.
Image data from the `camera/image_raw` topic can be used by a node that shows the image on the computer screen. The node that receives the information is said to subscribe to the topic being published, in this case `camera/image_raw`.
In some cases, a node can both publish and subscribe to one or more topics.

ROS messages

ROS messages are defined by the **type** of message and the data format. The ROS package named `std_msgs`, for example, has messages of type `String` which consist of a string of characters. Other message packages for ROS have messages used for robot navigation or robotic sensors. The `turtlesim` package has its own set of messages that pertain to the simulation.

We will see in the section, *Turtlesim – the first ROS robot simulation* that the turtlesim simulator has two nodes that are created when turtlesim is executed. Turtlesim has relatively few topics and messages so it is ideal for the initial study of ROS.

The ROS site `http://www.ros.org/core-components/` describes the communication and robot-specific features of ROS. Here, we will explore some of the main components of a ROS system including ROS nodes and the ROS Master. It is important for you to understand the ROS nodes, topics, and messages as they are involved in almost every ROS activity.

ROS Master

The ROS nodes are typically independent programs that can run concurrently on several systems. The ROS Master provides naming and registration services to the nodes in the ROS system. It tracks publishers and subscribers to the topics. Communication is established between the nodes by the ROS Master.

The role of the Master is to enable individual ROS nodes to locate one another. The most often used protocol for connection is the standard **Transmission Control Protocol/Internet Protocol (TCP/IP)** or **Internet Protocol** called TCPROS in ROS. Once these nodes are able to locate one another, they can communicate with each other peer-to-peer.

One responsibility of the Master is to keep track of nodes when new nodes are executed and come into the system. Thus, the Master provides a dynamic allocation of connections. The nodes cannot communicate however until the Master notifies the nodes of each other's existence. A simple example is shown at `http://wiki.ros.org/Master`.

Invoking the ROS Master using roscore

roscore starts processes that you *must* have running in order for ROS nodes to communicate. When it executes, roscore will start the following:

- A ROS Master
- A ROS Parameter Server
- A rosout logging node

The roscore command creates the Master so that nodes can register with the Master. You can view the ROS tutorial for roscore at http://wiki.ros.org/roscore.

Issue the following command to start the Master in a new terminal window and observe the output:

```
$ roscore
```

The output of the preceding command is as follows:

```
... logging to /home/linux/.ros/log/9c3776b4-09cd-11e7-bb39-1866da2351d7/
roslaunch-D158-45929-29790.log
Checking log directory for disk usage. This may take a while.
Press Ctrl-C to interrupt
Done checking log file disk usage. Usage is <1GB.


started roslaunch server http://D158-45929:34807/
ros_comm version 1.12.7



SUMMARY
========


PARAMETERS
 * /rosdistro: kinetic
 * /rosversion: 1.12.7


NODES


auto-starting new master
```

```
process[master]: started with pid [29802]
ROS_MASTER_URI=http://D158-45929:11311/

setting /run_id to 9c3776b4-09cd-11e7-bb39-1866da2351d7
process[rosout-1]: started with pid [29815]
started core service [/rosout]
```

In the preceding screen output, you will see information about the computer, parameters that list the name (kinetic) and version number of the ROS distribution, and other information. The Master is defined by its **Uniform Resource Identifier (URI)**. This identifies the location of the Master; in this case, it is running on the workstation used to execute the roscore command.

Parameter Server

The Parameter Server is a shared dictionary of parameters that nodes store and retrieve at runtime. The Parameter Server runs inside the Master and parameters are globally viewable so that nodes can access the parameters.

In the preceding screen output from the roscore command, the parameters associated with the Master are as follows:

* /rosdistro: kinetic
* /rosversion: 1.12.7

Kinetic is the ROS distribution release that we are using. As Kinetic is changed or packages are added, numbered versions such as 1.12.7 are released. Issuing the roscore command is a way to determining the version of ROS running on your computer.

Whenever ROS is executing, it is possible to list the nodes that are active and the topics that are used for communication. We will explore the information in the roscore output in more detail by invoking useful ROS terminal commands.

ROS commands to determine the nodes and topics

Three commands used extensively in ROS are as follows:

* roscore to start the Master and allow nodes to communicate
* rosnode list to list the active nodes
* rostopic list to list the topics associated with active ROS nodes

After the `roscore` command is executed, the terminal window used to execute `roscore` must remain active, but it can be minimized. In another terminal window, the `rosnode list` command will cause a list of the ROS nodes that are active to be displayed on the screen. After the command for `roscore` is executed, only one node `rosout` will be listed as an active node if you type the following command:

`$ rosnode list`

The output of the preceding command is as follows:

`/rosout`

In the second terminal window, list the active topics by typing:

`$ rostopic list`

The output of the preceding command is as follows:

`/rosout`

`/rosout_agg`

Notice that the `/rosout` node and the `/rosout` topic have the same designation. In ROS terms, the `rosout` node subscribes to the `/rosout` topic. All the active nodes publish their debug messages to the `/rosout` topic. We will not be concerned with these messages here; however, they can be useful to debug a program. For an explanation refer to the ROS wiki at `http://wiki.ros.org/rosout`.

The `rosout` node is connected to every other active node in the system. The `/rosout_agg` topic receives messages also, but just from the `rosout` node so it does not have to connect to all of the nodes and thus saves time at system startup.

The `rostopic` and `rosnode` terminal commands have a number of options that will be demonstrated by various examples in this book.

Most of the ROS commands have help screens that are usually helpful. Type the following command for the command options:

`$ rosnode -h`

For more detailed usage, use the subcommand name, for example:

`$ rosnode list -h`

This will list the subcommands and the options for the `rosnode` command.

There are a number of other important ROS terminal commands that you should know. They are introduced and explained using the turtlesim simulator in the upcoming section.

Turtlesim – the first ROS robot simulation

A simple way to learn the basics of ROS is to use the turtlesim simulator that is part of the ROS installation. The simulation consists of a graphical window that shows a turtle-shaped robot. The background color for the turtle's world can be changed using the Parameter Server. The turtle can be moved around on the screen by ROS commands or using the keyboard.

Turtlesim is a ROS package, and the basic concepts of package management were presented in the *Exploring the ROS packages* section, as discussed earlier. We suggest that you refer to this section before continuing.

We will illustrate a number of ROS commands that explore the nodes, topics, messages, and services used by the turtle simulator. We have already covered the `roscore`, `rosnode`, and `rostopic` commands. These commands will be used with turtlesim also.

Other important ROS terminal commands that will be covered in this section are as follows:

- `rosrun`: Finds and starts a requested node in a package
- `rosmsg`: Shows information about messages
- `rosservice`: Displays runtime information about nodes and can pass data between nodes in a request/response mode
- `rosparam`: Used to get and set parameters (data) used by nodes

Starting turtlesim nodes

To start turtlesim with ROS commands, we need to open two separate terminal windows. First, issue the following command in the first window if the Master is not already running:

```
$ roscore
```

Wait for the Master to complete startup. You can minimize this window but do not close it because the Master must run to allow the nodes to communicate.

The result on your screen will resemble the output discussed previously in the *Invoking the ROS Master using roscore* section, where `roscore` was described.

rosrun command

To display the turtle on the screen, use the rosrun command. It takes the arguments [package name] [executable name], and in this case, turtlesim as the package and turtlesim_node as the executable program.

In the second terminal window, issue the following command:

```
$ rosrun turtlesim turtlesim_node
```

You will see an output similar to this:

```
[ INFO] [1489616730.714683337]: Starting turtlesim with node name /
turtlesim
[ INFO] [1489616730.727083554]: Spawning turtle [turtle1] at
x=[5.544445], y=[5.544445], theta=[0.000000]
```

Wait for the display screen to appear with the image of a turtle at the center, as shown in the turtlesim screen in the following screenshot. The terminal window can be minimized, but keep the turtle display screen in view. The turtle is called turtle1 since this is the first and only turtle in our display.

After you have started turtlesim by executing the rosrun command, you will see information about the turtle's position on the screen. The /turtlesim node creates the screen image and the turtle. Here, the turtle is in the center at about $x = 5.5$, $y = 5.5$ with no rotation since angle theta is zero. The origin (0, 0) is at the lower-left corner of the screen:

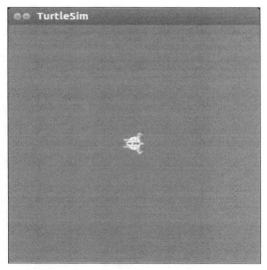

Turtlesim screen

Let's study the properties of the nodes, topics, services, and messages available with the `turtlesim` package in another terminal window. Thus, at this point, you will have three windows active but the first two can be minimized or dragged off to the side or the bottom. They should not be closed.

Turtlesim nodes

In the third window, issue the `rosnode` command to determine information about any node. First, list the active nodes, using the following command:

```
$ rosnode list
```

The output is as follows:

```
/rosout
```

```
/turtlesim
```

We will concentrate on the `/turtlesim` node. Note the difference in notation between the `/turtlesim` node and the `turtlesim` package.

To see the publications, subscriptions, and services of the `turtlesim` node, type the following command:

```
$ rosnode info /turtlesim
```

The output of the preceding command is as follows:

```
Node [/turtlesim]
Publications:
 * /turtle1/color_sensor [turtlesim/Color]
 * /rosout [rosgraph_msgs/Log]
 * /turtle1/pose [turtlesim/Pose]


Subscriptions:
 * /turtle1/cmd_vel [unknown type]


Services:
 * /turtle1/teleport_absolute
 * /turtlesim/get_loggers
 * /turtlesim/set_logger_level
 * /reset
 * /spawn
```

* `/clear`
* `/turtle1/set_pen`
* `/turtle1/teleport_relative`
* `/kill`

```
contacting node http://D158-45929:38895/ ...
Pid: 29981
Connections:
 * topic: /rosout
    * to: /rosout
    * direction: outbound
    * transport: TCPROS
```

The following diagram represents a graphical illustration of the relationship of the `turtlesim` node in elliptical shapes and topics in the rectangular boxes:

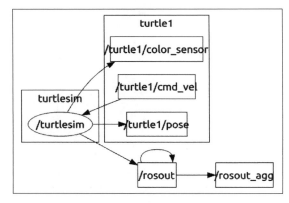

/turtlesim node

The graph was created using the `rqt_graph` command as described in the *Introducing RQT tools* section in *Chapter 3, Driving Around with TurtleBot.*

We read the output of the `rosnode info` command and the graph of the `turtlesim` node and topics in the preceding diagram as follows (ignoring the logging services and the `/rosout` and `/rosout_agg` nodes):

- The `/turtlesim` node publishes to two topics. These topics control the color of the turtle's screen and the position of the turtle on the screen when messages are sent from `/turtlesim`:

    ◦ `/turtle1/color_sensor` with the message type `[turtlesim/Color]`

    ◦ `/turtle1/pose` with the message type `[turtlesim/Pose]`

- The `/turtlesim` node subscribes to the `turtle1/cmd_vel` topic. The `/turtlesim` node is waiting for another node to publish on the `turtle1/cmd_vel` topic.

- There are a number of services associated with the `/turtlesim` node. The services can be used to move the turtle around (teleport), clear the screen, kill the nodes, and perform other functions. The services will be explained later in the section *ROS services to move turtle*.

Turtlesim topics and messages

A ROS message is a strictly typed data structure. In fact, the message type is not associated with the message contents. For example, one message type is `string`, which is just text. Another type of message is `uint8`, which means that it is an unsigned 8-bit integer. These are part of the `std_msg` package or standard messages. The command form `rosmsg list` lists the type of messages on your system; it is a long list! There are packages for messages of the type control, type geometry, and type navigation, among others to control robot actions. There are sensor message types used with laser scanners, cameras, and joysticks to name just a few of the sensors or input devices possible with ROS. Turtlesim uses several of the message types to control its simulated robot — the turtle.

For these exercises, keep the `roscore` and `/turtlesim` windows active. Open other terminal windows as needed. We will concentrate on the `turtle1/color_sensor` topic first. You will be typing in the third window.

 If the screen gets too cluttered, remember the `$ clear` command. Use the `$ history` command to see the commands you have used.

rostopic list

For the /turtlesim node, the topics are listed using the following command:

```
$ rostopic list
```

The output of the preceding command is as follows:

```
/rosout
/rosout_agg
/statistics
/turtle1/cmd_vel
/turtle1/color_sensor
/turtle1/pose
```

rostopic type

The topic type can be determined for each topic by typing the following command:

```
$ rostopic type /turtle1/color_sensor
turtlesim/Color
```

The message type in the case of the /turtle1/color_sensor topic is turtlesim/Color. This is the format of ROS message type names:

```
[package name]/[message type]
```

If a node publishes a message, we can determine the message type and read the message.

rosmsg list

The turtlesim package has two message types that are found with the following command:

```
$ rosmsg list | grep turtlesim
```

The output is as follows:

```
turtlesim/Color
turtlesim/Pose
```

The rosmsg list command displays all of the messages. Adding | grep turtlesim shows all messages of the turtlesim package. There are only two in the turtlesim package. From the message type, we can find the format of the message. Make sure that you note that Color in the message type starts with a capital letter.

rosmsg show

The `rosmsg show <message type>` command displays the fields in a ROS message type. For the `turtlesim/Color` type, the fields are integers:

```
$ rosmsg show turtlesim/Color
```

Output of the preceding command is as follows:

```
uint8 r
uint8 g
uint8 b
```

The format of values designating colors red (r), green (g), and blue (b) is unsigned, 8-bit integer.

To understand the message, it is necessary to find the message type. For example, `turtlesim/Color` is a message type for turtlesim that has three elements that define the color of the background. For example, the red color in the background is defined by `uint8 r`. This indicates that if we wish to modify the red value, an 8-bit unsigned integer is needed. The amount of red in the background is in the range of 0–255.

In general, the formats of numerical data include integers of 8, 16, 32, or 64 bits, floating point numbers, and other formats.

rostopic echo

To determine the color mixture of red, green, and blue in the background of our turtle, use the `rostopic echo [topic name]` command in the form, as follows:

```
$ rostopic echo /turtle1/color_sensor
```

Output of the preceding command is as follows:

```
r: 69
g: 86
b: 255
---
```

Press *Ctrl + C* to stop the output.

The website describing the *RGB Color Codes Chart* and the meaning of the numerical color values can be found at http://www.rapidtables.com/web/color/RGB_Color.htm.

The chart explains how to mix the **red, green, and blue (rgb)** color values to achieve any desired color. The color values are parameters that can be changed.

A simple table can clarify the relationship between the topics and the messages for the /turtlesim node:

Topics and messages for the /turtlesim node			
Topic name	Topic type	Message format	Message
$ rostopic list	$ rostopic type [topic name]	$ rosmsg show [topic type]	$ rostopic echo [topic name]
/turtle1 /color_sensor	turtlesim/Color	uint8 r uint8 g uint8 b	r: 69 g: 86 b: 255
/turtle1/pose	turtlesim/Pose	float32 x float32 y float32 theta float32 linear_ velocity float32 angular_ velocity	x: 5.54444456 y: 5.54444456 theta: 0.0 linear_velocity: 0.0 angular_ velocity: 0.0

The table of *Topics and messages* shows the topics, types, message formats, and data values for the two topics of the /turtlesim node that we explored. The commands to determine the information are also shown in the table.

Move the turtle by publishing /turtle1/cmd_vel

Start the Master and execute the turtlesim_node by typing:

```
$ roscore
```

In a second terminal window, issue the following command:

```
$ rosrun turtlesim turtlesim_node
```

Once the turtle screen is visible, there are a number of ways to move the turtle around.

The turtlesim_node subscribes to the /turtle1/cmd_vel topic, so the turtle can be commanded to move by sending messages on this topic. First, determine the type of messages for the topic by typing:

```
$ rostopic type /turtle1/cmd_vel
```

which displays the message type as the `Twist` message from the `geometry_msgs` package:

```
geometry_msgs/Twist
```

Next, the format of the message can be determined with the command:

```
$ rosmsg show geometry_msgs/Twist
```

The output shows that the message format allows six floating-point values which determine the linear and angular velocity of the turtle:

```
geometry_msgs/Vector3 linear
    float64 x
    float64 y
    float64 z
geometry_msgs/Vector3 angular
    float64 x
    float64 y
    float64 z
```

For the turtle in turtlesim that moves in a 2D space, the only motion allowed is forward motion in the turtle's *x* direction or rotation about the turtle's *z* axis that would extend out from the screen.

To move the turtle in a circle, the command

```
$ rostopic pub /turtle1/cmd_vel geometry_msgs/Twist -r 1 -- '[2.0, 0.0, 0.0]' '[0.0, 0.0, 1.8]'
```

causes motion forward at 2.0 meters/second as well as rotation at 1.8 radians/second. The command specifies the topic, type of message, the repeat option (`-r`) and the data values of the velocities. The data arguments are actually in YAML syntax, which is described in the YAML Command Line documentation at `http://wiki.ros.org/ROS/YAMLCommandLine`.

The ROS and Ubuntu command-line commands have **tab-completion** capability. For the previous `rostopic pub` command for example, much typing can be avoided by typing part of the command and hitting the *Tab* key. In particular, typing out the command up to the data values and hitting the *Tab* key will yield the format of the data that can be filled in by backspacing and entering the appropriate values.

Move the turtle using the keyboard or joystick

After the turtle screen is visible, type the command:

```
$ rosrun turtlesim turtle_teleop_key
```

activates the keyboard control of the turtle with this output:

```
Reading from keyboard
---------------------------
Use arrow keys to move the turtle.
Up arrow        Turtle up
Down arrow      Turtle down
Right arrow     Rotate CW
Left  arrow     Rotate CCW
```

In *Chapter 8, Controlling Your Robots with External Devices* in the section *Controlling Turtlesim with a custom game controller interface,* code is given to allow control of the turtle with a game controller (joystick).

Parameter Server of Turtlesim

The Parameter Server maintains a dictionary of the parameters. Thus, the /turtlesim node can read and write parameters held by the Parameter Server.

rosparam help

Use the help option to determine the form of the rosparam command:

```
$ rosparam help
```

Output of the preceding command is as follows:

```
rosparam is a command-line tool for getting, setting, and deleting
parameters from the ROS Parameter Server.   Commands:
rosparam set        set parameter
rosparam get        get parameter
rosparam list       list parameter names
<Edited>
```

rosparam list for the /turtlesim node

To list the parameters for the /turtlesim node, we will use the following command:

```
$ rosparam list
```

Output of the preceding command is as follows:

```
/background_b
/background_g
/background_r
/rosdistro
/roslaunch/uris/host_d158_45929__34807
/rosversion
/run_id
```

Note that the last four parameters were created by invoking the Master with the roscore command, as discussed previously. Also, the list defines the characteristics of the parameter but not the data value.

Change parameters for the color of the turtle's background

To change the background color parameters for turtlesim, let's change the turtle's background to red. To do this, make the blue and green data values equal to zero and saturate *red* = *255* using the rosparam set command. Note that the clear option from rosservice must be executed before the screen changes color.

rosparam get

The default turtle screen is blue. You can use rosparam get / to show the data contents of the entire Parameter Server:

```
$ rosparam get /
```

Output of the preceding command is as follows:

```
background_b: 255
background_g: 86
background_r: 69
rosdistro: 'kinetic

  '

roslaunch:
```

```
uris: {host_d158_45929__34807: 'http://D158-45929:34807/'}
rosversion: '1.12.7
```

```
'
```

```
run_id: 9c3776b4-09cd-11e7-bb39-1866da2351d7
```

rosparam set

You can change the colors of the turtle's screen to a full red background using the
rosparam set commands:

```
$ rosparam set background_b 0
```

```
$ rosparam set background_g 0
```

```
$ rosparam set background_r 255
```

```
$ rosservice call /clear
```

You will see a red background on the turtle screen. To check the numerical results,
use the rosparam get / command.

ROS services to move turtle

Another capability of nodes is to provide what in ROS terms is called a **service**. This
feature is used when a node requests information from another node. Thus, there is a
two-way communication between the nodes.

You can check the turtle's pose using the /turtle1/pose topic and the message
type, /turtlesim/Pose. Carefully note the different notations and meanings. To
determine the message type, run the following command:

```
$ rostopic type /turtle1/pose
```

The output is as follows:

```
turtlesim/Pose
```

To determine the format and meaning of the fields in the message, type:

```
$ rosmsg show turtlesim/Pose
```

The output is as follows:

```
float32 x
float32 y
float32 theta
float32 linear_velocity
float32 angular_velocity
```

We can find the turtle's position, orientation in angle (theta), and its velocity using the rostopic echo command:

```
$ rostopic echo /turtle1/pose
```

The output is as follows:

```
x: 5.544444561
y: 5.544444561
theta: 0.0
linear_velocity: 0.0
angular_velocity: 0.0
```

This command outputs the result continuously and is stopped by pressing the *Ctrl + C* keys. The result will show that the turtle is at the center of its screen with no rotation at angle zero and no movement since the velocities are zero.

rosservice call

The turtle can be moved using the rosservice teleport option. The format of the command is rosservice call <service name><service arguments>. The arguments here will be the turtle's position and orientation as x, y, and theta. The turtle is moved to position [1, 1] with theta = 0 by running the following command:

```
$ rosservice call /turtle1/teleport_absolute 1 1 0
```

The result can be seen in the following screenshot:

turtle after an absolute move

The relative teleport option moves the turtle with respect to its present position. The arguments are [linear distance, angle]. Here, the rotation angle is zero. The command for relative movement is as follows:

```
$ rosservice call /turtle1/teleport_relative 1 0
```

Your turtle should now move to *x=2* and *y=1*.

ROS commands summary

If you are communicating with ROS via the terminal window, it is possible to issue commands to ROS to explore or control nodes in a package from the command prompt, as listed in the following table:

Command	Action	Example usage and subcommand examples
roscore	Starts the Master	`$ roscore`
rosrun	Runs an executable program and creates nodes	`$ rosrun [package name] [executable name]`

rosnode	Shows information about nodes and lists the active nodes	`$ rosnode info [node name]`
		 `$ rosnode<subcommand>`
		 Subcommand: `list`

rostopic	Shows information about ROS topics	`$ rostopic<subcommand><topic name>` Subcommands: `echo`, `info`, and `type`
rosmsg	Shows information about the message types	`$ rosmsg<subcommand> [package name]/ [message type]` Subcommands: `show`, `type`, and `list`
rosservice	Displays the runtime information about various services and allows the display of messages being sent to a topic	`$ rosservice<subcommand> [service name]` Subcommands: `args`, `call`, `find`, `info`, `list`, and `type`
rosparam	Used to get and set parameters (data) used by nodes	`$ rosparam<subcommand> [parameter]` Subcommands: `get`, `set`, `list`, and `delete`

The website (`http://wiki.ros.org/ROS/CommandLineTools`) describes many ROS commands. The table lists some important ones. However, these examples only cover a few of the possible variations of the commands.

Summary

In this chapter, you first learned how to install and launch ROS. We discussed the ROS architecture and ROS packages, nodes, topics, messages, and services. To apply the knowledge, we used the turtlesim simulator was used to illustrate many ROS commands. For additional control of the turtlesim turtle, see *Chapter 8, Controlling Your Robots with External Devices*. There the turtle is controlled with a custom game controller.

In *Chapter 2, Creating Your First Two-Wheeled ROS Robot (in Simulation)*, we will show you how to build a robot model that ROS uses to display the robot and allows you to control it in a simulation. The chapter introduces the visualization tool called rviz to display the robot and the simulation tool Gazebo that includes the physics of the robot as you move it around in a simulated environment.

2
Creating Your First Two-Wheeled ROS Robot (in Simulation)

Your first robot will be created in simulation so that even if you do not have a physical robot to learn ROS on, you will be able to follow along and do the exercises in this book. We will build a simple two-wheeled robot named dd_robot (dd is short for differential drive). We will build a **Unified Robot Description Format** (**URDF**) file for the robot that will describe the main components of our robot and enable it to be visualized and controlled by ROS tools, such as rviz and Gazebo. Rviz is a visualization tool in which we will view our dd_robot URDF file as we build it in increments. When the visual model is complete, we will modify the URDF file for use in the Gazebo simulator. In Gazebo, we can view the effects of physics on our model as we move our model around the 3D environment.

In this chapter, we will cover the following topics:

- An introduction to rviz, installation instructions, and instructions for use
- How to create and build a ROS package
- An incremental approach to develop a URDF file and visualizing it in rviz
- ROS tools to verify the URDF file
- An introduction to Gazebo, installation instructions, and instructions for use
- Modifications necessary to visualize the URDF file in Gazebo
- Tools to verify your Gazebo URDF/**Simulation Description Format** (**SDF**) file
- A simple way to control a robot in Gazebo

We begin by learning about rviz.

Introducing rviz

Rviz, abbreviation for **ROS visualization**, is a powerful 3D visualization tool for ROS. It allows the user to view the robot model, display and/or log sensor information from the robot's sensors, and replay the logged sensor information. By visualizing what the robot is seeing, thinking, and doing, the user can debug a robot application from sensor inputs to planned (or unplanned) actions.

Rviz displays 3D sensor data from stereo cameras, lasers, Kinects, and other 3D devices in the form of point clouds or depth images. 2D sensor data from webcams, RGB cameras, and 2D laser rangefinders can be viewed in rviz as image data.

If an actual robot is communicating with a workstation that is running rviz, rviz will display the robot's current configuration on the virtual robot model. For example, if a real two-armed robot like Baxter has his arms in a certain pose, then the robot model will display that pose in rviz. The ROS topic containing arm configuration information as well as any ROS topic published to move the arm joints can be displayed in the information on the rviz screen. ROS topics can also display live representations, based on the sensor data published by any cameras, infrared sensors, and laser scanners that are part of the robot's system. This can be useful to develop and debug robot systems and controllers. Rviz provides a configurable **Graphical User Interface (GUI)** to allow the user to display only information that is pertinent to the present task.

In this chapter, we will use rviz to visualize our progress in creating a two-wheeled robot model. Rviz will use the URDF file that we create for our robot and display the visual representation.

We will begin by checking whether rviz has been downloaded and installed on your system.

Installing and launching rviz

To run rviz, you require a powerful graphics card, and the appropriate drivers need to be installed on your computer.

 If you have trouble with running rviz, refer to `http://wiki.ros.org/rviz/Troubleshooting` or search the ROS forum at `http://answers.ros.org/questions/`.

1. Follow these steps to install and run Rviz:
2. Rviz tool should have been installed on your computer as part of the `ros-kinetic-desktop-full` installation, as described in the *Installing and launching ROS* section in *Chapter 1, Getting Started with ROS*.

   To test whether rviz has been installed correctly, open a terminal window and start the ROS Master by typing the following command:

   ```
   $ roscore
   ```

   Next, open a second terminal window and type the following command:

   ```
   $ rosrun rviz rviz
   ```

   This will display an environment similar to the following screenshot:

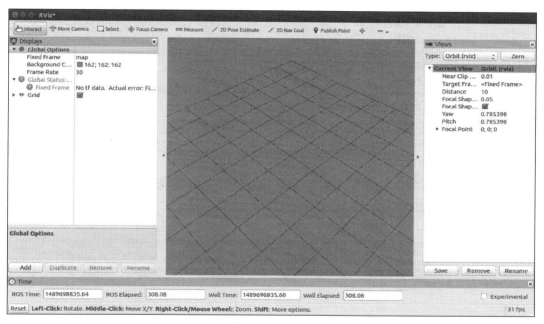

rviz main screen

   If the `$ rosrun rviz rviz` command generates a warning message, make sure that you have `source ~/catkin_ws/devel/setup.bash` in your `.bashrc` file, or this command is entered at the terminal window prompt. The `.bashrc` file resides in your home directory but cannot be seen unless you use the `$ ls -la` command option to list the directory and files. This option shows the hidden files that are preceded by a dot (`.`).

3. If rviz has not been installed, then install it from the Debian repository using the following command:

```
$ sudo apt-get install ros-kinetic-rviz
```

 If you wish to install rviz from source, refer to the rviz user guide at http://wiki.ros.org/rviz/UserGuide. This guide is also a good reference to learn additional features of rviz that are not covered in this book.

Getting familiar with rviz

The central window on the rviz main screen provides the world view of a 3D environment. Typically, only the grid is displayed in the center window or the window is blank.

The main screen is divided into four main display areas: the central window, the **Displays** panel to the left, the **Views** panel to the right, and the **Time** panel at the bottom. Across the top of these display areas are the toolbar and the main screen menu bar. Each of these areas of the rviz main screen is described in the following sections. This overview is provided so that you can gain familiarity with the rviz GUI.

Displays panel

On the left panel of the rviz main screen is the **Displays** panel, where the user can add, duplicate, remove, or rename the visualization elements in the 3D environment.

By clicking on the **Add** button on the **Displays** panel, the **Add** menu appears, as shown in the following screenshot. This menu displays the visualization elements that can be added to the environment, such as a camera image, point cloud, robot model, and so on. A brief description of each item is provided at the bottom of the window when that item is highlighted. A unique display name can be entered for the item to be added to the environment. For further details on the display types, go to http://wiki.ros.org/rviz/DisplayTypes. This site also identifies the ROS messages that provide the data for the display.

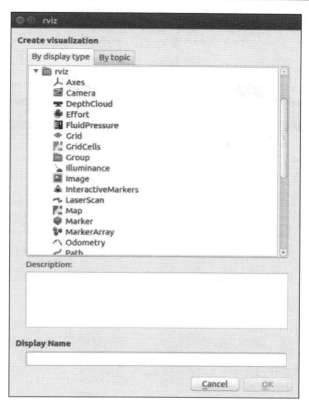

rviz Add display menu

Clicking on the triangle symbol on the left side of a panel item will expand or hide the details of the item.

The **Displays** panel also shows access to **Global Options**, such as **Background Color** and **Frame Rate**. The options under the **Grid** element allow the user to tailor the grid lines by changing the number of grid cells, line width, line color, and so on.

Views and Time panels

The **Views** panel on the right side of the rviz main screen and the **Time** panel at the bottom are not important at this point and so we have removed them from the rest of the screenshots in this chapter. We will work in the orbit view, which is the default camera view for rviz. In this view, the orbital camera will rotate around a focal point visualized as a small yellow disc in the 3D world view.

Mouse control

To move around the 3D world in the orbit view, use the mouse and keyboard as follows:

- **Left mouse button**: Click and drag to rotate the scene around the focal point. *Shift* key + Left mouse button: pan scene right-left-up-down.

- **Middle mouse button (if available)**: Click and drag to move the focal point in the plane formed by the camera's up and right vectors. (The *Shift* key and left mouse button combination also invokes this mode.)

- **Right mouse button**: Click and drag to zoom in/out of the focal point. Dragging up zooms in and down zooms out.

- **Scroll wheel**: Rotate to zoom in/out of the focal point. Press to pan right-left-up-down.

Toolbar

The toolbar at the top of the rviz main screen is shown in this screenshot and provides the corresponding functionalities described below:

rviz toolbar

- **Interact**: This shows interactive markers when present.

- **Move Camera** (default mode): This is a 3D view that responds to the mouse/keyboard, as described for the **Views** panel.

- **Select**: This allows items to be selected by a mouse click or drag box selection. The selected item will have a wireframe box placed around it.

- **Focus Camera**: A mouse click on a specific spot in the 3D view becomes the focal point of the camera.

- **Measure**: Mouse click on a start point then an end point. The distance between these two points will be shown at the bottom left of the rviz window.

- **2D Nav Goal** and **2D Pose Estimate**: These selections will be discussed in *Chapter 4, Navigating the World with TurtleBot*.

- **Publish Point**: A mouse click on a single point causes the coordinates of that point to be published to topic /clicked_point.

Main window menu bar

The top-most main window menu bar provides options under the basic **File**, **Panels**, and **Help** headings, as shown here:

- **File**: Options are **Open Config**, **Save Config**, **Save Config As**, **Recent Configs**, **Save Image**, and **Quit**
- **Panels**: Options are **Add Panel** and **Delete Panel**

  Other options for panels are: **Tools**, **Displays**, **Selection**, **Tool Properties**, **Views**, and **Time**
- **Help**: Options are **Show Help panel**, **Open rviz wiki in browser**, and **About**

These selections allow the user to customize the panels to be displayed for rviz. This custom configuration of rviz can be saved and reused.

In this chapter, we will use rviz to visualize the construction of our two-wheeled robot model in 3D. We will show you how to use rviz to visualize odometry data for navigation purposes in *Chapter 3*, *Driving Around with TurtleBot*.

For more in-depth tutorials on rviz, go to `http://wiki.ros.org/rviz/Tutorials`.

At this point, rviz can be exited by navigating to **File** | **Quit**. In the next section, we will create and build a ROS package to hold our URDF code and launch files.

Creating and building a ROS package

Before we begin to design and build our robot model in simulation, we should create our first ROS package. In *Chapter 1*, *Getting Started with ROS*, we created a ROS catkin workspace under `/home/<username>/catkin_ws`. The structure of a catkin workspace looks like this:

```
catkin_ws/                    -- WORKSPACE
build/                        -- BUILD SPACE
devel/                        -- DEVEL SPACE
src/                          -- SOURCE SPACE
CMakeLists.txt        -- 'Toplevel' CMake file, provided by catkin
```

 Make sure that you have source ~/catkin_ws/devel/ setup.bash in your .bashrc file, or this command is entered at the terminal window prompt.

We begin by moving to your catkin workspace source directory:

```
$ cd ~/catkin_ws/src
```

Now, let's create our first ROS package, ros_robotics:

```
$ catkin_create_pkg ros_robotics
```

This command will create a /ros_robotics directory under the ~/catkin_ws/ src directory. The /ros_robotics directory will contain a package.xml file and a CMakeLists.txt file. These files contain information generated from the $ catkin_ create_pkg command execution.

The catkin_create_pkg syntax

catkin_create_pkg requires a unique package name and, optionally, a list of dependencies for the package. The command format to create it is as follows:

```
$ catkin_create_pkg <package_name> [depend1] [depend2] [depend3]
```

[depend1], [depend2], and [depend3] specify software packages that are required to be present for this software package to be made.

We will not identify any dependencies for our ros_robotics package at this point.

Next, build the packages in the catkin workspace:

```
$ cd ~/catkin_ws
```
```
$ catkin_make
```

After the workspace has been built to include the ros_robotics package, the ~/catkin_ws/devel subdirectory will have a structure similar to the structure under the /opt/ros/kinetic directory.

Building a differential drive robot URDF

URDF is an XML format specifically defined to represent robot models down to their component level. These URDF files can become long and cumbersome on complex robot systems. **XML Macros (Xacro)** is an XML macro language created to make these robot description files easier to read and maintain. Xacro helps you reduce the duplication of information within the file.

For our first robot model, we will build a URDF file for a two-wheeled differential drive robot. The model will be created incrementally, and we will view the results at each step in rviz. When our simple two-wheeled robot is complete, we will add Gazebo formatting and view the model in Gazebo. In *Chapter 5, Creating Your First Robot Arm (in Simulation)*, we will expand our knowledge of URDF files and build a simple robot arm model using the Xacro notation.

Downloading the ros_robotics code

You can download the example code files and other support material for this book from the Packt Publishing website, http://www.PacktPub.com, or from https://github.com/FairchildC/ROS-Robotics-By-Example-2nd-Edition.

If you download the ros_robotics package from the website, replace the entire ~/catkin_ws/src/ros_robotics directory with the downloaded package. Instead, if you plan to enter the code from this book, begin by creating a /urdf directory under your ros_robotics package directory:

```
$ cd ~/catkin_ws/src/ros_robotics
$ mkdir urdf
$ cd urdf
```

Creating a robot chassis

Two basic URDF components are used to define a tree structure that describes a robot model. The **link** component describes a rigid body by its physical properties (dimensions, position of its origin, color, and so on). Links are connected together by **joint** components. Joint components describe the kinematic and dynamic properties of the connection (that is, links connected, types of joint, axis of rotation, amount of friction and damping, and so on). The URDF description is a set of these link elements and a set of the joint elements connecting the links together.

The first component of our robot is a simple chassis box. The downloaded dd_robot.urdf file contains the code for this exercise. Alternately, you can enter the code portion using your favorite editor and save the file as dd_robot.urdf to your ~/catkin_ws/src/ros_robotics/urdf directory:

```
<?xml version='1.0'?>
<robot name="dd_robot">

  <!-- Base Link -->
  <link name="base_link">
```

```
        <visual>
          <origin xyz="0 0 0" rpy="0 0 0" />
          <geometry>
            <box size="0.5 0.5 0.25"/>
          </geometry>
        </visual>
      </link>

   </robot>
```

 XML comments are bracketed by <!-- and -->.

This XML code defines a robot labeled dd_robot that has one link (also known as part) whose visual component is a box 0.5 meters long, 0.5 meters wide, and 0.25 meters tall. The box is centered at the origin (0, 0, 0) of the environment with no rotation in the roll, pitch, or yaw (rpy) axes. The link has been labeled base_link, and our model will use this box as the link on which our other links are defined.

(A base_link link should be identified as the URDF root link to create the beginning of the robot's kinematic chain.)

Using roslaunch

Roslaunch is a ROS tool that makes it easy to launch multiple ROS nodes as well as set parameters on the ROS Parameter Server. By using a roslaunch file, there is no need to start the ROS Master with the roscore command. The ROS Master starts automatically if it is not already running. Roslaunch configuration files are written in XML and typically end in a .launch extension. In a distributed environment, the .launch files also indicate the processor the nodes should run on.

 The roslaunch syntax is as follows:

```
$ roslaunch <package_name> <file.launch>
```

To use `roslaunch` for our URDF file, you will need to use one of the following ways:

- Download the `ddrobot_rviz.launch` file from the `ros_robotics/launch` directory from this book's website

- Create a `launch` directory under the `ros_robotics` package and create the `ddrobot_rviz.launch` file from the following XML code:

```xml
<launch>

  <!-- values passed by command line input -->
  <arg name="model" />
  <arg name="gui" default="False" />

  <!-- set these parameters on Parameter Server -->
  <param name="robot_description"
         textfile="$(find ros_robotics)/urdf/$(arg model)"
  />
  <param name="use_gui" value="$(arg gui)"/>

  <!-- Start 3 nodes: joint_state_publisher,
         robot_state_publisher and rviz -->

  <node name="joint_state_publisher"
        pkg="joint_state_publisher"
        type="joint_state_publisher" />

  <node name="robot_state_publisher"
        pkg="robot_state_publisher"
        type="state_publisher" />

  <node name="rviz" pkg="rviz" type="rviz"
        args="-d $(find ros_robotics)/urdf.rviz"
        required="true" />
</launch>
```

This `roslaunch` file performs the following:

- Loads the model specified in the command line into the Parameter Server.

- Starts nodes that publish the `JointState` and transforms (discussed later in this chapter).

- Starts rviz with a configuration file (`urdf.rviz`). It is important to use the `urdf.rviz` file that came with the book example code or save your own `urdf.rviz` file from rviz to be used with this launch file.

Type the following command to see the robot model in rviz:

```
$ roslaunch ros_robotics ddrobot_rviz.launch model:=dd_robot.urdf
```

At this point, your rviz screen should resemble one of the following two screenshots. Look carefully for a visual representation of your `dd_robot` box in the main screen and examine it under the **Displays** panel to decide how to proceed. Does your rviz screen look like the following screenshot?

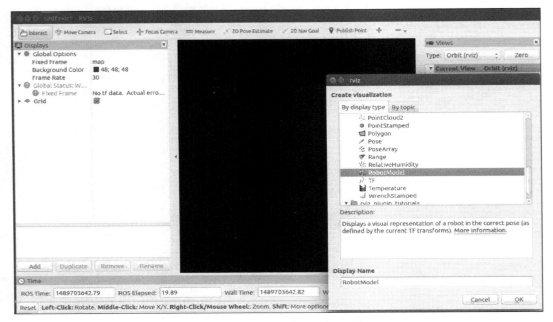

Rviz screen without the urdf.rviz file

If your rviz screen looks like the preceding screenshot with no box on the main screen and no **RobotModel** or **TF** under the **Displays** panel, then perform the following three steps in any order:

- Select the **Add** button under the **Displays** panel and add **RobotModel**
- Select the **Add** button under the **Displays** panel and add **TF**
- Select the field next to **Fixed Frame** (under **Global Options**), which in the preceding screenshot says map, and type in base_link

(The preceding screenshot shows the **Add** menu with the **RobotModel** selection highlighted.) When all the three steps are completed, your rviz screen will look similar to the following screenshot.

When you go to **File** | **Quit** to close your rviz session, you will be asked whether you want to save the configuration to a `urdf.rviz` file and it is recommended that you do. If you do not, you will have to perform the previous three steps each time to see your **RobotModel** and **TF** frames.

For the users who copied the `urdf.rviz` file from the book example code, the rviz screen will come up and look like the following:

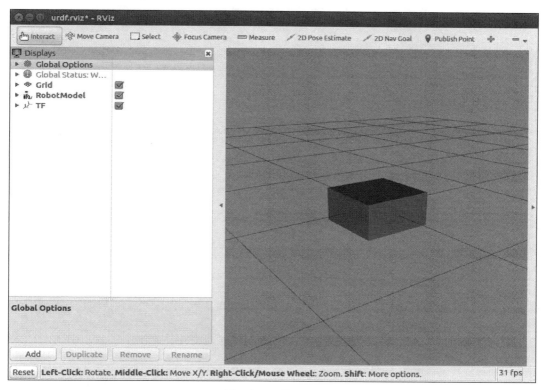

dd_robot.urdf in rviz

Things to note:

- The fixed frame is a transform frame where the center (origin) of the grid is located.

- In URDF, the `<origin>` tag defines the reference frame of the visual element with respect to the reference frame of the link. In `dd_robot.urdf`, the visual element (the box) has its origin at the center of its geometry by default. Half of the box is above the grid plane and half is below.

- The rviz display configuration has been changed to remove the **View** and **Time** displays. This configuration is defined in the `urdf.rviz` file that comes with the book's example code (refer to the `.launch` file commands).

- The **RobotModel** and **TF** displays have been added under the **Displays** panel. Under **RobotModel**, notice the following:

  ○ **Robot description**: `robot_description` is the name of the ROS parameter where the URDF file is stored on the Parameter Server. The description of the links and joints and how they are connected is stored here.

Adding wheels

Now, let's add shapes and links for wheels on our robot. When we add link elements to the URDF file, we must add joints to describe the relationship between the links. Joint elements define whether the joint is flexible (movable) or inflexible (fixed). For flexible joints, the URDF describes the kinematics and dynamics of the joint as well as its safety limits. In URDF, there are six possible joint types, which are as follows:

- **Fixed**: This is not really a joint because it cannot move. All degrees of freedom are locked. This type of joint does not require the axis, calibration, dynamics, limits, or safety controller.

- **Revolute**: This joint rotates around one axis and has a range specified by the upper and lower limits.

- **Continuous**: This is a continuous hinge joint that rotates around the axis and has no upper and lower limits.

- **Prismatic**: This is a sliding joint that slides along the axis and has a limited range specified by the upper and lower limits.

- **Floating**: This joint allows motion for all six degrees of freedom.

- **Planar**: This joint allows motion in a plane perpendicular to the axis.

For our robot wheels, we require continuous joints, which mean that they can respond to any rotation angle from negative infinity to positive infinity. They are modeled like this so that they can rotate in both directions forever.

The downloaded `dd_robot2.urdf` file contains the XML code for this exercise. Alternately, you can enter the new code portion to your previous URDF file to create the two wheels (lines from the previous code have been left in or omitted and new code are highlighted):

```
<?xml version='1.0'?>
<robot name="dd_robot">
```

```
<!-- Base Link -->
<link name="base_link">
...
</link>

<!-- Right Wheel -->
<link name="right_wheel">
  <visual>
    <origin xyz="0 0 0" rpy="1.570795 0 0" />
    <geometry>
      <cylinder length="0.1" radius="0.2" />
    </geometry>
  </visual>
</link>
<joint name="joint_right_wheel" type="continuous">
  <parent link="base_link"/>
  <child link="right_wheel"/>
  <origin xyz="0 -0.30 0" rpy="0 0 0" />
  <axis xyz="0 1 0" />
</joint>

<!-- Left Wheel -->
<link name="left_wheel">
  <visual>
    <origin xyz="0 0 0" rpy="1.570795 0 0" />
    <geometry>
      <cylinder length="0.1" radius="0.2" />
    </geometry>
  </visual>
</link>

<joint name="joint_left_wheel" type="continuous">
  <parent link="base_link"/>
  <child link="left_wheel"/>
  <origin xyz="0 0.30 0" rpy="0 0 0" />
  <axis xyz="0 1 0" />
</joint>

</robot>
```

Run your rviz `roslaunch` command:

```
$ roslaunch ros_robotics ddrobot_rviz.launch model:=dd_robot2.urdf
```

Rviz should come up and look like this:

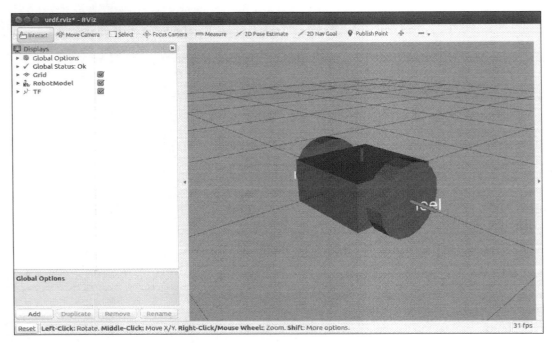

dd_robot2.urdf in rviz

Things to note in the URDF:

- Each wheel is defined visually as a cylinder of radius `0.2` meters and length of `0.1` meters. The wheel's visual origin defines where the center of the visual element should be, relative to its origin. Each wheel's origin is at (0, 0, 0) and is rotated by 1.560795 radians *(= pi/2 = 90 degrees)* about the *x* axis.

- The joint is defined in terms of a parent and a child. The URDF file is ultimately a tree structure with one root link. The `base_link` link is our robot's root link with the wheel's position dependent on position of the `base_link`.

- The wheel joint is defined in terms of the parent's reference frame. Therefore, the wheel's joint origin is `0.30` meters in the *x* direction is for the left wheel and `-0.30` meters for the right wheel.

- The axis of rotation is specified by a `xyz` triplet, indicating that the wheel's joint axis of rotation is around the *y* axis.

- These `<joint>` elements define the complete kinematic model of our robot.

Adding a caster

In the next step, we will add a caster to the front of our robot in order to keep the robot chassis balanced. The caster will only be a visual element added to the chassis and not a joint. The caster will slide along the ground plane as the robot's wheels move.

The downloaded `dd_robot3.urdf` file contains the XML code for this exercise. Alternately, you can enter the new code portion to your previous URDF file (new code has been highlighted):

```
<?xml version='1.0'?>
<robot name="dd_robot">

  <!-- Base Link -->
  ...
    <!-- Caster -->
    <visual name="caster">
      <origin xyz="0.2 0 -0.125" rpy="0 0 0" />
      <geometry>
        <sphere radius="0.05" />
      </geometry>
    </visual>

  </link>
  <!-- Right Wheel -->
  ...
  <!-- Left Wheel -->
  ...
</robot>
```

Run your rviz `roslaunch` command:

```
$ roslaunch ros_robotics ddrobot_rviz.launch model:=dd_robot3.urdf
```

Rviz should come up and look like this:

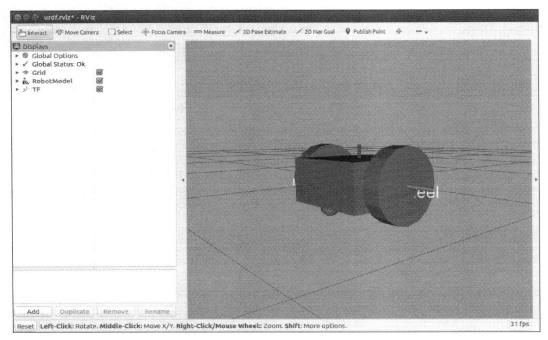

dd_robot3.urdf in rviz

Things to note in the URDF file:

- The caster is defined visually as a sphere with a radius of 0.05 meters. The center of the caster is 0.2 meters in the *x* direction and -0.125 meters in the *z* direction with respect to the origin of the `base_link`.

Adding color

A completely red robot has parts that are not distinctive enough; we will add some color to our model.

The downloaded `dd_robot4.urdf` file contains the XML code for this exercise. Alternately, you can enter the new code portions to your previous URDF file (new code has been highlighted):

```
<?xml version='1.0'?>
<robot name="dd_robot">

  <!-- Base Link -->
  ...
```

```
        <material name="blue">
          <color rgba="0 0.5 1 1"/>
        </material>
    </visual>

    <!-- Caster -->
    ...
  <!-- Right Wheel -->
    ...
        <material name="black">
          <color rgba="0.05 0.05 0.05 1"/>
        </material>
    </visual>
    ...
  <!-- Left Wheel -->
    ...
        <material name="black"/>
    </visual>
    ...
  </robot>
```

Run your rviz `roslaunch` command:

```
$ roslaunch ros_robotics ddrobot_rviz.launch model:=dd_robot4.urdf
```

Rviz should look like the following screenshot:

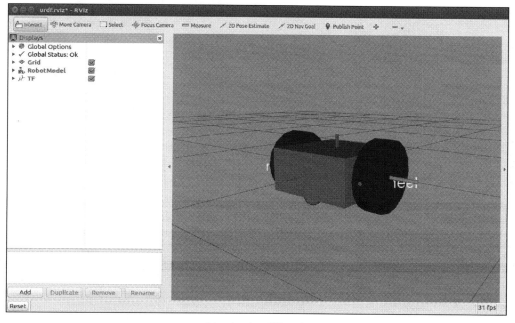

dd_robot4.urdf in rviz

Things to note in the URDF file:

- The `<material>` tag can define `<color>` in terms of red/green/blue/alpha, each in the range of [0, 1]. Alpha is the transparency level of the color. An alpha value of 1 is opaque and 0 is transparent. Once specified and labeled with a name, the material name can be reused without specifying the color values. (For example, note that the left wheel does not have a `<color rgba>` tag because it has been defined in the right wheel visual link.)

- Although the book may show this picture in shades of gray, the chassis of the robot is now blue and the wheels are black.

Adding collisions

Next, we will add the `<collision>` properties to each of our `<link>` elements. Even though we have defined the visual properties of the elements, Gazebo's collision detection engine uses the collision property to identify the boundaries of the object. If an object has complex visual properties (such as a mesh), a simplified collision property should be defined in order to improve the collision detection performance.

The downloaded `dd_robot5.urdf` file contains the XML code for this exercise. Alternately, you can enter the new code portions to your previous URDF file (new code has been highlighted):

```
<?xml version='1.0'?>
<robot name="dd_robot">

  <!-- Base Link -->
  ...
    <!-- Base collision -->
    <collision>
      <origin xyz="0 0 0" rpy="0 0 0" />
      <geometry>
        <box size="0.5 0.5 0.25"/>
      </geometry>
    </collision>

    <!-- Caster -->
    ...
    <!-- Caster collision -->
    <collision>
      <origin xyz="0.2 0 -0.125" rpy="0 0 0" />
      <geometry>
        <sphere radius="0.05" />
```

```
      </geometry>
    </collision>
  </link>

  <!-- Right Wheel -->
  ...
    <!-- Right Wheel collision -->
    <collision>
      <origin xyz="0 0 0" rpy="1.570795 0 0" />
      <geometry>
        <cylinder length="0.1" radius="0.2" />
      </geometry>
    </collision>
  ...

  <!-- Left Wheel -->
  ...
    <!-- Left Wheel collision -->
    <collision>
      <origin xyz="0 0 0" rpy="1.570795 0 0" />
      <geometry>
        <cylinder length="0.1" radius="0.2" />
      </geometry>
    </collision>
  </robot>
```

Adding the `<collision>` property does not change the visual model of the robot, and the rviz display will look the same as in the previous screenshot.

Moving the wheels

Now that we have the right and left wheel joints defined and we can see them clearly, we will bring up the GUI pop-up screen to control these joints. In the `ddrobot_rviz.launch` file, we start three ROS nodes: `joint_state_publisher`, `robot_state_publisher`, and `rviz`. The `joint_state_publisher` node finds all of the non-fixed joints and publishes a `JointState` message with all those joints defined. So far, the values in the `JointState` message have been constant, keeping the wheels from rotating. We bring up a GUI interface in rviz to change the value of each `JointState` and watch the wheels rotate.

Add the `gui` field to the rviz `roslaunch` command:

```
$ roslaunch ros_robotics ddrobot_rviz.launch model:=dd_robot5.urdf
gui:=True
```

Rviz should look like the following screenshot:

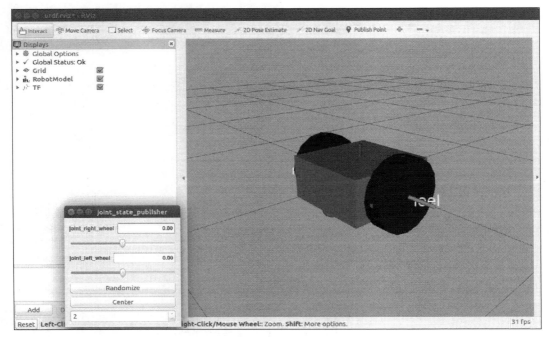

dd_robot5.urdf in rviz

Things to note:

- The joint positions in the window are sliders. The wheel joints are defined as continuous but this GUI limits each slider's value from –Pi to +Pi. Play with the sliders and see how the wheels move.

- The **Randomize** button will select a random value for both the joints.

- The **Center** button will move both the joints to the zero position. (Visually, the blue dot on both the wheels should be at the top.)

- The bottom selection allows the user to select the configuration of the slider display, either listed one below the other, or side-by-side.

A word about tf and robot_state_publisher

A robotic system is made up of a collection of 3D coordinate frames for every component in the system. In our dd_robot model, there is a base coordinate frame and a frame for each wheel that relates back to the base coordinate frame. The model's coordinate frames are also related to the world coordinate frame of the 3D environment. The tf package is the central ROS package used to relate the coordinate frames of our robot to the 3D simulated environment (or a real robot to its real environment).

The robot_state_publisher node subscribes to the JointState message and publishes the state of the robot to the tf transform library. The tf transform library maintains the relationships between the coordinate frames of each component in the system over time. The robot_state_publisher node receives the robot's joint angles as inputs and computes and publishes the 3D poses of the robot links. Internally, the robot_state_publisher node uses a kinematic tree model of the robot built from its URDF. Once the robot's state gets published, it is available to all components in the system that also use tf.

Adding physical properties

With the additional physical properties of mass and inertia, our robot will be ready to be launched in the Gazebo simulator. These properties are needed by Gazebo's physics engine. Specifically, every <link> element that is being simulated needs an <inertial> tag.

The two sub-elements of the inertial element we will use are as follows:

- <mass>: This is the weight defined in kilograms.

- <inertia>: This frame is a 3 x 3 rotational inertia matrix. Because this matrix is symmetrical, it can be represented by only six elements. The six highlighted elements are the six element <inertia> values. The other three values are not used:

ixx	ixy	Ixz
ixy	iyy	Iyz
ixz	iyz	Izz

Wikipedia's list of moment of inertia tensors (https://en.wikipedia.org/wiki/List_of_moments_of_inertia) provides the equations for the inertia of simple geometric primitives, such as a cylinder, box, and sphere. We use these equations to compute the inertia values for the model's chassis, caster, and wheels.

Do not use inertia elements of zero (or almost zero) because real-time controllers can cause the robot model to collapse without warning, and all links will appear with their origins coinciding with the world origin.

The downloaded `dd_robot6.urdf` file contains the XML code for this exercise. Alternately, you can enter the new code portions in your previous URDF file (new code has been highlighted):

```xml
<?xml version='1.0'?>
<robot name="dd_robot">

  <!-- Base Link -->
  ...
    <inertial>
      <mass value="5"/>
      <inertia ixx="0.13" ixy="0.0" ixz="0.0"
                iyy="0.21" iyz="0.0" izz="0.13"/>
    </inertial>

    <!-- Caster -->
    ...
    <inertial>
      <mass value="0.5"/>
      <inertia ixx="0.0001" ixy="0.0" ixz="0.0"
                iyy="0.0001" iyz="0.0" izz="0.0001"/>
    </inertial>
  </link>

  <!-- Right Wheel -->
  ...
    <inertial>
      <mass value="0.5"/>
      <inertia ixx="0.01"  ixy="0.0" ixz="0.0"
                iyy="0.005" iyz="0.0" izz="0.005"/>
    </inertial>
  ...
  <!-- Left Wheel -->
  ...
    <inertial>
      <mass value="0.5"/>
      <inertia ixx="0.01" ixy="0.0" ixz="0.0"
                iyy="0.005" iyz="0.0" izz="0.005"/>
    </inertial>
    ...
</robot>
```

Adding the `<inertial>` property does not change the visual model of the robot and the rviz display will look the same as the preceding screenshot.

Trying URDF tools

ROS provides command-line tools that can help verify and visualize information about your URDF. We will try out these tools on our robot URDF but first you will need to check whether the tools have been installed on your computer system. Type the following command:

```
$ sudo apt-get install liburdfdom-tools
```

check_urdf

`check_urdf` attempts to parse a URDF file description and either prints a description of the resulting kinematic chain or an error message. (Be sure to run this command from the directory containing the `dd_robot6.urdf` file.)

```
$ check_urdf dd_robot6.urdf
```

The output of the preceding command is as follows:

```
robot name is: dd_robot
---------- Successfully Parsed XML --------------
root Link: base_link has 2 child(ren)
child(1): left_wheel
child(2): right_wheel
```

urdf_to_graphiz

The `urdf_to_graphiz` tool creates a graphviz diagram of a URDF file and a diagram in the `.pdf` format. Graphviz is open-source graph visualization software.

To execute `urdf_to_graphiz`, type:

```
$ urdf_to_graphiz dd_robot6.urdf
```

The output is as follows:

```
Created file dd_robot.gv
Created file dd_robot.pdf
```

Open the `.pdf` file with the following command:

```
$ evince dd_robot.pdf
```

The `dd_robot.pdf` file should appear as follows:

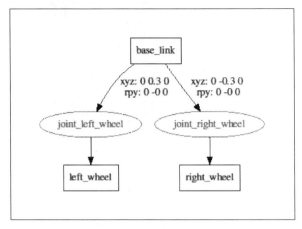

dd_robot.pdf

Now that we have a working URDF model of our two-wheeled robot, we are ready to launch it into Gazebo and move it around. First, we must make some modifications to our URDF file to add simulation-specific tags so that it properly works in Gazebo. Gazebo uses SDF, which is similar to URDF, but by adding specific Gazebo information, we can convert our `dd_robot` model file into an SDF-type format.

Gazebo

Gazebo is a free and open source robot simulation environment developed by Willow Garage. As a multifunctional tool for ROS robot developers, Gazebo supports the following:

- Designing of robot models
- Rapid prototyping and testing of algorithms
- Regression testing using realistic scenarios
- Simulation of indoor and outdoor environments
- Simulation of sensor data for laser range finders, 2D/3D cameras, kinect-style sensors, contact sensors, force-torque, and more
- Advanced 3D objects and environments utilizing **Object-Oriented Graphics Rendering Engine (OGRE)**
- Several high-performance physics engines (**Open Dynamics Engine (ODE)**, Bullet, Simbody, and **Dynamic Animation and Robotics Toolkit (DART)**) to model the real-world dynamics

In this section, we will load our two-wheeled robot URDF into Gazebo to visualize it in a 3D environment. Gazebo allows you to take control of some aspects of our model without an external control program. In the later chapters, we will be using simulated versions of robots in Gazebo to control joints, visualize sensor data, and test control algorithms.

Installing and launching Gazebo

To run Gazebo requires a powerful graphics card and the appropriate drivers be installed on your computer.

 If you have trouble with running Gazebo, refer to `http://answers.gazebosim.org/questions/` or search the ROS forum at `http://answers.ros.org/questions/`.

Gazebo should have been installed on your computer as part of the `ros-kinetic-desktop-full` installation, as described in the *Installing and launching ROS* section in *Chapter 1, Getting Started with ROS*. Gazebo 7.x is the default version of Gazebo for ROS-Kinetic/Ubuntu-Xenial and is the version recommended for the exercises in this book.

To test whether Gazebo has been installed correctly, open a terminal window and type the following command:

```
$ gazebo
```

This should display an environment similar to the following screenshot:

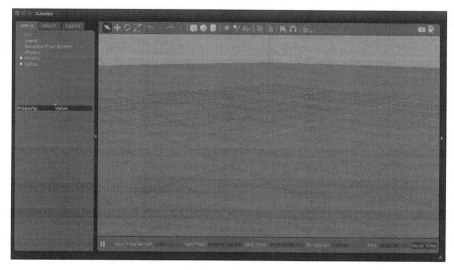

Gazebo main screen

If Gazebo has not been installed, refer to the ROS-Kinetic installation instructions at `http://wiki.ros.org/kinetic/Installation/Ubuntu` or the general Gazebo installation instructions at `http://gazebosim.org/tutorials?cat=install`. Make sure that you install the Gazebo 7 version.

The `$ gazebo` command runs two different executables: the Gazebo server and the Gazebo client. The Gazebo server `gzserver` will execute the simulation process, including the physics update loop and sensor data generation. This process is the core of Gazebo and can be used independently of any graphical interface. The Gazebo client `gzclient` command runs the Gazebo GUI. This GUI provides a nice visualization of simulation and handy controls for an assortment of simulation properties.

Tutorials for Gazebo can be found at `http://gazebosim.org/tutorials`.

To shut down Gazebo

Use the *Ctrl* + *C* keys to kill the terminal window process after you have closed the Gazebo window.

Important commands: If at any time, your command generates a warning or error command, type `$ rosnode list` to determine whether there are any active nodes still lingering after you have attempted to shut down Gazebo. If any nodes are still active, use the `$ rosnode kill` command to list them. Next, select the number of the ROS nodes that you wish to kill. Or you can use the `$ rosnode kill -a` command to kill all the active nodes.

Using roslaunch with Gazebo

Roslaunch is a standard method used to start Gazebo with world files and robot URDF models. To perform a basic test of Gazebo, an empty Gazebo world can be brought up with the following command:

```
$ roslaunch gazebo_ros empty_world.launch
```

This test will verify that Gazebo has been installed properly. If you wish to try other demo worlds, including the `gazebo_ros` package, try substituting one of the following with `empty_world.launch` in the previous command:

- `willowgarage_world.launch`
- `mud_world.launch`
- `shapes_world.launch`
- `rubble_world.launch`

For the exercises in this chapter, we created our own world, `ddrobot.world`. This world consists of a ground plane and two construction cones for you to drive the robot around. You will find this file in the `ros_robotics` package under `ros_robotics/worlds`. We will launch our `dd_robot` model into this world using the `ddrobot_gazebo.launch` launch file found in the `ros_robotics/launch` directory.

Getting familiar with Gazebo

The Gazebo GUI is similar to rviz in many ways. The central window provides the view for Gazebo's 3D world environment. The grid is typically configured to be the ground plane of the environment on which all the models are held due to gravity in the environment. A red-green-blue axis is provided at the origin of the 3D Cartesian co-ordinate system. The red axis represents the x axis, green is y and blue is z.

Gazebo also has mouse controls to navigate the scene as shown in the following image:

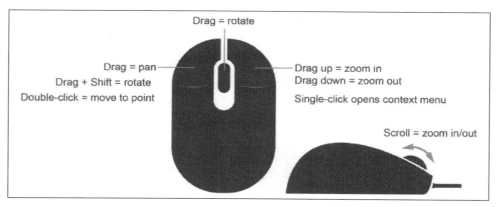

Gazebo mouse control

For Gazebo keyboard shortcuts, visit `http://gazebosim.org/hotkeys`.

Double-clicking on a spot in the environment will cause the display to be zoomed in to that spot.

 For Gazebo, the standard units of measurement are in terms of meters and kilograms (like rviz).

The main screen of Gazebo is divided into four main display areas: the central window, the **World, Insert** and **Layers** panels to the left, the **Joints** panel to the right, and the **Simulation** panel at the bottom. Across the top of these display areas are the **Environment** toolbar and the main screen menu bar. Each of the display areas of Gazebo will be described in the following sections. This overview should provide basic familiarity with the Gazebo GUI.

Environment toolbar

The toolbar at the top of the Gazebo environment display provides options for interacting with the simulation models and environment as shown in the following screenshot:

Gazebo environment toolbar

Each option represented by an icon has a label that is revealed when the cursor hovers over the icon. Keyboard shortcuts are also displayed in parentheses. The following labels appear on the toolbar icons (from left to right) and offer the following functionalities:

- **Selection Mode** (*Esc*): This selects a model in the environment when the cursor is clicked on it or a drag box is wrapped around it. The **World** panel displays the model's properties. When selected, a white outline 3D box is drawn around the model. A yellow disc is placed where the cursor is clicked and becomes the focal point when the mouse controls are used to move around the scene. (Hitting the *Esc* key will also activate this mode.)

- **Translation Mode** (*T*): This selects a model in the environment when the cursor is clicked on it or a drag box is wrapped around it. A 3D axis (red-green-blue) is drawn and centered on the model. Use the cursor and left mouse button to move the model anywhere in the *x, y,* and *z* planes. (Hitting the *T* key will also activate this mode.)

- **Rotation Mode** (*R*): This selects a model in the environment when the cursor is clicked on it or a drag box is wrapped around it. A 3D sphere (red-green-blue) is drawn and centered around the model. Use the cursor and left mouse button to rotate the model in the roll, pitch, or yaw directions using one of the rings. (Hitting the *R* key will also activate this mode.)

- **Scale Mode** (*S*): This selects a model in the environment when the cursor is clicked on it or a drag box is wrapped around it. A 3D axis (red-green-blue) with square endpoints is drawn and centered on the model. Scaling of a model is currently limited to only simple shapes. (A warning message will be displayed in the terminal window if the user attempts to scale other models.)

- **Undo** (*Ctrl + Z*): This reverses the last action.
- **Redo** (*Shift + Ctrl + Z*): This reverses the last undo.
- **The next set of icons is used to create simple shapes in Gazebo**: **Box**, **Sphere**, and **Cylinder**. Click on the icon and place the image shape anywhere in the 3D environment. The scale mode can then be used to resize the object.
- **The next set of icons is used for lighting**: **Point Light**, **Spot Light**, and **Directional Light**. Explore these if you wish to change the lighting and shadows in your environment.
- **Copy** (*Ctrl + C*): This copies the selected item to the clipboard.
- **Paste** (*Ctrl + V*): This pastes the item from the clipboard.
- **In Selection mode, hold Ctrl and select 2 objects to align**: Click on this icon when the objects are selected to align their axis in *x*, *y* or *z* and aligning to the minimum, center or maximum of the first or last object selected. (Lots of options here.)
- **Snap Mode** (*N*): In this mode, you can select the locations of two objects that you want to join.
- **Change the View Angle**: This changes the perspective view of the scene from various predefined angles.
- **Screenshot**: The camera icon will take a picture of the simulation scene and save it to your `~/gazebo/pictures` directory.
- **Log Data** (*Ctrl + D*): This will record the simulation to reproduce it later. A compressed `.log` file is produced which contains the initial full description of the whole world, then a series of *world states*. By default, the `.log` file is saved to the `~/.gazebo/log` directory. The following screenshot shows the window that allows you to start the recording and select where the log file is stored:

Gazebo Data Logger screen

World, Insert and Layers panels

The **World**, **Insert** and **Layers** panels are shown in the following screenshot:

Gazebo World, Insert and Layers panel

The **World** panel to the left of the 3D environment provides access to all of the environment elements. These environment elements are **GUI**, **Scene**, **Spherical Coordinates**, **Physics**, **Models**, and **Lights**. By clicking on any of these labels, a properties panel will appear below the **World** panel with a properties list specific for that element.

The **GUI** element displays the camera name and pose in x, y, z, roll, pitch and yaw. The **Scene** selections allow the user to alter the ambient environment, the background and the shadows. The **Spherical Coordinates** displays the **Surface Model** in use and the **Latitude**, **Longitude**, **Elevation** and **Heading**. The **Physics** selections check whether the physics engine is enabled. If the physics engine is enabled, the user can control the real-time update rate, gravity, and constraints under the **Physics** tab as well as other properties. The **Models** list will display all models active in the environment. When the $ gazebo command is used, the only active model will be the ground_plane model. By clicking on the ground_plane label, the properties displayed will be the model name, a checkbox to make the model static, the model's pose (x, y, z, roll, pitch, and yaw) in the environment, and its link information.

These details are lengthy so you can explore them at your leisure. The last element, **Lights**, displays all the light sources for the environment. For our default environment, the sun is the only source. The properties of the sun are its pose, diffuse, specular, range, and attenuation. Our primary interest for this book will be the **Models**.

The **Insert** tab is behind the **World** panel. The **Insert** panel accesses two locations to allow the user to select from a number of predefined models to be added to the environment. The first location, /home/<username>/.gazebo/models, is the user's repository of Gazebo models that they have selected from the main Gazebo repository. This repository is the second selection available at http://gazebosim. org/models/.

The **Layers** tab behind the **Insert** panel will initially be empty. Visualization layers are defined in a model's SDF file to create the capability to toggle visual parts of the model on and off through the Gazebo GUI. A layer may contain one or more models. Toggling a layer on or off will display or hide the model(s) in that layer.

Joints panel

The panels to the right and left of the center display can be revealed or hidden using the three tiny rectangles in the black vertical strip. On the right side, the user can click and drag these three tiny rectangles to reveal the **Joints** panel. (Widen the window if the panel is not responding.) Under the **Joints** panel, there are three tabs labeled: **Force**, **Position**, and **Velocity**. There is also a **Reset** button to return your model to its original state (if possible):

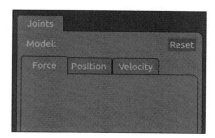

Gazebo Joints panel

To use these controls, the model must be selected to reveal the available model joints. For the joint control, we have the following values:

- **Force** values are in Newton meters
- **Position** values are in radians or degrees (make a selection from the drop-down window), **P Gain** (for proportional gain), **I Gain** (for integral gain), and **D Gain** (for derivative gain) (Scroll the window using the horizontal bar at the bottom of the panel to see all of these fields.)
- **Velocity** values are in m/s (for meters per second), **P Gain** (for proportional gain), **I Gain** (for integral gain), and **D Gain** (for derivative gain)

[The slider bar at the bottom of the **Joints** panel will help you see the information to the right of the display.]

Main window menu bar

The top-most main window menu bar provides options under the basic **File**, **Edit**, **Camera**, **View**, **Window**, and **Help** headings as shown here:

- **File**: **Save World**, **Save World As**, **Save Configuration**, **Clone World**, and **Quit**
- **Edit**: **Reset Model Poses**, **Reset World**, **Building Editor**, and **Model Editor**
- **Camera**: **Orthographic**, **Perspective**, **FPS View Control**, **Orbit View Control**, and **Reset View Angle**
- **View**: **Grid**, **Origin**, **Transparent**, **Wireframe**, **Collisions**, **Joints**, **Center of Mass**, **Inertias**, **Contacts**, **Link Frames**
- **Window**: **Topic Visualization**, **Oculus Rift**, **Show GUI Overlays**, **Show Toolbars**, and **Full Screen**
- **Help**: **Hot Key Chart** and **About**

These selections can be very useful. For example, if you wish to check the center of mass for your URDF in Gazebo, click on the **View** heading and select both the **Wireframe** and the **Center of Mass** options.

Simulation panel

At the bottom of the environment display is a handy tool used to run simulation scripts. It is useful when recording and playing back simulation runs.

Before we can load our `dd_robot` model into Gazebo, we must make a few modifications to the URDF file.

Modifications to the robot URDF

Gazebo expects the robot model file to be in SDF format. SDF is similar to the URDF, using some of the same XML descriptive tags. With the following modifications, Gazebo will automatically convert the URDF code into an SDF robot description. The following sections will describe the steps to be taken.

Adding the Gazebo tag

The `<gazebo>` tag must be added to the URDF to specify additional elements needed for simulation in Gazebo. This tag allows for identifying elements found in the SDF format that are not found in the URDF format. If a `<gazebo>` tag is used without a `reference=""` property, it is assumed that the `<gazebo>` elements refer to the whole robot model. The reference parameter usually refers to a specific robot link.

Other `<gazebo>` elements for both the links and joints can be applied to your robot but are not described in this book because of the extensive list and explanations of how they applied to the physics of Gazebo.

> Refer to the Gazebo tutorial at `http://gazebosim.org/tutorials/?tut=ros_urdf` for a list of these elements and their usage (*Elements for Links* and *Elements for Joints*).

Specifying color in Gazebo

The method of specifying link colors in rviz does not work in Gazebo since Gazebo has adopted OGRE's material scripts for coloring and texturing links. Therefore, a Gazebo `<material>` tag must be specified for each link. These tags can be placed in the model file just before the ending `</robot>` tag:

```
<gazebo reference="base_link">
  <material>Gazebo/Blue</material>
</gazebo>

<gazebo reference="right_wheel">
  <material>Gazebo/Black</material>
</gazebo>

<gazebo reference="left_wheel">
  <material>Gazebo/Black</material>
</gazebo>
```

A word about the <visual> and <collision> elements in Gazebo

Gazebo will not use the `<visual>` elements the same as the `<collision>` elements if you do not explicitly specify them for each link. Instead, Gazebo will treat your link as invisible to laser scanners and collision checking. If your model ends up partially embedded in Gazebo's ground plane, you should check your `<collision>` elements.

Verifying a Gazebo model

The dd_robot URDF has been updated with the <gazebo> tags and the <material> elements, as described earlier, and is stored in the downloaded file, dd_robot.gazebo. The .gazebo extension is used by the author to signify that this file is ready for use in Gazebo. An easy tool exists to check whether your URDF can be properly converted into an SDF. Simply run the following command:

```
$ gzsdf -p dd_robot.gazebo
```

or

```
$ gzsdf -p $(rospack find ros_robotics)/urdf/dd_robot.gazebo
```

This command outputs the entire SDF to the screen so you may wish to redirect the output to a file. The output will show you the SDF that has been generated from your input URDF as well as any warnings about the missing information required to generate the SDF.

Viewing the URDF in Gazebo

Viewing the dd_robot model in Gazebo requires a launch file obtained or created by one of the following ways:

- Using the downloaded ddrobot_gazebo.launch file from the ros_robotics/launch directory from the book's website

- Creating the ddrobot_gazebo.launch file from the following XML code:

```
<launch>
  <!-- We resume the logic in gazebo_ros package
       empty_world.launch,
       changing only the name of the
       world to be launched -->
  <include file="$(find
       gazebo_ros)/launch/empty_world.launch">
    <arg name="world_name"
       value="$(find ros_robotics)/worlds/ddrobot.world"/>

    <arg name="paused" default="false"/>
    <arg name="use_sim_time" default="true"/>
    <arg name="gui" default="true"/>
    <arg name="headless" default="false"/>
    <arg name="debug" default="false"/>
  </include>

  <!-- Spawn dd_robot into Gazebo -->
```

```
<node name="spawn_urdf" pkg="gazebo_ros"
    type="spawn_model" output="screen"
    args="-file
    $(find ros_robotics)/urdf/dd_robot.gazebo
        -urdf -model ddrobot" />

</launch>
```

This launch file inherits most of the necessary functionality from `empty_world.launch` from the `gazebo_ros` package. The only parameter that is changed is the `world_name` parameter by substituting the `ddrobot.world` world file. In addition to this, our URDF-based `dd_robot` model is launched into Gazebo using the ROS `spawn_model` service from the `gazebo_ros` ROS node. If you plan to reuse this code or share it, it is recommended that you add the dependency to your `package.xml` file for the `ros_robotics` package. The following statement should be added under dependencies:

```
<exec_depend>gazebo_ros</exec_depend>
```

The `ddrobot.world` world file contains a ground plane and two construction cones. This file can be found in the `ros_robotics/worlds` directory on the book's website, or you can create the `ddrobot.world` file from the following code:

```
<?xml version="1.0" ?>
<sdf version="1.4">
  <world name="default">
    <include>
      <uri>model://ground_plane</uri>
    </include>
    <include>
      <uri>model://sun</uri>
    </include>
    <include>
      <uri>model://construction_cone</uri>
      <name>construction_cone</name>
      <pose>-3.0 0 0 0 0 0</pose>
    </include>
    <include>
      <uri>model://construction_cone</uri>
      <name>construction_cone</name>
      <pose>3.0 0 0 0 0 0</pose>
    </include>
  </world>
</sdf>
```

> The ddrobot_gazebo.launch file should be found in the /launch directory and ddrobot.world should be found in the /worlds directory of the ros_robotics ROS package.

Now we are ready to launch our dd_robot model in Gazebo by typing the following command:

```
$ roslaunch ros_robotics ddrobot_gazebo.launch
```

This command will launch both the Gazebo server and GUI client with the dd_robot model and world automatically launched inside the Gazebo environment. Gazebo will look similar to the following screenshot:

dd_robot.gazebo in Gazebo

Tweaking your model

If your robot model behaves unexpectedly within Gazebo, it is likely because your model URDF needs further tuning to accurately represent its physics in Gazebo. Refer to the SDF user guide at http://sdformat.org/spec for more information on various properties available in Gazebo, which are also available in the URDF via the <gazebo> tag.

Moving your model around

To understand the physics of Gazebo, it is important to play with your model in Gazebo. Use the **Selection, Translation,** and **Rotation** modes on the **Environment** toolbar to move your model to different positions, and then watch how the gravity model works. If you are brave, you can even manipulate the environment to experiment with the relationship of the elements. For example, remove the ground plane and see what happens.

Simple joint control of our dd_robot model is possible by using the **Joints** panel, which is to the right of the center environment. In selection mode, click on the ddrobot model and the model will be highlighted with a white outline box. The joint_left_wheel and joint_right_wheel joints will appear under the tabbed sections with a value of 0.000 for each of the input windows. We will experiment by changing the values of the left and right wheel joints to see the dd_robot model move around on the ground plane. Play with the values for **Force, Position** and **Velocity** to move your dd_robot. The following screenshot shows our dd_robot ready to be controlled via the **Joints** panel:

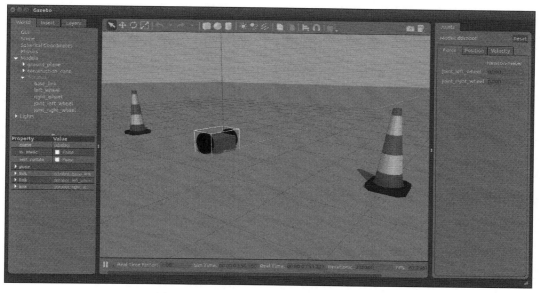

dd_robot.gazebo in Gazebo with the Joints panel

A greater control of our model can be achieved by adding transmission blocks to the URDF for the model joints. Gazebo plugins are also needed to simulate controllers that publish ROS messages for motor commands. A discussion of these advanced topics will be delayed until *Chapter 5, Creating Your First Robot Arm (in Simulation)*, when the reader has a better understanding of ROS messages for control of mobile robots. *Chapter 5, Creating Your First Robot Arm (in Simulation)* will walk you through the construction of a URDF/SDF for a robot arm with a joint control implemented via Gazebo plugins. The implementation of transmission blocks and plugins for our `dd_robot` model is left as an exercise on completion of *Chapter 5, Creating Your First Robot Arm (in Simulation)*.

Other ROS simulation environments

Gazebo is only one simulator that can interface to ROS and ROS models. A list of other simulators, both open source and commercial, is provided along with a website reference:

- MATLAB with Simulink is a commercially available, multi-domain simulation and modeling design package for dynamic systems. It provides support for ROS through its Robotics System Toolbox (`http://www.mathworks.com/hardware-support/robot-operating-system.html`). MATLAB ROS examples are available at the website `https://www.mathworks.com/help/robotics/examples/get-started-with-ros.html`. An introduction of the MATLAB ROS interface is presented in *Chapter 10, Controlling Baxter with MATLAB©*.

- Stage is an open source 2D simulator for mobile robots and sensors (`http://playerstage.sourceforge.net/index.php?src=stage/`).

- **Virtual Robot Experimentation Platform** (**V-REP**) is a commercially available robot simulator with an integrated development environment. Developed by Coppelia Robotics, V-REP lends itself to many robotic applications (`http://www.coppeliarobotics.com/`).

Summary

Your first robot design has been a simple two-wheeled differential drive model defined in URDF. There are many other properties that can be defined in the URDF file, and you are free to extend the dd_robot model. This introductory exercise was provided so that the elements of simulation can be understood by the reader. In an upcoming chapter, we will extend our understanding of URDF by learning about Xacro. We will build a Xacro file to define a robot model for a robot arm.

In *Chapter 3, Driving Around with TurtleBot*, we will use a simulated and a real TurtleBot to explore a variety of ROS control methods for mobile robot navigation. The rqt toolset will be introduced and used to monitor and control the TurtleBot's movements.

3
Driving Around with TurtleBot

It is time for a real ROS robot! A robot called TurtleBot will be discussed and described both in simulation and as the real robot. In this chapter, you will learn how to move TurtleBot as a simulated robot and as the real robot. Even if you do not have a real TurtleBot, the examples in this chapter will teach you the techniques to control a mobile robot.

After introducing TurtleBot 2, we will cover the following topics:

- Loading the TurtleBot simulation software and using Gazebo with TurtleBot
- Setting up your system to control a real TurtleBot from its own netbook computer or wirelessly from a remote computer
- Controlling the movement of the TurtleBot with ROS terminal commands or using the keyboard for control in teleoperation
- Creating a Python script which, when executed, moves TurtleBot
- Using rqt tools to provide a GUI that aids the user in analyzing robot programs and also monitoring and controlling the robot
- Exploring an environment using TurtleBot's odometry data
- Executing the automatic docking program of TurtleBot
- Introducing a newer version of TurtleBot, called TurtleBot 3, and describing the simulation and keyboard control of a real TurtleBot 3

Introducing TurtleBot 2

TurtleBot is a mobile robot that can be purchased as a kit or fully assembled. Several companies in North America and around the world sell TurtleBots. The TurtleBot 2 model is shown in the following image:

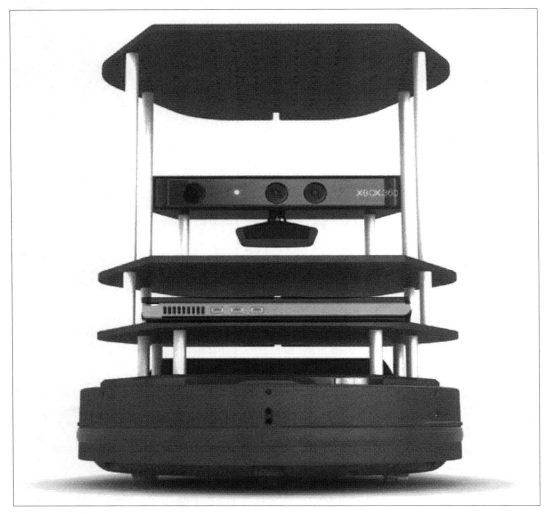

Turtlebot 2

A list of manufacturers can be found at http://www.turtlebot.com/ manufacturers/.

The main items that comprise the TurtleBot 2 model, from bottom to top in the preceding image, are as follows:

- A mobile base that also serves as support for the upper stages of the robot
- A netbook resting on a module plate
- Another module plate used to hold items
- A vision sensor with a color camera and 3D depth sensor
- The top most module plate used to hold items

We will discuss the main items briefly here and provide more details for the base and the netbook later in this chapter. Overall, the TurtleBot model stands about 420 mm (16.5 inches) high and the base is approximately 355 mm (14 inches) in diameter.

The particular base in the authors' TurtleBot is a Kobuki mobile platform produced by the Yujin Robot company. TurtleBot rests on the floor on two wheels and a caster. The base is configured as a differential drive base, which means that when the TurtleBot is moving, the rotational velocity of the wheels can be controlled independently. So, for example, TurtleBot can move back and forth in a straight line when the wheels are driven in the same direction, **clockwise (CW)** or **counterclockwise (CCW)**, with the same rotational velocity. If the wheels turn at different rotational velocities, TurtleBot can make turns as the velocity of the wheels is controlled. More details are available at http://kobuki.yujinrobot.com/about2/.

A model of a differential drive robot was built in the *Building a differential drive robot URDF* section in *Chapter 2, Creating Your First Two-Wheeled ROS Robot (in Simulation)*. The base has a battery pack and various power connections for accessories, including a USB connection and power plug for the netbook. TurtleBot also comes with a separate docking station for charging the Kobuki base.

The netbook is essentially a laptop computer but is lightweight with a small screen compared to many laptops. The netbook purchased with TurtleBot has Ubuntu and ROS packages installed. For remote control, the netbook is connected via Wi-Fi to a network and a remote computer. There are USB ports used to plug in the vision sensor or other accessories. The setup of the network is described in the *Networking the netbook and remote computer* section of this chapter.

The vision sensor, as shown in the preceding image of TurtleBot 2, is an Xbox 360 Kinect sensor manufactured by Microsoft. Originally designed for video games, the Kinect sensor is a popular vision and depth sensor for robotics.

The ROS wiki has a series of tutorials that cover TurtleBots 1, 2, and 3, including the Gazebo simulator, at the following link:
`http://wiki.ros.org/Robots/TurtleBot`

Loading TurtleBot 2 simulator software

This section deals with loading software packages for the TurtleBot simulator. The physical TurtleBot is not involved because these software packages are loaded on your laptop or desktop computer. It is assumed that Ubuntu 16.04 and ROS Kinetic software are installed on the computer that you will use for the simulation. This installation is described in the *Installing and launching ROS* section in *Chapter 1, Getting Started with ROS*.

Note that TurtleBot 2 software has not been completely upgraded to Kinetic as of this writing. On the ROS wiki, the latest supported release of TurtleBot 2 documentation is Indigo.

In a terminal window, type the following command:

```
$ sudo apt-get install ros-kinetic-turtlebot ros-kinetic-turtlebot-apps
ros-kinetic-turtlebot-interactions ros-kinetic-turtlebot-simulator
ros-kinetic-kobuki-ftdi ros-kinetic-turtlebot-gazebo
```

A large number of ROS packages are loaded by the `sudo apt-get` command. The groups are as follows:

- The TurtleBot software has ROS packages to simulate TurtleBot and control the real TurtleBot. The TurtleBot simulator download includes the `turtlebot_gazebo` package.
- The Kobuki software consists of ROS packages used to drive or simulate the mobile base.

To view the TurtleBot packages downloaded in each category, type the following command:

```
$ rospack list | grep turtlebot
```

To see the packages that apply to the base, type the following command:

```
$ rospack list | grep kobuki
```

The other software can be viewed in a similar way.

Launching TurtleBot 2 simulator in Gazebo

The simulator package Gazebo was introduced in *Chapter 2, Creating Your First Two-Wheeled ROS Robot (in Simulation)*. If you run the examples there using the differential drive robot, dd_robot, you should have a good understanding of Gazebo, including how to load models and worlds and manipulate the environment.

To run the simulator, you need to install the TurtleBot software, as described in the previous section.

To start the simulation, open a new terminal window and type the following command:

```
$ roslaunch turtlebot_gazebo turtlebot_world.launch
```

If all goes well, you will see a screenshot similar to this one:

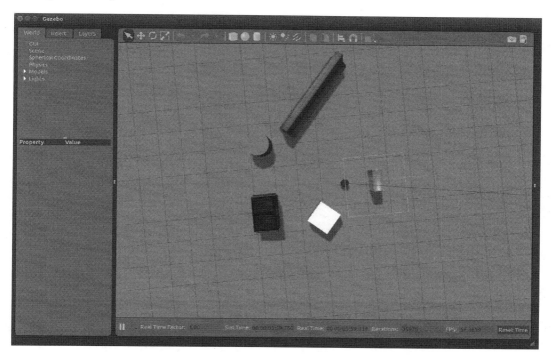

TurtleBot simulated in Gazebo

If you do not see Gazebo start, refer to the following *Problems and troubleshooting* section. If that is the case, there are a few issues that may help you if you are having problems with the simulation and the use of Gazebo.

TurtleBot is in the approximate center of the world view, as seen from an overhead camera. The initial position of TurtleBot in the Gazebo world is at the origin. To determine the pose of TurtleBot, choose **World** in the Gazebo left panel. Click on **Models**, click on `mobile_base`, and view the **Property** and **Value** window. Click on the arrowhead at **pose** and read the values. These values should be close to (0, 0, 0). The squares on the Gazebo ground-plane grid are 1 meter square.

Change the viewing angle to a side view and select the Translation-Mode on the environment toolbar and click on TurtleBot. A white outline box should appear around TurtleBot. If you move TurtleBot away from Gazebo's origin, you should see two coordinate axes, as in the following screenshot. One is for Gazebo showing the origin of the *world* coordinates and another coordinate system is attached to TurtleBot. In both cases, the x, y, and z axes are colored red, green, and blue respectively.

The Gazebo positions are absolute with respect to the Gazebo origin. In the screenshot shown, TurtleBot is moved ahead by 2 meters, as shown by the **pose** data for the `mobile_base` in the left panel. The other values are approximately zero:

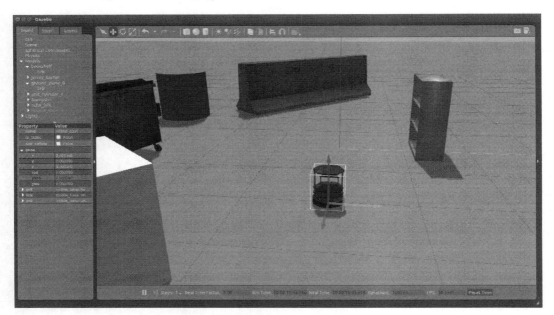

TurtleBot simulated with axes shown

The pose of any object in the Gazebo world can be found by selecting it in the left pane and viewing its pose. The bookcase is at approximately (0, 1.5) meters in (x, y).

If you have modified the scene, you can take a picture of it by left-clicking on the camera icon on the toolbar. This picture will be saved in `/home/<user_name>/.gazebo/pictures`.

Roll the cursor over the symbols on the Gazebo toolbar to obtain their meaning.

Problems and troubleshooting

The authors have tried their best to present the material in a clear manner so that you can follow along and achieve the same results. However, computers may differ in their abilities to run simulations that rely heavily on graphics, as Gazebo does.

We have run the code on relatively new laptops, older laptops, and on a powerful workstation. On a laptop, the response to commands from the keyboard may be slow, sometimes painfully so! Be patient: if the software is working, TurtleBot will respond if commanded to move.

Some serious problems that may occur are as follows:

- On some older laptops, the hardware accelerator will not allow Gazebo to run, but this can be fixed by adding the following statement to the `.bashrc` file, which disables the hardware accelerator:

  ```
  export LIBGL_ALWAYS_SOFTWARE=1
  ```

- Sometimes, it is necessary to close all the windows and start over if the system does not respond.

- If you execute the `roscore` or `roslaunch` command, and you have changed your ROS Master address using an `export` command to be linked to the TurtleBot network, as described later in this chapter, you may receive an error message similar to this:

  ```
  ERROR: unable to contact ROS master at [http://<IP Address>:11311]
  The traceback for the exception was written to the log file
  ```

  It probably means that the ROS addresses are incorrect for your local machine. Usually, the problem can be fixed by issuing the following commands:

  ```
  $ export ROS_MASTER_URI=http://localhost:11311
  $ export ROS_HOSTNAME=localhost
  ```

  This returns the ROS control to your local computer to run the simulator. You must run these export commands in each new terminal window that is opened or create a script file with these commands.

  Check the results for these environment variables with the following command:

  ```
  $ env | grep ROS
  ```

  Make sure that the `ROS_MASTER_URI` variable points to the proper location.

For more information on computer and network addresses, refer to the *Networking the netbook and remote computer* section in this chapter.

ROS commands and Gazebo

In the left side pane of the Gazebo window, the list of models will appear when you click on **Models**. Notice, particularly, the `mobile_base` link. You can find the position and orientation of the base with the `rosservice` command. In a new terminal window, type the following command:

```
$ rosservice call gazebo/get_model_state '{model_name: mobile_base}'
```

The output of the preceding command is similar to the following if TurtleBot is at the origin:

```
pose:
 position:
  x: 0.00161336508139
  y: 0.0091790167961
  z: -0.00113098620237
 orientation:
  x: -5.20108036968e-05
  y: -0.00399736084462
  z: -0.0191615228716
  w: 0.999808408868
 twist:
  linear:
   x: 9.00012388429e-06
   y: 6.54279879125e-05
   z: -1.4365465304e-05
  angular:
   x: -0.000449167550145
   y: 0.000197996689198
   z: -0.00047001444794 6
success: True
status_message: GetModelState: got properties
```

Looking at the position and orientation, we can see that the TurtleBot base is approximately at the center (*x=0, y=0, z=0*) of the grid, as you can see by zooming out in the world view. Since so many decimal places are shown, it appears that TurtleBot is off center.

However, if you notice, the first two decimal places in the position are zeros, and you can see that the values are very small, near zero. The orientation is also near zero and is represented in a special notation called a **quaternion**.

To see the complete list of services, type the following command:

```
$ rosservice list
```

You can also use the `rosnode list` or `rosmsg list` ROS commands, as was shown in *Chapter 1, Getting Started with ROS*, to list the nodes or messages.

With ROS commands, you can move the TurtleBot, as we did with the turtle in Turtlesim in *Chapter 1, Getting Started with ROS*. First, find the topic that will control the `mobile_base` link since that is the name given in Gazebo's left panel:

```
$ rostopic list | grep mobile_base
```

The output is as follows:

```
/mobile_base/commands/motor_power
/mobile_base/commands/reset_odometry
/mobile_base/commands/velocity
/mobile_base/events/bumper
/mobile_base/events/cliff
/mobile_base/sensors/bumper_pointcloud
/mobile_base/sensors/core
/mobile_base/sensors/imu_data
/mobile_base_nodelet_manager/bond
```

Now you can find the message type published by the `rostopic /mobile_base/commands/velocity` that moves the base by typing the following command:

```
$ rostopic type /mobile_base/commands/velocity
```

The output is as follows:

```
geometry_msgs/Twist
```

From the previously shown screen printout of the `rosservice` command to call `gazebo/get_model_state`, you can see that the twist is a six-dimensional value although all six need not be specified. The values represent velocities, which in the case of the TurtleBot represent the linear velocity along its forward x axis and the angular velocity about the vertical z axis. A reference is available at the following website:

`https://en.wikipedia.org/wiki/Screw_theory`

If you drive the TurtleBot with a command, the possible motions are linear along its x direction and angular rotation about the z axis since the TurtleBot moves on the xy plane and cannot fly. To drive it forward, run the following command:

```
$ rostopic pub -r 10 mobile_base/commands/velocity \geometry_msgs/Twist
'{linear: {x: 0.2}}'
```

Notice that the TurtleBot moves forward slowly until you stop it or it drives off the screen or it hits one of the objects in the environment. To stop its motion, press *Ctrl + C*. To bring the TurtleBot back, change the value of x to x: `-0.2` in the `rostopic` command and execute it.

There are many other features of Gazebo that can be explored, and you are encouraged to try various selections on the menu bar (**File**, **Edit**, **Camera**, **View**, **Window**, and **Help**). Also, you can open the rightmost third panel and change the values of **Force**, **Position**, or **Velocity** for the TurtleBot simulator.

Keyboard teleoperation of TurtleBot 2 in simulation

A command to launch the teleop mode using the keyboard keys to move TurtleBot on the screen is as follows:

```
$ roslaunch turtlebot_teleop keyboard_teleop.launch
```

This command allows keyboard keys to maneuver the TurtleBot on the screen. The keys to command the motion are as follows:

```
Control Your Turtlebot!
---------------------------
Moving around:
u    i    o
j    k    l
m    ,    .
q/z : increase/decrease max speeds by 10%
```

```
w/x : increase/decrease only linear speed by 10%
e/c : increase/decrease only angular speed by 10%
space key, k : force stop
anything else : stop smoothly
CTRL-C to quit
currently:  speed 0.2   turn 1
```

Think of the letter k as the center of TurtleBot looking down on it. Start with the letter i to move the TurtleBot straight ahead along its *x* axis and try the other keys.

Remember to click on the window in which you executed the `roslaunch` command to move TurtleBot. This is termed **focusing** on the window.

For now, we leave Gazebo and concentrate on installing software to control the real TurtleBot. However, even if you do not have access to a real TurtleBot, many of the commands and scripts that will be presented can also be used with the simulated TurtleBot. In fact, ideally, the Gazebo simulation should reflect the motion of the real TurtleBot in its environment.

For example, we later present a Python script that moves the real TurtleBot forward. You can use the command to run the script with Gazebo also.

Setting up to control a real TurtleBot 2

The TurtleBot 2 system consists of the TurtleBot base and its netbook that rides along with the TurtleBot and a separate remote computer that is used to control the robot. The netbook and computer communicate wirelessly once a network connection is established. This section describes the setup of the system, including the network.

A brief overview of the steps to set up and test the TurtleBot is as follows:

1. Set up the netbook with Ubuntu 16.04 and ROS Kinetic, and then load the TurtleBot software packages.
2. Set up the remote computer with similar software.
3. Test the TurtleBot in the standalone mode to assure proper operation.
4. Create the network of computers, being careful to define the TurtleBot netbook as the ROS Master to the remote computer.
5. Test the TurtleBot by communicating with commands wirelessly from the remote computer to the netbook of the TurtleBot.

With Ubuntu and the `ros-kinetic-desktop-full` installed, the packages for the TurtleBot are installed with the following command:

```
$ sudo apt-get install ros-kinetic-turtlebot ros-kinetic-turtlebot-apps
ros-kinetic-turtlebot-interactions ros-kinetic-turtlebot-simulator ros-
kinetic-kobuki-ftdi
```

To link the Kobuki base to the device folder of Ubuntu, find instructions at the following link:

`http://wiki.ros.org/kobuki_ftdi`

To set up your netbook battery monitor for the TurtleBot, visit: `http://wiki.ros.org/turtlebot/Tutorials/indigo/Netbook%20Battery%20Setup`.

There are many tutorials that cover TurtleBot. There is a website devoted to the TurtleBot at `http://learn.turtlebot.com/` with many interesting tutorials that cover the various aspects of the TurtleBot with details of setup, testing, and applications. This documentation is for Ubuntu 14.04 and ROS Indigo.

TurtleBot 2 standalone test

Before we make an attempt to network the TurtleBot to a remote computer, it is wise to test the TurtleBot in the standalone mode to determine whether the software has been installed properly. Now disconnect the netbook from any networks. Once the TurtleBot and its netbook are powered up, you can test software by opening a new terminal window on the netbook and executing the following command:

```
$ roscore
```

This should respond with a screen output that ends with the following message:

```
started core service [/rosout]
```

If there are no errors indicated in the screen output, the netbook is set up correctly with ROS.

After this, press *Ctrl + C* and close this terminal window. Open a new one to move the TurtleBot around, as was done previously in simulation. On the netbook, initialize the TurtleBot by typing the `roslaunch` command in the new window:

```
$ roslaunch turtlebot_bringup minimal.launch
```

Quite a bit of information is shown on the screen as the minimal launch proceeds, but most of this output is not of any concern for now. The ROS Master is the netbook indicated by the following lines:

```
auto-starting new master
ROS_MASTER_URI=http://localhost:11311
```

This will launch `roscore` and initialize the TurtleBot for control when the movement commands are issued. The importance of the `ROS_MASTER_URI` variable will be explained when networking the TurtleBot is discussed.

When the minimal launch is successful, you will hear TurtleBot play a jingle to indicate that it is ready.

To move the TurtleBot, open a new terminal window, and launch teleoperation by typing the following command:

```
$ roslaunch turtlebot_teleop keyboard_teleop.launch
```

Among other things, you will see a diagram of the control keys used to control the robot on the screen:

```
Control Your Turtlebot!
---------------------------
Moving around:
u    i    o
j    k    l
m    ,    .
```

These are the same keys as discussed previously for the TurtleBot simulator. If all goes well, the TurtleBot will move forward, backward, or turn according to the key pressed on the netbook.

Of course, controlling the TurtleBot from its netbook is not very satisfying. It is done only to see that the TurtleBot software is set up correctly. In the next section, we describe the setup of a network so that the robot can be controlled by a remote computer.

In particular, as discussed in the *Using keyboard teleoperation to move TurtleBot* section of this chapter, the keyboard keys of a remote computer are used to move TurtleBot after it is connected to a network.

Networking the netbook and remote computer

ROS has the ability to allow multiple computers to communicate and share nodes, topics, and services. In the case of TurtleBot, the netbook has limited capabilities for graphics applications, such as rviz. It is better to run rviz and other visualization software on a desktop computer or a powerful laptop, both of which will be called a remote computer here to distinguish it from the netbook that rides along with the TurtleBot.

The approach is to designate one computer in the network to run the ROS Master identified by the ROS_MASTER_URI variable and launch the roscore process from that computer. The choice is to set up TurtleBot's netbook as the Master since many applications of the TurtleBot require autonomous motion without the intervention of the remote computer.

Any other remote computer on the network will have its own IP address as the ROS_IP address but its ROS_MASTER_URI variable will be TurtletBot 2's netbook IP address.

Types of networks

Networks between computers can be set up in various ways. To link to the TurtleBot from a remote computer, there are several common ways to network wirelessly:

- Use a network with a server computer that allows access to the internet with Wi-Fi access, as might be found in a university or any other large organization.

- Use a router that allows local communication via Wi-Fi between the netbook and the remote computer. This is commonly used when setting up a private network to connect devices to each other wirelessly and to the internet.

The network system in an organization may have security limitations that cover computers that can access their network. It is best to check any such requirements. Also, many such networks have network addresses assigned by a server using **Dynamic Host Configuration Protocol (DHCP)**, which means that the IP address of a computer connected to a network can change if the computer is disconnected from the network and then reconnected. If the IP address changes, it is important to assign the ROS Master address as the new IP address of the TurtleBot's netbook connected to the wireless network.

Network addresses

A network identifies each computer on the network in one of several ways, but each computer connected to the network has a unique identity. If the computers communicate through the internet, you can refer to any internet-connected machine by its **Internet Protocol (IP)** address, which is a four-part number string (such as 192.168.11.xxx), in which the first part identifies the specific network to which the machine is connected. Another way to refer to the computer is by its hostname, which is usually a text string that consists of the machine name and the domain name.

You can determine the hostname of your computer with the `hostname` command and the username using the `whoami` command in the following forms:

```
$ hostname
```

```
$ whoami
```

In a ROS network, the Master is designated by a URI used to identify the name of the Master on a network. For example, the `ROS_MASTER_URI` variable for the TurtleBot in the authors' laboratory has the following address:

```
ROS_MASTER_URI=http://192.168.11.123:11311
```

The IP address in this case is 192.168.11.123. The IP address of a computer on the network can be determined by the following Ubuntu command:

```
$ ifconfig
```

This command will list the communication properties of the computer. The screen output will typically show an Ethernet connection (`eth0`) if any, a local loopback address (`lo`), and the wireless IP address (`wlan`), which is designated as `inetaddr`. The digits `11311` represent the port used by the ROS Master for communication on the computer.

The description of the ROS networking requirements can be viewed at the following websites:

- http://wiki.ros.org/ROS/NetworkSetup
- http://wiki.ros.org/ROS/Tutorials/MultipleMachines

There must be a network connection between the machines. Using the IP addresses of the machines to identify the machines is sufficient. Only one machine in the network can be the Master.

`ROS_IP` and `ROS_HOSTNAME` are environment variables that set the declared network address of a ROS node. The convention is to use `ROS_IP` if you are specifying an IP address, and `ROS_HOSTNAME` if you are specifying a hostname. The `ROS_HOSTNAME` variable takes precedence over the `ROS_IP` variable.

The ROS_MASTER_URI, ROS_IP, and ROS_HOSTNAME variables are described in the tutorial at: http://wiki.ros.org/ROS/EnvironmentVariables.

In the case of TurtleBot, the ROS Master resides on the netbook and the netbook's IP address must be indicated to the remote computer. On the remote computer, the ROS_MASTER_URI variable must be set to the address of the netbook so that its nodes can register with the Master. Once that is done, the nodes can communicate with the Master and other nodes wirelessly.

Remote computer network setup

To link the remote computer and the TurtleBot's netbook, make sure that both the computers communicate on the same network. This may involve changing the network choice of the computers if there are several networks available.

For your setup of the remote computer, determine the IP addresses of the netbook and your remote computer using the ifconfig command. Your commands will use your specific addresses, and you will use the following commands:

```
$ export ROS_MASTER_URI=http://<IP address of TurtleBot>:11311
$ export ROS_IP=<IP address of remote computer>
```

We recommend that you add these commands to the .bashrc file so that the TurtleBot is the ROS Master every time you open a new window.

To be more specific, on our remote computer, we edited our .bashrc file and added the following commands to create these environment variables for the TurtleBot:

```
export ROS_MASTER_URI=http://192.168.11.123:11311
export ROS_IP=192.168.11.139
```

The ROS Master address points to the TurtleBot netbook, and the ROS_IP variable is the IP address of our laptop used in this example. The examples just shown using the network addresses were taken from the actual computers used in the authors' laboratory to run TurtleBot. Of course, your addresses will be different.

To check the variables on the remote computer, type the following command to check the IP addresses of the ROS Master and the remote computer:

```
$ env | grep ROS
```

Netbook network setup

The netbook setup instructions can be found at the ROS wiki location at: http://wiki.ros.org/turtlebot/Tutorials/indigo/Network%20Configuration.

To set up the netbook addresses, you can type the following command at the netbook terminal window:

```
$ echo export ROS_MASTER_URI=http://<IP address of TurtleBot>:11311 >>
~/.bashrc

$ echo export ROS_IP=<IP address of TurtleBot> >> ~/.bashrc
```

Here `<IP address of TurtleBot>` is replaced with the IP address of the TurtleBot netbook, which is normally called the IP address of the TurtleBot. This sets the TurtleBot as the Master.

Secure Shell (SSH) connection

The **Secure Shell (SSH)** will be used to allow remote login to the TurtleBot's netbook from the remote computer. Check the SSH status with the following command:

```
$ sudo service ssh status
```

If the SSH service is not present, install it using this command:

```
$ sudo apt-get install openssh-server
```

Then run the previous command to check the SSH status. This software package should be installed on both the TurtleBot netbook and the remote computer.

For the authors' TurtleBot netbook, our username is `turtlebot`. Your username can be found by running the following command:

```
$ whoami
```

To communicate with the TurtleBot, on the remote computer, type the `ssh` command in the following form and enter your TurtleBot password when prompted:

```
$ ssh <username>@<IP address of TurtleBot>
```

Summary of network setup

In summary, to set up the communication between the TurtleBot 2 and the remote computer to control the robot, check the following on both the computers:

- TurtleBot's netbook hosts the ROS Master with:

  ```
  ROS_MASTER_URI= http://<IP address of TurtleBot>:11311
  ```

  and

  ```
  ROS_IP=http://<IP address of TurtleBot>
  ```

- The remote computer has:

  `ROS_MASTER_URI = http://<IP address of TurtleBot>:11311`

  and

  `ROS_IP=http://<IP address of remote computer>`

The addresses here are assumed to be the addresses of the TurtleBot netbook and the remote computer on a wireless network.

Troubleshooting your network connection

Many problems in networking ROS occur because the IP addresses of the netbook and the remote computer are not set correctly. Perform the following steps:

1. Check the computers' network settings.
2. Make sure that the network is working by communicating with the server or router for the network.
3. Use the `ifconfig` and `env | grep` ROS commands to check whether the network addresses are set correctly.
4. If your network has DHCP, see if the assigned IP addresses have changed.

 Some information about networks that may be helpful can be found at the following site:
`https://www.lifewire.com/networking-with-a-router-817719`

Testing the TurtleBot 2 system

To test the system and the communication, perform the following steps:

1. Make sure that the TurtleBot base battery and the netbook battery are charged.
2. Plug in the netbook to the base and power up the base.
3. Turn on the netbook and log on using the netbook's password and then connect to your network.
4. Give the TurtleBot room to move without obstacles in the way.
5. Log on to the remote computer and start communicating with the TurtleBot through your network.

This procedure is used to command the robot from the remote computer by typing the `ssh` command at the remote computer terminal and entering the TurtleBot password. The first example in the *Using keyboard teleoperation to move TurtleBot* section will allow you to control the TurtleBot using several keyboard keys.

To start communication with the TurtleBot from the remote computer, type the `ssh` command and enter the TurtleBot password when prompted:

```
$ ssh <username>@<IP address of TurtleBot>
```

(The output is not included for brevity.)

As described earlier, our TurtleBot IP address is `192.168.11.123`.

 The window prompt will change to the window prompt of the TurtleBot netbook. Our netbook prompt is `turtlebot@turtlebot-0428:~$` and has been left in the following command lines to identify where the commands are issued.

After the response, you can send commands to the TurtleBot by typing the following command:

```
turtlebot@turtlebot-0428:~$ roslaunch turtlebot_bringup minimal.launch
```

The output is as follows:

.

.

```
Checking log directory for disk usage. This may take awhile
```

After a long list of parameters and nodes, you will see the ROS Master address. In our system, the output is as follows:

```
auto-starting new master
process[master]: started with pid [23426]
ROS_MASTER_URI=http://192.168.11.123:11311
```

This line of the output shows that the TurtleBot is the ROS Master. It is followed by a list of the processes running and other information.

To view the nodes that are active after the minimal launch, in a second terminal use the following command:

```
$ rosnode list
```

TurtleBot 2 hardware specifications

Before driving the real TurtleBot around, it would be useful to understand the capabilities of the robot in terms of its possible speed, turning capability, carrying capacity, and other such properties. With this information, you can plan the motion and speed of TurtleBot and design interesting applications. The specifications here are taken from the information provided for the Kobuki base by the Yujin Robot company. Their website for general information and specifications can be found at the following site:

```
http://kobuki.yujinrobot.com/about2
```

A user's guide for the Kobuki base is included at the following site:

```
http://kobuki.yujinrobot.com/wiki/online-user-guide
```

The base has a rechargeable battery that powers the motors turning the wheels. The netbook has its own battery but is not charged when the TurtleBot is moving on its own. There are a number of sensors in the base.

In the previous examples of teleoperation, the TurtleBot linear speed in the forward or backward direction was 0.2 meters/second or 20 cm/second. That is a bit over 1 foot per second and is probably fast enough for a robot moving in a room with obstacles in its way. The turning rate was 1 radian/second. Since there are 2π (6.28) radians in a circle, the TurtleBot will rotate completely around in about 6 seconds or so.

According to the manufacturer, Yujin Robot, the maximum values are as follows:

- The maximum linear speed is 70 cm/second (27.5 inches/second)
- The maximum angular velocity is 180 degrees/second or π radians/second
- The payload is 5 kg (11 pounds) on a hard floor

Review the other functional and hardware specifications to familiarize yourself with TurtleBot and its capabilities and limitations. In our laboratory for safety reasons, we run the TurtleBot at a relatively slow speed compared to its maximum speed.

TurtleBot 2 dashboard

In this section, it is assumed that you have established communication with the TurtleBot and can send commands to start the minimal launch.

In a new terminal window on the remote computer, type the following command to bring up the dashboard:

```
$ roslaunch turtlebot_dashboard turtlebot_dashboard.launch
```

Wait for the image of the dashboard to appear.

In the following Turtlebot (Kobuki) dashboard screenshot, we have clicked on the diagnostic icon in the far upper-left corner of the screen to bring up the status messages on the dashboard:

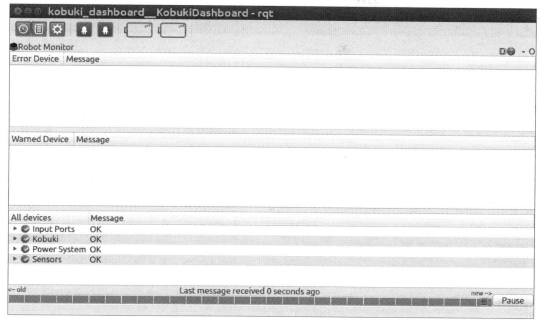

Kobuki dashboard

The dashboard indicates the status of various systems of the TurtleBot:

- A diagnostic indicator, /rosout messages, and motor control (OFF/ON) in the upper-left corner of the screen
- Controls for two colored LEDs on the base that can be turned on or off
- Battery monitor indicators for the netbook and the Kobuki base
- Status of the power system, the motors, and the sensors

If your netbook battery monitor does not work, check the directions in the *Setting up to control a real TurtleBot* section to select a proper battery for monitoring. The TurtleBot's dashboard is described at the site with the selection of the Groovy and Indigo versions: http://wiki.ros.org/turtlebot_dashboard.

Moving the real TurtleBot 2

There are a number of ways to move the TurtleBot using ROS. In this section, we present the following three methods:

- Using the keyboard
- Using ROS terminal window commands
- Using a Python script

Using keyboard teleoperation to move TurtleBot 2

In a new terminal window, launch the TurtleBot keyboard teleop program on the remote computer:

```
$ roslaunch turtlebot_teleop keyboard_teleop.launch
```

The output is as follows:

```
... logging to /home/harman/.ros/log/87ca9e6a-3c0c-11e7-a3ba-
6c71d9a711bd/roslaunch-D104-45931-5873.log
Checking log directory for disk usage. This may take a while.
Press Ctrl-C to interrupt
Done checking log file disk usage. Usage is <1GB.


started roslaunch server http://192.168.11.139:43506/


SUMMARY
========


PARAMETERS
 * /rosdistro: kinetic
 * /rosversion: 1.12.7
 * /turtlebot_teleop_keyboard/scale_angular: 1.5
 * /turtlebot_teleop_keyboard/scale_linear: 0.5
```

```
NODES
  /
turtlebot_teleop_keyboard (turtlebot_teleop/turtlebot_teleop_key)

ROS_MASTER_URI=http://192.168.11.123:11311

core service [/rosout] found
process[turtlebot_teleop_keyboard-1]: started with pid [5882]


Control Your Turtlebot!
---------------------------
Moving around:
u    i    o
j    k    l
m    ,    .


q/z : increase/decrease max speeds by 10%
w/x : increase/decrease only linear speed by 10%
e/c : increase/decrease only angular speed by 10%
space key, k : force stop
anything else : stop smoothly

CTRL-C to quit

currently:   speed 0.2   turn 1
```

We have left the entire output from the launch because it is useful to know the parameters and nodes involved when a package is launched. Make sure that the TurtleBot base and the netbook batteries are sufficiently charged so you can move the TurtleBot around to become familiar with its capabilities for straight-line motion and rotation. Now try the i key to move the TurtleBot forward or the , key to drive backward. The speed is 0.2 meters/second.

Using ROS commands to move TurtleBot 2 around

There are a number of ways to control the TurtleBot movement other than using the keyboard. There are several ROS commands that are useful to move and monitor the TurtleBot in motion:

- `rostopic pub` is used to publish commands to move the TurtleBot
- `rostopic echo` is used to display the messages sent

After the TurtleBot has been brought up with the minimal launch command, the `rostopic pub` command can be used to move and turn the TurtleBot. To move the TurtleBot forward, issue this command from the remote computer:

```
$ rostopic pub -r 10 /mobile_base/commands/velocity \geometry_msgs/Twist
'{linear: {x: 0.2}}'
```

TurtleBot should move forward continuously at 0.2 meters/second until you press *Ctrl* + *C* while the focus is on the active window.

This command publishes (`pub`) the `/mobile_base/commands/velocity` topic at the rate of 10 times per second. The `-r` variable indicates that the rate is repeated. To send the message once, use `-1` instead of `-r`.

To move the TurtleBot backward, issue the following command:

```
$ rostopic pub -r 20 /mobile_base/commands/velocity \geometry_msgs/Twist
'{linear: {x: -0.2}}'
```

Always press *Ctrl* + *C* to stop TurtleBot.

To cause the robot to turn in a circle requires some forward velocity and angular velocity, which the following command shows:

```
$ rostopic pub -r 10 /mobile_base/commands/velocity \geometry_msgs/Twist
'{linear: {x: 0.2}, angular: {x: 0, y: 0, z: 1.0}}'
```

The linear speed is 0.2 meters/second and the rotation is 1.0 radian (about 57 degrees) per second.

To view the messages sent, type the following command in a separate terminal window:

```
$ rostopic echo /mobile_base/commands/velocity
```

The output is as follows:

```
linear:
  x: 0.2
  y: 0.0
  z: 0.0
angular:
  x: 0.0
  y: 0.0
  z: 1.0
---
```

The message repeats the linear velocity and angular rotation values being sent 10 times a second. Use *Ctrl + C* to stop the display.

Writing your first Python script to control TurtleBot 2

We will present a simple Python script to move the TurtleBot in this section. The basic approach to create a script begins with a design. The design should detail the activity to be accomplished. For example, a script can command TurtleBot to move straight ahead, make several turns, and then stop. The next step is to determine the commands for TurtleBot to accomplish the tasks. Finally, a script is written and tested to see whether TurtleBot responds in the expected way. The remote computer will execute the Python script and TurtleBot will move as directed if the script is correctly written.

In terms of the TurtleBot commands that will be used, we can summarize the process as follows:

1. Design the program outlining the activities of TurtleBot when the script is executed

2. Determine the nodes, topics, and messages to be sent (published) or received (subscribed) from the TurtleBot during the activity

3. Study the ROS Python tutorials and examples to determine the way to write Python statements that send or receive messages between the remote computer and the TurtleBot

There is a great deal of documentation describing ROS Python scripts. The statement structure is fixed for many operations. The `http://wiki.ros.org/rospy` site briefly describes `rospy`, which is called the ROS client library for Python. The purpose is to allow statements written in Python language to interface with ROS topics and services.

The `http://wiki.ros.org/rospy_tutorials` site contains a list of tutorials. At the top of the tutorial page, there is a choice of distributions of ROS, and Kinetic is chosen for our discussions. A specific tutorial that describes many Python statements that are used in a typical script can be found at `http://wiki.ros.org/ROS/Tutorials/WritingPublisherSubscriber(python)`.

To find the nodes that are active after the `keyboard_teleop.launch` file is launched, type this command:

```
$ rosnode list
```

The output is as follows:

```
/bumper2pointcloud
/cmd_vel_mux
/diagnostic_aggregator
/mobile_base
/mobile_base_nodelet_manager
/robot_state_publisher
/rosout
/turtlebot_laptop_battery
/turtlebot_teleop_keyboard
```

The nodes are described in the Kobuki tutorial that can be found at:

`http://wiki.ros.org/kobuki/Tutorials/Kobuki's%20Control%20System`

According to the site, the `mobile_base` node listens for commands, such as velocity, and publishes sensor information. The `cmd_vel_mux` node serves to multiplex commands to assure that only one velocity command at a time is relayed to the mobile base.

In the previous example, we used the `rostopic pub` command to publish the linear and angular `geometry_msgs/Twist` data in order to move the TurtleBot. The Python script that follows will accomplish essentially the same thing. The script will send a `Twist` message on the `cmd_vel_mux/input/navi` topic.

A Python script will be created to move the TurtleBot forward in a simple example. If you are not very familiar with Python, it may be best to study and execute the example script and then refer to the ROS tutorials. The procedure to create an executable script on the remote computer is as follows:

1. Write the script with the required format for a ROS Python script using an ordinary text editor.

2. Give the script a name in the `<name>.py` format and save the script.

We have called our script `ControlTurtleBot.py` and saved it in our home directory.

To make the script executable, execute the Ubuntu command:

```
$ chmod +x ControlTurtleBot.py
```

Make sure that the TurtleBot is ready by running the minimal launch. Then, in a new terminal window, type this command:

```
$ python ControlTurtleBot.py
```

In our example, *Ctrl + C* is used to stop the TurtleBot. The comments in the script explain the statements. The tutorials listed previously give further details of Python scripts written using the ROS conventions:

```python
#!/usr/bin/env python
# Execute as a python script
# Set linear and angular values of TurtleBot's speed and turning.
import rospy       # Needed to create a ROS node
from geometry_msgs.msg import Twist     # Message that moves base

classControlTurtleBot():
  def __init__(self):
    # ControlTurtleBot is the name of the node sent to the #master
    rospy.init_node('ControlTurtleBot', anonymous=False)

    # Message to screen
    rospy.loginfo("Press CTRL+c to stop TurtleBot")

    # Keys CNTL + c will stop script
    rospy.on_shutdown(self.shutdown)

    # Publisher will send Twist message on topic
    # cmd_vel_mux/input/navi

    self.cmd_vel = rospy.Publisher('cmd_vel_mux/input/navi',
    Twist, queue_size=10)
```

```python
    # TurtleBot will receive the message 10 times per second.
    rate = rospy.Rate(10);
    # 10 Hz is fine as long as the processing does not exceed
    #   1/10 second.

    # Twist is geometry_msgs for linear and angular velocity
    move_cmd = Twist()
    # Linear speed in x in meters/second is + (forward) or -
    # (backwards)
    move_cmd.linear.x = 0.3
    # Modify this value to change speed
    # Turn at 0 radians/s
    move_cmd.angular.z = 0
    # Modify this value to cause rotation rad/s

    # Loop and TurtleBot will move until you type CNTL+c
    while not rospy.is_shutdown():
      # publish Twist values to TurtleBot node /cmd_vel_mux
      self.cmd_vel.publish(move_cmd)
      # wait for 0.1 seconds (10 HZ) and publish again
      rate.sleep()


  def shutdown(self):
    # You can stop turtlebot by publishing an empty Twist
    # message
    rospy.loginfo("Stopping TurtleBot")

    self.cmd_vel.publish(Twist())
    # Give TurtleBot time to stop
    rospy.sleep(1)

if __name__ == '__main__':
  try:
    ControlTurtleBot()
  except:
    rospy.loginfo("End of the trip for TurtleBot")
```

Introducing rqt tools

The rqt tools (ROS Qt GUI toolkit) that are part of ROS allow graphical representations of ROS nodes, topics, messages, and other information. The ROS wiki lists many of the possible tools that are added to the rqt screen as plugins: http://wiki.ros.org/rqt/Plugins.

The ROS tutorial on the topics also describes some of the features of the rqt tool is at:
`http://wiki.ros.org/ROS/Tutorials/UnderstandingTopics`.

rqt_graph

One of the common uses of rqt is to view the nodes and topics that are active. Bring the TurtleBot up with the minimal launch as previously described. Then, on the remote computer, issue the following command:

```
$ rqt_graph
```

Select the top-left box, **Nodes/Topics (all)**. The following screenshot of `rqt_graph` shows the nodes that are active and the connections between the publishers and subscribers that deal with moving the base of the TurtleBot. Pass the cursor over the various items to see the nodes and topics and see how they communicate:

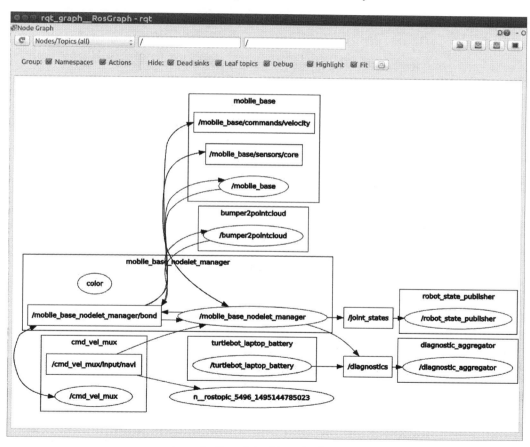

rqt_graph after minimal launch of TurtleBot

On the menu bar at the top of the screen, keep the dead sinks, leaf topics, and debug topics hidden to simplify the graph. Take a look at the preceding graph; the names, such as `mobile_base`, are called **namespaces** to identify the items. Ellipses (ovals) represent nodes while arrows represent connections through topics. The names in the rectangles represent topics.

For example, the `/mobile_base_nodelet_manager` node publishes on the `/joint_states` and `/diagnostics` topics.

After the minimal launch, the `keyboard_teleop.launch` command is issued in a separate terminal window, as described earlier. Issue the following command:

```
$ roslaunch turtlebot_teleop keyboard_teleop.launch
```

One of the screen outputs shows the name of the node that the `turtlebot_teleop` package is using, as follows:

NODES
```
  /turtlebot_teleop_keyboard (turtlebot_teleop/turtlebot_teleop_key)
```

The following screenshot portion shows selected nodes and topic after the launch of `keyboard_teleop.launch`. As shown in the following screenshot, a new `turtlebot_teleop_keyboard` node has appeared, publishing on the `/cmd_vel_mux/input/teleop` topic:

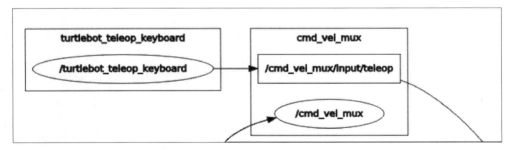

rqt_graph after TurtleBot teleoperation

To list all the active nodes, the `rosnode list` command, on the remote computer, can be issued. For details on a particular node, such as `/turtlebot_teleop_keyboard`, type the following command:

```
$ rosnode info /turtlebot_teleop_keyboard
```

The output is as follows:

```
--------------------------------------------------------------------------
-------

Node [/turtlebot_teleop_keyboard]
```

```
Publications:
 * /rosout [rosgraph_msgs/Log]
 * /cmd_vel_mux/input/teleop [geometry_msgs/Twist]
Subscriptions: None
Services:
 * /turtlebot_teleop_keyboard/get_loggers
 * /turtlebot_teleop_keyboard/set_logger_level


contacting node http://192.168.11.139:34375/ ...
Pid: 8593
Connections:
 * topic: /cmd_vel_mux/input/teleop
    * to: /mobile_base_nodelet_manager
    * direction: outbound
    * transport: TCPROS
 * topic: /rosout
    * to: /rosout
    * direction: outbound
    * transport: TCPROS
```

From the keyboard, the messages of the geometry_msgs/Twist type are sent when you press a key that moves TurtleBot as indicated by the node's publications.

rqt message publisher and topic monitor

There are a number of variations of the rqt command with options. The simplest command is as follows:

```
$ rqt
```

This brings up a display screen, as shown in the following screenshot. In the menu bar, there are drop-down menu items that allow you to make choices to perform the following steps:

1. Select the **Plugins** tab that will be displayed; in our screenshot, the **Message Publisher** and **Topic Monitor** options were chosen from the **Plugins** tab.

2. Select the topics or other information for your plugins.

3. Rearrange the screen to suit your preferences if you choose more than one plugin.

The `rqt` command and the drop-down menu selections are shown in the following screenshot:

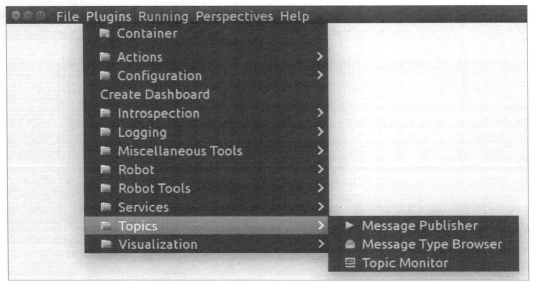

rqt command initial screen with plugin selections

For the following screenshot of rqt, the selections are made in the following order:

1. Issue the `rqt` command.
2. From the **Plugins** tab, select **Message Publisher** under the **Topics** tab.
3. From the **Plugins** tab, select **Topic Monitor** under the **Topics** tab.
4. Choose to publish the `Twist` message to `/cmd_vel_mux` and see the message monitored.
5. Rearrange the plugins on the screen for convenient viewing:

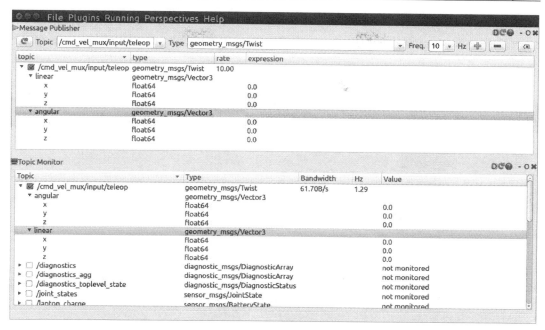

Two rqt plugins to publish and monitor messages

After you make the selections, there will be two plugins on the screen. You can rearrange them by clicking on the undocking symbol () in the upper-right corner of the plugins screen and dragging the window of the **Topic Monitor** below that of the **Message Publisher**.

Specifically, in the **Topic** entry box, type /cmd_vel_mux/input/teleop and click on the + button to add the topic. Left-click to check the topic's checkbox and right-click to expand the parameters of the message to see the angular and linear parameters of the Twist message. Note that the rate variable has been set to 10.00 from its original value of 1.00 so that the TurtleBot can move smoothly. When you click on the linear x or angular z variable, you can change the parameter under the column titled expression. Changing the values from 0.0 will cause the TurtleBot to move because the message will be published.

The result shows the **Message Publisher** and the **Topic Monitor** with the /cmd_vel_ mux/input/teleop topic selected. From the geometry_msgs package, the Twist message will be sent to the TurtleBot to move the robot.

From the screenshot showing the drop-down menu, it is clear that there are many options associated with the rqt tools. View the tutorials and try various options to experience the power of the rqt tools to allow you to control and monitor your robot's activities. One use is for **debugging** your scripts if the TurtleBot does not respond as expected, because you can monitor the messages sent to the TurtleBot.

TurtleBot's odometry

In this section, we explore the TurtleBot's odometry. The general definition of odometry is the use of data from motion sensors, such as wheel encoders, to estimate change in Turtlebot's position over time. Odometry is used by the TurtleBot to estimate its position and orientation relative to its starting location given in terms of an *x* and *y* position and an orientation around the *z* (upward) axis as the TurtleBot moves.

The odometry data to determine position and orientation can become very inaccurate as the TurtleBot moves a long distance. The inaccuracy can be due to errors in the robot's parameters such as incorrect wheel diameters used in calculation of distance or due to the uneven driving surfaces causing the wheel encoders to output inaccurate data. A comprehensive discussion of odometry is found in the paper *Measurement and Correction of Systematic Odometry Errors in Mobile Robots* by Johann Borenstein and Liqiang Feng. The paper can be found at the following site: http://www-personal.umich.edu/~johannb/Papers/paper58.pdf.

For the TurtleBot 2's Kobuki base, the odometry data published combines outputs from wheel encoders and the Kobuki's **Inertial Measurement Unit (IMU)** to determine TurtleBot's position and orientation relative to the starting pose. The form of the odometry data is found by typing several commands to determine the type and then the message format. First, type the following command:

```
$ rostopic type /odom
```

This yields the message type:

```
nav_msgs/Odometry
```

Then, determine the format of the message by typing the following command:

```
$ rosmsg show nav_msgs/Odometry
```

The message yields the following information:

```
std_msgs/Header header
  uint32 seq
  time stamp
  string frame_id
```

```
string child_frame_id
geometry_msgs/PoseWithCovariance pose
  geometry_msgs/Pose pose
    geometry_msgs/Point position
      float64 x
      float64 y
      float64 z
    geometry_msgs/Quaternion orientation
      float64 x
      float64 y
      float64 z
      float64 w
  float64[36] covariance
geometry_msgs/TwistWithCovariance twist
  geometry_msgs/Twist twist
    geometry_msgs/Vector3 linear
      float64 x
      float64 y
      float64 z
    geometry_msgs/Vector3 angular
      float64 x
      float64 y
      float64 z
  float64[36] covariance
```

The nav_msgs/Odometry type contains header and other information as well as geometry_msgs, which contain the position, orientation, linear velocity, and angular velocity of TurtleBot. The pose of TurtleBot is defined in terms of position and orientation by the geometry_msgs/Pose messages. The linear and angular velocities are given by the geometry_msgs/Twist messages. The structure for the pose is pose/pose/position or pose/pose/orientation. We will demonstrate several variations of the rostopic echo odom command to explain its use.

Typing the following command:

```
$ rostopic echo /odom
```

This yields a typical output similar to the following with TurtleBot stopped at an arbitrary position and orientation:

```
header:
  seq: 135240
  stamp:
    secs: 1496265119
    nsecs: 103228903
  frame_id: odom
child_frame_id: base_footprint
pose:
  pose:
    position:
      x: 0.190646478751
      y: 0.255858923656
      z: 0.0
    orientation:
      x: 0.0
      y: 0.0
      z: -0.634932792625
      w: 0.772567374958
  covariance: [0.1, 0.0, 0.0, 0.0, 0.0, 0.0, 0.0, 0.1, 0.0, 0.0,
0.0, 0.0, 0.0, 0.0, 1.7976931348623157e+308, 0.0, 0.0, 0.0, 0.0,
0.0, 0.0, 1.7976931348623157e+308, 0.0, 0.0, 0.0, 0.0, 0.0, 0.0,
1.7976931348623157e+308, 0.0, 0.0, 0.0, 0.0, 0.0, 0.0, 0.05]
twist:
  twist:
    linear:
      x: 0.0
      y: 0.0
      z: 0.0
    angular:
      x: 0.0
      y: 0.0
      z: -0.00174532925199
  covariance: [0.0, 0.0, 0.0, 0.0, 0.0, 0.0, 0.0, 0.0, 0.0, 0.0, 0.0,
0.0, 0.0, 0.0, 0.0, 0.0, 0.0, 0.0, 0.0, 0.0, 0.0, 0.0, 0.0, 0.0, 0.0,
0.0, 0.0, 0.0, 0.0, 0.0, 0.0, 0.0, 0.0, 0.0, 0.0, 0.0]
---
```

When you execute this `rostopic echo` command, the output will be updated continuously on the screen. The output here indicates that TurtleBot is at the point in x, y about (0.19, 0.26) meters from the (0,0) value of TurtleBot's original position.

To reset the odometry values to zero after the TurtleBot has moved, you can find the message type by typing:

```
$ rostopic type /mobile_base/commands/reset_odometry
std_msgs/Empty
```

Then publish the message to reset the odometry values by typing:

```
$ rostopic pub /mobile_base/commands/reset_odometry std_msgs/Empty
```

This yields the following output:

```
publishing and latching message. Press ctrl-C to terminate
```

If only the position and orientation of TurtleBot are desired, they can be found by typing:

```
$ rostopic echo /odom/pose/pose
```

with the result is as follows for TurtleBot at its origin:

```
position:
  x: 0.0
  y: 0.0
  z: 0.0
orientation:
  x: 0.0
  y: 0.0
  z: 0.0
  w: 1.0
```

This indicates that the TurtleBot is at the (0,0) position pointing in its $+x$ direction. This position and orientation occurs as a result of the TurtleBot minimal launch or after the odometry values are reset.

The IMU data can be displayed with the following command:

```
$ rostopic echo /mobile_base/sensors/imu_data
```

The IMU data for TurtleBot indicates the orientation as a quaternion, the angular velocity about the z axis, and the linear acceleration. The orientation values are the same as for the /odom topic since the orientation is determined by the IMU.

Using the numbers that are generated by the `/odom` topic can be useful in many cases. However, often we wish to display TurtleBot's motion using rviz. When the odometry option is chosen in rviz, the TurtleBot's position and orientation will be displayed with arrows that are generated as TurtleBot moves.

Odom for the simulated TurtleBot 2

The simulated TurtleBot will be used to demonstrate the odometry display possible in rviz.

> To run Gazebo on your remote computer, you must reassign the ROS Master if it is assigned to the TurtleBot in the `.bashrc` file. In each terminal window you open, type the following commands or put the commands in the `.bashrc` file:
>
> ```
> $ export ROS_MASTER_URI=http://localhost:11311
> $ export ROS_HOSTNAME=localhost
> ```

The commands executed on the remote computer to start Gazebo for simulation and rviz for visualization are as follows:

```
$ roslaunch turtlebot_gazebo turtlebot_world.launch
```

In another terminal window, run this command:

```
$ roslaunch turtlebot_rviz_launchers view_robot.launch
```

Gazebo includes the physics of the robot and rviz allows a variety of visualization options. In particular, it is useful to show the pose of the robot as indicated by arrows that point in the direction of the motion of the TurtleBot on the screen.

In rviz, it is necessary to choose several options to show the TurtleBot's odometry arrows on the screen. As shown in the following screenshot, we choose the following:

1. Under **Global** Options on the left side panel for **Fixed Frame**, change `base_link` or `base_footprint` to `odom`.
2. Click on **Add**, and select the **By topic** tab shown.
3. Choose **Odometry** and click on **OK**.
4. On the left side panel, click on the small arrow to the left of **Odometry** to show the various options. The topic is `odom` and the screen will keep 100 arrows that point to the direction of the simulated TurtleBot as it moves:

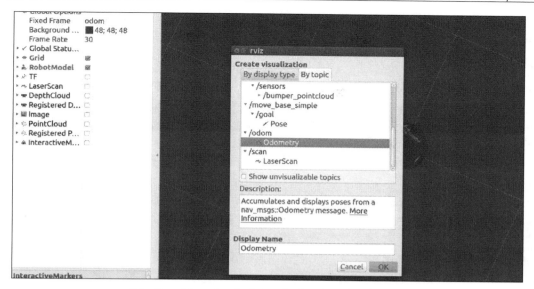

Selection of the odom topic in rviz showing a list of topics

5. Once these selections are made, the simulated TurtleBot will appear on the screen with an arrow pointing in its forward direction, as shown in the following screenshot:

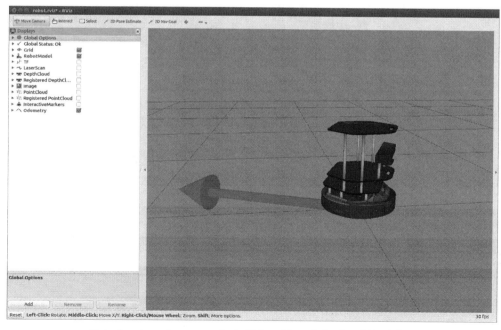

Rviz showing odom arrow for initial position of simulated TurtleBot

To track the motion of the simulated TurtleBot on the screen and display the arrows, we issue a movement command. Once the two screens are up for Gazebo and rviz, any commands to move the robot are possible, including the execution of a Python script. For example, in a third terminal window, issue one of the following commands to make the TurtleBot move in a circle on the screen:

```
$ rostopic pub -r 10 /cmd_vel_mux/input/teleop \geometry_msgs/Twist
'{linear: {x: 0.1, y: 0, z: 0}, angular: {x: 0, y: 0, z: -0.5}}'
```

```
$ rostopic pub -r 10 /mobile_base/commands/velocity \geometry_msgs/Twist
'{linear: {x: 0.1, y: 0, z: 0}, angular: {x: 0, y: 0, z: -0.5}}'
```

The result is the same in terms of the movement of the robot in our examples, but the `/mobile_base/commands/velocity` topic is used to control the mobile base as explained in the Kobuki tutorial at: `http://wiki.ros.org/kobuki/Tutorials/Kobuki%27s%20Control%20System`.

The `/cmd_vel_mux` node is used to multiplex velocity commands from different sources, such as the keyboard or a Python script. Either command makes the TurtleBot move in a circle, with the result shown in the following screenshot:

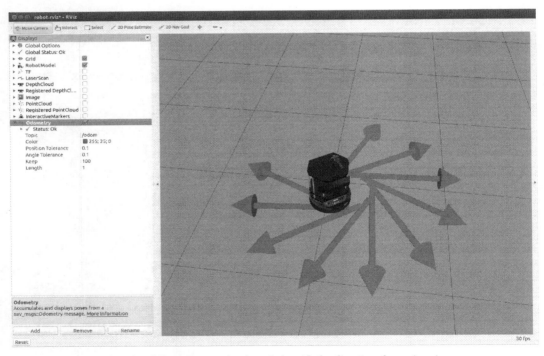

Simulated TurtleBot moving in a circle with the direction shown in rviz

Real TurtleBot 2's odometry display in rviz

The commands used in simulation can be used with the physical TurtleBot. After bringing up the real TurtleBot with the minimal launch, start rviz on the remote computer:

```
$ roslaunch turtlebot_rviz_launchers view_robot.launch
```

TurtleBot will appear in rviz, as shown in the following screenshot:

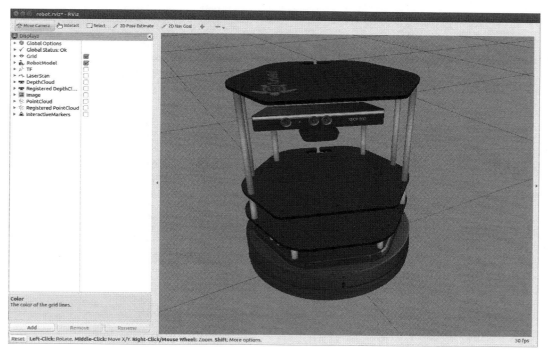

TurtleBot on rviz bringup

Then, set up rviz with odom for **Fixed Frame** and navigate to **Add | By topic | Odometry**, as was done with the simulated TurtleBot.

Run the following command to move TurtleBot in a circle:

```
$ rostopic pub -r 10 /mobile_base/commands/velocity \geometry_msgs/Twist
'{linear: {x: 0.1, y: 0, z: 0}, angular: {x: 0, y: 0, z: -0.5}}'
```

Stop the TurtleBot by pressing *Ctrl + C* with the focus on the window in which you executed the command to move the robot.

In the following screenshot, TurtleBot's turning was stopped by pressing *Ctrl + C*, and the Python script was executed that drives TurtleBot straightforward until the *Ctrl + C* keys are pressed again.

The command is as follows:

```
$ python ControlTurtleBot.py
```

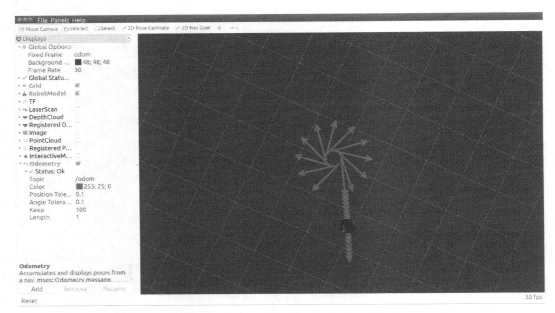

TurtleBot's path after the Twist message and running of the Python script

TurtleBot 2 automatic docking

TurtleBot 2 has the capability of finding its docking station and moving to that station for recharging as described in the tutorial available at:
`http://wiki.ros.org/kobuki/Tutorials/Automatic%20Docking`.

According to the tutorial, the TurtleBot must be placed in line-of-sight of the docking station since the robot homes on the station using an infrared beam. The docking station will show a solid red light when it is powered up. If the TurtleBot finds the station and docks properly, the red light will turn to blinking green when charging and solid green when TurtleBot's battery is fully charged.

Make sure that the minimal launch is active and the TurtleBot is within the line-of-sight to the docking station. On the remote computer, type the following command:

```
$ roslaunch kobuki_auto_docking minimal.launch
```

Then, in another terminal window, type the following command to cause the TurtleBot to start the search for the docking station:

```
$ roslaunch kobuki_auto_docking activate.launch
```

The following screenshot shows the TurtleBot rotating to find the IR signal and then heading toward the dock:

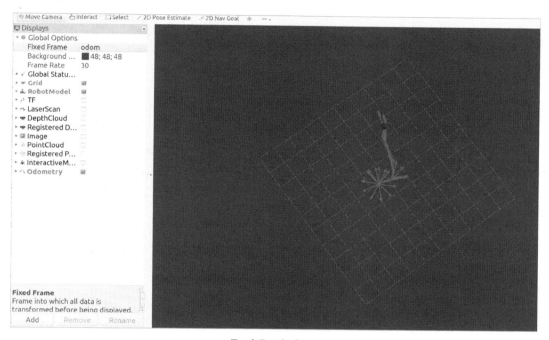

TurtleBot docking

In the preceding screenshot, the distance that the TurtleBot moved was about 2 meters (about 6 feet) to find the docking station and start recharging the base battery. The screen output as TurtleBot was completing the docking is as follows:

```
Feedback: [DockDrive: DOCKED_IN]:
Feedback: [DockDrive: DOCKED_IN]:
Result - [ActionServer: SUCCEEDED]: Arrived on docking station
successfully.
[dock_drive_client_py-1] process has finished cleanly
```

```
log file: /home/tlharmanphd/.ros/log/789b3ecc-6bca-11e5-b156-
6c71d9a711bd/dock_drive_client_py-1*.log
all processes on machine have died, roslaunch will exit
shutting down processing monitor...
... shutting down processing monitor complete
Done
```

As much as we enjoyed working with the TurtleBot 2, we have discovered a newer TurtleBot named TurtleBot 3. Our laboratory served as a beta test site for the new mobile robot. In the next section, we will introduce TurtleBot 3 and describe how to load its ROS software for simulation and for the real TurtleBot 3.

Introducing TurtleBot 3

At ROSCon 2016, a conference for developers, the TurtleBot 3 was introduced. TurtleBot 3 is a mobile robot designed and manufactured by ROBOTIS that is particularly suitable for education and hobbyist use. For remote control, the TurtleBot 3 must be connected via Wi-Fi to a network and a remote computer.

These ROS-based robots are smaller than the TurtleBot 2 described previously in this chapter. The two TurtleBot3 models are shown in the following image:

TurtleBot 3 Burger and Waffle

The Burger model has a small footprint with a wheelbase of 160 mm (6.29 in) and height of 192 mm (7.5 in) with a **Laser Distance Sensor** (**LDS**) on its top level. According to the specifications, the Burger version can carry 15 kg (33 lbs) and run for 2.5 hours. The Waffle model is larger with a wheelbase of 278mm (10.9 in) but with a height of only 141mm (5.5 in).

The TurtleBot 3 website describes the models presently available: `http://turtlebot3.robotis.com/en/latest/`.

In contrast to the TurtleBot 2, the TurtleBot 3 versions come with a powerful **single-board computer** (**SBC**) so there is no need for a netbook. Both versions have three-axis gyros, accelerometers, and magnetometers. Several types of 3D sensors are also available. The following websites have a great deal of information about the TurtleBot 3 versions, including links to the specifications of the SBC:

- `https://github.com/ROBOTIS-GIT/turtlebot3_wiki`
- `https://github.com/ROBOTIS-GIT/turtlebot3_wiki/blob/master/docs/source/specifications.rst`

Mounted on top of the TurtleBots are LDS to send distance data for navigation and obstacle detection to a SBC. The laser is connected to the SBC via a small interface board (USB2LDS). The Burger model computer board is a Raspberry Pi 3 Model B. The Waffle uses an Intel® Joule™ computer and incorporates an Intel® RealSense™ 3D sensor in addition to the laser sensor.

In both models, the SBC interfaces with a controller board, powered by an ARM Cortex-M7 (`https://developer.arm.com/products/processors/cortex-m/cortex-m7`), to which the motors and battery are connected. This board, developed by ROBOTIS and called the **Open-Source Control module for ROS** (**OpenCR**), is programmable with the Arduino software development environment. This OpenCR board is designed to be open source hardware as well as software. The following website describes the OpenCR board in detail:

`http://turtlebot3.robotis.com/en/latest/appendix_opencr.html`

In addition to the two basic kits for TurtleBot 3, instructions for other TurtleBot 3 configurations can be found at the following website:

`http://turtlebot3.robotis.com/en/latest/friends.html`

In the next sections, we will define first how to load the TurtleBot 3 simulation software and explore the TurtleBot 3 simulation that runs on rviz and Gazebo. Then the hardware and software for the real TurtleBot 3 will be discussed. Then, TurtleBot 3 will be driven around by keyboard teleoperation.

Loading TurtleBot 3 simulation software

The software packages for the TurtleBot 3 simulation will reside on the remote computer or any other desktop/laptop computer capable of running Gazebo simulations. This computer should be loaded with Ubuntu 16.04 and ROS Kinetic, as described in the *Installing and launching ROS* section in *Chapter 1, Getting Started with ROS.*

To begin, open a terminal window and type the following commands:

```
$ sudo apt-get install ros-kinetic-joy ros-kinetic-teleop-twist-joy ros-
kinetic-teleop-twist-keyboard ros-kinetic-laser-proc ros-kinetic-rgbd-
launch ros-kinetic-depthimage-to-laserscan ros-kinetic-rosserial-arduino
ros-kinetic-rosserial-python ros-kinetic-rosserial-server ros-kinetic-
rosserial-client ros-kinetic-rosserial-msgs ros-kinetic-amcl ros-kinetic-
map-server ros-kinetic-move-base ros-kinetic-urdf ros-kinetic-xacro
ros-kinetic-compressed-image-transport ros-kinetic-rqt-image-view ros-
kinetic-gmapping ros-kinetic-navigation
```

If you have not created a catkin workspace, refer to the *Creating a catkin workspace* section in *Chapter 1, Getting Started with ROS.*

For loading the TurtleBot 3 simulation software, we will also load all of the ROS catkin workspace packages developed for the TurtleBot 3 remote computer. We found that it was necessary to load both the remote computer software packages for the real TurtleBot 3 along with the simulation software package.

Type the following commands to load and compile these packages:

```
$ cd ~/catkin_ws/src/
$ git clone https://github.com/ROBOTIS-GIT/turtlebot3_simulations.git
$ git clone https://github.com/ROBOTIS-GIT/turtlebot3_msgs.git
$ git clone https://github.com/ROBOTIS-GIT/turtlebot3.git
$ cd ~/catkin_ws
$ catkin_make
```

Directories for `turtlebot3`, `turtlebot3_msgs`, and `turtlebot3_simulations` are created under the `src` directory of the catkin workspace. The `turtlebot3_simulations` directory contains the `turtlebot3_fake` package that is the TurtleBot 3 simulation in rviz. The `turlebot3_gazebo` package is also in the `turtlebot3_simulations` directory. This package contains the software for the TurtleBot 3 Gazebo simulation.

> When running TurtleBot 3 simulations in rviz and Gazebo, the environment variables should be set to return ROS control to your local computer. Use the following commands in every new window that is used or include them in a script file that is run when a new window is open:
> ```
> $ export ROS_MASTER_URI=http://localhost:11311
> $ export ROS_HOSTNAME=localhost
> ```

Launching TurtleBot 3 simulation in rviz

The TurtleBot 3 rviz simulation is created and controlled by the `turtlebot3_fake_node` node.

This node generates the model of the TurtleBot in rviz and allows for it to be run with a teleop node.

Be sure that your ROS IP environment variables are set to `localhost` or to the IP address of your computer. In your first terminal window, set the environment variable for the Turtlebot 3 model you wish to use in the rviz simulation. Either `burger` or `waffle` can be selected for the model parameter. For our examples, we have chosen the model to be `burger`:

```
$ export TURTLEBOT3_MODEL=burger
```

Then type the following command to launch the simulation:

```
$ roslaunch turtlebot3_fake turtlebot3_fake.launch
```

Three nodes are started: `robot_state_publisher`, `rviz`, and `turtlebot3_fake_node`. The following screenshot should appear:

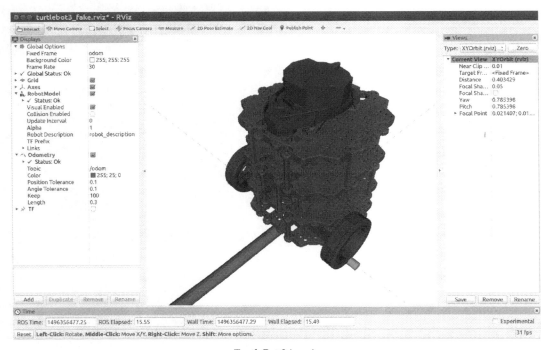

TurtleBot 3 in rviz

Now you can control the simulated TurtleBot with the keyboard. Open a second terminal window and type the following command:

```
$ roslaunch turtlebot3_teleop turtlebot3_teleop_key.launch
```

The `turtlebot_teleop_keyboard` node becomes active and allows for keyboard keys to be used to drive the TurtleBot across the rviz screen. The keys to control the robot are as follows:

```
Control Your Turtlebot3!
---------------------------

Moving around:
     w
a    s    d
     x


w/x : increase/decrease linear velocity
```

```
a/d : increase/decrease angular velocity
space key, s : force stop

CTRL-C to quit
```

```
(Be sure and focus on (select) the keyboard teleop window.)
```

Hitting the *W* key will slowly start the TurtleBot 3 moving forward and the following information will be displayed:

```
currently:   linear vel 0.01    angular vel 0
```

Hitting the *W* key a few more times will increase the speed slowly:

```
currently:   linear vel 0.02    angular vel 0
currently:   linear vel 0.03    angular vel 0
currently:   linear vel 0.04    angular vel 0
```

Hitting the *S* key will stop the robot and pressing the *A* key will make the robot turn left:

```
currently:   linear vel 0    angular vel 0
currently:   linear vel 0    angular vel -0.1
```

Enjoy moving the TurtleBot around in the rviz environment, but remember to use the spacebar or *S* key to stop its movement.

Next, we will try TurtleBot 3 in the Gazebo 3D simulator. Close all terminal windows before proceeding to the next section.

Launching TurtleBot 3 simulation in Gazebo

Before launching TurtleBot 3 in Gazebo, set the environment variable for the Turtlebot 3 model you wish to use in the Gazebo simulation. Either `burger` or `waffle` can be selected for the model parameter:

```
$ export TURTLEBOT3_MODEL=burger
```

To start the simulation, type the following command:

```
$ roslaunch turtlebot3_gazebo turtlebot3_empty_world.launch
```

You should see the words `Advertise odom on odom!` on the screen and a screenshot similar to the following:

TurtleBot 3 in Gazebo empty world

Now let us try a more interesting scene with objects for TurtleBot to drive around. Use **Quit** on the Gazebo application from the menu bar and press *Ctrl + C* in the terminal window to halt the process. If you close the terminal window at this point, make sure that you export the `TURTLEBOT3_MODEL` variable in a new terminal window.

Now, type the following command to spawn the TurtleBot 3 model on the TurtleBot 3 world map:

```
$ roslaunch turtlebot3_gazebo turtlebot3_world.launch
```

This command should produce a screenshot similar to the following:

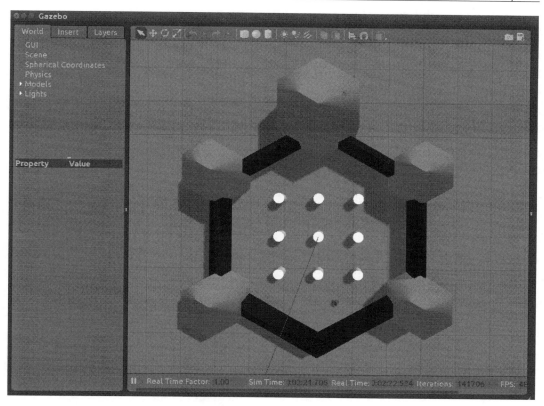

TurtleBot 3 in Gazebo TurtleBot3 world

Notice the small black dot between the large turtle's back legs. This is TurtleBot 3! You can use the keyboard control command that was used for rviz to drive TurtleBot around the TurtleBot 3 world. Open a second terminal window and type the following command:

```
$ roslaunch turtlebot3_teleop turtlebot3_teleop_key.launch
```

The TurtleBot 3 can also run autonomously, navigating around the TurtleBot 3 world. To view this application, hit *Ctrl + C* in the terminal window running the keyboard teleop process, and close the window. Open a new terminal window and type the following commands:

```
$ export TURTLEBOT3_MODEL=burger
$ roslaunch turtlebot3_gazebo turtlebot3_simulation.launch
```

The Gazebo window should show TurtleBot 3 actively running around the TurtleBot 3 world. Next, open another terminal window and launch rviz configured to visualize certain TurtleBot 3 published topics by typing the following commands:

```
$ export TURTLEBOT3_MODEL=burger
$ roslaunch turtlebot3_gazebo turtlebot3_gazebo_rviz.launch
```

The rviz screen should look similar to the following screenshot:

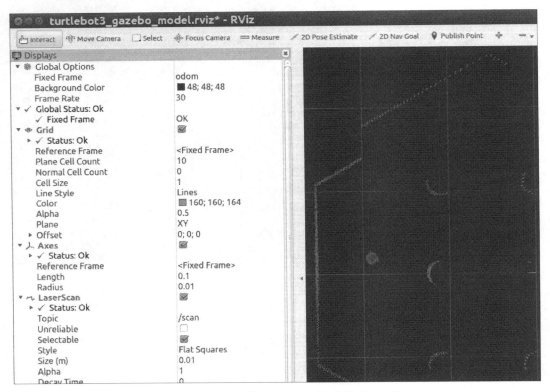

rviz visualization of TurtleBot 3 in TurtleBot 3 world

In the preceding screenshot, TurtleBot is near the left wall of the TurtleBot 3 world and the red line represents the laser scan data. This laser scan visualization will be discussed in more detail in the next chapter, *Chapter 4, Navigating the World with TurtleBot*.

Now, we will present the real TurtleBot 3 and describe how to get the robot up and running.

Hardware assembly and testing

TurtleBot 3 arrives as a kit of parts that must be assembled. Assembly instructions can be found in the *Hardware Setup* section at: `http://turtlebot3.robotis.com/en/latest/hardware.html`.

Testing the operation of the components while you are assembling the robot is important. We recommend running the Basic Operations identified for the OpenCR board when the OpenCR board, motors, and battery are all connected. This step will verify their operation before you attach the layers for the SBC and vision sensor(s). In addition, when power is applied, look for green LEDs to light on all the boards to indicate that they are operational.

The following sections will focus on the TurtleBot 3 Burger version since that was the version that the authors evaluated as beta testers. For instructions on the TurtleBot 3 Waffle and other versions, refer to the following website: `http://turtlebot3.robotis.com/en/latest/`.

Loading TurtleBot 3 software

TurtleBot 3 software resides in three locations: onboard the robot in the SBC, the OpenCR board, and on the remote computer. The remote computer can be a laptop or a desktop computer but must have Wi-Fi capability. Since the OpenCR board typically comes preloaded with software and is configured for the TurtleBot 3 model that is purchased, the instructions for loading the OpenCR software will not be described here. The next two sections will explain loading the software for the remote computer and loading the software for the SBC.

Installing remote computer software

 If you have already installed TurtleBot 3 simulation software, skip this section and proceed to *Installing SBC software*.

This section provides an explanation of loading software to control TurtleBot 3. It is assumed that Ubuntu 16.04 and ROS Kinetic software are installed on the computer that you will be using. Details for installing ROS Kinetic software are provided in the *Installing and launching ROS* section in *Chapter 1, Getting Started with ROS*.

The following steps reflect the instructions provided in the PC Software Setup section of the TurtleBot 3 documentation: `http://turtlebot3.robotis.com/en/latest/pc_software.html`.

Open a terminal window and type the following command:

```
$ sudo apt-get install ros-kinetic-joy ros-kinetic-teleop-twist-joy ros-kinetic-teleop-twist-keyboard ros-kinetic-laser-proc ros-kinetic-rgbd-launch ros-kinetic-depthimage-to-laserscan ros-kinetic-rosserial-arduino ros-kinetic-rosserial-python ros-kinetic-rosserial-server ros-kinetic-rosserial-client ros-kinetic-rosserial-msgs ros-kinetic-amcl ros-kinetic-map-server ros-kinetic-move-base ros-kinetic-urdf ros-kinetic-xacro ros-kinetic-compressed-image-transport ros-kinetic-rqt-image-view ros-kinetic-gmapping ros-kinetic-navigation
```

After these packages have been successfully installed, proceed with loading the remaining TurtleBot 3 packages into your catkin workspace and running `catkin_make`. If you have already loaded the TurtleBot 3 simulation software using the instructions from the previous section, *Loading TurtleBot 3 simulation software*, you will not need to perform the following commands. Proceed to the next section for instructions on loading the SBC software.

If you have not created a catkin workspace, refer to the *Creating a catkin workspace* section in *Chapter 1, Getting Started with ROS*. To download the TurtleBot 3 packages to your catkin workspace, type the following commands:

```
$ cd ~/catkin_ws/src/
```
```
$ git clone https://github.com/ROBOTIS-GIT/turtlebot3_msgs.git
```
```
$ git clone https://github.com/ROBOTIS-GIT/turtlebot3.git
```
```
$ cd ~/catkin_ws
```
```
$ catkin_make
```

If the last command executes without errors, you are ready to load the software on the SBC.

Installing SBC software

This section describes installing the TurtleBot 3 software on the Raspberry Pi 3. For instructions on installing TurtleBot 3 software on the Intel® Joule™, refer to the *SBC Software Setup* section at:

`http://turtlebot3.robotis.com/en/latest/sbc_software.html`

Loading Ubuntu MATE

The Linux operating system must be loaded onto the microSD card prior to installing it into the Raspberry Pi's microSD slot. The microSD card must be at least 8 GB and the operation of loading the operating system must be done on another computer. This can be your remote computer. Typically, an adapter card is needed to fit the microSD card into an SD card slot on the computer.

When you have the microSD card placed in the adapter and slid into the SD card slot of your computer, go to this website to download the latest version of Ubuntu MATE 16.04:

```
https://ubuntu-mate.org/download/
```

Select the release for Ubuntu MATE 16.04 LTS, then click on **Raspberry Pi** as the architecture. Next, scroll down to the *Via Direct Download* section and click on the **Bytemarktag** that shows the `.xz` file. The download will begin and an Ubuntu MATE `.xz` file will be placed in your computer's `Download` directory. When the download has completed, perform the following steps:

1. Select the `.xz` file and use the **Open With Disk Image Writer** option from the pop-up selection menu.

2. From the pop-up **Restore Disk Image** window, select the **Destination Drive** for your microSD card. This should be the 7.9 GB Drive if you are using an 8 GB microSD card.

3. Click the **Start Restoring...** button.

4. Click the **Restore** button when prompted with Are you sure you want to write the disk image to the device?

5. Type your user password to authenticate the action.

You should see a pop-up window similar to the following if all the steps have been done properly:

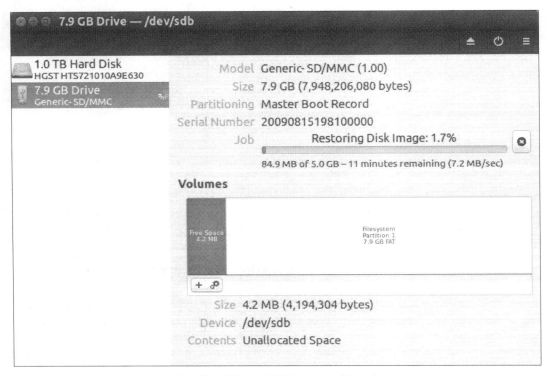

Installing Ubuntu MATE on microSD card

When the download is complete, the SD adapter can be removed from the computer and the microSD card can be removed from the adapter. The microSD card can then be inserted in the slot at the bottom of the Raspberry Pi 3 board.

For the next steps, an external keyboard, mouse, and monitor will need to be connected to the Raspberry Pi board. When these components have been connected, apply power to the Raspberry Pi board. If the Pi is not connected by I/O pins 4 and 6 to the OpenCR board, you can apply power using an external micro USB charger. The monitor should display a stream of text messages, then display the Ubuntu MATE GUI, as shown in the following screenshot:

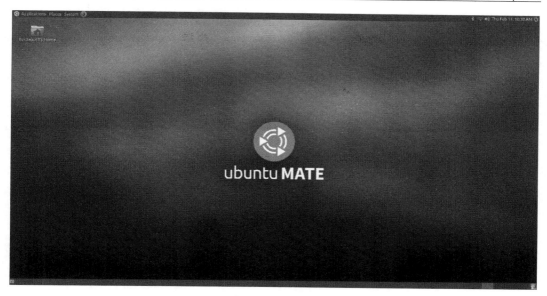

Ubuntu MATE GUI

As you will notice in the upper-left corner, the main menu bar has selections for the
Dash icon, **Applications**, **Places**, **System**, and the **Mozilla Foxfire** icon.

Loading ROS packages

The next steps will install ROS Kinetic on your Raspberry Pi 3 running Ubuntu
MATE (be sure that the Pi is connected to the internet to download the ROS
packages):

1. The first step is to configure the Ubuntu repositories to allow restricted,
    universe, and multiverse. For this step, find **System** on the main menu, then
    pull down the menu to find **Administration**, then continue over to **Software
    & Updates**. When the window pops up, the first four checkboxes should be
    checked. Then close this window.

2. From the main menu, select **Application**, pull down **System Tools**, and
    select **MATE Terminal** to open a terminal window. Next install the ROS
    packages with the following commands:

    ```
    $ sudo apt-get update
    ```

    ```
    $ sudo apt-get upgrade
    ```

    ```
    $ wget https://raw.githubusercontent.com/ROBOTIS-GIT/robotis_
    tools/master/install_ros_kinetic_rp3.sh && chmod 755 ./install_
    ros_kinetic_rp3.sh && bash ./install_ros_ kinetic_rp3.sh
    ```

The `wget` command retrieves the ROS Kinetic packages via an installation script, `install_ros_kinetic_rp3.sh`.

If the last command generates an error, add the option `--no-check-certificate` to the `wget` command.

3. Now reboot the Raspberry Pi.

Loading TurtleBot 3 packages

After successfully loading the ROS packages, the TurtleBot 3 packages should be installed with the following command:

```
$ sudo apt-get install ros-kinetic-joy ros-kinetic-teleop-twist-joy ros-
kinetic-teleop-twist-keyboard ros-kinetic-laser-proc ros-kinetic-rgbd-
launch ros-kinetic-depthimage-to-laserscan ros-kinetic-rosserial-arduino
ros-kinetic-rosserial-python ros-kinetic-rosserial-server ros-kinetic-
rosserial-client ros-kinetic-rosserial-msgs ros-kinetic-amcl ros-kinetic-
map-server ros-kinetic-move-base ros-kinetic-urdf ros-kinetic-xacro
ros-kinetic-compressed-image-transport ros-kinetic-rqt-image-view ros-
kinetic-gmapping ros-kinetic-navigation
```

After these packages have been successfully installed, proceed with loading the remaining TurtleBot 3 packages into your catkin workspace and running `catkin_make`. To download the TurtleBot 3 packages to your catkin workspace, type the following commands:

```
$ cd ~/catkin_ws/src/
$ git clone https://github.com/ROBOTIS-GIT/hls_lfcd_lds_driver.git
$ git clone https://github.com/ROBOTIS-GIT/turtlebot3_msgs.git
$ git clone https://github.com/ROBOTIS-GIT/turtlebot3.git
$ cd ~/catkin_ws
$ catkin_make
```

If the `git clone` commands produce a `fatal: unable to access` error message, use the following command to set the environment variable to disable security checking:

```
$ export GIT_SSL_NO_VERIFY=1
```

If the `catkin_make` command executes without errors, the SBC software has successfully been installed.

Setting up udev rules for TurtleBot 3

Ubuntu uses udev system software to dynamically manage devices connected to the computer system. The USB ports on the Raspberry Pi 3 need to be configured to operate without requiring root (sudo) permission. These ports are used for connections to the OpenCR board and USB2LDS. Type the following commands to establish special system configuration rules, called **udev rules**, to bypass this required permission:

```
$ cd ~/catkin_ws/src/turtlebot3
$ sudo cp ./99-turtlebot3-cdc.rules /etc/udev/rules.d/
$ sudo udevadm control --reload-rules
$ sudo udevadm trigger
```

Before disconnecting the monitor, keyboard, and mouse from the Raspberry Pi 3, be sure to complete the forthcoming section on TurtleBot 3 network setup and perform the steps there to identify and prepare the network connection for the robot.

Networking TurtleBot 3 and the remote computer

The TurtleBot 3 and remote computer must be configured to set up communications on the same network. Each computer's IP address should be identified and used to establish the ROS environment variable for the communication system. The following figure shows how these variables are identified:

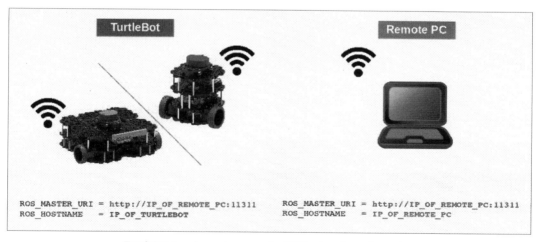

TurtleBot 3 and remote computer ROS network configuration

Note that the TurtleBot 3 and the remote computer identify the remote computer IP address as the `ROS_MASTER_URI` variable. This setup is different than that for the ROS variables for TurtleBot 2. For TurtleBot 3, the Master resides on the remote computer.

The next two sections will step through the network configuration setup process.

Remote computer network setup

The remote computer should be set to connect to the same network as the TurtleBot 3. Determine the remote computer's IP address on that network by typing:

```
$ ifconfig
```

From the screen output, look for the IP address of this computer on the wireless network:

```
wlan0     Link encap:Ethernet HWaddr 9c:b6:d0:0f:6f:89
          inet addr:192.168.11.139  Bcast:192.168.11.255
Mask:255.255.255.0
```

The IP address for our remote computer on our Buffalo router network is `192.168.11.139`, as shown in the preceding output. Your IP address will be different.

With the IP addresses of the remote computer, use the following commands with your specific IP addresses and assign the `ROS_MASTER_URI` and `ROS_HOSTNAME` variables:

```
$ export ROS_MASTER_URI=http://<IP address of remote computer>:11311
$ export ROS_HOSTNAME=<IP address of remote computer>
```

We recommend that you add these commands to the `.bashrc` script file of the remote computer so the ROS environment variables will always be set correctly. Use your favorite editor to add these lines to the `.bashrc` script, then save the file and run the following command:

```
$ source ~/.bashrc
```

To check that the ROS environment variables are set correctly, type:

```
$ env | grep ROS
```

Next, it is necessary to establish the TurtleBot 3 network configuration.

TurtleBot 3 network setup

While the Raspberry Pi is still connected to the monitor, keyboard, and mouse, set up TurtleBot's network configuration to always select the desired network on power up. Be sure that the Raspberry Pi is connected to the network that you plan to use for communication from the remote computer.

On the main menu of Ubuntu MATE, find the **System** option, pull down the menu and select **Preferences**. From the **Preferences** option, select **Internet and Network**, then **Network Connections**. Select the network connection you will be using and hit the **Edit** button. A pop-up window should appear. Make sure that the **General** tab is selected. A screen similar to the following screenshot should be displayed:

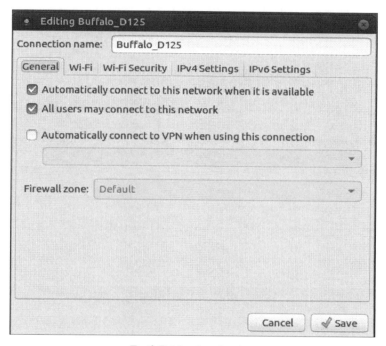

TurtleBot 3 network setup

Check the top two checkboxes in this window to set the network to always connect to your desired network. Then click on the **Save** button in the lower-right corner. Other network connections can be disabled by unchecking these two boxes for those network connections. Then close the network connection window.

Next, find the IP address of TurtleBot 3 using the following command:

```
$ ifconfig
```

From the screen output, look for the `wlan` settings similar to the following:

```
wlan0     Link encap:Ethernet  HWaddr b8:27:eb:b4:87:c4
          inet addr:192.168.11.127  Bcast:192.168.1.255
Mask:255.255.255.0
```

The IP address for our TurtleBot 3 on our Buffalo router network is `192.168.11.127`, as shown in the preceding output. Your IP address will be different.

With the IP addresses of the remote computer and the TurtleBot, use the following commands with your specific IP addresses and assign the `ROS_MASTER_URI` and `ROS_HOSTNAME` variables:

```
$ export ROS_MASTER_URI=http://<IP address of remote computer>:11311
$ export ROS_HOSTNAME=<IP address of TurtleBot 3>
```

We recommend that you modify these commands in the `.bashrc` script file for TurtleBot 3 so the ROS environment variables will always be set correctly. To open this script, type:

```
$ pluma ~/.bashrc
```

Look for the two lines at the end of the `.bashrc` script that assign the `ROS_MASTER_URI` and `ROS_HOSTNAME` variables. Change the word `localhost` to the appropriate IP address indicated previously. Save and close the script and then, run the following command:

```
$ source ~/.bashrc
```

To check that the ROS environment variables are set correctly, type:

```
$ env | grep ROS
```

One last check on the TurtleBot 3 will finish setting up the SSH connection from the Raspberry Pi.

SSH connection

While the Raspberry Pi is still connected to the monitor, keyboard, and mouse, check to make sure that you can SSH from the remote computer to the TurtleBot 3 SBC. On the Raspberry Pi, use the following command to check the SSH status:

```
$ sudo service ssh status
```

The output should show Active: active (running) when SSH is working properly. If the screen output lists Active: inactive (dead), the following command will restart the SSH services:

```
$ sudo service ssh restart
```

This command is only a temporary fix for the problem. To have SSH work automatically on boot up, use the following command:

```
$ sudo systemctl enable ssh
```

Next, the communication between the TurtleBot 3 and the remote computer will be verified.

Testing the SSH communication

To test the connection between your remote computer and TurtleBot 3, try to establish an SSH connection from your remote computer to the TurtleBot 3 by typing the following command on your remote computer:

```
$ ssh <username>@<IP address of TurtleBot>
```

For the authors' Raspberry Pi, the user account was set up with the username turtlebot3. The username for your Raspberry Pi can be found with the whoami command.

Troubleshooting your network connection

If an SSH connection cannot be established, check the following details:

- Both the Raspberry Pi and remote computer are set to the same network
- All network setup for the Raspberry Pi and remote computer were completed as described in the *Remote computer network setup* and *TurtleBot 3 network setup* sections
- The SSH service on the Raspberry Pi is set to automatically boot up on power up

If all of these troubleshooting steps have been completed, try to ping the TurtleBot with the following command:

```
$ ping <IP address of TurtleBot>
```

If the `ping` communication can be established but SSH does not work, then it is recommended to remove and re-install the `openssh` software on the Raspberry Pi. The following commands should be typed on the Raspberry Pi:

```
$ sudo apt-get remove openssh-client openssh-server
$ sudo apt-get install openssh-client openssh-server
```

Retry SSHing to the TurtleBot 3. When you have successfully established a communication link, the window prompt of the TurtleBot Raspberry Pi will be seen on the remote computer.

When you are able to SSH from the remote computer to the TurtleBot 3, proceed to the next section to operate TurtleBot 3 with the keyboard. You will no longer need the monitor, keyboard, and mouse connected to your TurtleBot 3.

Moving the real TurtleBot 3

As with TurtleBot 2, TurtleBot 3 has a number of ways to move using ROS. In the following section, we will present moving TurtleBot around using a keyboard.

To operate the TurtleBot 3 on you network, perform the following steps:

1. Make sure that the TurtleBot battery is charged.
2. Turn on the TurtleBot and make sure that green lights illuminate on the OpenCR board and the Raspberry Pi. A red light should also be lit on the Raspberry Pi. The green light on the USB2LDS board should also be lit.
3. Make sure the TurtleBot has room to move on the floor.
4. Connect the remote computer to the network for TurtleBot and start communicating.

This procedure will be used each time you set up to use the `ssh` command from the remote computer terminal. The TurtleBot 3 password will be required after using the `ssh` command described in the next section.

 While operating the TurtleBot 3, be aware that the buzzer will emit a warning sound when the battery is running low. The buzzer will sound continuously and the actuators will become disabled when the battery voltage level drops below 11V. The TurtleBot should then be connected to the charger to recharge the battery.

Using keyboard teleoperation to move TurtleBot 3

To bring up the TurtleBot from the remote computer, open a terminal window on the remote computer and start `roscore`:

```
$ roscore
```

In a second terminal window, start the communication with the TurtleBot from the remote computer using the `ssh` command:

```
$ ssh <username>@<IP address of TurtleBot>
```

After you have entered the TurtleBot password and see the window prompt change to the TurtleBot prompt, type in the following command to start the TurtleBot's basic operations:

```
$ roslaunch turtlebot3_bringup turtlebot3_robot.launch
```

When this command executes properly, the LDS sensor on the TurtleBot 3 will start spinning. This visual check and no errors in the terminal window will assure you that TurtleBot is up and running.

This command launches two nodes: `turtlebot3_core` and `turtlebot3_lds`. This command is similar to the minimal launch command of TurtleBot 2. The operations in the two terminal windows just described will be necessary to launch the TurtleBot and run most other applications on TurtleBot 3.

To view the real TurtleBot 3 in rviz, open a new terminal window and type the following commands:

```
$ export TURTLEBOT3_MODEL=burger
$ roslaunch turtlebot3_bringup turtlebot3_model.launch
```

An rviz screen should appear, similar to the following screenshot:

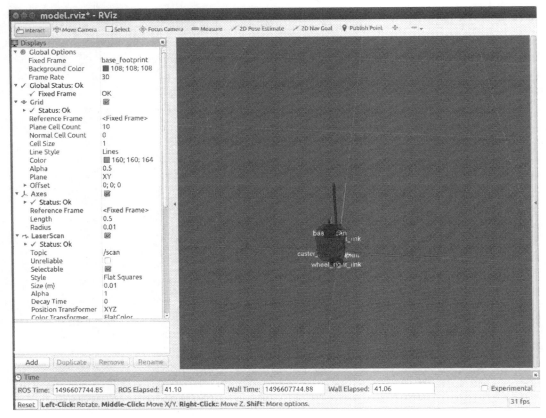

Real TurtleBot 3 in rviz

In rviz, the TurtleBot 3 model appears at the center of the environment and the `tf` frames for the robot are displayed. You should also see red dots surrounding the TurtleBot indicating the 3D points detected by the LDS sensor for objects detected at a distance. This sensor is essential for collecting the distance data required for **Simultaneous Localization and Mapping (SLAM)**.

To start the keyboard teleoperation, open another terminal window and enter the following command:

```
$ roslaunch turtlebot3_teleop turtlebot3_teleop_key.launch
```

This command will launch the `turtlebot3_teleop_keyboard` node to handle processing the keyboard input and sending the `cmd_vel` topics to the `turtlebot3_core` node. The `turtlebot3_core` node handles control of the wheel motors. On the screen in the terminal window, the keyboard control instructions will be displayed:

```
Control Your Turtlebot3!
---------------------------------

Moving around:
     w
a    s    d
     x


w/x : increase/decrease linear velocity
a/d : increase/decrease angular velocity
space key, s : force stop


CTRL-C to quit
```

Hitting the *W* key will cause the TurtleBot to start moving forward slowly and the following text will appear on the screen:

```
currently:  linear vel 0.01    angular vel 0
```

Repeatedly pressing the *W* key will increase the linear velocity by `0.01` each time. For angular velocity, the increments are increased or decreased by 0.1 m/s. Press the spacebar or the *S* key to stop all TurtleBot movement.

Now enjoy driving TurtleBot around your room.

Summary

This chapter introduced the TurtleBot 2 robot and described how to load the necessary software for this TurtleBot. The Gazebo simulator was used to show the capability of ROS to control the TurtleBot 2 in simulation.

To control a real TurtleBot 2 and allow it to roam autonomously, it is desirable to set up a wireless communication between a remote computer and the TurtleBot's netbook. The explanation given in this chapter will allow you to set up the network and remotely control TurtleBot 2.

The various methods to control TurtleBot 2 were presented. Teleoperation from the remote computer is one of the common methods used to control the robot's motion. A Python script was shown, which, when executed, will make the TurtleBot 2 move in a straight line. This chapter also covered the use of rqt tools to send commands to TurtleBot 2 and monitor them.

An important aspect of this chapter is that the TurtleBot 2 can be controlled in simulation or in a real environment with the same commands and scripts. This use of a simulator can save much time in planning, testing, and debugging the applications for TurtleBot 2 before the real robot is turned loose.

Odometry for the TurtleBot 2 was described for the simulated TurtleBot and the real TurtleBot using rviz for visualizing the robot's motion. The auto-docking feature of TurtleBot 2 was also demonstrated.

Finally, the Burger and Waffle TurtleBot 3 models were described. Simulations in rviz and Gazebo were presented. Next, loading the software to control a real TurtleBot 3 was presented for both the remote computer and the TurtleBot itself. Then, TurtleBot was controlled by keyboard teleoperation.

The next chapter explains TurtleBot's use of the vision sensor. The chapter shows in detail how to create a map for TurtleBot and enable it to autonomously navigate around its environment. The mapping and navigation capabilities for both TurtleBot 2 and TurtleBot 3 described.

4
Navigating the World with TurtleBot

In the previous chapter, the TurtleBot 2 robot was described as a two-wheeled differential drive robot developed by Willow Garage. The setup of the TurtleBot 2 hardware, netbook, network system, and remote computer were explained, so the user could set up and operate their own TurtleBot. Then, the TurtleBot 2 was driven around using keyboard control, command-line control, and a Python script. TurtleBot 3 was also introduced and driven around using keyboard control.

In this chapter, we will expand TurtleBot's capabilities by giving the robot vision. The chapter begins by describing 3D vision systems and how they are used to map obstacles within the camera's field of view. The four types of 3D sensors typically used for TurtleBot are shown and described, detailing their specifications. A 2D vision system is also introduced for TurtleBot 3.

Setting up the 3D sensor for use on TurtleBot 2 is described and the configuration is tested in a standalone mode. To visualize the sensor data coming from TurtleBot 2, two ROS tools are utilized: Image Viewer and rviz. Then, an important aspect of TurtleBot is described and realized: **navigation**. TurtleBot will be driven around and the vision system will be used to build a map of the environment. The map is loaded into rviz and used to give the user point and click control of TurtleBot so that it can autonomously navigate to a location selected on the map. Two additional navigation methods will be shown: driving TurtleBot to a location without a map and driving with a map and a Python script. The autonomous navigation ability using rviz is also shown for TurtleBot 3.

In this chapter, you will learn the following topics:

- How 3D vision sensors work
- The difference between the four primary 3D sensors for TurtleBot
- Details on a 2D vision system for TurtleBot 3
- Information on TurtleBot environmental variables and the ROS software required for the sensors
- ROS tools for the rgb and depth camera output
- How to use TurtleBot to map a room using **Simultaneous Localization and Mapping (SLAM)**
- How to operate TurtleBot in autonomous navigation mode by **adaptive monte carlo localization (amcl)**
- How to navigate TurtleBot to a location without a map
- How to navigate TurtleBot to waypoints with a Python script and a map

3D vision systems for TurtleBot

TurtleBot's capability is greatly enhanced by the addition of a 3D vision sensor. The function of 3D sensors is to map the environment around the robot by discovering nearby objects that are either stationary or moving. The mapping function must be accomplished in real time so that the robot can move around the environment, evaluate its path choices, and avoid obstacles. For autonomous vehicles, such as Waymo's self-driving cars, 3D mapping is accomplished by a high-cost LIDAR system that uses laser radar to illuminate its environment and analyze the reflected light. For our TurtleBot, we will present a number of low cost but effective options. These standard 3D sensors for TurtleBot include Kinect sensors, ASUS Xtion sensors, Carmine sensors, and Intel RealSense sensors. TurtleBot 3 navigates using a 2D low cost laser distance sensor, the Hitachi-LG LDS.

How these 3D vision sensors work

The 3D vision systems that we describe for TurtleBot have a common **infrared (IR)** technology to sense depth. This technology was developed by PrimeSense, an Israeli 3D sensing company and originally licensed to Microsoft in 2010 for the Kinect motion sensor used in the Xbox 360 gaming system. The depth camera uses an IR projector to transmit beams that are reflected back to a monochrome **Complementary Metal–Oxide–Semiconductor (CMOS)** sensor that continuously captures image data. This data is converted into depth information, indicating the distance that each IR beam has traveled. Data in x, y, and z distance is captured for each point measured from the sensor axis reference frame.

For a quick explanation of how 3D sensors work, the video *How the Kinect Depth Sensor Works in 2 Minutes* is worth watching at https://www.youtube.com/watch?v=uq9SEJxZiUg.

This 3D sensor technology is primarily for use indoors and does not typically work well outdoors. Infrared from the sunlight has a negative effect on the quality of readings from the depth camera. Objects that are shiny or curved also present a challenge for the depth camera.

Comparison of 3D sensors

Currently, many 3D vision sensors have been integrated with ROS and TurtleBot. Microsoft Kinect, ASUS Xtion, PrimeSense Carmine, and Intel RealSense have all been integrated with camera drivers that provide a ROS interface used for TurtleBot 2. The Intel RealSense sensors are also used with the TurtleBot 3 Waffle version, but navigation is performed using the (2D) LDS on both the Burger and Waffle versions of TurtleBot 3. The ROS packages that handle the processing for these sensors will be described in an upcoming section, but first, a comparison of these products is provided.

Microsoft Kinect

Kinect was developed by Microsoft as a motion sensing device for video games, but it works well as a mapping tool for TurtleBot. Kinect is equipped with an rgb camera, a depth camera, an array of microphones, and a tilt motor.

The rgb camera acquires 2D color images in the same way in which our smart phones or webcams acquire color video images. The Kinect microphones can be used to capture sound data and a three-axis accelerometer can be used to find the orientation of the Kinect. These features hold the promise of exciting applications for TurtleBot, but this book will not delve into the use of these Kinect sensor capabilities.

Kinect is connected to the TurtleBot netbook through a USB 2.0 port (USB 3.0 for Kinect v2). Software development on Kinect can be done using the **Kinect Software Development Kit (SDK)**, freenect, and **Open Source Computer Vision (OpenCV)**. The Kinect SDK was created by Microsoft to develop Kinect apps, but unfortunately, it only runs on Windows. OpenCV is an open source library of hundreds of computer vision algorithms that provides support for 2D image processing. 3D depth sensors, such as the Kinect, ASUS, PrimeSense, and RealSense are supported in the VideoCapture class of OpenCV. Freenect packages and libraries are open source ROS software that provides support for Microsoft Kinect. More details on freenect will be provided in an upcoming section titled *Configuring TurtleBot and installing 3D sensor software*.

Microsoft has developed three versions of Kinect to date: Kinect for Xbox 360, Kinect for Xbox One, and Kinect for Windows v2. The following figure presents images of the variations and the subsequent table shows their specifications:

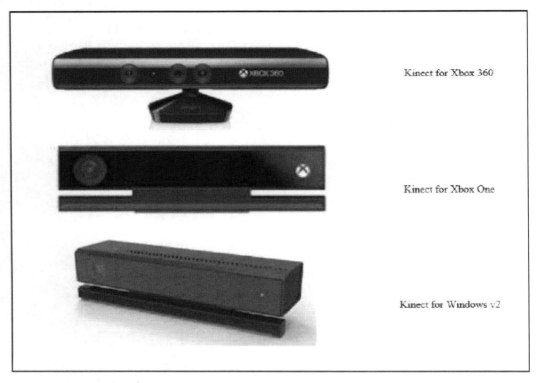

Kinect for Xbox 360

Kinect for Xbox One

Kinect for Windows v2

Microsoft Kinect versions

Microsoft Kinect version specifications:

Spec	Kinect 360	Kinect One	Kinect for Windows v2
Release date	November 2010	November 2013	July 2014
Horizontal field of view (degrees)	57	57	70
Vertical field of view (degrees)	43	43	60
Color camera data	640 x 480 32-bit @ 30 fps	640 x 480 @ 30 fps	1920 x 1080 @ 30 fps
Depth camera data	320 x 240 16-bit @ 30 fps	320 x 240 @ 30 fps	512 x 424 @ 30 fps
Depth range (meters)	1.2–3.5	0.5–4.5	0.5–4.5
Audio	16-bit @ 16 kHz	4 microphones	
Dimensions	28 x 6.5 x 6.5 cm	25 x 6.5 x 6.5 cm	25 x 6.5.x 7.5 cm
Additional information	Motorized tilt base range ± 27 degrees; USB 2.0	Manual tilt base; USB 2.0	No tilt base; USB 3.0 only
	Requires external power		

fps: **frames per second**

ASUS

ASUS Xtion, Xtion PRO, PRO LIVE, and the recently released Xtion 2 are also 3D vision sensors designed for motion sensing applications. The technology is similar to the Kinect, using an IR projector and a monochrome CMOS receptor to capture the depth information.

The ASUS sensor is connected to the TurtleBot netbook through a USB 2.0 port (or USB 3.0 for the Xtion 2) and no other external power is required. Applications for the ASUS Xtion sensors can be developed using the ASUS development solution software, OpenNI2, and OpenCV. **OpenNI2** packages and libraries are open source software that provides support for ASUS and PrimeSense 3D sensors. More details on OpenNI2 will be provided in the following section, *Configuring TurtleBot and installing 3D sensor software.*

The following figure presents images of the ASUS sensor variations and the subsequent table shows their specifications:

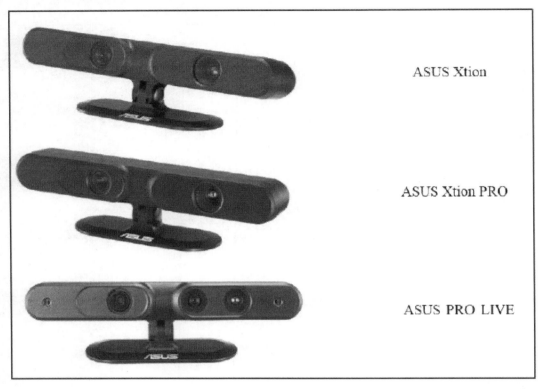

ASUS Xtion and PRO versions

ASUS Xtion and PRO version specifications:

Spec	Xtion	Xtion PRO	Xtion PRO LIVE	Xtion 2
Horizontal field of view (degrees)	58	58	58	74
Vertical field of view (degrees)	45	45	45	52
Color camera data	none	none	1280 x 1024	2592 x 1944
Depth camera data	unspecified	640 x 480 @ 30 fps 320 x 240 @ 60 fps	640 x 480 @ 30 fps 320 x 240 @ 60 fps	640 x 480 @ 30 fps 320 x 240 @ 60 fps
Depth range (meters)	0.8–3.5	0.8–3.5	0.8–3.5	0.8–3.5
Audio	none	none	2 microphones	none
Dimensions (cm)	18 x 3.5 x 5	18 x 3.5 x 5	18 x 3.5 x 5	11 x 3.5 x 3.5
Additional information	USB 2.0	USB 2.0	USB 2.0/ 3.0	USB 3.0
	No additional power required — powered through USB			

PrimeSense Carmine

PrimeSense was the original developer of the 3D vision sensing technology using near-infrared light. They also developed the NiTE software that allows developers to analyze people, track their motions, and develop user interfaces based on gesture control. PrimeSense offered its own sensors, Carmine 1.08 and 1.09, to the market before the company was bought by Apple in November 2013. The Carmine sensor is shown in the following image. ROS OpenNI2 packages and libraries also support the PrimeSense Carmine sensors. More details on OpenNI2 will be provided in the upcoming section titled *Configuring TurtleBot and installing 3D sensor software*:

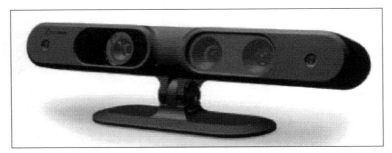

PrimeSense Carmine

PrimeSense has two versions of the Carmine sensor: 1.08 and the short range 1.09. The preceding image shows how the sensors look and the subsequent table shows their specifications:

Spec	Carmine 1.08	Carmine 1.09
Horizontal field of view (degrees)	57.5	57.5
Vertical field of view (degrees)	45	45
Color camera data	640 x 480 @ 30 Hz	640 x 480 @ 60 Hz
Depth camera data	640 x 480 @ 60 Hz	640 x 480 @ 60 Hz
Depth range (meters)	0.8–3.5	0.3–1.4
Audio	Two microphones	Two microphones
Dimensions	18 x 2.5 x 3.5 cm	18 x 3.5 x 5 cm
Additional information	USB 2.0 / 3.0	USB 2.0 / 3.0
	No additional power required—powered through USB	

Intel RealSense

Intel RealSense technology was developed to integrate gesture tracking, facial analysis, speech recognition, background segmentation, 3D scanning, augmented reality, and many more applications into an individual's personal computer experience. For TurtleBot, the RealSense series of 3D cameras can be combined with powerful and adaptable machine perception software to give TurtleBot the capability to navigate on its own. Given that these cameras are powered by a USB 3.0 interface, connecting to the TurtleBot's netbook or SBC is straightforward. Any of these cameras will provide color, depth, and IR video streams for navigation.

In the following paragraphs, we will introduce and describe the latest Intel RealSense series cameras: R200, SR300, and ZR300. Intel's Euclid Development Kit integrates the RealSense camera technology with a power computer to provide a compact all-in-one imaging system. The Euclid will be introduced and described also in a subsequent paragraph.

Intel RealSense Camera R200: It is a long range, stereo vision 3D imaging system. The R200 has two active IR cameras positioned on the left and right of an IR laser projector. These two cameras provide the ability to implement stereo vision algorithms to calculate depth. Images detected by these cameras are sent to the R200 **application-specific integrated circuit (ASIC)**. The ASIC is custom designed to calculate the depth value for each pixel in the image. The IR laser projector is a class-1 laser device that emits additional illumination to texture a scene for better stereo vision performance. The R200 also has a full HD color imaging sensor for color vision data. The R200 has the added advantage of outdoor use because of the IR projection system. Adjustments for a fully sunlit environment might be necessary. The product datasheet for the R200 can be found at the website: `https://software.intel.com/sites/default/files/managed/d7/a9/ realsense-camera-r200-product-datasheet.pdf`.

Intel RealSense Camera SR300: It's a short range, coded light 3D imaging system that is optimized for background segmentation and facial tracking applications. The SR300 is the second-generation improvement over the Intel RealSense F200 camera in depth range and higher quality depth data. The F200 and SR300 imaging systems use embedded coded light IR for depth measurement and full HD color for imaging. The SR300 camera contains an IR laser projector system and a fast **video graphics array (VGA)** IR sensor that work together using a coded light pattern projected on a 2D array of monochromatic pixel values. This coded light method provides depth imaging with reduced exposure time allowing for faster dynamic motion capture. This technology has two significant drawbacks:

1. Multiple SR300 (and F200) cameras used for the same scene degrade the cameras' performance.

2. The camera does not work well in outdoor environments due to ambient IR.

The camera can operate to produce independent color, depth, and IR video streams or synchronizes these video data streams to a client computer system. The SR300 product datasheet can be found at: `https://software.intel.com/sites/default/files/managed/0c/ec/realsense-sr300-product-datasheet-rev-1-0.pdf`.

Intel RealSense Camera ZR300: This variant is a mid-range, stereo vision 3D imaging system similar to the R200. The ZR300 stereo vision is implemented with a left IR camera, a right IR camera, and an IR laser projector. The image data is received from the cameras on the ZR300 ASIC, which calculates the depth values for each pixel in the image. The ZR300 also incorporates a six-degree of freedom IMU and a fisheye optical sensor. The ZR300 image streams have timestamp synchronization to a 50μs reference clock. The ZR300 product datasheet can be found at: `https://www.intel.com/content/dam/support/us/en/documents/emerging-technologies/intel-realsense-technology/ZR300-Product-Datasheet-Public.pdf`.

Intel Euclid Developer Kit: The Euclid combines a ZR300 camera with a full featured computer into the compact size of a candy bar. The computer is an Intel Atom x7-8700 Quad-Core processor with 4 GB of memory and 32 GB of storage. It comes pre-installed with Ubuntu 16.04 and ROS Kinetic Kame. The Euclid has both Wi-Fi and Bluetooth communication and USB 3.0, Micro HDMI, and USBOTG/Charging ports. Sensors within the Euclid include an IMU, barometric pressure sensor, GPS, and proximity sensor. It can be powered by its own lithium polymer battery pack or with external power. The Euclid comes ready to use out of the box and the developer uses a web interface from a phone or computer to run, monitor, and manage the application. Many more details on the Euclid Developer Kit are available at the following websites:

*   *Euclid Development Kit Datasheet*: `https://click.intel.com/media/productid2100_10052017/335926-001_public.pdf`

*   *Euclid Development Kit User Guide*: `https://click.intel.com/media/productid2100_10052017/euclid_user_guide_2-15-17_final3d.pdf`

*   *Euclid Operating Guide*: `https://click.intel.com/media/productid2100_10052017/euclid-operating-guide-final.pdf`

Software development tools for the RealSense cameras are available with any of the following software packages:

- The Intel RealSense SDK for Windows was created to encourage users to develop natural, immersive, and intuitive interactive applications with the 3D cameras. Each of the cameras requires **Depth Camera Manager (DCM)** software specific for that camera to be downloaded and installed for use with the SDK. This SDK makes it easy to incorporate human-computer interaction capabilities such as facial recognition, hand gesture recognition, user background segmentation/removal, 3D scanning, and more features into your apps. Unfortunately, Intel has decided to discontinue support of the SDK for Windows. The `librealsense` API (described next) is the recommended alternative software for developers. Information on the SDK for Windows is available at:
`https://software.intel.com/en-us/intel-realsense-sdk`.

- The `librealsense` API was developed by Intel as an open-source, cross-platform (Linux, OS X, and Windows) driver for streaming video data from the RealSense cameras. It provides image streams for color, depth, and IR as well as produces rectified and registered image streams. Librealsense also supports multi-camera capture from single or multiple RealSense models simultaneously. This API has been initiated to support developers in the areas of robotics, virtual reality, and internet of things. The GitHub repository is present at `https://github.com/IntelRealSense/librealsense`.

- The Intel RealSense SDK for Linux is a collection of software libraries, tools, and samples utilizing the `librealsense` API. The SDK libraries provide the ability to correlate color and depth images, create point clouds, and apply other advanced image processing. Tools and samples are provided to demonstrate the usage of the SDK libraries. `https://software.intel.com/sites/products/realsense/sdk/`.

- OpenCV software can also be used with the image streams produced by the RealSense cameras.

- ROS RealSense packages rely on the librealsense API described previously. The `librealsense` package is used by the ROS `realsense_camera` package, which creates the camera node for publishing streams of color, depth, and IR data. `http://wiki.ros.org/RealSense`.

More details on ROS RealSense software is provided in the upcoming section titled *Configuring TurtleBot and installing 3D sensor software*.

The Intel RealSense cameras currently considered for integrating with TurtleBot are the R200, SR300, ZR300, and the Euclid Development Kit as shown in the following figure. Specifications for the R200, SR300, and ZR300 cameras are shown in the subsequent table:

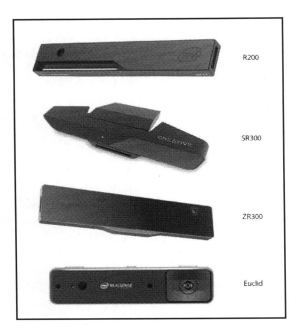

Intel RealSense cameras and the development kit

Intel RealSense camera's specifications:

Spec	R200	SR300	ZR300
Release Date	December 2015	July 2016	January 2017
Horizontal field of view (degrees)	70	71.5	68
Vertical field of view (degrees)	43	55	41.5
Color camera data	1920 x 1080 @ 30 fps	1920 x 1080 @ 30 fps	1920 x 1080
Depth camera data	640 x 480 @ 60 fps	640 x 480 @ 60 fps	640 x 480
IR camera data	640 x 480 @ 60 fps	640 x 480 @ 200 fps	640 x 480
Depth range (meters)	0.4–3.5	0.2–1.5	0.55–2.8
Audio	None	Dual-array Microphones	None

Spec	R200	SR300	ZR300
Dimensions	10.2 x. 1.0 x 0.4 cm 11 x 1.3 x 0.4 cm		15.5 x 3.2 x 0.9 cm
Additional information	Outdoor depth range up to 10 meters USB 3.0 only	USB 3.0 only	Includes: Fisheye Camera 640 x 480; IMU USB 3.0 only
	No additional power required—powered through USB		

Hitachi-LG LDS

The TurtleBot 3 LDS rotates in a continuous 360 degrees to collect 2D distance data that is transmitted to the SBC. The hardware configurations are described in the *Introducing TurtleBot 3* section in *Chapter 3, Driving Around with TurtleBot*. The distance data is used for obstacle detection, SLAM mapping, and navigation. The LDS uses a Class 1 laser with a semiconductor laser diode light source. Basic specifications for the device can be found at `http://wiki.ros.org/hls_lfcd_lds_driver?action=AttachFile&do=view&target=LDS_Basic_Specification.pdf`.

The software driver is contained in the ROS package `hls-lfcd-lds-driver`. The LDS starts operating as part of the basic TurtleBot 3 operation described in the *Using keyboard teleoperation to move TurtleBot 3* section in *Chapter 3, Driving Around with TurtleBot*. The following figure shows a side view and top view of the LDS and the subsequent table shows its specifications:

Hitachi-LG LDS

LDS specifications:

Spec	LDS
Distance range (meters)	0.120 – 3.5
Angular range (degrees)	360
Angular resolution (degrees)	1
Distance accuracy (meters) 0.120 – 0.499 0.500 – 3.500	± 0.015 ± 5.0%
Distance precision (meters) 0.120 – 0.499 0.500 – 3.500	 ± 0.010 ± 3.5%
Scan rate (rpm)	300 ± 10

TurtleBot uses 2D and 3D sensing for autonomous navigation and obstacle avoidance, as described later in this chapter. Other applications that these 3D sensors are used in include 3D motion capture, skeleton tracking, face recognition, and voice recognition.

Obstacle avoidance drawbacks

There are a few drawbacks that you need to know about when using the infrared 3D sensor technology for obstacle avoidance. These sensors have a narrow imaging area of about 58 degrees horizontal and 43 degrees vertical (typically), although those for Kinect for Windows v2 and Xtion 2 are slightly larger. These sensors can also not detect anything within the first 0.5 meters (~20 inches). Highly reflective surfaces, such as metals, glass, or mirrors cannot be detected by the 3D vision sensors.

Configuring TurtleBot and installing the 3D sensor software

There are minor but important environmental variables and software that are needed for the TurtleBot based on your selection of 3D sensors. We have attached a Kinect Xbox 360 sensor to our TurtleBot, but we will provide instructions to configure each of the 3D sensors mentioned in this chapter. These environmental variables are used by the ROS launch files to launch the correct camera drivers. In ROS Kinetic, the Kinect, ASUS, and RealSense sensors are supported by different camera drivers, as described in the following sections.

Kinect

The environmental variables for the Kinect sensors are as follows:

```
export KINECT_DRIVER=freenect
export TURTLEBOT_3D_SENSOR=kinect
```

These variables should be added to the `~/.bashrc` files of both the TurtleBot and the remote computer. For mapping and navigation a common `3dsensor` launch file is utilized and these environment variables identify the 3D vision sensor attached to TurtleBot.

Libfreenect is an open source library that provides an interface for Microsoft Kinect to be used with Linux, Windows, and Mac. ROS packages for Kinect 360 and Kinect One are installed with TurtleBot software installation described in the *Setting up to control a real TurtleBot 2* section in *Chapter 3, Driving Around with TurtleBot*. These ROS packages are:

- `ros-kinetic-libfreenect`
- `ros-kinetic-freenect-camera`
- `ros-kinetic-freenect-launch`
- `ros-kinetic-rgbd-launch`

Kinect for Windows v2 requires a different camera driver named `libfreenect2` and the `iai_kinect2` software toolkit. The installation of this software is described in *Chapter 9, Flying a Mission with Crazyflie*.

 For the latest information on the ROS freenect software, check the ROS wiki at `http://wiki.ros.org/freenect_launch`. Maintainers of the freenect software utilize as much of the OpenNI2 software as possible to preserve compatibility.

ASUS and PrimeSense

The TurtleBot software for ROS Kinetic is configured to work with the ASUS Xtion PRO as the default configuration. It is possible to add the following environmental variable:

```
export TURTLEBOT_3D_SENSOR=asus_xtion_pro
```

although, (at this time) it is not necessary.

The `openni2_camera` ROS package supports the ASUS Xtion, Xtion PRO, and the PrimeSense 1.08 and 1.09 cameras. The `openni2_camera` package does not support any Kinect devices. This package provides drivers for the cameras to publish raw rgb, depth, and IR image streams.

ROS packages for OpenNI2 are installed with the TurtleBot software installation described in the *Setting up to control a real TurtleBot 2* section in *Chapter 3, Driving Around with TurtleBot*. These ROS packages are:

- `ros-kinetic-openni2-camera`
- `ros-kinetic-openni2-launch`

 For the latest information on the ROS OpenNI2 software, check the ROS wiki at `http://wiki.ros.org/openni2_launch`.

Intel RealSense

The environmental variable for one of the Intel RealSense cameras is as follows:

```
export TURTLEBOT_3D_SENSOR=<R200, F200, SR300, ZR300>
```

Only one of the camera identifiers within the brackets should be used. This variable can be added to the `~/.bashrc` files of both TurtleBot and the remote computer.

The RealSense ROS packages enable the use of Intel's RealSense cameras with ROS. Librealsense is the underlying library of drivers for communicating with all the cameras. The ROS package `realsense_camera` is the software for the camera node that publishes the image data. These packages are installed with the TurtleBot software installation described in the *Setting up to control a real TurtleBot 2* section in *Chapter 3, Driving Around with TurtleBot*. For installing these packages on the TurtleBot 3 Waffle SBC, use the following commands:

```
$ sudo apt-get install ros-kinetic-librealsense
$ sudo apt-get install ros-kinetic-realsense-camera
```

Camera software structure

The `freenect_camera`, `openni2_camera` and `realsense_camera` packages are ROS `nodelet` packages used to streamline the processing of an enormous quantity of image data. Initially, a nodelet manager is launched and then nodelets are added to the manager. The default 3D sensor data type for the camera nodelet processing is `depth_image`. The camera driver software publishes the `depth_image` message streams. These messages can be converted to point cloud data types to make them more usable for **Point Cloud Library** (**PCL**) algorithms. Basic navigation operations on TurtleBot use `depth_images` for faster processing. Launching nodelets to handle the conversion of raw depth, rgb, and IR data streams to the `depth_image`, `disparity_image`, and `registered_point_cloud` messages is the method of handling all the conversions in one process. Nodelets allow multiple algorithms to be running in a single process without creating multiple copies of the data when messages are passed between processes.

The `depthimage_to_laserscan` package uses the `depth_image` data to create `sensor_msgs/LaserScan` in order to utilize more processing power to generate maps. For more complex applications, converting `depth_images` to the point cloud format offers the advantage of using the PCL algorithms.

Defining terms

The important terms that are used in configuring TurtleBot are as follows:

- **Depth cloud**: Depth cloud is another name for the `depth_image` produced by a 3D sensor, such as the Kinect, ASUS, PrimeSense, and RealSense depth cameras.

- **Point cloud**: A point cloud is a set of points with x, y, and z coordinates that represent the surface of an object.

- **Registered DepthCloud** and **Registered PointCloud**: These terms are used by ROS for special `DepthCloud` or `PointCloud` data colored by the rgb image data. These data streams are available when the `depth_registration` option is selected (set to `true`).

Testing the 3D sensor in standalone mode

Before we make an attempt to control the TurtleBot 2 from a remote computer, it is wise to test the TurtleBot 2 in standalone mode. TurtleBot will be powered on and we will use its netbook to check whether the robot is operational on its own.

To prepare the TurtleBot, the following steps should be performed:

1. Plug in the power to the 3D sensor via the TurtleBot base connection (Kinect only).
2. Plug in the power to the netbook via the TurtleBot base connection.
3. Power on the netbook and establish the network connection on the netbook. This should be the network used for TurtleBot's ROS_MASTER_URI IP address.
4. Power on the TurtleBot base.
5. Plug in the 3D sensor to the netbook through a USB 2.0 port (for Kinect) or a USB 3.0 port (for Windows v2, Xtion 2, and RealSense).

Ensure that ROS environment variables are configured correctly on the netbook. Refer to the *Netbook network setup* section in *Chapter 3*, *Driving Around with TurtleBot*, and the *Configuring TurtleBot and installing 3D sensor software* section of this chapter.

To test the operation of the TurtleBot 2's 3D sensor in standalone mode, perform the following steps on the netbook:

1. On the TurtleBot netbook, bring up a terminal window and run the TurtleBot minimal launch:

   ```
   $ roslaunch turtlebot_bringup minimal.launch
   ```

2. Open another terminal window and start the camera nodelets for Kinect:

   ```
   $ roslaunch freenect_launch freenect.launch
   ```

   If you are using an ASUS or Carmine sensor, start the camera nodelets using the following command:

   ```
   $ roslaunch openni2_launch openni2.launch
   ```

   If you are using an Intel RealSense camera, start the camera nodelets using the following command that corresponds to the correct camera type:

   ```
   $ roslaunch realsense_camera r200_nodelet_default.launch
   $ roslaunch realsense_camera sr300_nodelet_default.launch
   $ roslaunch realsense_camera zr300_nodelet_default.launch
   ```

If these commands run on TurtleBot with no errors, you are ready to proceed with running 3D visualizations from the remote computer. If you receive errors, such as `No devices connected...`, make sure that the correct camera drivers are installed, as described in the *Configuring TurtleBot and installing 3D sensor software* section of this chapter. Also, make sure that the TurtleBot base is powered on.

Running ROS nodes for visualization

Viewing images on the remote computer is the next step to setting up TurtleBot 2. Two ROS tools can be used to visualize the rgb and depth camera images. Image Viewer and rviz are used in the following sections to view the image streams published by the Kinect sensor.

Visual data using Image Viewer

A ROS node can allow us to view images that come from the rgb camera on Kinect. The `camera_nodelet_manager` node implements a basic camera capture program using OpenCV to handle publishing ROS image messages as a topic. This node publishes the camera images in the `/camera` namespace.

Three terminal windows will be required to launch the base and camera nodes on TurtleBot and launch the Image Viewer node on the remote computer. The steps are as follows:

1. Terminal Window 1: Minimal launch of TurtleBot:

   ```
   $ ssh <username>@<TurtleBot's IP Address>
   $ roslaunch turtlebot_bringup minimal.launch
   ```

2. Terminal Window 2: Launch freenect camera:

   ```
   $ ssh <username>@<TurtleBot's IP Address>
   $ roslaunch freenect_launch freenect.launch
   ```

   This `freenect.launch` file starts the `camera_nodelet_manager` node, which prepares to publish both the rgb and depth stream data. When the node is running, we can check the topics by executing the `rostopic list` command. The topic list shows the `/camera` namespace with multiple `depth`, `depth_registered`, `ir`, `rectify_color`, `rectify_mono`, and `rgb` topics.

3. To view the image messages, open a third terminal window and type the following command to bring up the Image Viewer:

   ```
   $ rosrun image_view image_view image:=/camera/rgb/image_color
   ```

This command creates the /image_view node that opens a window, subscribes to the /camera/rgb/image_color topic, and displays the image messages. These image messages are published over the network from the TurtleBot to the remote computer (a workstation or laptop). If you want to save an image frame, you can click on the disk icon on the main menu of the viewer.

If you are using an ASUS sensor and openni2_launch, the /camera/rgb/image_color topic does not exist. Instead, use the /camera/rgb/image_raw topic.

The following screenshot from the Image Viewer shows the rgb image of the Baxter robot in our laboratory:

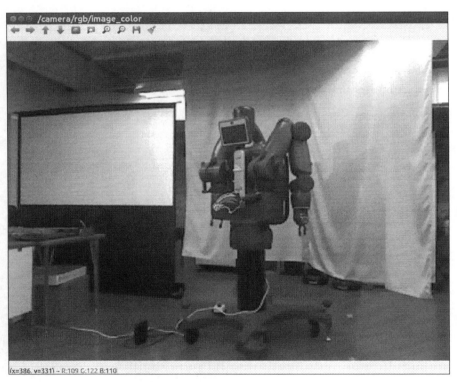

An image view of an rgb image

4. To view depth camera images, press the *Ctrl* + *C* keys to end the previous image_view process. Then, type the following command in the third terminal window:

```
$ rosrun image_view image_view image:=/camera/depth/image
```

A pop-up window for Image Viewer will appear on your screen. Our view is shown in the following screenshot:

An image view of a depth image

To close the Image Viewer and other windows, press the *Ctrl + C* keys in each terminal window.

Visual data using rviz

To visualize the 3D sensor data from the TurtleBot using rviz, begin by launching the TurtleBot minimal launch software. Next, a second terminal window should be opened to start the launch software for the 3D sensor:

1. Terminal Window 1: Minimal launch of TurtleBot:

   ```
   $ ssh <username>@<TurtleBot's IP Address>
   $ roslaunch turtlebot_bringup minimal.launch
   ```

2. Terminal Window 2: Launch 3D sensor software:

   ```
   $ ssh <username>@<TurtleBot's IP Address>
   $ roslaunch turtlebot_bringup 3dsensor.launch
   ```

The 3dsensor.launch file within the turtlebot_bringup package configures itself based on the TURTLEBOT_3D_SENSOR environment variable set by the user. Using this variable, it includes a custom Kinect or ASUS Xtion PRO or RealSense R200 launch.xml file that contains all of the unique camera and processing parameters set for that particular 3D sensor. The 3dsensor.launch file turns on all the sensor processing modules as the default. These modules include the following:

- ○ rgb_processing
- ○ ir_processing
- ○ depth_processing
- ○ depth_registered_processing
- ○ disparity_processing
- ○ disparity_registered_processing
- ○ scan_processing

It is typically not desirable to generate so much sensor data for an application. The 3dsensor.launch file allows users to set arguments to minimize the amount of sensor data generated. Typically, TurtleBot applications only turn on the sensor data needed in order to minimize the amount of processing performed. This is done by setting selected roslaunch arguments to false when particular sensor data is not needed.

When the 3dsensor.launch file is executed, the turtlebot_bringup package launches a /camera_nodelet_manager node with multiple nodelets. Nodelets were described in the *Camera software structure* section. The following is a list of nodelets that are started:

```
NODES
  /camera/
    camera_nodelet_manager (nodelet/nodelet)
    depth_metric (nodelet/nodelet)
    depth_metric_rect (nodelet/nodelet)
    depth_points (nodelet/nodelet)
    depth_rectify_depth (nodelet/nodelet)
    depth_registered_hw_metric_rect (nodelet/nodelet)
    depth_registered_metric (nodelet/nodelet)
    depth_registered_rectify_depth (nodelet/nodelet)
    depth_registered_sw_metric_rect (nodelet/nodelet)
    disparity_depth (nodelet/nodelet)
    disparity_registered_hw (nodelet/nodelet)
```

```
disparity_registered_sw (nodelet/nodelet)
driver (nodelet/nodelet)
ir_rectify_ir (nodelet/nodelet)
points_xyzrgb_hw_registered (nodelet/nodelet)
points_xyzrgb_sw_registered (nodelet/nodelet)
register_depth_rgb (nodelet/nodelet)
rgb_debayer (nodelet/nodelet)
rgb_rectify_color (nodelet/nodelet)
rgb_rectify_mono (nodelet/nodelet)
/
depthimage_to_laserscan (nodelet/nodelet)
```

Next, launch rviz to allow various forms of visualization data to be seen.

3. Terminal Window 3: View sensor data on rviz:

```
$ roslaunch turtlebot_rviz_launchers view_robot.launch
```

The turtlebot_rviz_launchers package provides the view_robot.launch file for bringing up rviz and is configured to visualize the TurtleBot and its sensor output.

Within rviz, the 3D sensor data can be displayed in many formats. If images are not visible in the environment window, set the **Fixed Frame** (under **Global Options**) on the **Displays** panel to /camera_link. Try checking the box for the **Registered PointCloud** and rotating the TurtleBot's screen environment in order to see what the Kinect is sensing. Zoom out to see the entire screen. Then wait. Patience is required because displaying a point cloud involves a lot of processing power.

The following screenshot shows the rviz display of a **Registered PointCloud** image in our lab:

A Registered PointCloud image

On the rviz **Displays** panel, the following display types can be added and checked for viewing in the environment window:

- **DepthCloud**
- **Registered DepthCloud**
- **Image**
- **LaserScan**
- **PointCloud**
- **Registered PointCloud**

If the sensor display does not appear, then the topic is not being published. You can check whether the topic is being published with the `rostopic echo` command. The processing modules for these topics are selected in the `3dsensor.launch` file.

The following table describes the different types of image sensor displays available in rviz and the message types that they display:

Sensor name	Description	Messages used
Camera	This creates a new rendering window from the perspective of a camera and overlays the image on top of it.	sensor_msgs/Image, sensor_msgs/CameraInfo
DepthCloud, Registered DepthCloud	This displays point clouds based on depth maps.	sensor_msgs/Image
Image	This creates a new rendering window with an image. Unlike the camera display, this display does not use camera information.	sensor_msgs/Image
LaserScan	This shows data from a laser scan with different options for rendering modes, accumulation, and so on.	sensor_msgs/LaserScan
Map	This displays an occupancy grid on the ground plane.	nav_msgs/OccupancyGrid
PointCloud, PointCloud2, and Registered PointCloud	This shows data from a point cloud with different options for rendering modes, accumulation, and so on.	sensor_msgs/PointCloud, sensor_msgs/PointCloud2

Navigating with TurtleBot

Launch files for TurtleBot will create ROS nodes either remotely on the TurtleBot netbook (via SSH to TurtleBot) or locally on the remote computer. As a general rule, the launch files (and nodes) that handle the GUI and visualization processing should run on the remote computer while the minimal launch and camera drivers should run on the TurtleBot netbook or SBC. Note that we will specify when to SSH to TurtleBot for a ROS command or omit the SSH for using a ROS command on the remote computer.

Mapping a room with TurtleBot 2

TurtleBot can autonomously drive around its environment if a map is made of the environment. The 3D sensor is used to create a 2D map of the room as the TurtleBot is driven around either by a joystick, keyboard, or any other method of teleoperation.

Since we are using the Kobuki base, calibration of the gyro inside the base is not necessary. If you are using the Create base, make sure that you perform the gyro calibration procedure in the TurtleBot ROS wiki at `http://wiki.ros.org/turtlebot_calibration/Tutorials/Calibrate%20Odometry%20and%20Gyro` before you begin with the mapping operation.

Defining terms

The core terms that are used in TurtleBot navigation are as follows:

- **Odometry**: Data gathered from moving sensors is used to estimate the change in a robot's position over time. This data is used to estimate the current position of the robot relative to its starting location.
- **Map**: For TurtleBot, a map is a 2D representation of an environment encoded with occupancy data.
- **Occupancy Grid Map (OGM)**: An OGM is a map generated from the 3D sensor measurement data and the known pose of the robot. The environment is divided into an evenly spaced grid in which the presence of obstacles is identified as a probabilistic value in each cell on the grid.
- **Localization**: Localization determines the present position of the robot with respect to a known map. The robot uses features in the map to determine where its current position is on the map.

Building a map

The following steps are fairly complex and will require the use of four or five terminal windows. Be conscious of which commands are on TurtleBot (requiring SSH from the remote computer) and those that are on the remote computer (not requiring SSH). In each terminal window, enter the commands following the $ prompt:

1. Terminal window 1: Minimal launch of TurtleBot:

   ```
   $ ssh <username>@<TurtleBot's IP Address>
   $ roslaunch turtlebot_bringup minimal.launch
   ```

   These commands are the now familiar process of setting the many arguments and parameters and launching nodes for the TurtleBot mobile base functionality.

2. Terminal window 2: Launch the gmapping operation as follows:

```
$ ssh <username>@<TurtleBot's IP Address>
$ roslaunch turtlebot_navigation gmapping_demo.launch
```

Look for the following text on your window:

```
odom received!
```

The `gmapping_demo` launch file launches the `3dsensor.launch` file, specifying turning off the `rgb_processing`, `depth_registration`, and `depth_processing` modules. This leaves the modules for `ir_processing`, `disparity_processing`, `disparity_registered_processing`, and `scan_processing`. The `.xml` files for `gmapping.launch` and `move_base.launch` are also invoked. The `gmapping.launch.xml` file launches the `slam_gmapping` node and sets multiple parameters in the `.xml` file. The `move_base.launch.xml` file launches the `move_base` node and also starts the nodes for `velocity_smoother` and `safety_controller`. A more complete description of this processing is provided in the following *How does TurtleBot accomplish this mapping task?* section.

3. Terminal window 3: View navigation on rviz by running the following command:

```
$ roslaunch turtlebot_rviz_launchers view_navigation.launch
```

Rviz should come up in the **TopDownOrtho** view identified in the **Views** panel on the right side of the screen. This environment shows a map that is the initial OGM, which shows occupied space, free space, and unknown space.

If a map is not displayed, make sure that the following display checkboxes have been selected on the **Displays** panel (on the left side):

- **Grid**
- **RobotModel**
- **LaserScan**
- **Bumper Hit**
- **Map**
- **Global Map**
- **Local Map**
- **Amcl Particle Swarm**
- **Full Plan**

Examine the rviz screen; the grid is the coordinate system for the map you will be making. TurtleBot is located at the origin of the grid and map. TurtleBot's *x* direction is pointing along the positive *x* axis of the grid. If you align the direction TurtleBot is facing perpendicular to the wall of the room then the map will squarely overlay the grid. From TurtleBot's starting point for the map (the origin of the grid), locations ahead of it will be positive in *x*, to the left will be positive in *y*, behind will be negative in *x*, and to the right will be negative in *y*.

Your rviz screen should display results similar to the following screenshot:

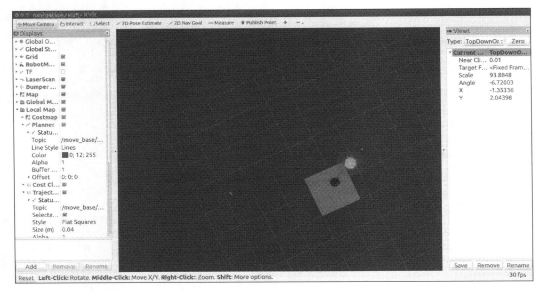

An initial gmapping screen in rviz

4. Terminal window 4: Keyboard control of TurtleBot:

```
$ roslaunch turtlebot_teleop keyboard_teleop.launch
```

 Here, the keyboard navigation command is used, but the joystick teleop or interactive marker navigation can be used instead.

At this point, you should use keyboard commands to navigate TurtleBot completely around the environment. A representation of the map is built and can be viewed in rviz as TurtleBot's 3D sensor detects objects within its range.

The following screenshot shows a map of our lab that TurtleBot produced on rviz:

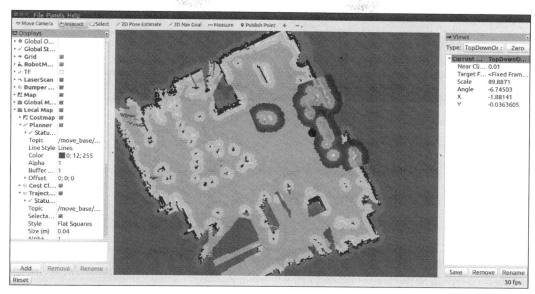

TurtleBot mapping a room

Notice that light gray areas are clear, unoccupied space, dark gray areas are unexplored areas, black indicates a solid border, such as a wall, and colored spots are obstacles in the room. The area of the brightest color is TurtleBot's local map (the area the sensor is currently detecting).

When a complete map of the environment appears on rviz, the map should be saved. Without killing any of the prior processes, open another terminal window and type the following commands:

```
$ ssh <username>@<Turtlbot's IP Address>
$ rosrun map_server map_saver -f /home/<TurtleBot's username>/my_map
```

If you do not know the TurtleBot's username, after *SSH'ing* to TurtleBot, use the pwd command to find it.

The process creates two files: my_map.yaml and my_map.pgm and places them in your TurtleBot netbook home directory. The path and filename can be changed as you desire, but files should be saved on the TurtleBot.

The .yaml file contains configuration information of the map and the path and name of the .pgm image file. The .pgm file is in portable gray map format and contains the image of the OGM.

The map configuration information includes the following:

- The absolute pathname to the .pgm image file
- The map resolution in meters per pixel
- Coordinates (*x*, *y*, and *yaw*) of the origin on the lower-left corner of the grid
- A flag to reverse the *white pixel=free* and *black pixel=occupied* semantics of the map color space
- The lowest threshold value at which pixels will be considered completely occupied
- The highest threshold value at which pixels will be considered completely free

In the next section, we will examine TurtleBot's mapping process from a more in-depth ROS perspective.

How does TurtleBot accomplish this mapping task?

TurtleBot builds maps using the ROS gmapping package. The gmapping package is based on OpenSlam's Gmapping (http://openslam.org/gmapping.html), which is a highly efficient Rao-Blackwellized particle filter algorithm. This approach is based on a laser scan-based SLAM implementation. Although a laser scanner would work the best for SLAM, the Kinect will provide a simulated laser scan for the TurtleBot. The ROS gmapping package contains the slam_gmapping node that takes the incoming laser scan stream and transforms it to the odometry tf reference frame.

The gmapping process is implemented by a set of parameters within the gmapping_demo.launch file in the turtlebot_navigation package. This launch file initiates the 3dsensor.launch file from the turtlebot_bringup package to handle the processing of the 3D sensor. Some of the sensor processing modules are turned off to minimize processing for this task.

The slam_gmapping node subscribes to the sensor_msgs/LaserScan messages from the camera_nodelet_manager node and the tf/tfMessage messages containing the odometry frames. The following diagram from rqt_graph shows the /tf and /tf_static topics (with tf/tfMessage messages) and the /scan topic (with sensor_msgs/LaserScan messages) being subscribed to by the slam_gmapping node. The slam_gmapping node combines this data to create an OGM of the environment. As the robot is driven around the room, the slam_gmapping node publishes the /map topic to update the OGM with an estimate of TurtleBot's location and the surrounding environment based on data from the laser scan.

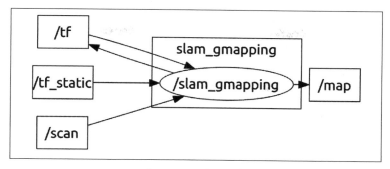

slam_gmapping node

When you issue the command to save the map, the `map_saver` node of the `map_server` package gets activated. The `map_saver` node provides a ROS service to take the OGM data and saves it to a pair of files (the `.pgm` and `.yaml` files described in the previous section). Each cell of the OGM records its occupancy state as a color for the corresponding pixel. Free space is identified as white with a value of `0` and occupied space is identified as black with a value of `100`. A special value of `-1` is used for unknown (unmapped) space. The threshold values within the `.yaml` file make the pixel values between 0 and 100 categorized as occupied, free, or in-between.

Autonomous navigation with TurtleBot 2

ROS has implemented the concept of a **Navigation Stack**. ROS stacks are a collection of packages that provide a useful functionality, in this case navigation. Packages in the Navigation Stack handle the processing of odometry data and sensor streams into velocity commands for the robot base. As a differential drive base, TurtleBot takes advantage of the ROS Navigation Stack to perform tasks, such as autonomous navigation and obstacle avoidance. Therefore, understanding TurtleBot's navigation processes will provide the knowledge base for many other ROS mobile robots as well as a basic understanding of navigation for aerial and underwater robots.

In this section, we will use the map that we created in the *Mapping a room with TurtleBot 2* section. As an alternative, you can use a bitmap image of a map of the environment, but you will need to build the `.yaml` file by hand. Values for map resolution, coordinates of the origin, and the threshold values will need to be selected. With the environment map loaded, we will command TurtleBot to move from its present location to a given location on the map defined as its goal.

At this point, understand that:

- TurtleBot is publishing odometry data and accepting velocity commands
- Kinect is publishing 3D sensor data (fake laser scan data)
- The `tf` library is maintaining the transformations between `base_link`, odom frame, and the depth sensor frame of Kinect
- Our map (`my_map`) will identify the environment locations that have obstacles

Defining terms

The following are the core terms used for autonomous navigation with TurtleBot:

- **Amcl**: The amcl algorithm works to figure out where the robot would need to be on the map in order for its laser scans to make sense. Each possible location is represented by a particle. Particles with laser scans that do not match well are removed, resulting in a group of particles representing the location of the robot in the map. The `amcl` node uses the particle positions to compute and publish the transform from map to `base_link`.
- **Global navigation**: These processes perform path planning for a robot to reach a goal on the map.
- **Local navigation**: These processes perform path planning for a robot to create paths to nearby locations on a map and avoid obstacles.
- **Global costmap**: This costmap keeps information for global navigation. Global costmap parameters control the global navigation behavior. These parameters are stored in `global_costmap_params.yaml`. Parameters common to global and local costmaps are stored in `costmap_common_params.yaml`.
- **Local costmap**: This costmap keeps information for local navigation. Local costmap parameters control the local navigation behavior and are stored in `local_costmap_params.yaml`.

Driving without steering TurtleBot 2

To navigate the environment, TurtleBot needs a map, a localization module, and a path planning module. TurtleBot can safely and autonomously navigate the environment if the map completely and accurately defines the environment.

Before we begin with the steps for autonomous navigation, check the location of your `.yaml` and `.pgm` map files created in the previous section.

As in the previous section, be conscious of which commands are on TurtleBot (requiring `ssh` from the remote computer) and those that are on the remote computer (not requiring `ssh`). At this point, all terminal windows should be closed. Then, open a window as indicated and enter the commands following the `$` prompt:

1. Terminal Window 1: Minimal launch of TurtleBot:

   ```
   $ ssh <username>@<TurtleBot's IP Address>
   $ roslaunch turtlebot_bringup minimal.launch
   ```

2. Terminal Window 2: Launch amcl operation:

   ```
   $ ssh <username>@<TurtleBot's IP Address>
   $ roslaunch turtlebot_navigation amcl_demo.launch map_file:=/
   home/<TurtleBot's username>/my_map.yaml
   ```

   Look for the following text on your window:

   ```
   odom received!
   ```

   The `amcl_demo` launch file launches the `3dsensor.launch` file, specifying to turn off the `rgb_processing`, `depth_registration`, and `depth_processing` modules. This leaves the modules for `ir_processing`, `disparity_processing`, `disparity_registered_processing`, and `scan_processing`. The `map_server` node is launched to read the map data from the file. The `.xml` files for `amcl.launch` and `move_base.launch` are also invoked. The `amcl.launch.xml` file launches the `amcl` node and processing sets multiple parameters in the `.xml` file. The `move_base.launch.xml` file launches the `move_base` node and also starts the nodes for `velocity_smoother` and `safety_controller`. A more complete description of this processing is provided in the following *How does TurtleBot accomplish this navigation task?* section.

3. Terminal Window 3: View navigation on rviz:

   ```
   $ roslaunch turtlebot_rviz_launchers view_navigation.launch
   ```

This command launches the rviz node and rviz will come up in the **TopDownOrtho** view. Your rviz screen should display results similar to the following screenshot:

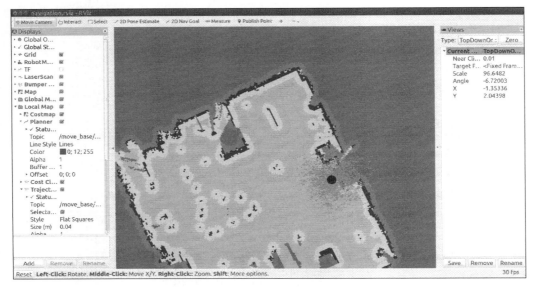

An initial amcl screen in rviz

rviz control

When `amcl_demo` loads the map of the environment, TurtleBot does not know its current location on the map. It needs a little help. Locate TurtleBot's position in the rviz environment and let TurtleBot know this location by performing the following steps:

1. Click on the **2D Pose Estimate** button on the tool toolbar at the top of the main screen.

2. Click the cursor on the location on the map where TurtleBot is located. A large green arrow will appear. Drag the mouse to extend the arrow in the direction TurtleBot is facing.

The giant green arrow helps you align the direction of TurtleBot's orientation. An example is shown in the following screenshot:

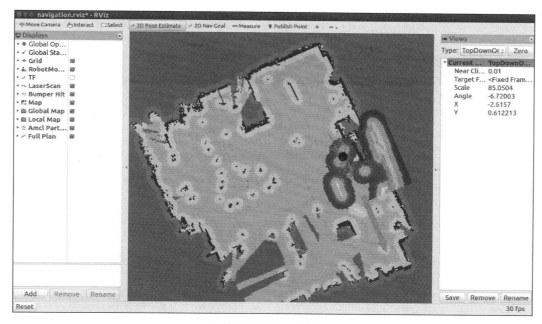

TurtleBot 2D Pose Estimate

When the mouse button is released, a collection of small arrows will appear around TurtleBot to show the direction. If the location and/or orientation are not correct, these steps can be repeated.

The previous steps seed TurtleBot's localization, so it has some idea where it is on the environment map. To improve the accuracy of the localization, it is best to drive TurtleBot around a bit so that the estimate of its current position converges when comparing data from the map with TurtleBot's current sensor streams. Use one of the teleoperation methods previously discussed. Be careful driving around the environment because there is no obstacle avoidance software running at this point. TurtleBot can be driven into obstacles even though they appear on its map.

Next, we can command TurtleBot to a new location and orientation in the room by identifying a goal:

1. Click on the **2D Nav Goal** button on the tool toolbar at the top of the main screen.

2. Click the cursor on the location on the map where you want TurtleBot to go. A large green arrow will appear. The point you clicked will be the final location of the TurtleBot. The arrow extending from that point indicates the direction TurtleBot should be facing when it is finished.

Warning:

Try to avoid navigating near obstacles that have low protrusions that will not be detected by the 3D sensor. In our lab, the extensions at the base of the Baxter robot cannot be seen by the TurtleBot.

The following screenshot shows setting the navigation goal for our TurtleBot:

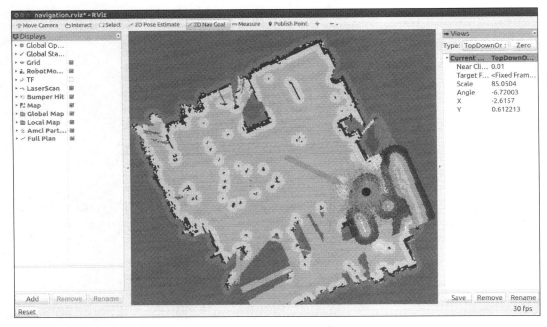

TurtleBot 2D Nav Goal

The following screenshot shows our TurtleBot accomplishing the goal:

TurtleBot reaches its goal

TurtleBot can also perform obstacle avoidance during autonomous navigation. While TurtleBot is on its way to a goal, step in front of it (at least 0.5 meters (1.6 feet) in front of the Kinect) and see that TurtleBot will move around you. Objects can be moved around or doors can be opened or closed to alter the environment. TurtleBot can also respond to the teleoperation control during this autonomous navigation.

In the next section, we will examine TurtleBot's autonomous navigation process from a more in-depth ROS perspective.

How does TurtleBot accomplish this navigation task?

At the highest level of processing, ROS navigation acquires odometry data from the robot base, 3D sensor data, and a goal robot pose. To accomplish the autonomous navigation task, safe velocity commands are sent to the robot to move it to the goal location.

TurtleBot's navigation package, `turtlebot_navigation`, contains a collection of launch and YAML configuration files to launch nodes with the flexibility to modify process parameters on the fly. The following diagram shows an overview of the navigation process:

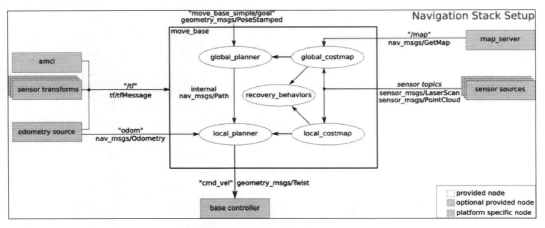

The ROS navigation process

When the `amcl` node is launched, it begins providing localization information about the location of the robot based on the current 3D sensor scans (`sensor_msgs/LaserScan`), tf transforms (`tf/tfMessage`), and the OGM (`nav_msgs/OccupancyGrid`). When a 2D Pose Estimate is input by the operator, an `initialpose` message (`geometry_msgs/PoseWithCovaianceStamped`) resets the localization parameter and reinitializes the amcl particle filter. As laser scans are read, amcl resolves the data to the odometry frame. The `amcl` node provides TurtleBot's estimated position in the map (`geometry_msgs/PoseWithCovarianceStamped`), a particle cloud (`geometry_msgs/PoseArray`), and the tf transforms for odom (`tf/tfMessage`).

The main component of the TurtleBot navigation is the `move_base` node. This node performs the task of commanding the TurtleBot to make an attempt to reach the goal location. This task is set as a preemptable action based on its implementation as a ROS action and TurtleBot's progress toward the goal is provided as feedback. The `move_base` node uses a global and a local planner to accomplish the task. Two costmaps, `global_costmap` and `local_costmap`, are also maintained for the planners by the `move_base` node.

The behavior of the `move_base` node relies on the following YAML files:

- `costmap_common_params.yaml`
- `local_costmap_params.yaml`

- `global_costmap_params.yaml`
- `dwa_local_planner_params.yaml`
- `move_base_params.yaml`
- `global_planner_params.yaml`
- `navfn_global_planner_params.yaml`

The global planner and costmap are used to create long-term plans over the entire environment, such as path planning for the robot to get to its goal. The local planner and costmap are primarily used for interim goals and obstacle avoidance.

The `move_base` node receives the goal information as a pose with position and orientation of the robot in relation to its reference frame. A `move_base_msg/MoveBaseActionGoal` message is used to specify the goal. The global planner will calculate a route from the robot's starting location to the goal taking into account data from the map. The 3D sensor will publish `sensor_msgs/LaserScan` with information on obstacles in the world to be avoided. The local planner will send navigation commands for TurtleBot to steer around objects even if they are not on the map. Navigation velocity commands are generated by the `move_base` node as `geometry_msgs/Twist` messages. TurtleBot's base will use the `cmd_vel.linear.x`, `cmd_vel.linear.y`, and `cmd_vel.angular.z` velocities for the base motors.

Goal tolerance is a parameter set by the user to specify the acceptable limit for achieving the goal pose. The `move_base` node will attempt certain recovery behaviors if TurtleBot is stuck and cannot proceed. These recovery behaviors include clearing out the supplied map and using sensor data by rotating in place.

Navigating to a designated location

In the *ROS commands and Gazebo* section of *Chapter 3, Driving Around with TurtleBot*, we used the `mobile_base` node from the Kobuki base of TurtleBot 2 to move the real TurtleBot. The node subscribes to the topic `/mobile_base/commands/velocity` topic with the `geometry_msgs/Twist` message type. The message is a movement command with `linear.x` pointing forwards as velocity in meters per second. The `angular.z` is interpreted as angular velocity in the *xy* plane in radians per second. The positive angular velocity values are rotations left or counterclockwise when the robot is viewed from above.

The websites `http://wiki.ros.org/kobuki_node` and `http://wiki.ros.org/kobuki/Tutorials/Kobuki%27s%20Control%20System` describe the Kobuki base that subscribes to the topic `commands/velocity` with message type `geometry_msgs/Twist` that sets the desired velocity of the robot. The relative movement of the robot can be monitored with the topic `/odom` with `nav_msgs/odometry` type message. The odometry of the robot is based on the gyro and motor encoders.

In this section, we use the `move_base` package to move the real TurtleBot by specifying a target pose as position and orientation with respect to a designated frame of reference. The topic `move_base_simple/goal` with message type `geometry_msgs/PoseStamped` defines the goal pose of the robot. The website `http://wiki.ros.org/move_base` describes the `move_base` package and the `move_base_simple/goal`.

Similar to the instructions in the *Building a map* section in this chapter, you can command the TurtleBot minimal launch, launch the `gmapping_demo.launch`, and move the TurtleBot from its initial position forward in its *x* direction as an example. Be sure TurtleBot has a clear space to move.

This will require four terminals to command TurtleBot. Enter the commands as shown:

1. Terminal Window 1: Minimal launch of TurtleBot:

   ```
   $ ssh <username>@<TurtleBot's IP Address>
   $ roslaunch turtlebot_bringup minimal.launch
   ```

2. Terminal Window 2: Check initial pose after minimal launch by typing:

   ```
   $ rostopic echo /odom/pose/pose
   ```

   You should see the following:

   ```
   position:
   x: 0.0
   y: 0.0
   z: 0.0
   orientation:
   x: 0.0
   y: 0.0
   z: 0.0
   w: 1.0
   ---
   ```

   Use *Ctrl* + *C* to stop the display.

3. Terminal Window 3: Launch the `gmapping_demo` by typing the following commands:

   ```
   $ ssh <username>@<TurtleBot's IP Address>
   $ roslaunch turtlebot_navigation gmapping_demo.launch
   ```

As previously described, this launches the `move_base` node, which will be used to move TurtleBot to a specific location with a designated pose. It is not necessary to move TurtleBot around to create a map. The `gmapping_demo` creates an initial map that consists of values `-1` indicating an unknown or unmapped space.

The `move_base_simple/goal` topic will be used to issue a non-action command to TurtleBot to move to the desired location. The action based implementation of `move_base` is described in the next section.

4. Terminal Window 4: To move TurtleBot ahead about 1 meter, type the command:

```
$ rostopic pub /move_base_simple/goal geometry_msgs/PoseStamped '{
header: { frame_id: "map" }, pose: { position: { x: 1.0, y: 0, z:
0 }, orientation: { x: 0, y: 0, z: 0, w: 1 } } }'
```

and watch TurtleBot move.

5. Terminal Window 2 again: Check the final pose with the command:

```
$ rostopic echo /odom/pose/pose
```

Our results showed the following:

```
position:
x:  0.908365634848
y:  -0.0158582614505
z:  0.0
orientation:
x:  0.0
y:  0.0
z:  -0.0352483477781
w:  0.99937858391
```

In our laboratory, our TurtleBot moved ahead with an error in the x distance of about 9% based on the odometry data.

Navigating to waypoints with a Python script using a map

In this section, we present a Python script that causes the real TurtleBot 2 to move from one position to another using locations on a map created in our laboratory. In the previous section, *Driving without steering TurtleBot 2*, the rviz **2D Nav Goal** option was used to select the goal location of TurtleBot.

In the example, the initial pose of the TurtleBot will be set on the map using **2D Pose Estimate**. Then, the **Publish Points** icon will be used to select goal points that act as waypoints for TurtleBot on the map. A Python script will be executed to move the real TurtleBot to several goal positions in our room as determined by the positions on the map.

In each terminal window, enter the following commands to initialize TurtleBot, select the map, and display the map with TurtleBot on the map:

1. Terminal Window 1: Minimal launch of TurtleBot:

   ```
   $ ssh <username>@<TurtleBot's IP Address>
   $ roslaunch turtlebot_bringup minimal.launch
   ```

2. Terminal Window 2: Launch amcl operation:

   ```
   $ ssh <username>@<TurtleBot's IP Address>
   $ roslaunch turtlebot_navigation amcl_demo.launch map_file:=/
   home/<TurtleBot's username>/my_map.yaml
   ```

3. Terminal Window 3: Launch rviz and display the map:

   ```
   $ roslaunch turtlebot_rviz_launchers view_navigation.launch
   ```

The following screenshot shows TurtleBot on the map in rviz:

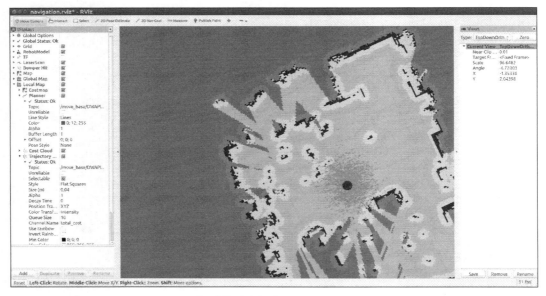

TurtleBot's initial position in rviz

Defining TurtleBot's position on a map

To determine TurtleBot's initial pose on the map, type the following:

```
$ rostopic echo /initialpose
```

This will display the initial pose after using the **2D Pose Estimate** in rviz to identify the initial position and orientation of TurtleBot in the room.

Our result for the initial pose was as follows:

```
header:
  seq: 1
  stamp:
    secs: 1500506112
    nsecs: 896815961
  frame_id: map
pose:
  pose:
    position:
      x: 0.172010675073
      y: 0.0527899339795
      z: 0.0
    orientation:
      x: 0.0
      y: 0.0
      z: -0.0139684328787
      w: 0.999902436682
  covariance: [0.25, 0.0, 0.0, 0.0, 0.0, 0.0, 0.0, 0.25, 0.0, 0.0, 0.0,
0.0, 0.0, 0.0, 0.0, 0.0, 0.0, 0.0, 0.0, 0.0, 0.0, 0.0, 0.0, 0.0,
0.0, 0.0, 0.0, 0.0, 0.0, 0.0, 0.0, 0.0, 0.0, 0.0, 0.06853891945200942]
---
```

For the map we created, TurtleBot's position is roughly in the middle of the map representing the middle of our laboratory.

Defining waypoints on a map

Using the **Publish Point** icon, select several points on the map and record the *x* and *y* coordinates of each point. The position of the cursor at any point will be displayed in a panel at the lower left of the screen. Alternatively, echo the topic `/clicked_point` with the following command line:

```
$ rostopic echo /clicked_point
```

Our results for two points were as follows:

```
header:
  seq: 6
  stamp:
    secs: 1500506877
    nsecs: 337500725
  frame_id: map
point:
  x: 3.00541186333
  y: -0.0026988487225
  z: -0.0013427734375
---
header:
  seq: 7
  stamp:
    secs: 1500506893
    nsecs: 543592195
  frame_id: map
point:
  x: 3.03029751778
  y: 3.57522583008
  z: 0.00247192382812
```

Our map overlays a 10 by 10 grid of squares 1 meter on a side with the origin in the center. Your map, however, may be rotated with respect to the grid, so use the **Publish Point** method to determine the values on your map so that they can be related to real positions in the room.

Using our map, we chose the following points from the map that indicate locations in our laboratory: (3.0, 0.0, 0.0) for the first goal point and (3.0, 3.6, 0.0) for the final position. The first point is near the wall on the right in the map and the second is near the door to the lab at the upper right corner of the map. At initialization and at the first waypoint, the orientation of TurtleBot will be chosen to be straight ahead as defined by the quaternion (0, 0, 0, 1) along the x axis. At the second waypoint, TurtleBot will be aligned with the y axis of the map with quaternion (0, 0, 0.707, 0.707) indicating approximately a 90 degree change in orientation. The following modified screenshot shows these locations:

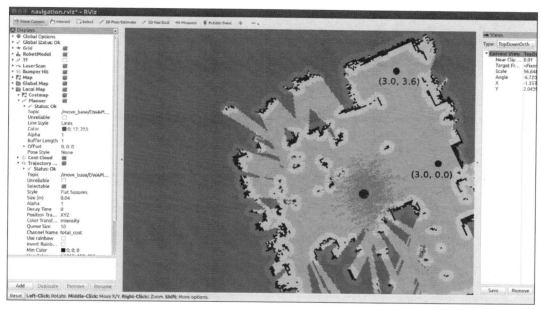

Goal locations chosen in rviz

Using Python code to move TurtleBot

You should choose goal points that relate to your map and replace the items in the list GoalPoints in the following Python script. Execute our Python script by typing in a new terminal:

```
$ python MoveTBtoGoalPoints.py
```

The following Python script named MoveTBtoGoalPoints.py moves TurtleBot to the various goal positions:

```
#!/usr/bin/env python

import rospy
```

```
import actionlib      # Use the actionlib package for client and
server

from move_base_msgs.msg import MoveBaseAction, MoveBaseGoal

# Define Goal Points and orientations for TurtleBot in a list
GoalPoints = [ [(3.0, 0.0, 0.0), (0.0, 0.0, 0.0, 1.0)] ,
               [(3.0, 3.6, 0.0), (0.0, 0.0, 0.707, 0.707)]]

# The function assign_goal initializes goal_pose variable as a
MoveBaseGoal action type.
def assign_goal(pose):
    goal_pose = MoveBaseGoal()
    goal_pose.target_pose.header.frame_id = 'map'
    goal_pose.target_pose.pose.position.x = pose[0][0]
    goal_pose.target_pose.pose.position.y = pose[0][1]
    goal_pose.target_pose.pose.position.z = pose[0][2]
    goal_pose.target_pose.pose.orientation.x = pose[1][0]
    goal_pose.target_pose.pose.orientation.y = pose[1][1]
    goal_pose.target_pose.pose.orientation.z = pose[1][2]
    goal_pose.target_pose.pose.orientation.w = pose[1][3]

    return goal_pose

if __name__ == '__main__':
    rospy.init_node('MoveTBtoGoalPoints')

    # Create a SimpleActionClient of a move_base action type and wait
for server.
    client = actionlib.SimpleActionClient('move_base', MoveBaseAction)
    client.wait_for_server()

    # for each goal point in the list, call the action server and move
to goal
    for TBpose in GoalPoints:
        TBgoal = assign_goal(TBpose)  # For each goal point assign
pose
        client.send_goal(TBgoal)
        client.wait_for_result()

    # print the results to the screen
    if(client.get_state() == GoalStatus.SUCCEEDED):
        rospy.loginfo("success")
    else:
        rospy.loginfo("failed")
```

When the program finishes, the terminal display should show `success`.

This Python script sends goal poses to TurtleBot one pose at a time to move it to a particular location. This code uses the navigation stack as described in the *How does TurtleBot accomplish this navigation task?* section. The `rospy` and `actionlib` packages and the `MoveBaseAction` and `MovBaseGoal` messages are used within the script and are imported at the beginning of the code. The `MoveBaseAction` message defines the action goal, action result, and action feedback specifically for behaviors regarding TurtleBot's movement. The `MoveBaseGoal` message is used to define the target pose.

The goal poses for TurtleBot are identified in the list `GoalPoints`. For the Python script, the goal poses in terms of position x, y, z and the orientation in terms of a quaternion were chosen as: `[[(3.0, 0.0, 0.0), (0.0, 0.0, 0.0, 1.0)]` and `[(3.0, 3.6, 0.0), (0.0, 0.0, 0.707, 0.707)]]`.

Next in the code is the definition of the `assign_goal` function. The `assign_goal` function creates a message of type `MoveBaseGoal` and assigns the values from the pose item in `GoalPoints` to target pose in this message.

When the main function of this program runs, it creates the ROS node `MoveTBtoGoalPoints`. Then it creates an action client for the `SimpleActionServer`, which is configured to communicate with the `move_base` server and adhere to the behaviors defined in the `MoveBaseAction` message. The wait statement indicates that a response from the action server is necessary before proceeding to the next lines of code.

The `for` loop increments through each of the goal poses in the `GoalPoints` list and causes each of these poses to be processed by the `move_base` action server. The first statement in the loop calls the `assign_goal` function to create a `MoveBaseGoal` message and assign the values of that message to be the values of the goal pose. The second statement calls the action client `send_goal` function to send the goal to the action server. The process then waits for the server to return the results of the action and the appropriate message is displayed. When we tested our example, the `success` message appeared on the screen.

TurtleBot at final goal point

As a result in our laboratory, TurtleBot moved toward the wall on the right of the map and turned approximately 90 degrees left and moved toward the door at the upper right. The script completes with the reply:

```
[INFO] [1499983063.642908]: success
```

The following screenshot shows the final location of TurtleBot after the Python script is executed:

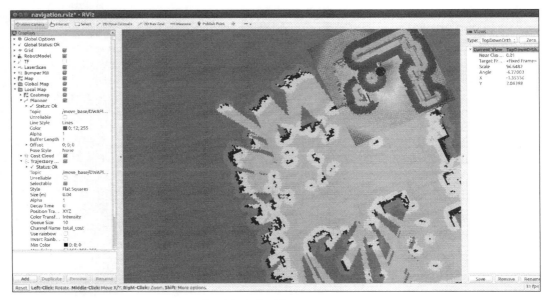

TurtleBot's final location in rviz

You can check the robot's final position as it moves on the map by typing:

```
$ rostopic echo /amcl_pose
```

Our final pose from topic `/amcl_pose` was as follows:

```
header:
  seq: 72
  stamp:
    secs: 1500584344
    nsecs: 824573719
  frame_id: map
pose:
  pose:
    position:
      x: 2.95402869322
      y: 3.30398805405
      z: 0.0
    orientation:
```

```
x: 0.0
y: 0.0
z: 0.666663241366
w: 0.745359056168
covariance: [0.02732330983433684, -0.001682319824116263, 0.0, 0.0, 0.0,
0.0, -0.001682319824116263, 0.002880105195270488, 0.0, 0.0, 0.0, 0.0,
0.0, 0.0, 0.0, 0.0, 0.0, 0.0, 0.0, 0.0, 0.0, 0.0, 0.0, 0.0, 0.0, 0.0,
0.0, 0.0, 0.0, 0.0, 0.0, 0.0, 0.0, 0.0, 0.0, 0.004937415284215015]
```

The indicated position and orientation is reasonably close to the selected values. The pose only can be viewed by typing:

```
$ rostopic echo /odom/pose/pose
```

since the covariance is not relevant in this case.

TurtleBot 3 has SLAM and autonomous navigation applications similar to those described for TurtleBot 2. The sequences and commands will be briefly described in the next two sections.

SLAM for TurtleBot 3

Before proceeding with the next two sections, check to verify your network configuration and ROS environment variables for both the TurtleBot 3 and the remote computer are set as described in the *Networking TurtleBot 3 and the remote computer* section of *Chapter 3, Driving Around with TurtleBot*.

The same launch procedure will be used as was described previously in the *Moving the real TurtleBot 3* section of *Chapter 3, Driving Around with TurtleBot*:

1. On the remote computer, start the ROS Master with the following command:

    ```
    $ roscore
    ```

2. In a second terminal window, ssh to the TurtleBot from the remote computer and then launch the TurtleBot basic operations with the following commands:

    ```
    $ ssh <username>@<IP address of TurtleBot>
    $ roslaunch turtlebot3_bringup turtlebot3_robot.launch
    ```

3. Next launch the SLAM software in a new terminal window with the following commands:

    ```
    $ export TURTLEBOT3_MODEL=burger
    $ roslaunch turtlebot3_slam turtlebot3_slam.launch
    ```

4. After the `turtlebot3_slam_gmapping` node has launched, information regarding the laser scans will begin to appear on the screen and run continuously updating data with each scan performed. To visualize the TurtleBot and the area that will become the map, start rviz with the following `roslaunch` command:

```
$ rosrun rviz rviz -d `rospack find turtlebot3_slam`/rviz/
turtlebot3_slam.rviz
```

An rviz window should be displayed similar to the following screenshot:

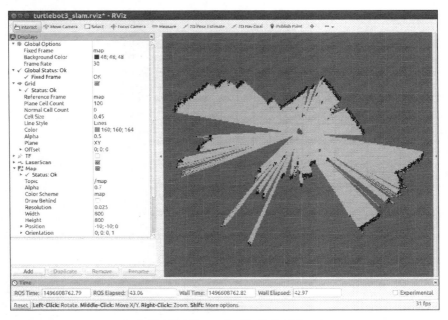

An initial SLAM map for TurtleBot 3 in rviz

This is very similar to the rviz window that is generated by SLAM gmapping for the TurtleBot 2.

5. Now, move the TurtleBot around the environment with keyboard control by using the following command in a new terminal window:

```
$ roslaunch turtlebot3_teleop turtlebot3_teleop_key.launch
```

6. When you have completely driven the robot around your environment and are happy with your map, open one additional terminal window and save the map to a file with the following command:

```
$ rosrun map_server map_saver -f ~/map
```

The map will be saved to the home directory of your remote computer, not on TurtleBot 3. Two files will be created for the map: map.pgm and map.yaml. These files are the same type as those described for TurtleBot 2.

7. Next, this map will be used to autonomously navigate TurtleBot around the area that was just mapped. Use *Ctrl + C* in each terminal window to kill all the processes and then close the windows.

Autonomous navigation with TurtleBot 3

As in the previous section, verify the network configuration and ROS environment variables for the TurtleBot 3 and the remote computer. Also, start the ROS Master and launch the basic operation of TurtleBot 3.

To launch the navigation software for the TurtleBot 3 Burger, use the following commands in a new terminal window:

```
$ export TURTLEBOT3_MODEL=burger
```

```
$ roslaunch turtlebot3_navigation turtlebot3_navigation.launch map_file:=~/map.yaml
```

If you named the map file with a name other than map, substitute that name with the .yaml extension in the preceding command. To visualize the map and Turtlebot, start rviz with the following rosrun command:

```
$ rosrun rviz rviz -d `rospack find turtlebot3_navigation`/rviz/turtlebot3_nav.rviz
```

The rviz screen should display the map with TurtleBot 3 located within the map surrounded by a cloud of small green arrows similar to the following screenshot:

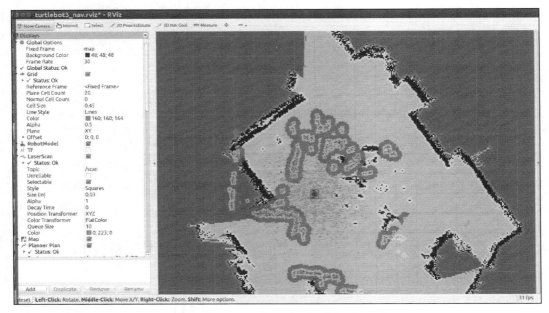

An initial navigation map for TurtleBot 3 in rviz

In the same manner as was done for TurtleBot 2, rviz should be updated with the initial location and orientation of the TurtleBot 3. To perform this update:

1. Click on the **2D Pose Estimate** button on the top toolbar.

2. Click the cursor on the location on the map where TurtleBot is located. A large green arrow will appear. Drag the mouse to extend the arrow in the direction TurtleBot is facing.

The giant green arrow that appears will help to align the direction TurtleBot is facing. When the mouse button is released, the map will update with the new location and orientation of the TurtleBot and its surrounding area.

To autonomously navigate TurtleBot to another location on the map, indicate a goal location and orientation by performing the following steps:

1. Click on the **2D Nav Goal** button on the top toolbar.
2. Click the cursor on the location on the map where you want TurtleBot to go. A large green arrow will appear. The point you clicked will be the final location of the TurtleBot. The arrow extending from the point indicates the direction TurtleBot should be facing when it is finished.

When the mouse button is released, TurtleBot will create a path to the goal location and begin executing the path plan. It will avoid obstacles detected by the LDS sensor. Be aware that the LDS sensor will only detect objects at the level of its own height. Objects above or below this height will not be sensed.

rqt_reconfigure

The many parameters involved in TurtleBot 2 navigation can be tweaked on the fly by using the `rqt_reconfigure` tool. This tool was previously named Dynamic Reconfigure and this name still appears on the screen. To activate this rqt plugin, use the following command:

```
$ rosrun rqt_reconfigure rqt_reconfigure
```

Nodes that have been programmed using the `rqt_reconfigure` API will be visible on the `rqt_reconfigure` GUI. On the GUI, nodes can be selected and a window with the nodes' parameters will appear with the current values and range limits. Sliders and input boxes allow the user to enter new values that will dynamically overwrite the current values. At present, TurtleBot 2 has implemented the `rqt_reconfigure` API as shown in the following screenshots. The following screenshot shows configuration parameters that can be changed for the `/camera/depth`, `/camera/depth_registered`, and `/camera/driver`:

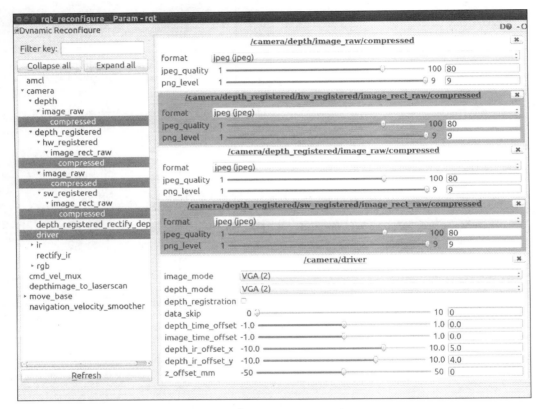

rqt_reconfigure camera parameters

The parameters for the `move_base` node control can be accessed through `rqt_reconfigure`. These parameters are set by the `move_base_params.yaml` file mentioned in the previous section. This screen identifies the `base_global_planner` and the `base_local_planner` as well as how often to update the planning process (`planner_frequency`), and so on. These parameters allow the operator to tweak the performance of the software during an operation.

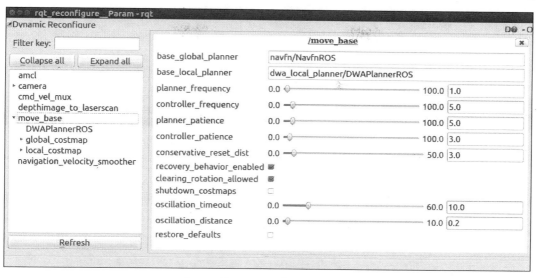

rqt_reconfigure move_base parameters

Exploring ROS navigation further

The ROS wiki provides extensive information on all aspects of setting up and configuring the navigation parameters. The following links are provided to enhance your understanding:

- http://wiki.ros.org/navigation
- http://wiki.ros.org/navigation/Tutorials/RobotSetup
- http://wiki.ros.org/navigation/Tutorials/Navigation%20Tuning%20 Guide

The following book is worth reading to gain a deeper understanding of amcl and robotic navigation:

Probabilistic Robotics by *Thrum, Burgard,* and *Fox* by *MIT Press*

Summary

TurtleBot comes with its own 3D vision system that is a low-cost laser scanner. The Kinect, ASUS, PrimeSense, or RealSense devices can be mounted on the TurtleBot base and provide a 3D depth view of the environment. This chapter provided a comparison of these four types of sensors and identified the software that is needed to operate them as ROS components. We checked their operation by testing the sensor on TurtleBot in standalone mode. To use the devices, we can utilize Image Viewer or rviz to view image streams from the rgb or depth cameras.

For TurtleBot 3, the LDS sensor was described and ROS software and camera driver software was identified.

The primary objective is for TurtleBot to see its surroundings and be able to autonomously navigate through them. First, TurtleBot is driven around in teleoperation mode to create a map of the environment. The map provides the room boundaries and obstacles so that TurtleBot's navigation algorithm, amcl, can plan a path through the environment from its start location to a user-defined goal.

Navigation to a designated location is also performed without a map. Additionally, an example of a Python script is used to navigate with the move_base action using a map of the environment.

In the next chapter, we will return to the ROS simulation world and create a robot arm. The development of a URDF for a robotic arm and control of it in simulation will then prepare us to examine the robotic arms of Baxter in *Chapter 6, Wobbling Robot Arms Using Joint Control*. Using Baxter's robot arms, we will explore the complexities of multiple joint control and the mathematics of kinematic solutions for positioning multiple joints.

5
Creating Your First Robot Arm (in Simulation)

In this chapter, you will begin to understand the control of robot arms with ROS. We will show a simple three-link, two-joint, articulated robotic arm in simulation. The simulated robot arm, `rrbot`, has two revolute joints that will help you to understand the operations of a physical robot arm, without the complexities that more joints would create. We will use the URDF elements described in *Chapter 2, Creating Your First Two-Wheeled ROS Robot (in Simulation)* and incorporate the advantages of Xacro to make our code more modular and efficient. We will also include a mesh design for our gripper, and add control elements for the arm and gripper to our URDF. Next, we will show various ways to control the robot arm in Gazebo.

In this chapter, you will learn the following:

- The advantages of using Xacro in a URDF
- Designing a three-link, two-joint robotic arm using Xacro and mesh files
- Controlling the arm in Gazebo using ROS commands and rqt

We will begin by expanding your 3D modeling skills in order to create a robot arm URDF using Xacro. First, the advantages of Xacro are described.

Features of Xacro

Xacro is the XML macro language for ROS. Xacro provides a set of macro operations to replace some repetitive statements with shorter, concise macros that will expand into full XML statements when processed. Xacro can be used with any XML document, but is most useful with long, complex URDF files. Xacro allows you to create shorter and more readable XML files for the robot URDF. Xacro provides advantages in many different areas:

- **Properties and property blocks**: If repeated information is used in a URDF/SDF file, the `<property>` tag can be used to specify these constant values in a central location. Property blocks are snippets that can contain one or more XML definitions. These are typically parameters that can be changed later. Properties and property blocks are usually declared at the beginning of the file, although this is not required. They can be found anywhere in the XML file at any level. It does not matter whether the property declaration is before or after its use.

  Here is an example of how to implement a property:

  ○   `<xacro:property name="my_name" value ="Robby" />`

  This is a property declaration for `my_name`.

  - ○   This property is used in the expression `"${my_name}"`, which is evaluated as the value of `my_name`, and can be used to substitute the text `"Robby"` into an attribute.

- **Simple math**: Math expressions can be constructed using the four basic operations: `+`, `-`, `/`, and `*`. The unary minus and parentheses can also be used. The expression must be enclosed in the `${}` construct. Numeric values are floating point numbers.

- **Macros**: This is the main feature of Xacro. When creating a macro, a simple `<xacro>` tag can expand into a statement or sequence of statements in the URDF/SDF file. Macros are extremely useful when statements are repeated or reused with modifications defined by parameters.

- **Use of rospack commands**: Xacro supports the use of `rospack` commands, just as `roslaunch` does for substitution arguments (`args`) (http://wiki. ros.org/roslaunch/XML). The `rospack` commands enclosed within `$()` will be resolved during Xacro processing. For example, `$(find ros_robotics)` will find the relative pathname for the `ros_robotics` package. The `$(arg var1)` argument will be resolved to a value passed by an Xacro statement or the command line. Arguments passed via the command line must use the `myvar:=true` flag.

- **Combining multiple Xacro files**: Other Xacro files can be included in the main URDF file to allow you to modularize the URDF file into component files. The tag is as follows:

```
<xacro:include filename="path to filename/filename" />
```

- Other features of Xacro can be found at `http://wiki.ros.org/xacro`.

These features will be used in the URDF file for `rrbot` throughout this chapter. The order in which Xacro processes all these features is as follows:

1. Includes
2. Properties and property blocks
3. Macro definitions
4. Instantiation of macros
5. Expression evaluation

Building an articulated robot arm URDF using Xacro

Our simple robot arm model `rrbot` consists of three link elements of various heights and two joint elements that join the links together. The joint elements each connect two of the links and enable the links to rotate around one of its axes.

In the next few sections, the `rrbot` URDF will be created and incrementally built to incorporate the advantages of each of the Xacro features we discussed in the last section. If you have not created the `ros_robotics` package, refer to the *Creating and building a ROS package* section in *Chapter 2, Creating Your First Two-Wheeled ROS Robot (in Simulation)*.

Specifying a namespace

In order to create the URDF file from Xacro files, the Xacro file must contain an XML namespace declaration using the `xmlns` attribute with the `xacro` tag and corresponding URI. Here is the XML namespace (`xmlns`) attribute for our `rrbot` robot arm:

```
<robot name="rrbot" xmlns:xacro="http://www.ros.org/wiki/xacro">
```

This declaration is vital for the file to parse properly. This statement appears as the second line in the main Xacro file, following the XML version reference.

Using the Xacro property tag

For the first iteration of our `rrbot` robot arm, we will build a URDF file that defines three links with the `<visual>`, `<collision>`, and `<inertial>` tags, and two joints with the `<parent>`, `<child>`, `<origin>`, and `<axis>` tags. This is a very similar format to the `dd_robot` URDF file that you are familiar with from *Chapter 2, Creating Your First Two-Wheeled ROS Robot (in Simulation)*. The differences for the Xacro format are listed here and explained in more detail after the code is presented:

- Addition of the XML namespace declaration on the second line
- Use of the Xacro `<property>` tag to define constant values
- Addition of property names instead of values within the `<box>` and `<origin>` tags
- Simple math (along with property names) to calculate link `<origin>` *z* values
- Joints for this arm are revolute and have the additional tags of `<dynamics>` and `<limit>`

The `rrbot.xacro` file can be downloaded from the Packt website. Otherwise, you can enter the following code into your favorite editor and place the file in your catkin workspace in the `ros_robotics` package:

```
<?xml version="1.0"?>
<!-- Revolute-Revolute Manipulator -->
<robot name="rrbot" xmlns:xacro=http://www.ros.org/wiki/xacro>

  <!-- Constants for robot dimensions -->
  <xacro:property name="width" value="0.1" />
  <xacro:property name="height1" value="2" />
  <xacro:property name="height2" value="1" />
  <xacro:property name="height3" value="1" />
  <xacro:property name="axle_offset" value="0.05" />
  <xacro:property name="damp" value="0.7" />

  <!-- Base Link -->
  <link name="base_link">
    <visual>
      <origin xyz="0 0 ${height1/2}" rpy="0 0 0" />
      <geometry>
        <box size="${width} ${width} ${height1}" />
      </geometry>
    </visual>

    <collision>
```

```
      <origin xyz="0 0 ${height1/2}" rpy="0 0 0" />
      <geometry>
        <box size="${width} ${width} ${height1}" />
      </geometry>
    </collision>

    <inertial>
      <origin xyz="0 0 ${height1/2}" rpy="0 0 0" />
      <mass value="1" />
      <inertia ixx="1.0" ixy="0.0" ixz="0.0"
               iyy="1.0" iyz="0.0" izz="1.0"/>
    </inertial>
  </link>

  <!-- Joint between Base Link and Middle Link -->
  <joint name="joint_base_mid" type="revolute">
    <parent link="base_link" />
    <child link="mid_link" />
    <origin xyz="0 ${width} ${height1 - axle_offset}"
    rpy="0 0 0"/>
    <axis xyz="0 1 0"/>
    <dynamics damping="${damp}"/>
    <limit effort="100.0" velocity="0.5" lower="-3.14"
           upper="3.14"/>
  </joint>

  <!-- Middle Link -->
  <link name="mid_link">
    <visual>
      <origin xyz="0 0 ${height2/2 - axle_offset}" rpy="0 0 0" />
      <geometry>
        <box size="${width} ${width} ${height2}" />
      </geometry>
    </visual>

    <collision>
      <origin xyz="0 0 ${height2/2 - axle_offset}" rpy="0 0 0" />
      <geometry>
        <box size="${width} ${width} ${height2}" />
      </geometry>
    </collision>

    <inertial>
      <origin xyz="0 0 ${height2/2 - axle_offset}" rpy="0 0 0" />
```

```
        <mass value="1" />
        <inertia ixx="1.0" ixy="0.0" ixz="0.0"
                 iyy="1.0" iyz="0.0" izz="1.0" />
      </inertial>
   </link>

   <!-- Joint between Middle Link and Top Link -->
   <joint name="joint_mid_top" type="revolute">
     <parent link="mid_link" />
     <child link="top_link" />
     <origin xyz="0 ${width} ${height2 - axle_offset*2}"
     rpy="0 00"/>
     <axis xyz="0 1 0" />
     <dynamics damping="${damp}" />
     <limit effort="100.0" velocity="0.5" lower="-3.14"
            upper="3.14"/>
   </joint>

   <!-- Top Link -->
   <link name="top_link">
     <visual>
       <origin xyz="0 0 ${height3/2 - axle_offset}" rpy="0 0 0" />
       <geometry>
         <box size="${width} ${width} ${height3}" />
       </geometry>
     </visual>

     <collision>
       <origin xyz="0 0 ${height3/2 - axle_offset}" rpy="0 0 0" />
       <geometry>
         <box size="${width} ${width} ${height3}" />
       </geometry>
     </collision>

     <inertial>
       <origin xyz="0 0 ${height3/2 - axle_offset}" rpy="0 0 0" />
       <mass value="1" />
       <inertia ixx="1.0" ixy="0.0" ixz="0.0"
                iyy="1.0" iyz="0.0" izz="1.0"/>
     </inertial>
   </link>

</robot>
```

This file and all the `.xacro` files should be saved in the `/urdf` directory of your `ros_robotics` package.

The preceding XML code defines a robot arm, labeled `rrbot`, which has three links that are 0.1 meters deep and wide. The `base_link` link is 2 meters tall, and the `mid_link` and `top_link` links are both 1 meter tall. The origin of the `base_link` is at (0, 0, 1) in order for the arm to be above the ground plane in rviz. The reference frame of the box is 1 meter in the z direction above the reference frame of the link. This `base_link` is identified as the URDF root link, and is the beginning of the kinematic chain for the arm. The collision elements of each link match their visual elements. Each inertial element indicates that each link weighs 1 kilogram and has the same basic inertia matrix values (we will utilize this duplication of the inertial element when we improve the code for `rrbot` later in the section *Using the Xacro include and macro tags*).

In `rrbot.xacro`, the `<property>` elements are used for the dimensions of the links, the offset for the axis of rotation, and for the damping coefficient, which are all constant values. These values are declared at the beginning of the XML code, making it easy to change the size of the links, the limits of the joints' rotation, or the damping characteristics of the arm.

Two new tags have been added to the joint elements: `<dynamics damping>` and `<limit>`. The `dynamics damping` coefficient is set to 0.7 Nms/rad. This damping is the amount of opposing force applied to the joint velocity that slows down the moving arms to a rest position. Using the `<property>` element, this damping value can be changed in one location. You are encouraged to change the value when you run the `rrbot` URDF/SDF with Gazebo and see the change made to the pendulum's swinging motion. The `<limit>` tag is required for revolute joints. The limit effort for the maximum joint effort that can be commanded is set to 100.0 N-m. The joint velocity is limited to a magnitude of 0.5 rad/s, with a damping effort applied when the joint is commanded beyond this limit. The upper and lower limits of the joint are set to pi radians and -pi radians, respectively.

Expanding Xacro

To generate a URDF file, the `xacro` program (from the `xacro` package) expands all the macros and outputs a resulting URDF file. Make sure that you are in the same directory as the `rrbot.xacro` file, then run the following command:

```
$ rosrun xacro xacro --inorder rrbot.xacro > rrbot.urdf
```

This command will pull together all of the xacro include files, expand the xacro macros in rrbot.xacro, and output the result to rrbot.urdf. The --inorder option mandates that the file be processed in read order. This processing will enable the latest property or macro to overlay a previous definition with the same name. This command is not necessary for running in rviz or Gazebo, but it can be a handy tool when used to examine the full URDF. The URDF XML file is generated with a heading comment warning that the file is autogenerated and that editing the file is not recommended.

The most common way to generate the URDF is in a launch file. The following line of code can be added to a launch file to create the most current robot_description from the Xacro file:

```
<param name="robot_description"
    command="$(find xacro)/xacro --inorder
      '$(find ros_robotics)/urdf/rrbot.xacro'" />
```

For complex robots, generating the URDF file at launch time will require a bit more time to process. The advantages are that the URDF is up to date and does not require a lot of memory to be stored.

Using roslaunch for rrbot

Modifications made to the launch file in rviz are necessary, but you will notice similarities to the ddrobot_rviz.launch file in *Chapter 2*, *Creating Your First Two-Wheeled ROS Robot (in Simulation)*. Either download the rrbot_rviz.launch file from the ros_robotics/launch directory on this book's website, or create the rrbot_rviz.launch file from the following code:

```
<launch>
  <!-- set parameter on Parameter Server -->
  <arg name="model" />
  <param name="robot_description"
      command="$(find xacro)/xacro --inorder
              '$(find ros_robotics)/urdf/$(arg model)'" />

  <!-- send joint values from gui -->
  <node name="joint_state_publisher" pkg="joint_state_publisher"
      type="joint_state_publisher">
    <param name="use_gui" value="TRUE"/>
  </node>

  <!-- use joint positions to update tf -->
```

```
    <node name="robot_state_publisher" pkg="robot_state_publisher"
        type="state_publisher"/>

    <!-- visualize robot model in 3D -->
    <node name="rviz" pkg="rviz" type="rviz"
        args="-d $(find ros_robotics)/urdf.rviz" required="true"/>

</launch>
```

The main difference in this rviz launch file is the execution of xacro with the argument passed as the model parameter. This process will generate the robot_description parameter to be loaded on the Parameter Server. Make sure that you place this rrbot_rviz.launch file in the /launch directory of your ros_robotics directory.

> If you have added the ROS_MASTER_URI and ROS_HOSTNAME or ROS_IP environment variables to your .bashrc file, you will need to comment out these lines with # as the first character of the line. Add the following two commands to your .bashrc file so that you can execute the ROS commands used in this chapter:
> ```
> export ROS_MASTER_URI=http://localhost:11311//
> export ROS_HOSTNAME=localhost
> ```

Next, run your rviz roslaunch command:

```
$ roslaunch ros_robotics rrbot_rviz.launch model:=rrbot.xacro
```

The rviz screen will look similar to the following screenshot:

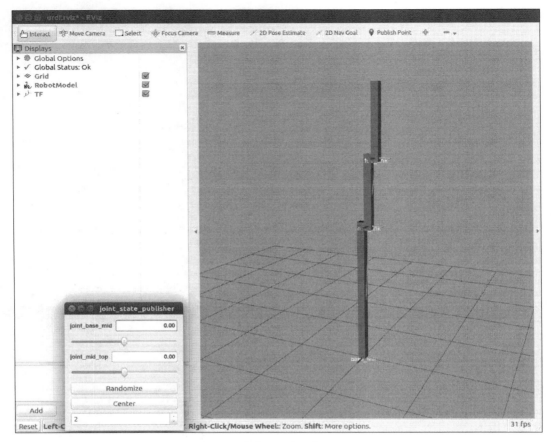

rrbot.xacro in rviz

In the preceding screenshot, notice the pop-up window with two joint control sliders for `joint_base_mid` and `joint_mid_top`. The center (`0.00`) position for both the joints puts the arm in a vertical position. You are encouraged to play with the sliders and the **Randomize** and **Center** buttons to understand the controls for the arm joints. The selection of `1` or `2` in the bottom field changes the format of the pop-up window.

Using the Xacro include and macro tags

In the following increment of the rrbot Xacro file, we will use an Xacro <include> tag to specify colors for each link of the robot arm. The materials.xacro file must be in the ros_robotics/urdf directory. To create the materials.xacro file, use the following code:

```
<?xml version="1.0"?>
<robot>

  <material name="black">
    <color rgba="0.0 0.0 0.0 1.0"/>
  </material>

  <material name="blue">
    <color rgba="0.0 0.0 0.8 1.0"/>
  </material>

  <material name="green">
    <color rgba="0.0 1.0 0.0 1.0"/>
  </material>

  <material name="grey">
    <color rgba="0.2 0.2 0.2 1.0"/>
  </material>

  <material name="orange">
    <color rgba="${255/255} ${108/255} ${10/255} 1.0"/>
  </material>

  <material name="brown">
    <color rgba="${222/255} ${207/255} ${195/255} 1.0"/>
  </material>

  <material name="red">
    <color rgba="0.8 0.0 0.0 1.0"/>
  </material>

  <material name="white">
    <color rgba="1.0 1.0 1.0 1.0"/>
  </material>

</robot>
```

Color values can be modified to your preferences for colors and textures. Within each `<visual>` element of the arm link, the following code should be added with any appropriate color:

```
<material name="any color defined in materials.xacro"/>
```

An Xacro `<macro>` block is also added to the `rrbot` Xacro file to replace the duplicate inertial elements in each link. The macro for `<inertial>` is as follows:

```
<xacro:macro name="default_inertial" params="z_value i_value mass">
  <inertial>
    <origin xyz="0 0 ${z_value}" rpy="0 0 0"/>
    <mass value="${mass}" />
    <inertia ixx="${i_value}" ixy="0.0" ixz="0.0"
             iyy="${i_value}" iyz="0.0"izz="${i_value}" />
  </inertial>
</xacro:macro>
```

Within each `<link>` of the arm, the entire `<inertial>` block is replaced with the following code:

```
<xacro:default_inertial
        z_value="${computation for <origin> in z-axis}"
        i_value="1.0" mass="1"/>
```

Study the following code to understand the computation for `<origin>` in the *z* axis. This code is in the `rrbot2.xacro` file available for download on this book's website, or can be entered as shown in the following lines (lines from the previous code have been left in or omitted and new code has been highlighted):

```
<?xml version="1.0"?>
<!-- Revolute-Revolute Manipulator -->
...

  <!-- Import Rviz colors -->
  <xacro:include
         filename="$(find ros_robotics)/urdf/materials.xacro" />

  <!-- Default Inertial -->
  <xacro:macro name="default_inertial"
         params="z_value i_value mass">
    <inertial>
      <origin xyz="0 0 ${z_value}" rpy="0 0 0"/>
```

```
        <mass value="${mass}" />
        <inertia ixx="${i_value}" ixy="0.0" ixz="0.0"
                 iyy="${i_value}" iyz="0.0"
                 izz="${i_value}" />
    </inertial>
</xacro:macro>

<!-- Base Link -->
...
    </collision>

    <xacro:default_inertial z_value="${height1/2}"
                            i_value="1.0" mass="1"/>
</link>
...
<!-- Middle Link -->
...
    </collision>

    <xacro:default_inertial z_value="${height2/2 - axle_offset}"
                            i_value="1.0" mass="1"/>
</link>
...
<!-- Top Link -->
...
    </collision>

    <xacro:default_inertial z_value="${height3/2 - axle_offset}"
                            i_value="1.0" mass="1"/>
</link>

</robot>
```

Next, run the rviz roslaunch command:

```
$ roslaunch ros_robotics rrbot_rviz.launch model:=rrbot2.xacro
```

The rviz screen will look similar to the following screenshot:

rrbot2.xacro in rviz

Although the book may show the screenshot in shades of gray, the `base_link` of the arm is now red, the `mid_link` is green, and the `top_link` is blue. On your screen, you will see the colors specified in your `rrbot2.xacro` file. The arm is shown in a random pose.

Adding mesh to the robot arm

A **mesh** is a collection of polygonal surfaces that provides a more realistic shape for an object in 3D. Although adding a mesh to the URDF is not unique to Xacro, we include the exercise here to give you the experience of using meshes and to append a more realistic gripper to our robot arm.

For the next upgrade to our robot arm, we will add a composite mesh image of a gripper to the `top_link` of the arm. To make our code design modular, we will create the gripper code in a separate file and use an Xacro `<include>` statement in the main `rrbot3.xacro` file:

```
<xacro:include filename="$(find ros_robotics)/urdf/gripper.xacro" />
```

Using this `<include>` statement, the `gripper.xacro` file must be in the `ros_robotics/urdf` directory.

The gripper is defined as four links with the `<visual>`, `<collision>`, and `<inertial>` tags, and four joints with the `<parent>`, `<child>`, `<origin>`, and `<axis>` tags. The four links are identified as `left_gripper`, `left_tip`, `right_gripper`, and `right_tip`. The links utilize the mesh files from the PR2 robot for their `<visual>` and `<geometry>` definitions. The PR2 robot is another famous Willow Garage robot, now mainly used for academic research. The `pr2_description` Xacro files are part of the `ros-kinetic-desktop-full` installation described in the *Installing and launching ROS* section in *Chapter 1, Getting Started with ROS*. The files used for the gripper are found in the `/opt/ros/kinetic/share/pr2_description/meshes/gripper_v0` directory. The `l_finger.dae` and `l_finger_tip.dae` files should be copied to a `/meshes` directory under your `ros_robotics` package directory, or they can be downloaded from the example code on this book's website.

The code to add the mesh file to the `left_gripper` link:

```
<link name="left_gripper">
  <visual>
    <origin xyz="0 0 0" rpy="0 0 0"/>
    <geometry>
      <mesh
          filename="package://ros_robotics/meshes/l_finger.dae"/>
    </geometry>
  </visual>
```

The other links follow the same format with the `left_tip` and `right_tip` links both utilizing the `l_finger_tip.dae` file. The `.dae` file is a **Digital Asset Exchange** file in the COLLADA format, representing a 3D image. These images can be created in Photoshop, SketchUp, AutoCAD, Blender, and other graphics software.

You can use the same geometry or meshes for both the `<collision>` and `<visual>` elements, although for performance improvements, we strongly suggest that you have simplified models/meshes for your collision geometry. A good open-source tool used to simplify meshes is Blender. There are many closed-source tools, such as Maya and 3DS Max, that can also simplify meshes. In the case of our robot arm, we specify simple rectangular shapes to be `<collision><geometry>` for each of these links.

Two types of joints are used for our gripper. The `left_gripper` and `right_gripper` links are connected to `top_link` of our robot arm using a revolute joint to restrict the range of movement of the joint. A `<limit>` tag is required for a revolute joint to define the `<effort>`, `<velocity>`, `<lower>`, and `<upper>` limits of the range. The effort limit is set to 30 Nm, the velocity limit is 0.1 rad/s, and the range is from -0.548 to 0.0 radians for the `left_gripper_joint` and `right_gripper_joint`.

A fixed joint is specified between the `left_gripper` and the `left_tip` and also between the `right_gripper` and the `right_tip`. There is no movement between these links.

This following code is provided for `gripper.xacro`, or it can be downloaded from the Packt website for this book:

```
<?xml version="1.0"?>
<robot xmlns:xacro="http://www.ros.org/wiki/xacro">

  <!-- Gripper -->
  <joint name="left_gripper_joint" type="revolute">
    <parent link="top_link"/>
    <child link="left_gripper"/>
    <origin xyz="0 0 ${height2 - axle_offset}" rpy="0 -1.57 0"/>
    <axis xyz="0 0 -1"/>
    <limit effort="30.0" lower="-0.548" upper="0.0"
    velocity="0.1"/>
  </joint>

  <link name="left_gripper">
    <visual>
      <origin xyz="0 0 0" rpy="0 0 0"/>
      <geometry>
        <mesh
          filename="package://ros_robotics/meshes/l_finger.dae"/>
      </geometry>
    </visual>

    <collision>
      <origin xyz="0.05 0.025 0" rpy="0 0 0"/>
      <geometry>
```

```
        <box size="0.1 0.05 0.05"/>
      </geometry>
    </collision>
    <xacro:default_inertial z_value="0" i_value="1e-6" mass="1"/>
  </link>

  <joint name="left_tip_joint" type="fixed">
    <parent link="left_gripper"/>
    <child link="left_tip"/>
  </joint>

  <link name="left_tip">
    <visual>
      <origin xyz="0.09137 0.00495 0" rpy="0 0 0"/>
      <geometry>
        <mesh
        filename="package://ros_robotics/meshes/l_finger_tip.dae"/>
      </geometry>
    </visual>

    <collision>
      <origin xyz="0.11 0.005 0"rpy="0 0 0"/>
      <geometry>
        <box size="0.02 0.03 0.02"/>
      </geometry>
    </collision>
    <xacro:default_inertial z_value="0" i_value="1e-6"
                              mass="1e-5"/>
  </link>

  <joint name="right_gripper_joint" type="revolute">
    <parent link="top_link"/>
    <child link="right_gripper"/>
    <origin xyz="0 0 ${height2 - axle_offset}" rpy="0 -1.57 0"/>
    <axis xyz="0 0 1"/>
    <limit effort="30.0" lower="-0.548" upper="0.0" velocity="0.1"/>
  </joint>

  <link name="right_gripper">
    <visual>
      <origin xyz="0 0 0" rpy="3.1415 0 0"/>
      <geometry>
        <mesh
```

```
            filename="package://ros_robotics/meshes/l_finger.dae"/>
      </geometry>
    </visual>

    <collision>
      <origin xyz="0.05 -0.025 0" rpy="0 0 0"/>
      <geometry>
        <box size="0.1 0.05 0.05"/>
      </geometry>
    </collision>
    <xacro:default_inertial z_value="0" i_value="1e-6" mass="1"/>
  </link>

  <joint name="right_tip_joint" type="fixed">
    <parent link="right_gripper"/>
    <child link="right_tip"/>
  </joint>

  <link name="right_tip">
    <visual>
      <origin xyz="0.09137 0.00495 0" rpy="-3.1415 0 0"/>
      <geometry>
        <mesh
        filename="package://ros_robotics/meshes/l_finger_tip.dae"/>
      </geometry>
    </visual>

    <collision>
      <origin xyz="0.11 -0.005 0" rpy="0 0 0"/>
      <geometry>
        <box size="0.02 0.03 0.02"/>
      </geometry>
    </collision>
    <xacro:default_inertial z_value="0" i_value="1e-6"
                mass="1e-5"/>
  </link>
</robot>
```

Next, run the rviz `roslaunch` command:

```
$ roslaunch ros_robotics rrbot_rviz.launch model:=rrbot3.xacro
```

 Note that a number of warning messages similar to `TIFFFieldWithTag: Internal error, unknown tag xxxxxx` may be displayed. This message is not an indication of any operational problem, and you may continue without difficulty.

A close-up view of the gripper should look similar to the following screenshot:

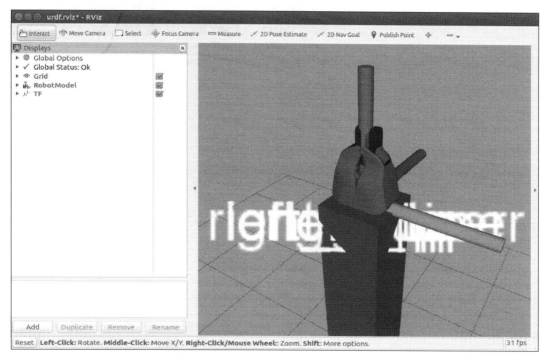

rrbot gripper in rviz

The controls for the arm and gripper are accessible via the four joint control sliders, as shown in the following screenshot. Controls for `left_gripper_joint` and `right_gripper_joint` have been added to the arm joints. The robot arm is shown in a random pose:

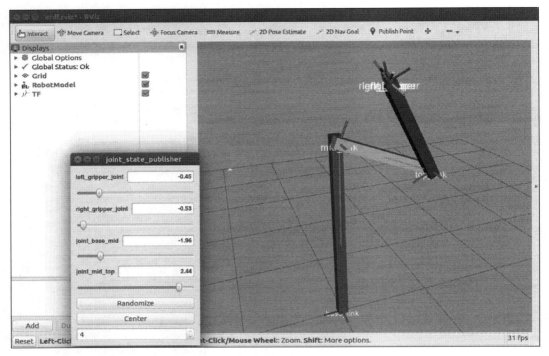

rrbot3.xacro in rviz

With our robot arm built using Xacro, we are ready to add modifications to the Xacro file so that it can be recognized as an SDF by Gazebo. Then, we will add transmission and control plugins to enable our robot arm to be controlled by ROS commands from the command line or rqt.

Controlling an articulated robot arm in Gazebo

The *Modifications to the robot URDF* section in *Chapter 2, Creating Your First Two-Wheeled ROS Robot (in Simulation)*, describes changes that need to be made to the URDF model so that Gazebo recognizes it as an SDF. The next section identifies the changes needed for our robot arm, `rrbot`.

Adding Gazebo-specific elements

Specific elements unique to the Gazebo simulation environment are grouped into the following areas:

- The `<material>` tags are used to specify the Gazebo color or texture for each link

- The `<mu1>` and `<mu2>` tags are used to define the friction coefficients for the contact surfaces of four of the robot's links

- A plugin is added for control of the revolute joints of `rrbot` (included here, but described in the *Adding a Gazebo ROS control plugin* section)

These specific Gazebo XML elements needed for simulation are split into a separate file labeled `rrbot.gazebo`, and an Xacro `<include>` statement is used in the main `rrbot4.xacro` file:

```
<xacro:include filename="$(find ros_robotics)/urdf/rrbot.gazebo" />
```

Using this `<include>` statement, the `rrbot.gazebo` file must be located in the `ros_robotics/urdf` directory.

To create the `rrbot.gazebo` file, use the following code:

```
<?xml version="1.0"?>
<robot>

  <!-- Base Link -->
  <gazebo reference="base_link">
    <material>Gazebo/Red</material>
  </gazebo>

  <!-- Middle Link -->
  <gazebo reference="mid_link">
    <mu1>0.2</mu1>
    <mu2>0.2</mu2>
    <material>Gazebo/Green</material>
  </gazebo>

  <!-- Top Link -->
  <gazebo reference="top_link">
    <mu1>0.2</mu1>
    <mu2>0.2</mu2>
```

```
        <material>Gazebo/Blue</material>
      </gazebo>

      <!-- Gripper Elements -->
      <gazebo reference="left_gripper">
        <mu1>0.2</mu1>
        <mu2>0.2</mu2>
      </gazebo>

      <gazebo reference="right_gripper">
        <mu1>0.2</mu1>
        <mu2>0.2</mu2>
      </gazebo>

      <gazebo reference="left_tip" />
      <gazebo reference="right_tip" />

      <!-- ros_control plugin -->
      <gazebo>
        <plugin name="gazebo_ros_control"
                filename="libgazebo_ros_control.so">
          <robotNamespace>/rrbot</robotNamespace>
          <robotSimType>
            gazebo_ros_control/DefaultRobotHWSim
          </robotSimType>
        </plugin>
      </gazebo>

    </robot>
```

Fixing the robot arm to the world

Since Gazebo simulates the physics of the real world, a robot arm, as we have
defined it, will not stand up for long as the force of gravity will cause it to topple.
Therefore, we need to attach our robot arm model to Gazebo's world frame. In the
rrbot4.xacro version of our code, a world link has been added and a fixed joint
attaching the robot's base_link to the world link:

```
    <link name="world"/>

    <joint name="fixed" type="fixed">
      <parent link="world"/>
      <child link="base_link"/>
    </joint>
```

With the `base_link` of the arm fixed to the `world` link, the `mid_link` and `top_link` will still succumb to the force of gravity. Although the robot arm appears to be standing straight up when the arm is launched in Gazebo, you will see that these top two links of the arm fall. The arm will swing and slow down due to the `<dynamics damping>` element defined for the joint, until it comes to a complete stop. We encourage you to play with the `<dynamics damping>` value in order to understand its property in relation to the Gazebo simulation.

Viewing the robot arm in Gazebo

Before we continue to add control elements to our URDF, we need to launch the `rrbot4.xacro` file in Gazebo. This launch file is similar to the `ddrobot_gazebo.launch` file in *Chapter 2, Creating Your First Two-Wheeled ROS Robot (in Simulation)*. This launch file can be downloaded from the book's website, or created as `rrbot_gazebo.launch` from the following XML code:

```
<launch>
  <!-- We resume the logic in gazebo_ros packageempty_world.launch,
       changing only the name of the world to be launched -->
  <include file="$(find gazebo_ros)/launch/empty_world.launch">
    <arg name="world_name"
         value="$(find ros_robotics)/worlds/rrbot.world"/>

    <arg name="paused" default="false"/>
    <arg name="use_sim_time" default="true"/>
    <arg name="gui" default="true"/>
    <arg name="headless" default="false"/>
    <arg name="debug" default="false"/>

  </include>

  <!-- Load the URDF into the ROS Parameter Server -->
  <param name="robot_description"
    command="$(find xacro)/xacro--inorder
      '$(find ros_robotics)/urdf/rrbot4.xacro'" />

  <!-- Spawn rrbot into Gazebo -->
  <node name="spawn_urdf" pkg="gazebo_ros"
    type="spawn_model" respawn="false" output="screen"
      args="-param robot_description -urdf -model rrbot" />
</launch>
```

The `rrbot.world` file from this book's website can be downloaded and used, or you can use the `ddrobot.world` file created in *Chapter 2, Creating Your First Two-Wheeled ROS Robot (in Simulation)*. You can even just omit the argument for `world_name` in the `include` statement and use `empty_world` from the `gazebo_ros` package.

The command to launch the robot arm in Gazebo is as follows:

```
$ roslaunch ros_robotics rrbot_gazebo.launch
```

The Gazebo screen should look similar to the following screenshot after the top two links of the arm have fallen and slowed to a stop:

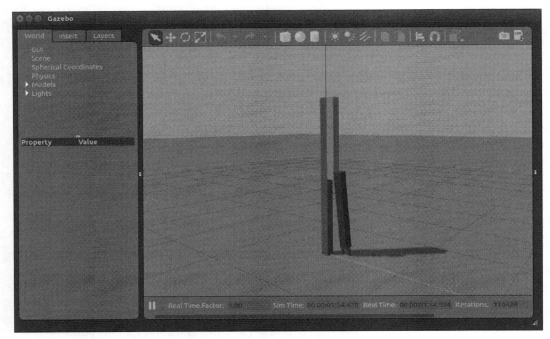

rrbot4.xacro in Gazebo

After verifying the model in Gazebo, additional control elements should be added to the robot arm URDF.

Adding controls to Xacro

The following are the steps used to set up controls for this robot arm in the Gazebo simulation:

1. Define transmission elements for the joints in the `rrbot` and gripper Xacro files.
2. Add a `gazebo_ros_control` plugin to our file of Gazebo-specific elements.
3. Create a YAML configuration file for control parameters.
4. Create a control launch file to launch the robot joint controllers.

To begin with, we need to install four packages: `gazebo_ros_pkgs`, `gazebo_ros_control`, `ros_control`, and `ros_controllers`. `gazebo_ros_pkgs` is a set of ROS packages (**metapackage**) that provides the interface and control for a robot in Gazebo. `ros_control` and `ros_controllers` provide generic controllers for ROS robots. For ROS Kinetic, the Debian packages should be installed with the following command:

```
$ sudo apt-get install ros-kinetic-gazebo-ros-pkgs ros-kinetic-gazebo-
ros-control ros-kinetic-ros-control ros-kinetic-ros-controllers
```

The `gazebo_ros_control` package integrates the `ros_contol` controller software with the Gazebo simulator. The `gazebo_ros_control` package instantiates the `ros_control` metapackage `controller_manager` package to provide simulation of the robot's controllers. The controller manager will be used by our control launch file to spawn controllers for the `joint_state_controller` and controllers for all four of the robot arm's revolute joints.

More details on the ROS controllers and the `ros_control` packages can be found at http://wiki.ros.org/ros_control.

Defining transmission elements for joints

Specific elements must be added to the URDF/SDF in order for a model to be controlled in the Gazebo simulation environment. The `<transmission>` element is used to define the relationship between the robot joint and the actuator. This `<transmission>` element encapsulates the details of the mechanical coupling with specific gear ratios and parallel linkages defined. For the `rrbot` robot, we have simple mechanical joints and do not require complex transmission element definitions.

The `rrbot` robot arm requires a `<transmission>` element for each of the `rrbot` revolute joints (`joint_base_mid`, `joint_mid_top`, `left_gripper`, and `right_gripper`). Each `<transmission>` element has a unique `<name>` and is associated with one of the `<joint names>` for the revolute joints. The `<type>` is `transmission_interface/SimpleTransmission`. In the `<joint>`, the `<hardwareInterface>` is `hardware_interface/EffortJointInterface` because we will be using simulated `ros_control hardware_interface::RobotHW`. This interface corresponds to the control plugin selected in the next section, *Adding a Gazebo ROS control plugin*. Each of the four `<transmission>` elements will look similar to the following code:

```
<transmission name="transmission1">
  <type>transmission_interface/SimpleTransmission</type>
  <joint name="joint_base_mid">
    <hardwareInterface>hardware_interface/EffortJointInterface
    </hardwareInterface>
  </joint>
  <actuator name="motor1">
    <mechanicalReduction>1</mechanicalReduction>
  </actuator>
</transmission>
```

This code should be duplicated twice and added to the `joint_base_mid` joint and `joint_mid_top` joint in the `rrbot4.xacro` file. It should also be duplicated twice and added to the `left_gripper` joint and `right_gripper` joint in the `gripper.xacro` file.

More details on the `<transmission>` elements can be found at `http://wiki.ros.org/urdf/XML/Transmission`.

Adding a Gazebo ROS control plugin

The `gazebo_ros_control` plugin defined previously in the *Adding Gazebo-specific elements* section is as follows:

```
<!-- ros_control plugin -->
<gazebo>
  <plugin name="gazebo_ros_control"
          filename="libgazebo_ros_control.so">
    <robotNamespace>/rrbot</robotNamespace>
    <robotSimType>
        gazebo_ros_control/DefaultRobotHWSim
    </robotSimType>
  </plugin>
</gazebo>
```

This plugin will parse the `<transmission>` elements in the `rrbot4.xacro` and `gripper.xacro` files and load the identified hardware interfaces and controller managers. The preceding control plugin is a custom simulation plugin that should already be in the `rrbot.gazebo` file.

Creating a YAML configuration file

YAML is a markup language commonly used for ROS parameters. It is convenient to use YAML-encoded files to set ROS parameters on the Parameter Server. For `rrbot`, a YAML file is created to hold the joint controller configurations, and this YAML file is loaded via the control launch file. The controller type is defined for the `joint_state_controller`, as well as for all the four `rrbot` joint controllers. The four `rrbot` controllers also have **proportional–integral–derivative (pid)** gains defined. These pid gains have been tuned to the control of the `rrbot` arm and gripper. The `rrbot_control.yaml` file contains the following code:

```
rrbot:
  # Publish all joint states
  joint_state_controller:
    type: joint_state_controller/JointStateController
    publish_rate: 50

  # Position Controllers
  joint_base_mid_position_controller:
    type: effort_controllers/JointPositionController
    joint: joint_base_mid
    pid: {p: 100.0, i: 0.01, d: 10.0}
  joint_mid_top_position_controller:
    type: effort_controllers/JointPositionController
    joint: joint_mid_top
    pid: {p: 100.0, i: 0.01, d: 10.0}
  left_gripper_joint_position_controller:
    type: effort_controllers/JointPositionController
    joint: left_gripper_joint
    pid: {p: 1.0, i: 0.00, d: 0.0}
  right_gripper_joint_position_controller:
    type: effort_controllers/JointPositionController
    joint: right_gripper_joint
    pid: {p: 1.0, i: 0.00, d: 0.0}
```

The `rrbot_control.yaml` file should be saved to a `/config` directory under the `ros_robotics` package directory.

Creating a control launch file

The best way to initiate control of our `rrbot` robot arm is to create a launch file to load the parameters into the Parameter Server and start all the `ros_control` controllers. The `rosparam` statement loads the controller settings to the Parameter Server from the YAML configuration file. Next, the `control_spawner` node creates the five controllers for `rrbot` using the `controller_manager` package. Another node is started for the `robot_state_publisher`. This `rrbot_control.launch` control file contains the following code, and is stored in the `/launch` directory of the `ros_robotics` package directory:

```
<launch>

  <!-- Load joint controller configurations from YAML file to
          parameter server -->
  <rosparam file="$(find ros_robotics)/config/rrbot_control.yaml"
          command="load"/>

  <!-- load the controllers -->
  <node name="control_spawner" pkg="controller_manager"
    type="spawner" respawn="false"
    output="screen" ns="/rrbot" args="joint_state_controller
    joint_base_mid_position_controller
    joint_mid_top_position_controller
    left_gripper_joint_position_controller
    right_gripper_joint_position_controller"/>

  <!-- convert joint states to TF transforms for rviz, etc -->
  <node name="robot_state_publisher" pkg="robot_state_publisher"
    type="robot_state_publisher" respawn="false" output="screen">
    <remap from="/joint_states" to="/rrbot/joint_states" />
  </node>

</launch>
```

After the nodes are started, the `joint_state_controller` begins publishing all the (nonfixed) joint states of `rrbot` on the `JointState` topic. The `robot_state_publisher` node subscribes to the `JointState` messages and publishes the robot's transforms to the `tf` transform library. Each of the other joint position controllers manages the control for its particular revolute joint.

To start the `rrbot` simulation, launch `rrbot` in Gazebo using the following command:

```
$ roslaunch ros_robotics rrbot_gazebo.launch
```

When `rrbot` is visible in the Gazebo window, open a second terminal window and launch the controllers using the following command:

```
$ roslaunch ros_robotics rrbot_control.launch
```

In the previously created control launch file, both the `controller_manager` and `robot_state_publisher` packages are used. If you plan to reuse this code or share it, it is recommended that you add these dependencies to your `package.xml` file for the `ros_robotics` package. The following statements should be added under the dependencies:

```
<exec_depend>controller_manager</exec_depend>
<exec_depend>robot_state_publisher</exec_depend>
```

Controlling your robot arm with the ROS command line

Now, we are able to send commands via a third terminal window to control our `rrbot` robot arm. The `rostopic pub` command is used to publish our command data to a specific joint position controller.

To command the top link of the arm to move to a 1.57radian (90degree) position, relative to the middle link, type the following command:

```
$ rostopic pub -1 /rrbot/joint_mid_top_position_controller/command std_
msgs/Float64 "data: 1.57"
```

On the terminal, the following screen message is displayed:

```
publishing and latching message for 3.0 seconds
```

On the Gazebo screen, the `rrbot` arm should look similar to the following screenshot. The view has been rotated to make the arm more visible to the reader:

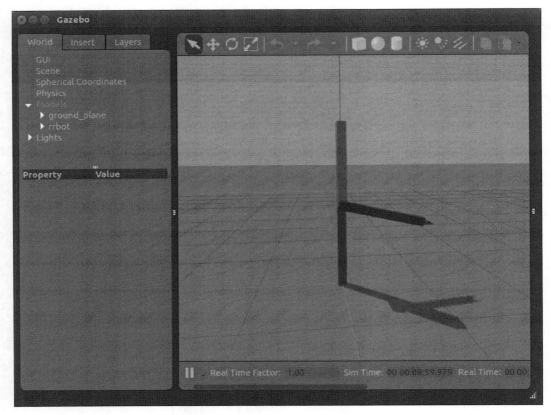

rrbot joint_mid_top at 1.57 radians

 Note that the top link of the arm may not be at a true 90 degree angle to the middle link because of the gravitational effects of the environment and the action of the controller. The proportional gain of the pid controls can be increased to improve these results. This can be done by changing the `rrbot` controller gains in the YAML file or in real-time using the Dynamic Reconfigure tool described in the upcoming section.

To open the gripper, two commands can be sent consecutively to move the right gripper and then the left gripper -0.5 radians from their center position:

```
$ rostopic pub -1 /rrbot/right_gripper_joint_position_controller/command
std_msgs/Float64 "data: -0.5"; rostopic pub -1 /rrbot/left_gripper_joint_
position_controller/command std_msgs/Float64 "data: -0.5"
```

On the Gazebo screen, the `rrbot` gripper should look similar to the following screenshot. Joint axes and rotation are shown in the Gazebo view:

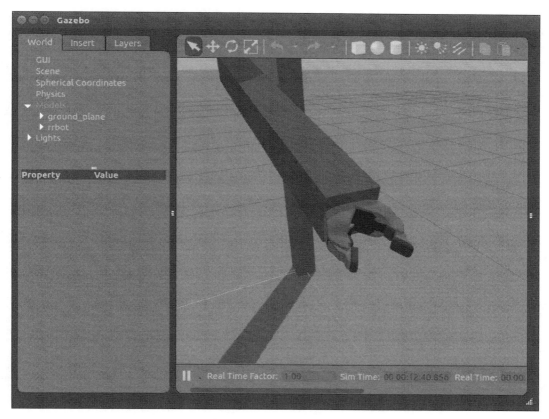

rrbot gripper open 1.0 radians

Controlling your robot arm with rqt

Another tool that we can use to control our `rrbot` arm is rqt, the ROS plugin-based user interface described in the *Introducing rqt tools* section of *Chapter 3, Driving Around with TurtleBot*. The command to start rqt is as follows:

```
$ rosrun rqt_gui rqt_gui
```

Or simply:

```
$ rqt
```

Under the **Plugins** menu in the rqt main window menu bar, select the **Topics |
Message Publisher** plugin. From the **Topics** drop-down box, at the top of the
Message Publisher plugin, select the command for the particular controller that
you want to publish to and add it to the **Message Publisher** main screen. The green
plus sign button at the top-right corner of the window will add the command to the
main screen. In the following screenshot, the `/rrbot/joint_base_mid_position_controller/command` and`/rrbot/joint_mid_top_position_controller/command` topics have been added to the **Message Publisher** main screen:

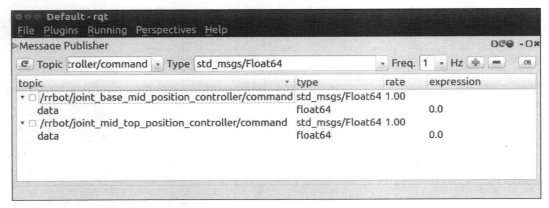

rqt Message Publisher screen for rrbot

To change the position of the `rrbot` arm, expand the topic by clicking on the triangle symbol on the left side. Next, select and change the expression field of one of the topics and check the checkbox on the left of the topic to publish the message. In the following screenshot, the value of the `/rrbot/joint_base_mid_position_controller/command` topic has been changed to -1.57 radians. In addition to this, the plugin for **Topic Monitor** has been displayed so that the change in the published state of the `/rrbot/joint_base_mid_position_controller/state` topic `set_point` field can be verified:

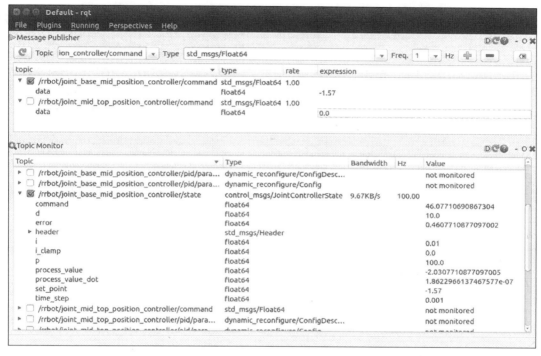

rqt Message Publisher and Topic Monitor

The following screenshot shows both rqt and Gazebo with the `rrbot` arm positioned with its `joint_base_mid` at -1.57 radians. The `joint_mid_top` is set at 0.0 radians:

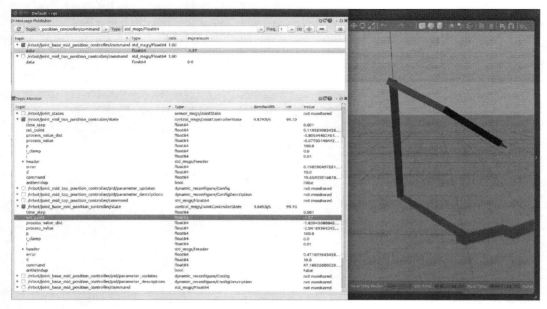

rrbot arm controlled via rqt

Trying more things in rqt

The following suggestions are additional starting points for using rqt with your `rrbot` arm:

- **Message Publisher** expression values can also be equations, such as *sin(i/10)*, where *i* is an rqt variable for time. Inserting this equation into one of the joint commands will make the joint vary sinusoidally with respect to time.

- The rqt **Plot** plugin is found under **Plugins | Visualization | Plot**. Choose to plot `joint_xxx_position_controller/command/data` to the screen or even `joint_xxx_position_controler/state/error`. The error plot will visually display how well the pid control eliminates the error on the joint.

- The rqt **Dynamic Reconfigure** plugin is found under **Plugins | Configuration | Dynamic Reconfigure**. Click on **Expand All** to see all the options and select **pid** for any of the joint controllers. A pop-up window will allow you to dynamically change **p**, **i**, **d**, **i_clamp_min**, and **i_clamp_max** to tune that controller's performance.

Moving the robot arm with a Python script is also possible, but this is left as an exercise for the reader.

Summary

This chapter helped you to develop an understanding of how robot arms are modeled and controlled. We created a URDF/SDF for a simple three-link, two-joint robot arm to be used in a Gazebo simulation. Xacro was used to make the URDF/SDF modular and efficient. Mesh files were incorporated into the gripper design to give it a more realistic look. Control plugins and transmission elements were added to the robot model code to enable control of the robot arm in simulation. Then, ROS commands were used via the command-line and rqt tools to control the arm's position in Gazebo.

In *Chapter 6, Wobbling Robot Arms Using Joint Control,* we will extend our control of robot arms to the 7-DOF dual-armed Baxter. You will learn multiple ways to command and control Baxter's arms using both forward kinematic and inverse kinematic methods.

6
Wobbling Robot Arms Using Joint Control

Mobile robots are good at getting from one location to another without running into objects around them. Making them even more useful, a robot arm can grasp and manipulate objects in its environment. This chapter features a leading-edge robot that uses its two arms to perform tasks from manufacturing to human assistance and more. The Baxter robot by Rethink Robotics is a collaborative robot that works safely alongside humans without the need for safety precautions. The Gazebo simulated version of Baxter is included in this book for those who do not have access to a real Baxter.

In this chapter, you will be introduced to Baxter in both real and simulated forms. The software for Baxter Simulator will be installed and executed to bring up the Gazebo environment with a Baxter model in it. Baxter's arms will be controlled using a variety of methods: keyboard, joystick, and Python script. Demonstrations of the different types of joint controls for Baxter's arms will be provided.

A more in-depth look at **tf**, ROS **transform reference** frames, is included in this chapter. These reference frames are critical to maintaining the complex kinematic equations that are required for Baxter's arm joints. Another ROS tool, MoveIt!, will be introduced and used to manipulate Baxter's arms. MoveIt! provides a framework for motion planning for either both of Baxter's arms, an individual arm, or a subset of joints in an arm.

A section on the real Baxter is included and describes the configuration of Baxter with a workstation computer. This setup is the standard for what is referred to as *the research Baxter*. In the *Introducing Baxter* section, the different versions of Baxter will be described. All of the commands and controls described for Baxter Simulator will also apply to the real Baxter. The use of MoveIt! to plan Baxter's arm movements to avoid obstacles will be presented. Then, the versatile ROS package for state machines, SMACH, will be introduced and a fun example using Baxter's arms will be implemented.

In this chapter, you will learn the following topics:

- Baxter and the robot's hardware
- Loading and using Baxter Simulator with Gazebo
- Using MoveIt! to create trajectories for Baxter's arms
- Controlling the real Baxter with applications
- Implementing a state machine for Baxter arm poses

Introducing Baxter

Baxter is a two-armed robot created by Rethink Robotics designed to be a collaborative worker in the manufacturing industry. Each of Baxter's arms has seven **degrees of freedom** (**DOF**) and a series of joint actuators, which makes Baxter unique as a manufacturing robot. Baxter's joints are composed of **series-elastic actuators** (**SEAs**) that have a spring between the motor/gearing and the output of the actuator. This *springiness* makes Baxter's arms compliant and capable of detecting external forces, such as contact with a human. This advantage makes Baxter safe to work alongside people without a safety cage. The SEAs also provide greater flexibility for control using the torque deflection as feedback for the control system.

Baxter, shown in the following image, has a number of sensors that enable Baxter to perform many tasks:

- A 360-degree sonar sensor at the top of Baxter's head
- A 1024 x 600 pixel screen face with a built-in camera
- A camera, infrared sensor, and accelerometer on the cuff at the end of each arm

- A gripper mount that can easily mount a variety of end-effectors
- Navigator buttons with a scroll-wheel dial on each forearm and torso side

Baxter on a pedestal

The manufacturing version of Baxter is programmed by moving the arms to the desired locations and interacting with the navigator buttons on the arm or torso to store the positions. Gripper control is achieved by activating the buttons located on each cuff. An indented spot on Baxter's cuff places the arm in **Zero Force Gravity (Zero-G)** mode to allow the arm's joints to be moved effortlessly into position. Baxter can be taught different arm positions and trajectories, and these can be collected into a sequence and stored as a type of program. The display-screen face is used as a GUI for the worker to build and store these programs. No special programming language or mathematics is required; only arm manipulation, button presses, and the use of the scroll-wheel dial located alongside the navigator buttons.

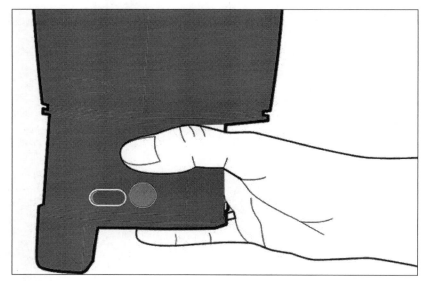

Position to activate Zero-G mode

More information on Baxter's technical specifications can be found at the following websites:

- `http://www.rethinkrobotics.com/baxter/tech-specs/`
- `http://sdk.rethinkrobotics.com/wiki/Hardware_Specifications`
- `https://www.active8robots.com/wp-content/uploads/Baxter-Hardware-Specification-Architecture-Datasheet.pdf`

Information on the manufacturing version of Baxter can be found at `http://www.rethinkrobotics.com/baxter/`.

Baxter, the research robot

A second version of Baxter was introduced by Rethink the year after the manufacturing version was released. This later version is primarily for the use of academic and research organizations. The hardware for the research version of Baxter is identical to the manufacturing version, however, the software for the two versions is not the same.

The Baxter research robot is configured with an SDK that runs on a remote computer workstation and allows researchers to develop custom software for Baxter. The SDK provides an open source ROS **application programming interface (API)** to directly run ROS commands and scripts to operate Baxter. Baxter runs as the ROS Master and any remote workstation (on Baxter's network) launches ROS nodes to connect to Baxter and control its joints and sensors.

An alternative arrangement of configuring the SDK directly on the physical Baxter is possible, but that scenario will not be covered in this book.

For information on the Baxter on-robot workspace setup and code execution, visit http://sdk.rethinkrobotics.com/wiki/SSH.

Researchers have been able to develop applications with Baxter in numerous areas. Rethink Robotics hosts a web page to link many of these accomplishments.

For videos, visit http://sdk.rethinkrobotics.com/wiki/Customer_Videos.

For research papers, visit http://sdk.rethinkrobotics.com/wiki/Published_Work.

Baxter Simulator

Baxter Simulator has been developed by Rethink Robotics to provide a comparable simulation experience for controlling Baxter using Gazebo. The simulation software for Baxter is contained in the `baxter_simulator` ROS metapackage. Baxter's URDF is used to create the simulated Baxter model and an emulation of the hardware interfaces to the research Baxter is provided by the `baxter_sim_hardware` ROS package. This package allows models of the position and velocity controllers to be modified using the ROS rqt tool. The arm and head controllers are found in the `baxter_sim_controllers` package. These controller plugins for Gazebo are for arm position, arm velocity, and arm torque control, and position control for the head and the electric grippers. Interfaces are also simulated for the following Baxter components:

- The head sonar ring
- The infrared sensors on each cuff
- The cameras on each cuff and head
- The navigator lights and buttons
- The shoulder buttons
- The head screen display (xdisplay)

Baxter Simulator can also be used with the ROS tools, rviz and MoveIt!. Details on rviz can be found in the *Introducing rviz* section of *Chapter 2, Creating Your First Two-Wheeled ROS Robot (in Simulation)*; details on MoveIt! will be provided later in this chapter, in the *Introducing MoveIt!* section. Further details on Baxter Simulator will be supplied in the section *Installing Baxter Simulator* as we install the software and learn to control the simulated Baxter in Gazebo.

For details on the Baxter Simulator ROS packages and API, refer to the following Rethink websites:

- `http://sdk.rethinkrobotics.com/wiki/Simulator_Architecture`
- `http://sdk.rethinkrobotics.com/wiki/Baxter_Simulator`
- `http://sdk.rethinkrobotics.com/wiki/API_Reference#tab.3DSimulator_API`
- `https://github.com/RethinkRobotics/baxter_simulator`

Baxter's arms

Baxter has seven rotary joints, as shown in the following figure. Each arm is often referred to as a 7-DOF arm, since motion of the arm is controlled by seven actuators (motors), which are capable of independent rotation.

Baxter's 7-DOF arms are described on the Rethink Robotics site at `http://sdk.rethinkrobotics.com/wiki/Arms`.

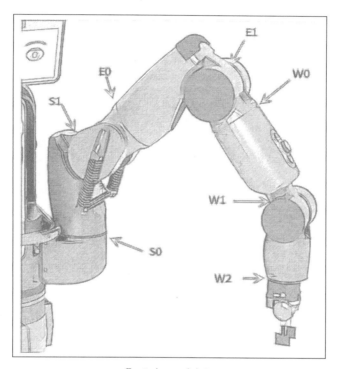

Baxter's arm joints

The arm joints are named in the following manner:

- **S0**: Shoulder Twist (Roll)
- **S1**: Shoulder Bend (Pitch)
- **E0**: Elbow Twist (Roll)
- **E1**: Elbow Bend (Pitch)
- **W0**: Wrist Twist (Roll)
- **W1**: Wrist Bend (Pitch)
- **W2**: Wrist Twist (Roll)

The designation of the joints as S0, S1, E0, E1, W0, W1, and W2 enables us to define, and even monitor, each of the angles for these joints with respect to the coordinates of the joints. In ROS, the angles are measured in radians. As there are 2π radians in a complete circle, one radian is *360/(2π)*, or about 57.3 degrees. A 90-degree angle is $\pi/4$, or about 0.7854 radians. These conversion values are given because it is often necessary to move the joints to a 90-degree position or another angle defined in radians and it is usual for us to think in terms of degrees of rotation.

The joints of the arms are connected by links of various lengths. Although all the joints are rotary joints, there is a distinction between bend joints and twist joints. The bend joints, also called pitch joints, are S1, E1, and W1. They pitch up and down on the arm and rotate about their axis perpendicular to the joint. The twist or roll joints S0, E0, W0, and W2 rotate about an axis that extends along their centerline.

Information on maximum joint speeds, joint flexure stiffness, peak torque, and other detailed arm specifications can be found at `http://sdk.rethinkrobotics.com/wiki/Hardware_Specifications`.

Baxter's bend joints

Three of the arm joints, S1, E1, and W1, are defined as bend joints and are labeled in the following figure for positive and negative direction:

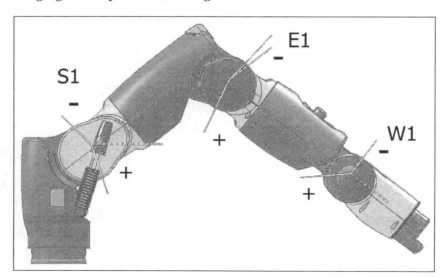

Baxter's bend joints

The following table shows Baxter's bend joint limits and range of motion measured in both degrees and radians for each joint:

Joint	Min limit	Max limit	Range	Min limit	Max limit	Range
	in degrees			in radians		
S1	-123	+60	183	-2.147	+1.047	3.194
E1	-2.864	+150	153	-0.05	+2.618	2.67
W1	-90	+120	210	-1.5707	+2.094	3.6647

Baxter's twist joints

Four of Baxter's arm joints, **S0**, **E0**, **W0**, and **W2**, are defined as twist or roll joints and are labeled in the following figure for positive and negative direction:

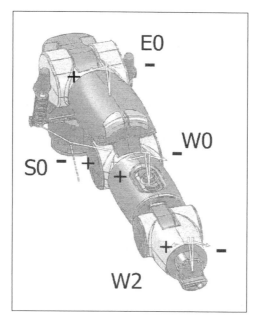

Baxter's twist joints

The following table shows Baxter's twist joint limits and range of motion measured in both degrees and radians for each joint:

Joint	Min limit	Max limit	Range	Min limit	Max limit	Range
	in degrees			in radians		
S0	-97.494	+97.494	194.998	-1.7016	+1.7016	3.4033
E0	-174.987	+174.987	349.979	-3.0541	+3.0541	6.1083
W0	-175.25	+175.25	350.5	-3.059	+3.059	6.117
W2	-175.25	+175.25	350.5	-3.059	+3.059	6.117

Baxter's coordinate frame

Before we discuss the details of the arm positions and orientations, it is necessary to define a **base coordinate system** from which other positions are measured. The following figure shows Baxter's reference coordinate system:

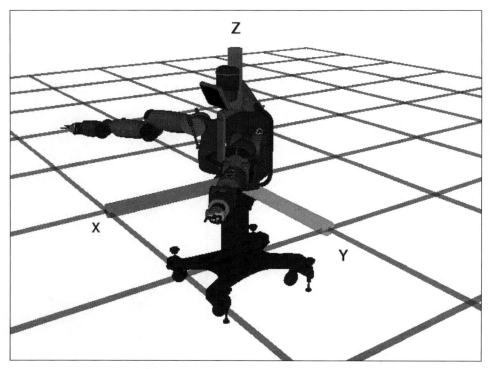

Baxter's base coordinate system

Standing behind Baxter, the positive x axis runs forward, along the centerline of Baxter, the positive y axis runs to the left from the centerline, and the positive z axis runs up vertically. The z axis center of Baxter's base coordinate system is at the base of Baxter's torso. This is the $z=0$ position. The $x=0$, $y=0$ position is behind Baxter's front plate, along the centerline on the vertical axis.

An important use of this base coordinate system is to define the position of the grippers at the end of Baxter's arms in terms of the distance in x, y, and z from the base origin considered (0, 0, 0). This is useful because, when positioned on a pedestal, Baxter has a base coordinate system that does not move during operations. However, the coordinates of each joint and the grippers will change as Baxter performs various tasks.

Cartesian positions are defined in meters in ROS, as defined in REP 103, titled *Standard Units of Measure and Coordinate Conventions* (http://www.ros.org/reps/rep-0103.html).

Another measure for a three-dimensional object is its orientation or angles with respect to a given coordinate system, usually a coordinate system centered on the object itself if it is stationary. We will discuss the orientation of Baxter's grippers when the transformation of coordinate systems, tf, is introduced.

In the previous figure, Baxter's outstretched arms represent the joint angles of zero degrees for all its joints. The various conventions for measuring the distance and rotation of Baxter's grippers will be presented later.

Control modes for Baxter's arms

There are four modes of controlling Baxter's arms: joint position, joint velocity, joint torque, and raw joint position control. Note the descriptions and the important differences between these four joint control modes:

- **Joint position control**: This mode is the most fundamental control mode and is the primary method for controlling Baxter's arms. The angle of each of Baxter's joints is specified in a message to the motor controllers, which contains seven values—one value for each of the seven joints. The motor controller processes the message, checking for collisions in the URDF model between the two arms and also between the arms and the torso. If a potential collision is detected, the collision-avoidance model plans offsets to the commanded path to avoid impact.

- **Joint velocity control**: This mode is for advanced control of Baxter's arms. Joint velocities are specified for the joints to simultaneously achieve. The joint command message will contain seven velocity values for the controllers to achieve. Collision avoidance and detection is applied. If the velocity given in a command would take a joint to a position beyond its limits, no joints will move. *This mode is dangerous and extreme caution should be used.*

- **Joint torque control**: This mode is also for the advanced control of Baxter's arms. Joint torques are specified in the command message, which will contain seven torque values for the controllers to simultaneously perform. Collision avoidance and detection is *not* applied. *This mode is dangerous and extreme caution should be used.*

- **Raw joint position control**: This mode provides a more direct position control, leaving the execution of joint commands primarily for the controllers. Collision avoidance and detection is *not* implemented and motor velocity limits are *not* monitored. *This mode is dangerous and extreme caution should be used.*

For an in-depth description of the joint control modes, refer to Rethink's wiki at `http://sdk.rethinkrobotics.com/wiki/Arm_Control_Modes`.

Baxter's grippers

Rethink provides two options for grippers Baxter can have: electric grippers and suction grippers. The electric gripper, as shown on the left in the following image, has two fingers with removable inserts to allow different configurations of the gripping surface. Force control of the grippers allows them to pick up rigid and semirigid objects. The electric grippers can grasp an object from the inside or outside. The gripper can open to 144 mm (approximately 5.6 inches) to grasp an object, though the fingers have various configurations within this grasping range.

The suction gripper supports the attachment of a single vacuum cup or a multicup vacuum manifold. The image shows a single suction gripper (on the right). The gripper is powered by an external air supply line. This gripper works well on smooth, nonporous, or flat objects:

Baxter's electric and suction grippers

Baxter's arm sensors

Each of Baxter's arms has a number of sensors on the cuff at the end of the arm. An integrated camera is mounted on the cuff and is pointed toward objects that the gripper could potentially pick up. The camera has a frame rate of 30 frames per second and a maximum resolution of 1280 x 800 pixels. An infrared sensor pointing in the same direction can detect distances from 4 to 40 cm (1.5–15 inches). The following image shows the positions of the cuff camera and the infrared sensor. Each cuff also contains a three-axis accelerometer:

Baxter's cuff camera and infrared sensor

Additional information on these sensors can be found at the following websites:

- `http://sdk.rethinkrobotics.com/wiki/Hardware_Specifications`
- `https://github.com/RethinkRobotics/sdk-docs/wiki/API-Reference#Sensors`
- `http://sdk.rethinkrobotics.com/wiki/API_Reference#Cameras`

Loading Baxter software

This section describes how to load software packages for the SDK, Baxter Simulator, and MoveIt. It is assumed that Ubuntu 16.04 and ROS Kinetic software are installed on the computer to be used for the Baxter Simulator and software development. The steps for installing Ubuntu and ROS are described in *Chapter 1, Getting Started with ROS*, in the *Installing and launching ROS* section.

Installing Baxter SDK software

The installation of Baxter Simulator requires the SDK to already have been downloaded and installed into a ROS catkin workspace on the workstation computer. Instructions for the installation are presented here and can also be found on the Rethink website at `http://sdk.rethinkrobotics.com/wiki/Workstation_Setup`. These instructions are for installing with Ubuntu 14.04 and ROS Indigo. *We have updated the instructions here for Ubuntu 16.04 and ROS Kinetic.*

In *Chapter 1, Getting Started with ROS*, we created the `catkin_ws` catkin workspace and used this workspace in *Chapter 2, Creating Your First Two-Wheeled ROS Robot (in Simulation)*, to create the `ros_robotics` ROS package. For the Baxter SDK packages, we will create another catkin workspace, `baxter_ws`, to contain the Rethink ROS packages and be the development space for the new software we wish to create. If you wish to use the `catkin_ws` workspace for your Baxter software, skip to the step where the Baxter SDK dependencies are installed. (Afterwards, remember to replace the `baxter_ws` name in each of the command lines with `catkin_ws`.)

At the system level, the Baxter software can also be installed for all users of the workstation computer. Administrator privileges are necessary. We have installed our Baxter workspace under the `/opt` directory using the following instructions by replacing `~/baxter_ws` with `/opt/baxter_ws`.

For a user-level installation, create the Baxter catkin workspace `baxter_ws` by typing these commands:

```
$ mkdir -p ~/baxter_ws/src
$ cd ~/baxter_ws/src
$ catkin_init_workspace
```

Build and install the Baxter workspace:

```
$ cd ~/baxter_ws
$ catkin_make
```

Next, source the `setup.bash` file within the Baxter workspace to overlay this workspace on top of the ROS environment for the workstation:

```
$ source ~/baxter_ws/devel/setup.bash
```

Remember to add this source command to your `.bashrc` file:

```
$ echo "source ~/baxter_ws/devel/setup.bash" >> ~/.bashrc
```

Make sure that the `ROS_PACKAGE_PATH` environment variable includes the path you just sourced by typing this command:

```
$ echo $ROS_PACKAGE_PATH
```

The `/home/<username>/baxter_ws/src` path should be displayed as one of the paths on the screen.

Now that the Baxter catkin workspace has been created, the Baxter SDK dependencies are installed by typing the following commands:

```
$ sudo apt-get update
$ sudo apt-get install git-core python-argparse python-wstool python-
vcstools python-rosdep ros-kinetic-control-msgs ros-kinetic-joystick-
drivers
```

Next, the ROS `wstool` workspace tool is used to check out all the required Baxter SDK packages from the GitHub repository and place them in the Baxter workspace source directory:

```
$ cd ~/baxter_ws/src
$ wstool init
$ wstool merge https://raw.githubusercontent.com/RethinkRobotics/baxter/
master/baxter_sdk.rosinstall
$ wstool update
```

Then, the workspace is built and installed:

```
$ cd ~/baxter_ws
$ catkin_make
$ catkin_make install
```

These instructions install the latest version of the Baxter SDK source, which is version 1.2 at the time of writing. In the next section, installation instructions for the Baxter Simulator software packages will be described.

Installing Baxter Simulator

Since Rethink has made the packages for Baxter Simulator open source, owning a real Baxter robot is no longer necessary to gain access to the GitHub files. The instructions for loading the Baxter Simulator software on your computer presented here can also be found at `http://sdk.rethinkrobotics.com/wiki/Simulator_Installation`.

To ensure that you have the supporting ROS packages required for Baxter Simulator, we recommend that you execute the following two commands in preparation for loading the Baxter Simulator packages:

```
$ sudo apt-get update
$ sudo apt-get install gazebo7 ros-kinetic-qt-build ros-kinetic-gazebo-
ros-control ros-kinetic-gazebo-ros-pkgs ros-kinetic-ros-control ros-
kinetic-control-toolbox ros-kinetic-realtime-tools ros-kinetic-ros-
controllers ros-kinetic-xacro python-wstool ros-kinetic-tf-conversions
ros-kinetic-kdl-parser
```

A large number of ROS packages are loaded by the `sudo apt-get` command. These packages are as follows:

- `Gazebo7`: This is the correct version of Gazebo to work with ROS Kinetic.
- `qt_build`: This is necessary for building qt and rqt applications such as `rqt_reconfigure`.
- `gazebo_ros_control`, `ros_control`, `control_toolbox`, and `ros_controllers`: These provide the simulated control software, as well as the real-time control software for Baxter Simulator.
- `gazebo_ros_pkgs`: This provides the interface between Gazebo and ROS, enabling robots to be simulated in the Gazebo environment.
- `realtime_tools`: This provides a real-time publisher that publishes ROS messages to a topic from a real-time thread.

- xacro: This package is used with Baxter's URDF to generate the robot_description parameter. Xacro is described in some detail in *Chapter 5, Creating Your First Robot Arm (in Simulation)*.

- tf_conversions: This package and kdl_parser work together to support the tf transforms of Baxter. The tf_conversion package provides conversions for the user to obtain the data type they require from the transform library. **KDL** stands for **Kinematics and Dynamics Library**. The kdl_parser package provides the tools to construct the full KDL tree from the URDF. If you are not familiar with URDF, *Chapter 2, Creating Your First Two-Wheeled ROS Robot (in Simulation)* and *Chapter 5, Creating Your First Robot Arm (in Simulation)*, provide an understanding of how the URDF describes the robot, its kinematics structure, and its dynamic movement.

The ROS wstool workspace tool is used to check out all the required Baxter Simulator packages from the GitHub repository and place them in the Baxter workspace source directory:

```
$ cd ~/baxter_ws/src
$ wstool init
```

(If your baxter_ws already exists, skip the preceding step.)

```
$ wstool merge https://raw.githubusercontent.com/RethinkRobotics/baxter_
simulator/kinetic-devel/baxter_simulator.rosinstall
```

(Say yes when prompted.)

```
$ wstool update
```

Then, the workspace is built and installed:

```
$ cd ~/baxter_ws
$ catkin_make
```

Configuring the Baxter shell

The Baxter SDK requires the baxter.sh script file to establish the connections between the Baxter robot and the workstation computer. This connection will depend on how your network is set up. Further details on a network connection to a real Baxter will be discussed in the *Configuring a real Baxter setup* section.

Baxter Simulator additionally uses the `baxter.sh` file to establish a simulation mode where the ROS environment variables are set up to identify the host workstation computer. The `baxter.sh` script file contains a *special hook* for Baxter Simulator.

1. First, the file must be copied to the `baxter_ws` directory and the file permissions changed to grant execution privileges to all users:

   ```
   $ cp ~/baxter_ws/src/baxter/baxter.sh ~/baxter_ws
   $ chmod +x baxter.sh
   ```

2. Next, open the `baxter.sh` script in your favorite editor and find the `your_ip` parameter (around line 26). Change the `your_ip` value to the IP address of your workstation computer:

   ```
   your_ip="192.168.XXX.XXX"
   ```

   If the IP address of your computer is unknown, connect to the network used for Baxter, then use the `ifconfig` command:

   ```
   $ ifconfig
   ```

   The screen results will contain the `inet_addr` field for the IP address of the workstation computer.

3. Alternatively, if you wish to use the hostname, comment out the line for `your_ip` and uncomment the line for `your_hostname`. To use the real hostname of your workstation computer, use the following command:

   ```
   $ hostname
   ```

   Then, add this to the `your_hostname` parameter.

   These parameters will assign either the `ROS_IP` or `ROS_HOSTNAME` environment variable. If both are present, the `ROS_HOSTNAME` variable takes precedence.

4. Also, near line 30, change `ros_version` to `kinetic`. Then, save and close the `baxter.sh` script.

Installing MoveIt!

MoveIt! is an important ROS tool for path planning and can be used with Baxter Simulator or a real Baxter. The installation of MoveIt! is described here, while the operation of MoveIt! is detailed later in the chapter, in the *Introducing MoveIt!* section. Instructions for the installation can also be found on the Rethink website at http://sdk.rethinkrobotics.com/wiki/MoveIt_Tutorial. *These instructions are for ROS Indigo, but they have been updated for ROS Kinetic here.*

The MoveIt! software should be loaded into the source (`src`) directory of the catkin workspace `baxter_ws` created earlier in the chapter in the section *Loading the Baxter software*. The commands are as follows:

```
$ cd ~/baxter_ws/src
$ git clone https://github.com/ros-planning/moveit_robots.git
$ sudo apt-get update
$ sudo apt-get install ros-kinetic-moveit
```

Then, new additions to the workspace are incorporated with the `catkin_make` command:

```
$ cd ~/baxter_ws
$ catkin_make
```

To verify that all the Baxter SDK, simulator, and MoveIt packages were downloaded and installed, type the following command:

```
$ ls ~/baxter_ws/src
```

The output should be as follows:

```
baxter            baxter_examples      baxter_simulator     CMakeLists.txt
baxter_common     baxter_interface     baxter_tools         MoveIt!_robots
```

Launching Baxter Simulator in Gazebo

Before launching Baxter Simulator in Gazebo, it is important to check the ROS environment variables. To start up Baxter Simulator, use the following commands to get to your Baxter catkin workspace and run your `baxter.sh` script with the `sim` parameter:

```
$ cd ~/baxter_ws
$ ./baxter.sh sim
```

The command prompt should return with the following tag appended to the beginning of the prompt:

```
[baxter - http://localhost:11311]
```

You are now talking to the simulated Baxter! At this point, check your ROS environment with the following command:

```
$ env | grep ROS
```

Within the output screen text, look for the following result:

```
ROS_MASTER_URI=http://localhost:11311
ROS_IP= <your workstation's IP address>
```

or

```
ROS_HOSTNAME=<your workstation's hostname>
```

The `ROS_HOSTNAME` field need not be present.

If the `ROS_IP` or `ROS_HOSTNAME` environment variables does not match the IP address of your workstation (use `ifconfig` to check), type `exit` to stop communication with the simulated Baxter. Then, edit the `baxter.sh` script to change the `your_ip` variable (near line 26) to the current IP address of your workstation. To continue, repeat the preceding steps for a final check.

If there are issues with Baxter's hardware, software, or network, refer to the general Baxter troubleshooting website at `http://sdk.rethinkrobotics.com/wiki/Troubleshooting`.

The `baxter.sh` script should run without errors and the ROS environment variables should be correct. The next section covers running Baxter Simulator for the first time.

Bringing Baxter Simulator to life

To start Baxter Simulator, go to the `baxter_ws` workspace and run the Baxter shell script with the sim parameter specified:

```
$ cd ~/baxter_ws
$ ./baxter.sh sim
```

Next, call the `roslaunch` command to start the simulation with controllers:

```
$ roslaunch baxter_gazebo baxter_world.launch
```

The following lines are some of the results you will see on the screen while Baxter Simulator starts:

```
NODES
  /
    base_to_world (tf2_ros/static_transform_publisher)
    baxter_emulator (baxter_sim_hardware/baxter_emulator)
    baxter_sim_io (baxter_sim_io/baxter_sim_io)
    baxter_sim_kinematics_left (baxter_sim_kinematics/kinematics)
    baxter_sim_kinematics_right (baxter_sim_kinematics/kinematics)
    gazebo (gazebo_ros/gzserver)
    gazebo_gui (gazebo_ros/gzclient)
    robot_state_publisher (robot_state_publisher/robot_state_publisher)
    urdf_spawner (gazebo_ros/spawn_model)
  /robot/
    controller_spawner (controller_manager/controller_manager)
    controller_spawner_stopped (controller_manager/controller_manager)
    left_gripper_controller_spawner_stopped (controller_manager/
controller_manager)
    right_gripper_controller_spawner_stopped (controller_manager/
controller_manager)
```

As the process is completing, look for these lines:

```
[ INFO] [1502315064.794924787, 0.718000000]: Simulator is loaded and
started successfully
[ INFO] [1502315064.905968083, 0.830000000]: Robot is disabled
[ INFO] [1502315064.906014361, 0.830000000]: Gravity compensation was
turned off
```

The following screenshot should appear with Baxter in a disabled state:

Baxter's initial state in Gazebo

If Gazebo and Baxter Simulator fail to appear or there are red error messages in your terminal window, refer to the Gazebo Troubleshooting page provided by Rethink Robotics at `http://sdk.rethinkrobotics.com/wiki/Gazebo_Troubleshooting`.

 To remove all Gazebo processes after shutdown, use the command:
`$ killall gzserver`

For an introduction to using Gazebo, refer to the *Gazebo* section in *Chapter 2, Creating Your First Two-Wheeled ROS Robot (in Simulation)*. In that section, the various Gazebo display panels, menus, and toolbars are explained. Gazebo uses similar cursor/mouse controls to those of rviz, and these mouse/cursor actions are described in the *Introducing rviz: Mouse control* section of *Chapter 2, Creating Your First Two-Wheeled ROS Robot (in Simulation)*.

In the previous screenshot, the **World** panel on the left shows the **Models** element open to reveal the two models in the environment: ground_plane and baxter. Under the baxter model, all of Baxter's links are listed and you are welcome to select the links to explore the details about each one. The screenshot also shows the smaller display window that contains Baxter's IO. Baxter's four navigators, located one on each side of the rear torso (near the shoulders) and one on each arm, are also shown. The oval-shaped navigators have three push buttons, one of which is a scroll wheel. Baxter's cuff buttons are also shown in this window. There are two buttons and one touch sensor on each cuff.

The terminal window in which the roslaunch command was performed will be unable to run additional commands, so a second terminal window should be opened. In this window, go to the baxter_ws workspace and run the baxter.sh script with the sim parameter:

```
$ cd ~/baxter_ws
$ ./baxter.sh sim
```

 For each additional terminal window opened, go to the baxter_ws workspace and run the baxter.sh script with the sim parameter.

Baxter (in simulation) is initially in a disabled state. To confirm this, use the enable_robot script from the baxter_tools package using the following command:

```
$ rosrun baxter_tools enable_robot.py -s
```

The screen should display the following output:

```
ready: False
enabled: False
stopped: False
error: False
estop_button: 0
estop_source: 0
```

To enable Baxter, use the same enable_robot script with the -e option:

```
$ rosrun baxter_tools enable_robot.py -e
```

The output is similar to the following:

```
[INFO] [1501189929.999603, 141.690000]: Robot Enabled
```

Confirm Baxter is enabled using the following command:

```
$ rosrun baxter_tools enable_robot.py -s
```

The output should be as follows:

```
ready: False
enabled: True
stopped: False
error: False
estop_button: 0
estop_source: 0
```

 Always enable Baxter Simulator before attempting to control any of the motors.

At this point, a **cheat sheet** for use with Baxter Simulator is provided for you to use with the example programs that follow. The commands for launching, enabling, and untucking are provided here for your reference:

 Baxter Simulator cheat sheet

To launch Baxter Simulator in Gazebo, use the following commands:

```
$ cd ~/baxter_ws
$ ./baxter.sh sim
$ roslaunch baxter_gazebo baxter_world.launch
```

For subsequent terminal windows, use the following commands:

```
$ cd ~/baxter_ws
$ ./baxter.sh sim
```

To enable the robot, use the following command:

```
$ rosrun baxter_tools enable_robot.py -e
```

To enable and set the arms in a known position, use the following command:

```
$ rosrun baxter_tools tuck_arms.py -u
```

With Baxter enabled, the next section describes some of Baxter's example scripts using the head display screen.

Warm-up exercises

Rethink Robotics has provided a collection of example scripts to demonstrate Baxter's interfaces and features. These example programs are contained in the `baxter_examples` package and work primarily with a real Baxter and the SDK. A portion of these example programs also work with Baxter Simulator.

The `baxter_examples` are Python programs that access Baxter's hardware and functionality through the `baxter_interface` package. The `baxter_examples` programs are written to demonstrate how to use Baxter interfaces. The `baxter_interface` package is a repository of Python APIs to use for interacting with the Baxter Research Robot. The repository contains a set of classes that are ROS wrappers to communicate with and control Baxter's hardware and functionality. These Python classes are built on top of the ROS API layer.

This section and the following sections present SDK example programs that can be used with Baxter Simulator. To find additional information on the SDK example programs implemented in Baxter Simulator, visit the following website:

`http://sdk.rethinkrobotics.com/wiki/API_Reference#tab=Simulator_API`

The first example program will display an image on Baxter's (simulated) head display screen using the following command:

```
$ rosrun baxter_examples xdisplay_image.py --file=`rospack find baxter_
examples`/share/images/baxterworking.png
```

Your screen should look similar to the following screenshot:

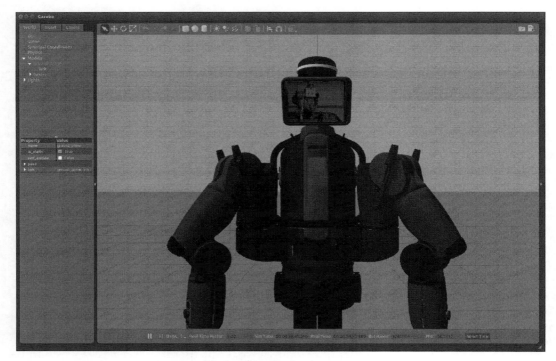

Baxter after xdisplay_image.py

The `xdisplay_image.py` program locates the `baxterworking.png` image in the specified location under the `baxter_examples` package. This image data is published as a `sensor_msgs/Image` ROS message. The display image must be a `.png` or `.jpg` file with a display resolution of 1024 x 600 pixels or smaller. Smaller images will appear in the top-left corner of Baxter's display screen.

A second `baxter_examples` program will cause Baxter Simulator to nod Baxter's head up and down, then turn from side to side:

```
$ rosrun baxter_examples head_wobbler.py
```

The simulated Baxter should randomly wobble its head until *Ctrl* + *C* is pressed. The movement demonstrates both the head pan motion (side to side) and head nod motion (up and down) interfaces. This program shows the use of the `baxter_interface Head` class (`head.py`). The `command_nod` function is called first to trigger an up-down motion of the head. It is not possible to command a specific angle for the nod motion. The pan motion is achieved with several calls to the `set_pan` function, with random angles provided as the parameter.

Another `baxter_examples` program also moves Baxter's head through a set of head positions and velocities. The Head Action Client Example demonstrates the use of the Head Action Server. This example is similar to the head wobble just performed, but provides a good example of an action server and client interaction. If you wish to try the Head Action Client Example, access the instructions and explanations at `http://sdk.rethinkrobotics.com/wiki/Head_Action_Client_Example`.

The next section will demonstrate some example programs for Baxter's arms.

Flexing Baxter's arms

The focus of the following sections will be on Baxter's arms. The section on *Bringing Baxter Simulator to life* should be completed before starting these sections. Baxter Simulator should be launched in Gazebo and the robot should be enabled with its arms untucked.

The following example programs use the `baxter_interface Limb` class (`limb.py`) to create instances for each arm. The `joint_names` function is used to return an array of all the joints in the limb.

Commands for the joint control modes are via ROS messages within the `baxter_core_msgs` package. To move the arm, a `JointCommand` message must be published on the `robot/limb/<left/right>/joint_command` topic. Within the `JointCommand` message, a mode field indicates the control mode to the Joint Controller Boards as `POSITION_MODE`, `VELOCITY_MODE`, `TORQUE_MODE`, or `RAW_POSITON_MODE`.

In the following sections, various methods of controlling Baxter's arm movements will be demonstrated. After several example arm programs have been presented, a Python script to command Baxter's arms to move to a home position will be shown.

Untucking Baxter's arms

Before Baxter's arms can be commanded, Baxter must be enabled. This can be accomplished using the `tuck_arms.py` program provided by Rethink using the `untuck` option. During untuck movements, Baxter's collision avoidance is disabled. Collision avoidance for Baxter Simulator is modeled as part of the URDF. Each of Baxter's links is tagged with a collision block that is slightly larger than the visual element. For further details on the URDF, collision blocks, and the visual element, refer to *Chapter 2, Creating Your First Two-Wheeled ROS Robot (in Simulation)*. Typically, when the position of the arms places the collision blocks into contact with each other, the collision model detects the contact and ends the movement to avoid the parts colliding.

To command Baxter into the untuck position, use the following command:

```
$ rosrun baxter_tools tuck_arms.py -u
```

The output should be similar to the following:

```
[INFO] [1501190044.262606, 0.000000]: Untucking arms
[INFO] [1501190044.375889, 255.938000]: Moving head to neutral position
[INFO] [1501190044.376109, 255.938000]: Untucking: Arms already Untucked;
Moving to neutral position.
[INFO] [1501190045.673587, 257.234000]: Finished tuck
```

The following screenshot shows the simulated Baxter in the untucked position:

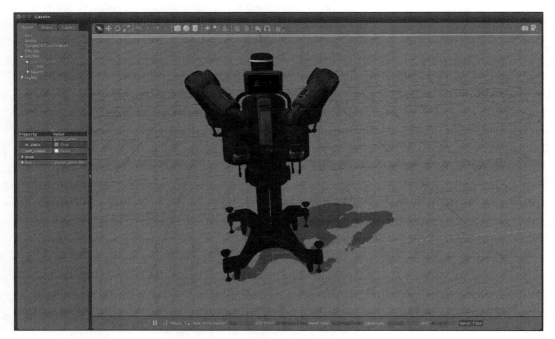

Baxter untucked

To explore Baxter's untuck operation further, refer to the Rethink wiki *Tuck Arms Tool* information at http://sdk.rethinkrobotics.com/wiki/Tuck_Arms_Tool.

Wobbling arms

The next example program provides a demonstration of controlling Baxter's arms using joint velocity control. The joint control modes for Baxter's arms were described in the *Baxter's arms* section. In simulation, the joint velocity wobble can be observed by typing the following command:

```
$ rosrun baxter_examples joint_velocity_wobbler.py
```

The output should be as follows:

```
Initializing node...
Getting robot state...
Enabling robot...
[INFO] [1501190177.147845, 388.564000]: Robot Enabled
Moving to neutral pose...
Wobbling. Press Ctrl-C to stop...
```

The program will begin by moving Baxter's arms to a preset neutral starting position. Next, random velocity commands are sent to each arm to create a sinusoidal motion across both limbs. The following screenshot shows Baxter's neutral starting position:

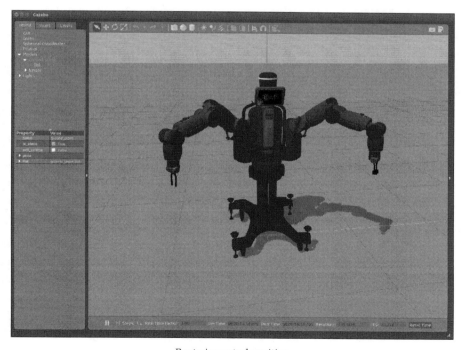

Baxter's neutral position

To explore Baxter's arms' `joint_velocity_wobbler` operation in more detail, refer to the Rethink wiki *Wobbler Example* information at `http://sdk.rethinkrobotics.com/wiki/Wobbler_Example`.

Controlling arms and grippers with a keyboard

Baxter's arms can also be controlled with keyboard keystrokes. Keystrokes are used to control the positions of the joints, with each keyboard key mapped to either increase or decrease the angle of one of Baxter's 14 arm joints. Keys on the right side of the keyboard are mapped to Baxter's left arm and keys on the left side of the keyboard are mapped to Baxter's right arm.

This example demonstrates another of Baxter's arm control modes: joint position control.

To start the keyboard joint position control example, use the following command:

```
$ rosrun baxter_examples joint_position_keyboard.py
```

This should be the output on the screen:

```
Initializing node...
Getting robot state...
Enabling robot...
[INFO] [1501190427.217690, 638.355000]: Robot Enabled
Controlling joints. Press ? for help, Esc to quit.
key bindings:
  Esc: Quit
  ?: Help
```

`/: left: gripper calibrate`	`b: right: gripper calibrate`
`,: left: gripper close`	`c: right: gripper close`
`m: left: gripper open`	`x: right: gripper open`
`y: left_e0 decrease`	`q: right_e0 decrease`
`o: left_e0 increase`	`r: right_e0 increase`
`u: left_e1 decrease`	`w: right_e1 decrease`
`i: left_e1 increase`	`e: right_e1 increase`
`6: left_s0 decrease`	`1: right_s0 decrease`
`9: left_s0 increase`	`4: right_s0 increase`
`7: left_s1 decrease`	`2: right_s1 decrease`
`8: left_s1 increase`	`3: right_s1 increase`
`h: left_w0 decrease`	`a: right_w0 decrease`
`l: left_w0 increase`	`f: right_w0 increase`
`j: left_w1 decrease`	`s: right_w1 decrease`
`k: left_w1 increase`	`d: right_w1 increase`
`n: left_w2 decrease`	`z: right_w2 decrease`
`.: left_w2 increase`	`v: right_w2 increase`

 The output has been modified to aid ease of use.

Controlling arms and grippers with a joystick

This example program uses a joystick to control Baxter's arms. The `joint_position_joystick` program uses the ROS drivers from the `joy` package to interface with a generic Linux joystick. Joysticks with a USB interface are supported by the `joy` package. The `joy` package creates a `joy_node` to generate a `sensor_msgs/Joy` message containing the various button-push and joystick-move events.

The first step is to check for the joystick driver package `joy` using the following command:

```
$ rospack find joy
```

If the ROS package is on the computer, the screen should display this:

```
/opt/ros/kinetic/share/joy
```

If it is not, then an error message is displayed:

```
[rospack] Error: stack/package joy not found
```

If the joy package is not present, install it with the following command:

```
$ sudo apt-get install ros-kinetic-joystick-drivers
```

For a PS3 joystick controller, you will need the ps3joy package. Instructions can be found at http://wiki.ros.org/ps3joy/Tutorials/ PairingJoystickAndBluetoothDongle.

Next, type the command to start the joint_position_joystick program using one of the joystick types (xbox, logitech, or ps3):

```
$ roslaunch baxter_examples joint_position_joystick.launch
joystick:=<joystick_type>
```

We used the Xbox controller joystick in our example; the output is as follows:

```
...
NODES
  /
    joy_node (joy/joy_node)
    rsdk_joint_position_joystick (baxter_examples/joint_position_
joystick.py)
...
[INFO] [1501196267.914400, 251.752000]: Robot Enabled
Press Ctrl-C to quit.
rightTrigger: left gripper close
rightTrigger: left gripper open
leftTrigger: right gripper close
leftTrigger: right gripper open
leftStickHorz: right inc right_s0
leftStickHorz: right dec right_s0
rightStickHorz: left inc left_s0
rightStickHorz: left dec left_s0
leftStickVert: right inc right_s1
leftStickVert: right dec right_s1
rightStickVert: left inc left_s1
rightStickVert: left dec left_s1
rightBumper: left: cycle joint
```

```
leftBumper: right: cycle joint
btnRight: left calibrate
btnLeft: right calibrate
function1: help
function2: help
Press Ctrl-C to stop.
```

The preceding output shows the Xbox joystick buttons and knobs to move Baxter's joints. The joystick controls two joints at a time on each of Baxter's two arms using the **Left Stick** and the **Right Stick** (see the following diagram). The up-down (vertical) control of the stick controls increasing and decreasing one of the joint angles. The side-to-side (horizontal) control increases and decreases another joint angle. The **Left Bumper** and **Right Bumper** cycle the joystick control through all of Baxter's arm joints in the order: S0-S1-E0-E1-W0-W1-W2. For example, initially, the Left Stick control will be in command of the (right arm) S0 joint using horizontal direction, and the S1 joint using vertical direction. When the Left Bumper is pressed, the **Left Stick** horizontal control will command the S1 joint, and the vertical control will command the E0 joint. Cycling the joints continues in a continuous loop, where the S0 joint will be selected after the W2 joint.

 The joystick mapping of *joystick left* = *robot right* allows the operator ease of use while the operator is positioned facing Baxter.

The following image and table describe the mapping of the Xbox joystick controls:

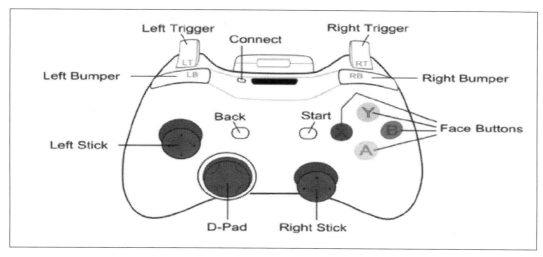

Xbox joystick controls

Buttons	Action for RIGHT Arm	Buttons	Action for LEFT Arm
Back	Help	*Ctrl + C or Ctrl + Z*	Quit
Left Button (*X*)	gripper calibrate	Right Button (*B*)	gripper calibrate
Top Button (*Y*)	none	Bottom Button (*A*)	none
Left Trigger [PRESS]	gripper close	Right Trigger[PRESS]	gripper close
Left Trigger [RELEASE]	gripper open	Right Trigger[RELEASE]	gripper open
Left Bumper	cycle joints	Right Bumper	cycle joints
Stick Axes	**Action**		
Left Stick Horizontal	right: increase/decrease <current joint 1> (S0)		
Left Stick Vertical	right: increase/decrease <current joint 2> (S1)		
Right Stick Horizontal	left: increase/decrease <current joint 1> (S0)		
Right Stick Vertical	left: increase/decrease <current joint 2> (S1)		

Controlling arms with a Python script

In this section, we will create a simple Python script to command Baxter's arms into a specific pose. The following script commands Baxter's arms to a home position, similar to the untuck position. Comments have been placed throughout the code to provide information on the process. Further explanation of this Python code operation is given following the script:

```python
#!/usr/bin/env python

"""
Script to return Baxter's arms to a "home" position
"""

# rospy - ROS Python API
import rospy

# baxter_interface - Baxter Python API
import baxter_interface

# initialize our ROS node, registering it with the Master
```

```
rospy.init_node('Home_Arms')

# create instances of baxter_interface's Limb class
limb_right = baxter_interface.Limb('right')
limb_left = baxter_interface.Limb('left')

# store the home position of the arms
home_right = {'right_s0': 0.08, 'right_s1': -1.00, 'right_w0': -0.67,
'right_w1': 1.03, 'right_w2': 0.50, 'right_e0': 1.18, 'right_e1':
1.94}
home_left = {'left_s0': -0.08, 'left_s1': -1.00, 'left_w0': 0.67,
'left_w1': 1.03, 'left_w2': -0.50, 'left_e0': -1.18, 'left_e1': 1.94}

# move both arms to home position
limb_right.move_to_joint_positions(home_right)
limb_left.move_to_joint_positions(home_left)

quit()
```

This code can be placed in a file named home_arms.py. Then, it can be made executable using the Ubuntu chmod + x command. Execute this Python script with this terminal command:

```
$ python home_arms.py
```

In this script, the rospy ROS-Python interface package is used to create ROS components from Python code. The rospy client API provides software routines for initializing the ROS node, Home_Arms, to invoke the process. The baxter_interface package provides the API for interacting with Baxter. In the script, we instantiate instances of the Limb class for both the right and left arms. A Python dictionary is used to assign joint angles to specific joints for both the right and left arms. These joint angle dictionaries are passed to the move_to_joint_positions method to command the respective arm to the provided position. The move_to_joint_positions method is also a part of the baxter_interface package.

Recording and replaying arm movements

Another capability provided by the `baxter_examples` programs is the ability to record and play back arm positions. A recorder program captures the time and joint positions in an external file. The `armRoutine` filename is used in the following command lines, but you may substitute your own filename instead. After the command for the recorder program is executed, the operator should move Baxter's arms manually or using the keyboard, joystick, ROS commands, or a script. When the operator wishes to end the recording, *Ctrl + C* or *Ctrl + Z* must be pressed to stop the recording. The playback program can be executed with the external file passed as a parameter. The playback program will run through the arm positions in the file once and then exit. The following instructions show the commands and the order of operation:

```
$ rosrun baxter_examples joint_recorder.py -f armRoutine
```

The output should be as follows:

```
Initializing node...
Getting robot state...
Enabling robot...
[INFO] [1501198989.301174, 2970.058000]: Robot Enabled
Recording. Press Ctrl-C to stop.
```

At this time, you should use your hands or the joystick, keyboard, Python script, and/or commands to move Baxter's arms. Press *Ctrl + C* when you are finished moving Baxter's arms. Next, execute the following command to play the file back:

```
$ rosrun baxter_examples joint_position_file_playback.py -f armRoutine
```

The output on the screen should be similar to the following:

```
Initializing node...
Getting robot state...
Enabling robot...
[INFO] [1501199319.366765, 3299.749000]: Robot Enabled
Playing back: armRoutine
Moving to start position...
  Record 10462 of 10462, loop 1 of 1
Exiting example...
```

If the file `armRoutine` is brought up in an editor, you should see that it contains data similar to the following:

```
time,left_s0,left_s1,left_e0,left_e1,left_w0,left_w1,left_w2,left_
gripper,right_s0,right_s1,right_e0,right_e1,right_w0,right_w1,right_
w2,right_gripper
0.221000,-0.0799704928309,-1.0000362209,-0.745950772448,-
0.0499208630966,-1.6948350728,1.03001017593,-0.500000660376,0.0,-
1.04466483018,-0.129655442605,1.5342459042,1.94952695585,-
0.909650985497,1.03000093981,0.825985250377,0.0
...
```

As shown, the first line contains the labels for the data on each of the subsequent rows. As the first label indicates, the first field contains the timestamp. The subsequent fields hold the joint positions for each of the left and right arm joints and grippers.

Baxter's arms and forward kinematics

Considering Baxter's arms up to the wrist cuff, each arm has seven values that define the rotation angle of each joint. Since the link lengths and joint angles are known, it is possible to calculate the position and orientation of the gripper attached to the wrist. This approach to calculating the **pose** of the gripper, given the configuration of the arm is called **forward kinematic analysis**.

Fortunately, ROS has programs that allow the calculation and publishing of the joint angles, given a particular position and orientation of the gripper. The particular topic for Baxter is `/robot/joint_states`.

Joints and joint state publisher

Baxter has seven joints in each of its two arms and two more joints in its head. The `/robot/joint_states` topic publishes the current joint states of the head pan (side-to-side) joint and the 14 arm joints. These joint states show position, velocity, and effort values for each of these joints. Joint position values are in radians, velocity values are in radians per second, and torque values are in Newton meters. The robot state publisher internally has a kinematic model of the robot. So, given the joint positions of the robot, the robot state publisher can compute and broadcast the 3D pose of each link in the robot.

For the examples in this section, it is assumed that Baxter Simulator is running, `baxter_world` is launched from `baxter_gazebo`, and the simulated robot is enabled:

```
$ cd baxter_ws
$ ./baxter.sh sim
$ roslaunch baxter_gazebo baxter_world.launch
```

In a second terminal, type the following commands:

```
$ cd baxter_ws
$ ./baxter.sh sim
$ rosrun baxter_tools enable_robot.py -e
```

Baxter's arms will be placed in the *home* position using the Python script presented previously via the following command:

```
$ python home_arms.py
```

The joint states will be displayed with the screen output edited to show the arm positions as angles of rotation in radians. To view one output of the joint states, type this:

```
$ rostopic echo /robot/joint_states -n1
```

Here is our output on the screen:

```
header:
  seq: 42448
  stamp:
    secs: 850
    nsecs: 553000000
  frame_id: ''


name: ['head_pan', 'l_gripper_l_finger_joint', 'l_gripper_r_finger_
joint', 'left_e0', 'left_e1', 'left_s0', 'left_s1', 'left_w0', 'left_
w1', 'left_w2', 'r_gripper_l_finger_joint', 'r_gripper_r_finger_joint',
'right_e0', 'right_e1', 'right_s0', 'right_s1', 'right_w0', 'right_w1',
'right_w2']


position: [9.642012118504795e-06 (Head),
```

```
Left: -9.409649977892339e-08, -0.02083311343765363, -1.171334885477055,
1.9312641121225074, -0.07941855421008803, -0.9965989736590268,
0.6650922280384437, 1.0314330310192892, -0.49634000104265397,


Right: 0.020833000098799456, 2.9266103072174966e-10, 1.1714460516466971,
1.9313701087550257, 0.07941788278369621, -0.9966421178258322,
-0.6651529936706897, 1.0314155121179436, 0.49638770883940264]


velocity: [8.463358573117045e-09, 2.2845555643152853e-05,
2.766005018018799e-05, 6.96516608889685e-08, -1.4347584964474649e-07,
5.379243329637427e-08, -3.07783563763457e-08, -5.9625446169838476e-06,
-2.765075210928186e-06, 4.37915209815064e-06, -1.9330586583769175e-08,
-3.396963606705046e-08, -4.1024914575147146e-07, -6.470964538079114e-07,
1.2464164369422782e-07, -3.489373517131325e-08, 1.3838850846575283e-06,
1.1659521943505596e-06, -3.293066091641411e-06]


effort: [0.0, 0.0, 0.0, -0.12553439407980704, -0.16093410986695034,
1.538268268319598e-06, -0.1584186302672208, 0.0026223415490989055,
-0.007023475006633362, -0.0002595722218323715, 0.0, 0.0,
0.12551329635801522, -0.16096013901023554, -1.4389475655463002e-05,
-0.1583874287014453, -0.0026439994199378702, -0.007005447407815685,
0.00024931690616014635]
```

Compare the radian values from home_arms.py and the result of rostopic echo of joint states, but watch the order of listing of the joints:

```
# store the home position of the arms
home_right = {'right_s0': 0.08, 'right_s1': -1.00, 'right_w0': -0.67,
'right_w1': 1.03, 'right_w2': 0.50, 'right_e0': 1.18, 'right_e1':
1.94}
home_left = {'left_s0': -0.08, 'left_s1': -1.00, 'left_w0': 0.67,
'left_w1': 1.03, 'left_w2': -0.50, 'left_e0': -1.18, 'left_e1': 1.94}
```

The velocity and effort (torque) terms are essentially zero, since Baxter's arms are not moving. Rounding off the arm joint position values to two places shows that the angular positions of the arm joints are equivalent to the values in the Python script.

We find the type of messages for joint states from sensor_msgs using this command:

```
$ rostopic type /robot/joint_states
```

The output is as follows:

```
sensor_msgs/JointState
```

To show the `home_arms` pose for Baxter in Gazebo, follow these steps:

1. Go to **World | Models**, click on **baxter**, and then select **left_s0**.

2. Pull the **Property** window into view by clicking and dragging the three small ticks above this panel.

   The figure should look like this:

Baxter home position

3. Choose **pose** and look at the value of `angle_0: -0.07886530088`. Rounded off, this is `left_s0: -0.08` selected in `home_arms.py`. You can view other information by selecting another joint or link of Baxter from the **World** panel.

Another command shows the position and orientation of the end of the left arm:

```
$ rostopic echo /robot/limb/left/endpoint_state/pose -n1
```

The output should be similar to the following:

```
---
header:
  seq: 62403
  stamp:
    secs: 1249
    nsecs: 653000000
  frame_id: ''
pose:
  position:
    x: 0.582326339279
    y: 0.191017651504
    z: 0.111128161508
  orientation:
    x: 0.131168552915
    y: 0.991040351028
    z: 0.0117205349262
    w: 0.0222814367168
```

Yet another way to see the values is to start rqt and select **Topics** as **Plugins** and **Topic Monitor**. Select the `/robot/limb/left/endpoint_state` and `/robot/limb/right/endpoint_state` topics. The result is shown in the following screenshot:

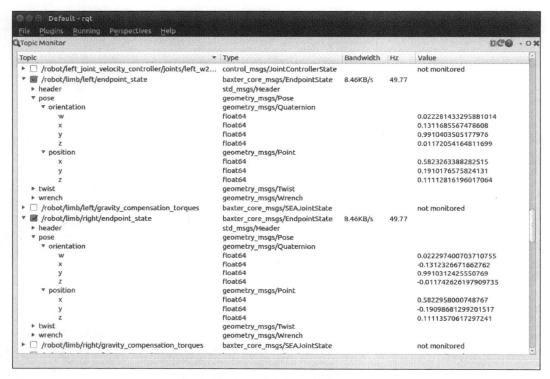

Topic Monitor in rqt for endpoint states

The left arm's endpoint x, y, and z position agrees with the output from the `rostopic echo` command for the left `endpoint_state` topic. The right arm endpoint has the same x and z positions, but a negative value for y. This indicates that it is to the right of Baxter's vertical centerline.

Understanding tf

Tf is a transform system used to keep track of the relation between different coordinate frames in ROS. The relationship between the coordinate frames is maintained in a tree structure that can be viewed. In Baxter's example, the robot has many coordinate frames that can be referenced to Baxter's base frame.

Tutorials about tf are given on the ROS wiki at `http://wiki.ros.org/tf/Tutorials`.

To demonstrate the use of tf, the following Baxter examples will be provided:

- Show tf in rviz after Baxter's arms are moved to a position in which the angles of the joints are zero
- Show various coordinate frames for Baxter's elements, such as cameras or grippers

A program to move Baxter's arms to a zero angle position

With Baxter Simulator running (Gazebo), executing the Python script `arms_to_zero_angles.py` will move Baxter's arms to a position in which all the joint angles are zero.

The following code simply sets the joint angles to zero:

```python
#!/usr/bin/env python    # arms_to_zero_angles.py
#
"""
Script to return Baxter's arms to a " zero" position
"""


# rospy - ROS Python API
import rospy

# baxter_interface - Baxter Python API
import baxter_interface

# initialize our ROS node, registering it with the Master
rospy.init_node('Zero_Arms')

# create instances of baxter_interface's Limb class
limb_right = baxter_interface.Limb('right')
limb_left = baxter_interface.Limb('left')

# store the zero position of the arms
zero_zero_right = {'right_s0': 0.0, 'right_s1': 0.00, 'right_w0':
0.00, 'right_w1': 0.00, 'right_w2': 0.00, 'right_e0': 0.00, 'right_
e1': 0.00}
zero_zero_left = {'left_s0': 0.0, 'left_s1': 0.00, 'left_w0': 0.00,
'left_w1': 0.00, 'left_w2': 0.00, 'left_e0': 0.00, 'left_e1': 0.00}

# move both arms to zero position
```

```
limb_right.move_to_joint_positions(zero_zero_right)
limb_left.move_to_joint_positions(zero_zero_left)

quit()
```

Make the Python script executable:

```
$ chmod +x arms_to_zero_angles.py
```

Then, run the script:

```
$ python arms_to_zero_angles.py
```

The position of the arms can be visualized in Gazebo and the values for position, velocity, and effort can be displayed. In the following Gazebo window, Baxter has arms outstretched at an angle from its torso:

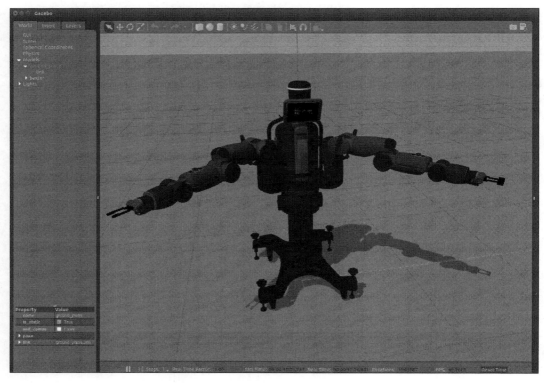

Baxter's joints at zero degrees

The results of the joint states showing only the name and position are as follows:

```
---
header:
  seq: 120710
  stamp:
    secs: 2415
    nsecs: 793000000
  frame_id: ''
```

```
name: ['head_pan', 'l_gripper_1_finger_joint', 'l_gripper_r_finger_
joint', 'left_e0', 'left_e1', 'left_s0', 'left_s1', 'left_w0', 'left_
w1', 'left_w2', 'r_gripper_1_finger_joint', 'r_gripper_r_finger_joint',
'right_e0', 'right_e1', 'right_s0', 'right_s1', 'right_w0', 'right_w1',
'right_w2']
```

```
position: [2.1480795875383762e-05,
0.02083300010459807, 7.094235804419552e-09,
 -0.0052020885142498585, 0.008648349108503872, -0.000352622473348773,
-0.004363080957646481, 0.0029469234535000055, 0.004783709772852696,
-0.0022098995590349446,
-4.685055459408831e-10, -0.02083300002921974, 0.005137618938708677,
0.008541712202397633, 0.0003482148331919177, -0.004308001456631239,
-0.0029103069740452625, 0.004726431947482013, 0.002182588672263286]
```

Within numerical error tolerance, the values are zero for the arm joint angles.

Commanding the joint angles directly

You can send joint angles directly to Baxter using the `JointCommand` message from the `baxter_core_messages` package.

The `JointCommand` message is defined as follows:

```
int32 mode
float64[] command
string[] names

int32 POSITION_MODE=1
int32 VELOCITY_MODE=2
int32 TORQUE_MODE=3
int32 RAW_POSITION_MODE=4
```

The message defines the control mode, the command as an angle for the joints, and the names of the joints being controlled. The details of this are discussed on the following website:

```
http://sdk.rethinkrobotics.com/wiki/Arm_Control_Modes
```

As an example, move Baxter's arms into an arbitrary pose and then, to set the angles of four of Baxter's joints to zero using position control, type this command:

```
$ rostopic pub /robot/limb/left/joint_command baxter_core_msgs/
JointCommand
"{mode: 1, command: [0.0, 0.0, 0.0, 0.0], names: ['left_w1', 'left_e1',
'left_s0', 'left_s1']}" -r 10
```

rviz tf frames

With Gazebo running and Baxter's arms in a zero-angle pose, start rviz:

```
$ rosrun rviz rviz
```

Now select the parameters for rviz:

1. Select the field next to **Fixed Frame** (under **Global Options**) and select `base`.
2. Select the **Add** button under the **Displays** panel, add **Robot Model**, and you will see Baxter appear.
3. Select the **Add** button under the **Displays** panel, add **TF**, and see all the frames that are too complicated to use.
4. Arrange the windows to see the left panel and the figure. Close the **Views** window on the right panel.
    ◦ Expand **TF** in the **Displays** panel by clicking on the triangle symbol on the left
    ◦ Under **TF**, expand **Frames** by clicking on the left triangle
    ◦ Uncheck the checkbox next to **All Enabled**
5. Now, check `left_gripper` to display the axes.

The rviz display looks similar to the following screenshot:

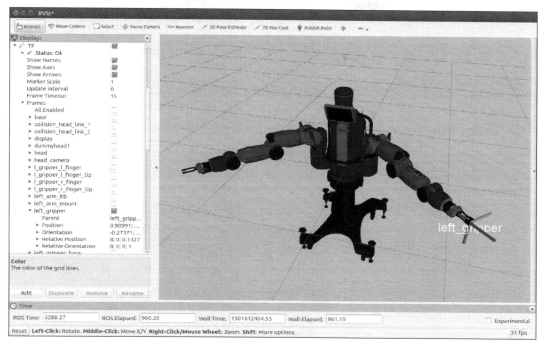

tf transform base and left gripper

You will see the left gripper axes in color on your screen: x is down (red), y is to the right (green), and z is forward (blue) in the preceding screenshot.

Now you can choose various elements of Baxter to see the tf coordinate axes.

Viewing a tf tree of robot elements

The `view_frames` program can generate a PDF file with a graphical representation of the complete tf tree. To try the program, Baxter Simulator or the real Baxter should be communicating with the terminal window. To run `view_frames`, use the following command:

```
$ rosrun tf view_frames
```

In the current working folder, you should now have a file called `frames.pdf`. Open the file with the following command:

```
$ evince frames.pdf
```

More information about the tf frames can be found at `http://wiki.ros.org/tf/Tutorials/Introduction%20to%20tf`.

Introducing MoveIt!

One of the challenging aspects of robotics is defining a path for the motion of a robot's arms to grasp an object, especially when obstacles may obstruct the most obvious path of motion. Fortunately, a ROS package called MoveIt! allows us to plan and execute a complicated trajectory.

A video created by Rethink Robotics shows how to use MoveIt! to plan the motion of Baxter's arms and then have MoveIt! actually cause a real or simulated Baxter to execute that motion. To see the video, go to: `https://www.youtube.com/watch?feature=player_detailpage&v=1Zdkwym42P4`.

A tutorial is available on the Rethink wiki site at `http://sdk.rethinkrobotics.com/wiki/MoveIt_Tutorial`.

First, start the Baxter simulator in Gazebo:

```
$ cd baxter_ws
$ ./baxter.sh sim
$ roslaunch baxter_gazebo baxter_world.launch
```

In a second terminal window, untuck Baxter's arms and start the Python script that starts `joint_trajectory_action_server`:

```
$ cd baxter_ws
$ ./baxter.sh sim
$ rosrun baxter_tools tuck_arms.py -u
$ rosrun baxter_interface joint_trajectory_action_server.py
```

The output on the screen should be as follows:

```
Initializing node...
Initializing joint trajectory action server...
Running. Ctrl-c to quit
```

In a third terminal, start MoveIt! and wait for the response:

```
$ cd baxter_ws
$ ./baxter.sh sim
$ roslaunch baxter_moveit_config baxter_grippers.launch
```

Look for the output:

. . .

```
You can start planning now!
```

Looking at the Gazebo window and the MoveIt! window, you'll see that Baxter looks the same in terms of the positions of its arms:

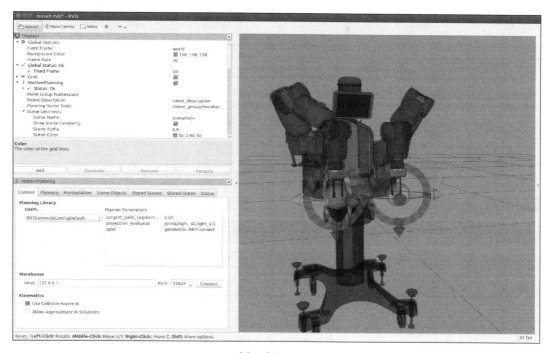

MoveIt! startup

In the screenshot, which is the rviz screen, the **Displays** and **Motion Planning** windows are shown on the left with the **Context** tab information showing. On the right, you can see the simulated Baxter in the starting position of MoveIt! with its arms untucked.

You can select any one of the **Displays** categories and modify the parameters. For example, the screenshot shows Baxter with a lightened **Background Color** chosen under **Global Options**.

Under the **MotionPlanning** panel, the **Context/Planning/Manipulation/Scene Objects/Stored Scenes/Stored States/Status** tabs are defined in the following table:

Tab	Uses
Context	Select the planning library and planner parameters; set collision awareness for IK solver
Planning	Set the start state, the goal state, and plan and execute moves of Baxter's arms
Manipulation	Object detection and manipulation
Scene Objects	Import or export scenes such as pillars or tabletops from a disk file or database, manipulate objects, and Publish Scene
Stored Scenes	Stored scenes on a database
Stored States	Store and load robot states
Status	Status

Planning a move of Baxter's arms with MoveIt!

Click on the **Planning** tab under **MotionPlanning**. On the **Planning** panel, look for the **Query** field and the **Select Start State** heading. Click on **Select Start State** to reveal a menu box and set it to <current>. Then, click on the **Update** button.

Now to move Baxter's arms, we will do the following:

1. Use arrows and rings to move Baxter's simulated arms to the desired positions. The desired goal positions should appear in orange in the simulation window.

2. Under the **Commands** area, choose the **Plan** button to see the trajectory of Baxter's arms in MoveIt!.

3. Choose the **Execute** button to see Baxter's arms move to the goal positions.

4. You should see red arms move from the start state to the final (goal) states:

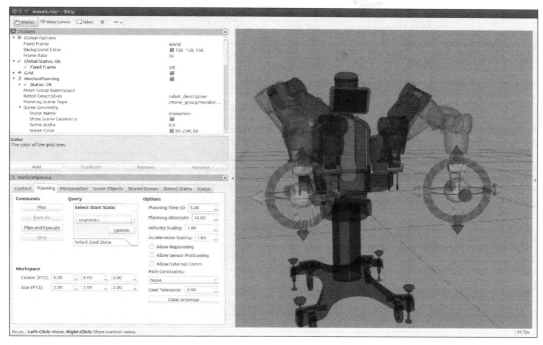

Baxter's arms and goal state for its arms

Next, have the arms move back to the original start positions to perform another move. To do this, under the **Query** field, click on **Select Goal State** to reveal the menu box and set it to <same as start>. Then, click on the **Update** button:

Query field to return arms to start positions

Adding objects to a scene

Select the **Scene Objects** tab from the **MotionPlanning** frame. If you have scenes in your computer's directories, you can import them using the **Scene Geometry** field by selecting **Import From Text**. Alternatively, use the following scene, which we created in the `PillarTable.scene` file. Make sure that this file is saved as a text file.

```
(noname)+
* pillar
1
box
0.308 0.13056 0.6528
0.7 -0.01 0.03
0.0108439 0.706876 0.0103685 0.707178
0 0 0 0
* tabletop
1
box
0.7 1.3 0.02
0.7 0.04 -0.13
0 0 0 1
0.705882 0.705882 0.705882 1
.
```

The first line of dimensions under `box` in the file represents the height, width, and length of the pillar in meters. The next line defines the position from Baxter's origin. The third line is the pose of the pillar as a quaternion. The following screenshot shows the results of importing the scene elements:

Baxter with tabletop and pillar

To manipulate the objects by moving or rotating them, select the object name (not the checkbox), and the arrows and rings should appear. Change their position with the green and blue arrows and rotate them with the ring. Moving the **Scale** slider will change the size of the object. Move the mouse to rotate the object, and roll the mouse wheel, if you have one, to zoom the object's size. You can save the scene (**Export As Text**) after you finish manipulating it.

Next, on the **Scene Objects** panel, click on the **Publish Scene** button under the **Scene Geometry** field. *This step is important and tells MoveIt! to plan around obstacles in the environment!*

Position of objects

When **pillar** is selected under **Current Scene Objects** (select the word, not the checkbox), values for its **Position (XYZ)** and **Rotation (RPY)** appear under **Manage Pose and Scale**. The position of x, y, and z of the centroid of the pillar is shown with respect to Baxter's origin. Baxter's x axis extends outward toward the viewer. The positive y axis is to the right in the view and the z axis runs upward. Note that the roll, pitch, and yaw are about the x, y, and z axes, respectively.

Planning a move to avoid obstacles with MoveIt!

In the following example, the left arm is going to move to the other side of the obstacle. MoveIt! will plan the trajectory so that Baxter's arm will not hit the pillar.

Return to the **Planning** tab on the **MotionPlanning** panel. First, move Baxter's right arm away from the pillar. **Plan** and then **Execute** moving the right arm.

We can now drag our interactive markers for Baxter's left arm to move the goal state to a location on the opposite side of the pillar. Each time you click on the **Plan** button, a different arm trajectory path is shown on the virtual Baxter. Each path avoids collision with the pillar.

Caution!

We move Baxter's other arm (the right arm, in this case) out of the way to avoid any possible collisions. This is necessary if the MoveIt! trajectories are used on the real Baxter. Move the right arm with the markers and choose **Plan** and **Execute**.

The following screenshot shows Baxter prior to moving the left arm around the pillar. Notice that the right arm is moved out of the way:

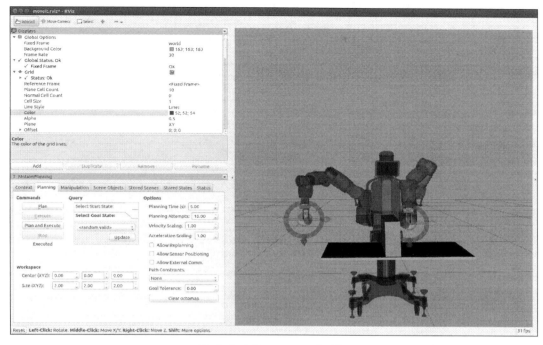

Baxter's right arm moved aside

Caution!

When using MoveIt! with the real Baxter, the arms sometimes move into odd positions. If this happens, move them apart and restart MoveIt!.

Now, click on **Execute** to see Baxter's arm avoid the obstacle and move to the goal position on the other side of the pillar. The following screenshot shows that Baxter's left arm has moved around the pillar to the other side of it:

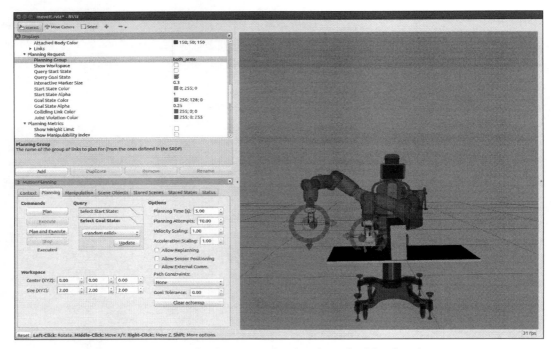

Baxter's simulated arm moved to the other side of the obstacle

Configuring a real Baxter setup

In the *Installing Baxter SDK software* section, we loaded the workstation computer SDK software used to control Baxter. This control can be either through the `baxter_example` programs described previously, through Python scripts, or using the command line. To control the real Baxter, the `baxter.sh` script is used to set up the environmental variables for configuring the network for Baxter. Ensure that you have completed the *Configuring Baxter shell* section before continuing.

The Baxter Research Robot can be configured to communicate with a development workstation computer over various network configurations. An Ethernet network or a wireless network can be established between Baxter and the workstation computer for bi-directional communication. For full descriptions of the various network configurations for Baxter and the workstation, refer to the Rethink wiki at `http://sdk.rethinkrobotics.com/wiki/Networking`.

To communicate with Baxter, the `baxter.sh` script must be edited (again) to modify the `baxter_hostname` variable. The default for `baxter_hostname` is the robot's serial number, located on the back of the robot, next to the power button. An alternative method is to assign a new robot hostname using the **Field Service Menu (FSM)**, accessed by plugging a USB keyboard into the back of Baxter. Refer to the Rethink wiki for more details (`http://sdk.rethinkrobotics.com/wiki/Field_Service_Menu_(FSM)`).

Using Baxter's serial number or assigned hostname within the `baxter.sh` script, find and edit the following line:

```
baxter_hostname="baxter_hostname.local"
```

Next, verify that either the `your_ip` variable *or* the `your_hostname` variable is set to specify the IP address or hostname of your workstation computer. The IP address should be the one assigned for the network connection. (When using the `$ ifconfig` command, this would be the IP address associated with the `inet addr` field.) The hostname must be resolvable by Baxter to identify the workstation computer hostname.

If there is any doubt, use the `ping <IP address>` or `ping <hostname>` command to verify that the network communication is working.

Find and modify one of the following variables inside the `baxter.sh` script:

```
your_ip="192.168.XXX.XXX"
your_hostname="my_computer.local"
```

Do not use both of these variables; otherwise `your_hostname` will take precedence. The unused variable should be commented out with a # symbol. Save your changes to `baxter.sh`.

To verify the ROS environment setup for Baxter, it is wise to run the `baxter.sh` script and verify the ROS variables. To do so, use the following commands:

```
$ cd ~/baxter_ws
$ ./baxter.sh
$ env | grep ROS
```

Check whether these important fields are set with the correct information:

- `ROS_MASTER_URI`: This should now contain Baxter's hostname
- `ROS_IP`: This should contain the workstation computer's IP address
  Or:
- `ROS_HOSTNAME`: If not using the IP address, this field should contain the workstation computer's hostname

Again, a cheat sheet for use with the real Baxter is provided for you to use with the example programs that follow. The commands for communicating, enabling, and untucking are provided here for your reference:

> **Real Baxter cheat sheet**
>
> To communicate with the real Baxter, use the following commands:
>
> ```
> $ cd ~/baxter_ws
> $ ./baxter.sh
> ```
>
> For subsequent terminal windows, use the following commands:
>
> ```
> $ cd ~/baxter_ws
> $ ./baxter.sh
> ```
>
> Be sure that Baxter is enabled and untucked for the examples using the real Baxter:
>
> ```
> $ rosrun baxter_tools enable_robot.py -e
> $ rosrun baxter_tools tuck_arms.py -u
> ```

If there are issues with Baxter's hardware, software, or network, refer to the general Baxter troubleshooting website at `http://sdk.rethinkrobotics.com/wiki/Troubleshooting`.

If there are problems with the workstation computer setup, refer to the Rethink wiki site at `http://sdk.rethinkrobotics.com/wiki/Workstation_Setup`.

Controlling a real Baxter

The `baxter_examples` programs described in the subsections within the *Launching Baxter Simulator in Gazebo* section also work on a real Baxter robot. Some additional arm control programs that work on a real Baxter but not on Baxter Simulator are described in the following sections.

Commanding joint position waypoints

This program is another example of joint position control for Baxter's arms. Baxter's arm is moved using the Zero-G mode to freely configure the arm's joints to the desired position. When the desired position is attained, the corresponding navigator button on the arm is pressed to record the waypoint position. This `baxter_examples` program is executed with the following command, specifying either right or left for the arm that is to be moved:

```
$ rosrun baxter_examples joint_position_waypoints.py -l <right or left>
```

The output should be as follows:

```
...

Press Navigator 'OK/Wheel' button to record a new joint position
waypoint.
Press Navigator 'Rethink' button when finished recording waypoints to
begin playback.

...
```

On the navigator, the center button (scroll wheel) is the control used to record all seven joint angles of the specified arm's current position. Waypoints can be recorded repeatedly until the lower button (the button with the Rethink icon) is pressed. This Rethink button activates playback mode, when the arm will begin going back to the waypoint positions in the order that they were recorded. This playback mode will continue to loop through the waypoints until the *Ctrl + C* or *Ctrl + Z* key combination is pressed. Parameters for speed and accuracy can be passed with the `joint_position_waypoints.py` command. Refer to Rethink's wiki site at http://sdk.rethinkrobotics.com/wiki/Joint_Position_Waypoints_Example.

Commanding joint torque springs

This `baxter_examples` program provides an example of Baxter's joint torque control. This program moves the arms into a neutral position, then applies joint torques at 1000 Hz to create an illusion of virtual springs. The program calculates and applies linear torques to any offset from the arm's starting position. When the arm is moved, these joint torques will return the arm to the starting position. Depending on the stiffness and damping applied to the joints, oscillation of the joints will occur.

This joint torque springs program is executed with the following command, specifying right or left for the arm that is to be manipulated:

```
$ rosrun baxter_examples joint_torque_springs.py -l <right or left>
```

The joint torques are configurable using the rqt reconfigure tool. To adjust the torque settings, type the following command in a new terminal:

```
$ rosrun rqt_reconfigure rqt_reconfigure
```

The following screenshot shows the `rqt_reconfigure` screen for `joint_torque_springs.py` for the left arm:

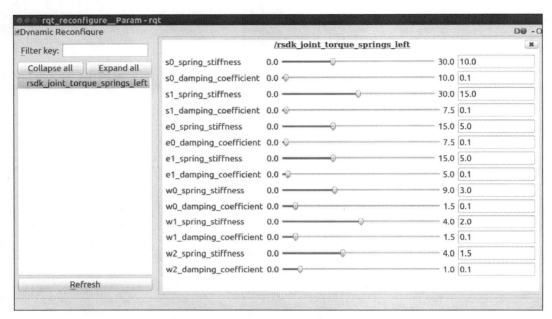

rqt reconfigure joint torque springs

Select `rsdk_joint_torque_springs` from the left panel to view the control menu. The spring stiffness and damping coefficient can be varied for each joint of the arm specified.

Be careful when changing these values!

If you experiment with Baxter's control system, you should record the initial values and reset the values to the originals after changing them.

Demonstrating joint velocity

Rethink provides a simple `baxter_examples` program to demonstrate the joint velocity control mode for Baxter's arms. This program begins by moving the arms into a neutral position. The joint velocity puppet program simply mirrors the movement of Baxter's arm when the other arm is moved in Zero-G mode. This `baxter_examples` program is executed with the following command, specifying either right or left for the arm that is to be moved:

```
$ rosrun baxter_examples joint_velocity_puppet.py -l <right or left>
```

A parameter for amplitude can be passed with this command to change the velocity applied to the puppet response. For more information on this command, refer to Rethink's wiki site at `http://sdk.rethinkrobotics.com/wiki/Puppet_Example`.

Additional examples

The `baxter_examples` programs also include programs for gripper control, camera control, and analog and digital input/output control. Refer to the Rethink wiki Baxter examples program site to get details on these programs: `http://sdk.rethinkrobotics.com/wiki/Examples`.

In addition, Rethink offers a series of video tutorials that provide information on everything from setting up Baxter to running the example programs. Referring to these videos may provide some help if you have problems with executing the example programs (`http://sdk.rethinkrobotics.com/wiki/Video_Tutorials`).

Visual servoing and grasping

One of the greatest features of a real Baxter is the capability to detect and grasp an object. This capability is called **visual servoing control**. Baxter's cuff camera and gripper combination makes this a determined objective.

Baxter's cuff camera provides 2D camera images that can be processed by computer vision software such as OpenCV. OpenCV provides a vast library of functions for processing real-time image data. Computer vision algorithms for thresholding, shape recognition, feature detection, edge detection, and many more are useful for 2D (and 3D) perception.

An example of visual servoing from the Rethink website is available at `http://sdk.rethinkrobotics.com/wiki/Worked_Example_Visual_Servoing`.

This is a basic implementation linking object detection with the autonomous movement of the arm to grasp the object. This project is a good example of the technique described previously. Unfortunately, this example works with ROS Hydro and uses OpenCV functions that have been deprecated.

Only using Baxter's 2D cameras limits the accuracy of grasping objects, making the depth of objects in the entire scene hard to determine. Typically, programs such as the one previously mentioned require a setup phase, in which an infrared sensor measurement to the table surface is required. An alternative is to use an external 3D camera such as the Kinect, ASUS, PrimeSense, or RealSense to detect the depth of objects and match that information with the RGB camera data. This requires calibrating the two image data streams. The Open Source Robotics Foundation has demo software for both 2D perception and manipulation and 3D perception at `https://github.com/osrf/baxter_demos`.

The calculation of inverse kinematics to move the gripper to the desired location is also crucial to this process.

Inverse kinematics

Using forward kinematics, we can determine the position of the gripper at any time. The inverse kinematic problem is to place the gripper at a desired location and orientation. This requires the calculation of the joint angles, then sending Baxter the seven joint angles and commanding the arm to move.

Rethink Robotics provides an **Inverse Kinematic (IK)** example that sets a specific endpoint position and orientation in the script and solves the required joint angles. The example and the Python script are described on these websites:

- `http://sdk.rethinkrobotics.com/wiki/IK_Service_Example`
- `http://sdk.rethinkrobotics.com/wiki/IK_Service_-_Code_Walkthrough`

To run the IK example to find the joint angles of the left limb (arm) for the fixed position and orientation in the Python script, type this command:

```
$ rosrun baxter_examples ik_service_client.py -l left
```

The pose of the left end-effector taken from the `ik_service_client.py` script is as follows:

```
'left': PoseStamped(
        header=hdr,
        pose=Pose(
            position=Point(
                x=0.657579481614,
                y=0.851981417433,
                z=0.0388352386502,
            ),
            orientation=Quaternion(
                x=-0.366894936773,
                y=0.885980397775,
                z=0.108155782462,
                w=0.262162481772,
            ),
        ),
    ),
```

Executing this yields the joint angles to move Baxter's left arm to the pose defined in the script. These angles would be used to move Baxter's arm to this pose from an arbitrary position, as shown by the example in the next section.

The script also sets an initial pose for the right arm. The endpoint position and orientation of the right arm can be found using the same command but with the `right` option. See the code to find the specific pose assigned for this.

Moving Baxter's arms with IK

To demonstrate the IK service example using the real Baxter's left arm, we will perform the following steps:

1. Power up Baxter and untuck both arms. This is the home position for the arms.

2. Record the endpoint state in the position and orientation of the left arm.

3. Move Baxter's left arm to an arbitrary position.

4. Modify the `ik_service_client.py` script in the `baxter_examples` package by entering the position and orientation of the untucked left arm and save the file under a different name in `catkin_workspace`.

5. Execute the script to get the joint angles of the left arm.

6. Type the angles into a modified `home_arms.py` script and execute it.

7. Record the new endpoint positions and orientations and compare them to the original values recorded in step 2.

First, execute the script to move Baxter's arms to the untucked position:

```
$ cd baxter_ws
$ ./baxter.sh
$ rosrun baxter_tools tuck_arms.py -u
```

Then, display the left-arm endpoint pose position and orientation and record the values to two decimal places with the following command:

```
$ rostopic echo /robot/limb/left/endpoint_state/pose -n1 -w4
```

Our output for the pose of the left arm is as follows:

```
position:

  x: 0.57
  y: 0.18
  z: 0.10
orientation:
  x: 0.13
  y: 0.99
  z: 0.00
  w: 0.02
```

The endpoint of Baxter should be out about 0.57 meters in x, 0.18 meters to the left of Baxter's vertical centerline in y, and about 0.10 meters up from the base in z. Next, by hand, move Baxter's arms arbitrarily so that you can test the IK server routine.

To modify the script `ik_service_client.py`, first use the following command:

```
$ roscd baxter_examples/scripts
```

Find the Python script to modify in this directory. To use the IK service with the endpoints of the untucked position and get angles for the left limb, put the x, y, z values and the orientation into the script `ik_service_client.py` file by editing the script with the values shown here, or use the values you obtained:

```
poses = {
        'left': PoseStamped(
            header=hdr,
            pose=Pose(
                position=Point(
                    x=0.57,
                    y=0.18,
                    z=0.10,
                ),
                orientation=Quaternion(
                    x=0.13,
                    y=0.99,
                    z=0.00,
                    w=0.02,
                ),
            ),
        ),
```

After editing `ik_service_client.py`, you should rename the file. Our new file was named `ik_home_arms_ch6RealBaxter.py`. To make it executable, type the following command:

```
$ chmod +x ik_home_arms_ch6RealBaxter.py
```

To run this script to find the joint angles of the left arm that would move Baxter's arm to the specific endpoint position, type this:

```
$ python ik_home_arms_ch6RealBaxter.py -l left
```

The output should be similar to the following:

```
SUCCESS - Valid Joint Solution Found from Seed Type: Current Joint Angles


IK Joint Solution:
{'left_w0': -1.8582664616409326, 'left_w1': -1.460468102595922,
'left_w2': 2.2756459061545797, 'left_e0': -1.6081637990992477, 'left_
e1': 1.9645288022495901, 'left_s0': 0.044896665837355125, 'left_s1':
-0.3326492980686455}

------------------
```

Your results will probably be different, but the end position of Baxter's arms should be the same as in this Python example, which moves the arms to the home (untucked) position.

Use the resulting angles to move Baxter's arms using the edited Python script, home_ arms.py. Change the values of the left arm joints and save the file with a new name. We used the MoveLeftArmToHome.py filename. Make the file executable using this command:

```
$ chmod +x MoveLeftArmToHome.py
```

Execute the new script and watch Baxter's left endpoint return to the desired position, if all goes well:

```
$ python MoveLeftArmToHome.py
```

Finally, display the left arm endpoint pose position and orientation and record the values to compare them to the original values for position and orientation:

```
$ rostopic echo /robot/limb/left/endpoint_state/pose -n1 -w4
```

After Baxter's arm moved, our values were fairly close to the originals:

```
position:
    x: 0.57
    y: 0.18
    z: 0.09
orientation:
    x: 0.12
    y: 0.99
    z: 0.00
    w: 0.02
```

Using a state machine to perform YMCA

Finite-state machines are powerful mechanisms for controlling the behavior of a system, especially robotic systems. ROS has implemented a state machine structure and behaviors in a Python-based library called **SMACH**. The SMACH library is independent of ROS and can be used with any Python project. SMACH provides an architecture for implementing hierarchical tasks and mechanisms to define transitions between these tasks. The advantages of using SMACH for a system include the following:

- Rapid prototyping of a state machine for testing and use

- Defining complex behaviors using a clear, straightforward method for design, maintenance, and debugging

- Introspection of the state machine, its transitions, and data flow using SMACH tools

For a complete set of documentation and tutorials on SMACH, examine these websites:

- `http://wiki.ros.org/smach`

- `http://wiki.ros.org/smach/Tutorials`

Some basic rules for implementing state machines on a robot are as follows:

- A robot can be in one—and only one—state at a time.

- A finite number of states must be identified.

- The state that a robot transitions to, will depend on the state that just completed. These behaviors are encapsulated in the states to which they correspond.

- Transitions between states are specified by the structure of the state machine.

- All possible outcomes of a state should be identified and corresponding behaviors should address those outcomes.

- States that only have one transition condition cannot fail and only have one outcome.

To underscore the usefulness of the SMACH package, we devised a simple and fun example for Baxter, which has been implemented by Mikal Cristen, a recent UHCL graduate. Because the UHCL Baxter is such a main attraction on our campus, this project was to endow the robot with an entertainment skill, specifically, dancing to YMCA.

This state machine has five states corresponding to Baxter's arm poses for each letter: Y, M, C, A, and a fifth state for a neutral pose. When one pose of the arms completes, the state will successfully complete and the next state will begin. The code for this state machine is implemented in the `YMCAStateMach.py` code that follows and will be described in subsequent paragraphs.

> The code for `YMCAStateMach.py` and `MoveControl.py` can be found in the `Chapter 6` folder of the Packt GitHub website for this book or at the website `https://github.com/FairchildC/ROS-Robotics-By-Example-2nd-Edition`

SMACH compels state machines to be implemented using Python procedures to provide flexibility in their implementation. Notice in the following code, the ROS convention for state machines is that the state names are identified in ALL_CAPS and the transition names are in lowercase:

```python
#!/usr/bin/env python

import rospy
from smach import State,StateMachine

from time import sleep
from MoveControl import Baxter_Arms

class Y(State):
  def __init__(self):
    State.__init__(self, outcomes=['success'])

    self.letter_y = {
        'letter': {
            'left':  [0.0, -1.0, 0.0, 0.0,  0.0, 0.0, 0.0],
            'right': [0.0, -1.0, 0.0, 0.0,  0.0, 0.0, 0.0]
                    } }
            #DoF Key [s0,s1,e0,e1,w0,w1,w2]

  def execute(self, userdata):
    rospy.loginfo('Give me a Y!')
    barms.supervised_move(self.letter_y)
    sleep(2)
    return 'success'

class M(State):
```

```
    def __init__(self):
      State.__init__(self, outcomes=['success'])

      self.letter_m = {
          'letter': {
              'left': [0.0, -1.50, 1.0, -0.052, 3.0, 2.094, 0.0],
              'right':[0.0, -1.50, -1.0, -0.052, -3.0, 2.094, 0.0]
                    } }
              #DoF Key [s0,s1,e0,e1,w0,w1,w2]

    def execute(self, userdata):
      rospy.loginfo('Give me a M!')
      barms.supervised_move(self.letter_m)
      sleep(2)
      return 'success'

class C(State):
  def __init__(self):
    State.__init__(self, outcomes=['success'])

    self.letter_c = {
        'letter': {
            'left': [0.80, 0.0, 0.0, -0.052,  3.0, 1.50, 0.0],
            'right':[0.0, -1.50, -1.0, -0.052, -3.0, 1.0, 0.0]
                  } }
            #DoF Key [s0,s1,e0,e1,w0,w1,w2]

  def execute(self, userdata):
    rospy.loginfo('Give me a C!')
    barms.supervised_move(self.letter_c)
    sleep(2)
    return 'success'

class A(State):
  def __init__(self):
    State.__init__(self, outcomes=['success'])

    self.letter_a = {
        'letter': {
            'left': [0.50, -1.0, -3.0, 1.0, 0.0, 0.0, 0.0],
            'right':[-0.50, -1.0, 3.0, 1.0,  0.0, 0.0, 0.0]
                  } }
```

```
                    #DoF Key [s0,s1,e0,e1,w0,w1,w2]

      def execute(self, userdata):
        rospy.loginfo('Give me an A!')
        barms.supervised_move(self.letter_a)
        sleep(2)
        return 'success'

  class Zero(State):
    def __init__(self):
      State.__init__(self, outcomes=['success'])

      self.zero = {
          'letter': {
              'left': [0.00, 0.00, 0.00, 0.00, 0.00, 0.00, 0.00],
              'right':[0.00, 0.00, 0.00, 0.00,  0.00, 0.00, 0.00]
                      } }
                        #DoF Key [s0,s1,e0,e1,w0,w1,w2]

      def execute(self, userdata):
        rospy.loginfo('Ta-da')
        barms.supervised_move(self.zero)
        sleep(2)
        return 'success'

if __name__ == '__main__':

  barms = Baxter_Arms()
  rospy.on_shutdown(barms.clean_shutdown)

  sm = StateMachine(outcomes=['success'])
  with sm:
    StateMachine.add('Y', Y(), transitions={'success':'M'})
    StateMachine.add('M', M(), transitions={'success':'C'})
    StateMachine.add('C', C(), transitions={'success':'A'})
    StateMachine.add('A', A(), transitions={'success':'ZERO'})
    StateMachine.add('ZERO', Zero(),         transitions={'success':'s
uccess'})

  sm.execute()
```

This Python script imports the following packages:

- `rospy`: This ROS package is used for information messages and to control Baxter's arms in the event a system shutdown occurs.

- `smach`: This ROS package imports the `State` and `StateMachine` classes and their methods.

- `time`: This Python package imports the `sleep` function.

- `MoveControl`: This package imports the `Baxter_Arms` class and the methods for interacting with Baxter's arms. Look for this Python script in the `Chapter06` folder of the Packt GitHub website for this book.

Next, classes are defined for each of the states of the state machine: `Y`, `M`, `C`, `A`, and `Zero`. Each of these classes creates a new, initialized instance of the SMACH `State` class, identifying all of the possible outcomes for that state. For these states, `success` is the only outcome. Next, each of Baxter's 14 arm joints are assigned a value (in radians). These values are assigned in the specific order they are expected (ultimately) by the `baxter_interface` package. This order, as indicated in the code comment, is S0, S1, E0, E1, W0, W1, W2.

Each of the states also implements an execute method, where the actual work is done. In each of these state execute methods, the `supervised_move` function for moving Baxter's arms is called passing the argument with all of the joint angles for Baxter's arms. After the function is called, the process sleeps for 2 seconds to allow all of Baxter's arm movements to stop. When the state finishes, the `success` flag is returned as an outcome to the calling function.

The main program of `YMCAStateMach.py` creates an instance of the `Baxter_Arms` class and initializes the attributes for the instance. An instance of a `StateMachine` class is also created and a list of possible outcomes is passed as an argument. The empty `StateMachine` (`sm`) instance is opened and populated with the different states we defined. Each state is added with the add function. For example, the first `StateMachine.add` function adds the state `Y`, with an instance of the class `Y()` and, on completion with a successful outcome, the `StateMachine` class will transition to state `M`. Similarly, the state `M` is added with an instance of the class `M()` and, with a successful outcome, will transition to state `C`. The states `C` and `A` are added in a similar manner, as is the last state `ZERO`. Upon completion, the state `ZERO` will return the successful outcome for `StateMachine`.

Be sure that the `MoveControl.py` and `YMCAStateMach.py` scripts are in your directory and have execute permissions. Real Baxter or Baxter Simulator should be running and enabled (preferably in an untucked pose). Then, run the state machine with the following command:

```
$ python YMCAStateMach.py
```

You should see Baxter's arms transition to a Y pose, then an M pose, then a C pose, then an A pose, and end in a pose similar to the `arms_to_zero_angles.py` pose. The `INFO` messages to the terminal window should be similar to the following:

```
[ INFO ] : State machine starting in initial state 'Y' with userdata:
[]
[INFO] [1502141862.054272]: Give me a Y!
[INFO] [1502141862.054742]: Movement in progress.
[INFO ] : State machine transitioning 'Y':'success'-->'M'
[INFO] [1502141867.569880]: Give me a M!
[INFO] [1502141867.570851]: Movement in progress.
[INFO] [1502141872.782220]: Robot Disabled
[ INFO ] : State machine transitioning 'M':'success'-->'C'
[INFO] [1502141874.784842]: Give me a C!
[INFO] [1502141874.785353]: Movement in progress.
[INFO] [1502141876.906888]: Robot Disabled
[INFO ] : State machine transitioning 'C':'success'-->'A'
[INFO] [1502141878.909487]: Give me an A!
[INFO] [1502141878.910383]: Movement in progress.
[INFO ] : State machine transitioning 'A':'success'-->'ZERO'
[INFO] [1502141889.262132]: Ta-da
[INFO] [1502141889.262614]: Movement in progress.
[ INFO ] : State machine terminating 'ZERO':'success':'success'
```

Summary

In this chapter, we described a real and popular robot called Baxter, manufactured by Rethink Robotics Corporation. Many of the details of the robot can be discovered using Baxter Simulator, which displays a simulated Baxter using the Gazebo program. Since Baxter has two movable arms, much of the chapter describes the arms and control of them.

The chapter started with a description of Baxter in both the research and the manufacturing versions. Baxter's arms and sensors and the control modes for the arms were described.

After downloading the Baxter Simulator software, the simulator was used to demonstrate various examples of controlling Baxter with Python scripts supplied by Rethink Robotics. Baxter can be controlled using ROS commands, a keyboard, or a joystick. We have also included several Python scripts that will make the control of Baxter easier if joint angles are specified for the movement of the arms.

The ROS frame transform package tf was used to show the relationship between the coordinate frames of Baxter's base and other elements of the arms. The view in rviz displays these frames.

MoveIt! is another package that works with a simulated Baxter, as well as with the real robot. MoveIt! was explained and the method of planning and executing arm trajectories even with obstacles in Baxter's path was discussed.

Finally, we were introduced to the real Baxter by explaining the setup procedure for communication between a workstation and Baxter. Various examples showing control of the real Baxter were also discussed. A state machine using the ROS SMACH package was implemented to move Baxter's arms into different positions.

In the next chapter, a ROS view of quadrotors will be described using both simulated and real air vehicles. The simulated air vehicle is a generalized representation of a quadrotor and is great for learning to control the craft before you decide to try flying a real one.

In addition to this action packed chapter for Baxter, *Chapter 10, Controlling Baxter with MATLAB©* presents the **Robotics System Toolbox**. This MATLAB toolbox allows ROS commands to be used with MATLAB scripts to control Baxter.

Making a Robot Fly

7

Today, flying vehicles are very popular. Even in their primary configuration, controlled by a radio controller, some flying vehicles can be considered robots that respond to their environment to stay in the air. Flying robots that have altitude sensors can hover in place. If they have **Global Positioning System** (**GPS**) sensors, they know where they are and can fly to a specific location. As more sensors are added, their capabilities increase.

As you will see in this chapter, there are some commonalities between mobile robots and flying robots in terms of their command and control. ROS utilizes these commonalities in the structure of the nodes, topics, messages, and services of these two categories of robots. The topic cmd_vel, which was used for Turtlesim and TurtleBot earlier in this book, is again used for the simulated and real quadrotors presented in this chapter. For sensors and devices that are common between mobile robots and flying robots, ROS takes advantage of these commonalities through its standard topic and message interfaces. Just as with other robots, ROS standard topics and messages communicate information from the onboard sensors about the state of the quadrotor and its environment.

This chapter begins by providing an overview of how a quadrotor works to stay in the air. The basic steps of learning to fly a quadrotor are discussed so that you can quickly gain expertise in flying. Three ROS quadrotors are introduced: one simulated quadrotor, Hector, which exists only in Gazebo, and two real quadrotors, a tiny Crazyflie and the Bebop. The Hector and Crazyflie quadrotors will be controlled through a common Xbox 360 controller interface. The advanced capabilities for SLAM and autonomous navigation will be explored. References are also given for controlling multiple quadrotors using ROS.

We will cover the following topics in this chapter:

- How quadrotors fly
- The capability of the sensors that are used in quadrotors
- Techniques and rules for flying quadrotors
- Examples of quadrotors using ROS
- Flying the simulated Hector Quadrotor
- Flying real quadrotors: Crazyflie and Bebop

Introducing quadrotors

Quadrotors, sometimes called quadcopters, are part of a broad category of robots called **Unmanned Aerial Vehicles (UAVs)** that have four motors and propellers to provide lift for the craft. In this chapter, we will introduce some of these flying robots that are controlled by ROS. The chapter will consider both simulations and flying the real thing.

The following figure shows the Crazyflie quadrotor that will be discussed later in this chapter:

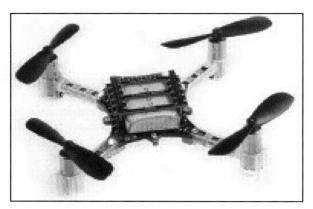

Crazyflie quadrotor

In the image, notice the four propellers or rotors that act to lift the craft vertically for takeoff and keep it in flight at a certain altitude when flying. First, such crafts are classified as **rotocrafts** because lift is generated by the rotors shown in the figure, rather than the wings of an airplane. Second, they are not helicopters, because the main propeller and the tail rotor control the flight of a helicopter. The tail rotor of a helicopter keeps the craft from rotating itself due to the rotation of the main horizontal propeller.

With a quadrotor, all flight maneuvers are made by varying the speed of one or more propellers. The propellers are called **fixed-pitch** propellers, since their angle with respect to the quadrotor body cannot be changed. There are more sophisticated quadrotors available with propellers that have variable pitch, but they will not be considered in this chapter. On helicopters, the main propeller is a variable-pitch propeller to control the craft's direction of flight.

For a general discussion of quadrotors, visit `https://en.wikipedia.org/wiki/Quadcopter`.

Why are quadrotors so popular?

Quadrotors are a popular option for hobbyists and researchers. They have a number of attractive characteristics; primarily:

- Relatively low-cost compared to other aerial craft
- Not too difficult to fly due to electronic stabilization during flight
- Depending on the size and type, some quadrotors can be flown indoors as well as outdoors
- With the addition of a camera, the quadrotor is excellent for outdoor aerial photography

Defining roll, pitch, and yaw

As in any field of robotics, there is a vocabulary which is important for speaking precisely about the operations and tasks involved. A flying craft is said to have six DOF because the position of the craft can be located in space (x, y, and z coordinates) and in orientation with respect to three axes. This position is usually defined in terms of the position of a fixed point, usually on the ground, such as the point of takeoff. The figure of the plane here shows how the orientation of the plane is defined in terms of angles around the coordinate axes of the airplane itself. The same definition would apply to the quadrotor:

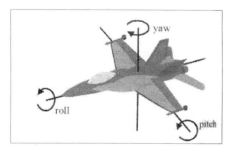

Roll, pitch, and yaw for an airplane

Pitch is the movement of the nose, up or down in forward flight. **Roll** is rotation around the longitudinal axis that runs along the length of the aircraft. **Yaw** is the movement of the nose to the left or right, which is rotation about the vertical axis. The amount of rotation is typically stated in degrees.

You can imagine two coordinate systems involved in flight. The fixed system usually defined at a ground point and the system belonging to the flying craft. The relationship between these coordinate systems becomes important for flight maneuvers and when making a flight plan.

The important difference between airplane flight control and quadrotor control is that in an airplane, turns and other maneuvers are controlled by the movement of flight surfaces, such as ailerons to control roll and a rudder to control yaw. Pitch is controlled by the elevator. For fixed-pitch quadrotors, only the speed of the propellers can be controlled. This control determines the direction and orientation of the quadrotor, as well as the speed over the ground.

Turning an aircraft to change its heading is called **banking**, because this requires the aircraft to roll to achieve an angle of bank. When the plane returns to level flight on a new heading, the plane would have no pitch, roll, or yaw with respect to its own coordinate system during straight and level flight. A quadrotor craft is different in that it can turn on its own yaw axis without banking. It can even fly backwards!

How do quadrotors fly?

The quadrotor has two pairs of counter-rotating propellers. When hovering, the propellers rotate at the same speed and provide **lift** to keep the craft in the air, overcoming the pull of gravity. They are counter-rotating to negate the torque that would cause the body of the quadrotor to rotate in the opposite direction if only one propeller turned. Since the propellers cannot change pitch, the lift vector is always in a direction perpendicular to the plane of the rotors. The gravity vector is always perpendicular to the ground.

According to our previous discussion of the airplane flying, we expect to control the pitch, roll, and yaw of the quadrotor to control banking and heading, as well as the forward speed. A throttle control varies the speed of rotation of the propellers. For example, in level flight, if the rotational speed of the propellers is increased, the craft will rise. Thus, what is often called a **throttle** on the user's flight controller is really an altitude control for a hovering quadrotor. In forward or backward motion, the throttle does control speed over the ground.

To move the quadrotor forward, the vehicle must tilt in the forward direction, which causes the front of the craft to pitch down. This is done by increasing the rotational speed of the rear pair of propellers. As shown in the figure, the lift vector now has a component in the forward direction, so the craft moves forward. Thus, the lift vector overcomes the downward force of gravity and the drag force caused by the air resistance as the quadrotor moves through the air. A component of lift is in the forward direction and causes the craft to fly forward. However, the lift component opposing gravity is slightly reduced. The amount of lift increase to keep the craft level is determined by the flight control software for the quadrotor:

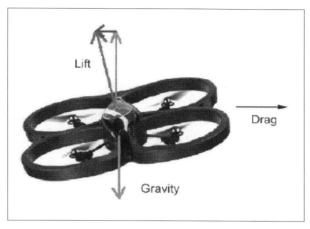

Quadrotor flying forward

The next figure shows a top view of a quadrotor in flight with the forward propeller **1** rotating **clockwise (CW)** and propeller **4** rotating **counterclockwise (CCW)**. To achieve forward motion, increasing the speed of motor **2** (rotating CW) and motor **3** (rotating CCW) with respect to motors **1** and **4** will cause the craft to pitch down and fly forward:

Quadrotor propellers

If you want to roll the quadrotor, the speed of the propellers on one or other of the lateral sides has to be increased, such as motors **2** and **4**. To yaw the craft, the speed of the two motors across from each other diagonally is decreased, and the other two motors are speeded up. This imparts angular torque to the aircraft, which makes it turn. An example of this would be to increase the speed of motors **3** and **4**.

If you own a quadrotor, notice the pitch (tilt) of the propeller blades on the propellers that rotate CW and those that rotate CCW. The upward tilt of the blades causes lift by the propeller rotating, with the upward edge cutting into the air.

Unfortunately, determining and setting the rotational speeds of the four propellers for such control in flight is quite difficult. Fortunately, in practice, the calculations for the speed of the propellers are carried out by a microcontroller and the appropriate software when commands are given to maneuver the quadrotor. The results of the calculations by the microcontroller are output to an electronic motor control unit, which adjusts the speed of the individual propellers.

The algorithm that converts commands from the ground-based control device to the motor controller is typically a **PID controller**. For those interested in the math, the following website explains PID for quadrotors: `http://blog.oscarliang.net/ quadcopter-pid-explained-tuning/`.

In manual flight, the operator commands various maneuvers, such as takeoff, forward flight, and landing using a flight-control unit with joystick-like controls. Many quadrotors also allow control by smartphones, tablets such as iPads, and similar devices. The software interfaces for many quadrotors are provided by the manufacturer and are unique to that quadrotor. We have chosen quadrotors that can be controlled by ROS to illustrate the use of ROS in flying them.

The basic control of the quadrotor from the ground is to command its altitude by causing it to rise or descend and control its direction and attitude. The attitude of a flying craft represents its pitch and roll or bank with respect to the Earth's horizon. The electronic motor control unit of the craft makes the necessary changes or corrections to the speed of the propellers to achieve the result commanded.

Components of a quadrotor

The main components for the flight of a quadrotor craft are the frame, or body, the motors, and the propellers. The body holds onboard flight and motor control circuitry, communications circuitry, and a battery. In flight, the quadrotor reports its condition and other flight information to the ground-based control device using **telemetry**.

For the quadrotor, telemetry is the wireless transmission of various parameters, such as the battery condition and the position and orientation of the craft. On the craft, there is a set of measuring units called **sensors** that measure the parameters that are encoded and transmitted to the ground-based control device.

Adding sensors

One important application of quadrotors is for aerial photography. Some models have a camera built directly into the body. Other models have cameras attached underneath the body. Usually, the camera is controlled from the ground to take pictures or videos.

In addition, some quadrotors may have a GPS receiver on board. The position of the craft over the Earth is available and some quadrotors can be guided to traverse a selected course through a series of GPS waypoints.

For more information about the GPS system, visit `http://www.gps.gov/systems/gps/`.

There are many models of quadrotors on the market. For a comparison, visit `http://quadcopterhq.com/best-quadcopters/`.

Since manufacturers are producing new quadrotors in complete or kit form, you should check websites that review the latest craft if you are in the market to buy one.

Quadrotor communications

There are a number of communication methods that allow quadrotors to be controlled for autonomous or manually controlled flight. Here are a few examples:

- **GPS** provides position data for your quadrotor if it has a GPS receiver. Using maps for GPS that can be downloaded, you can plot a course for the craft and it will fly that course autonomously.

- **Wi-Fi** communication can allow manual control of the quadrotor using smartphones and tablets. After downloading the manufacturer's software from a website, a screen appears with an image of flight controls that mimic joysticks that you can use to fly and control the quadrotor. Data from the quadrotor can also be received on these devices. If the drone has a camera, the camera view can be seen on these devices. Some quadrotors come with their own controllers that usually include joystick-type controls to fly the craft.

- **Bluetooth** connection provides another method for transmitting information to and from the quadrotor. The range of the signal is limited to 10 meters (32 feet) for mobile devices.

- Some quadrotors may use **Radio Frequency (RF)** signals to communicate with the craft. Radio-controlled crafts, such as model airplanes, have been available for many years. These signals allow for a much longer range of communication.

Understanding quadrotor sensors

The onboard flight controller circuitry receives information from sensors that provide data about the craft in flight. Some of the possible sensors that determine the attitude, altitude, and direction of flight include:

- A **gyroscope** that determines the attitude of the craft, including its pitch and roll. This indicates the rotational motion of the craft.

- An **accelerometer** that determines the rate of change of velocity of the craft with respect to the three axes.

- An **altimeter** or **barometer** that determines the altitude of the craft above ground. At low altitudes, a down-looking sonar sensor may be used to determine altitudes up to several meters or more.

- A **magnetometer** that serves as a compass to indicate the craft's direction by using the Earth's magnetic field as a reference.

The accelerometer and magnetometer need calibration to initialize their readings to the conditions where the flights will take place. For each quadrotor, it is therefore important to follow the manufacturer's instructions carefully to setup the craft before flights.

Inertial measurement unit

The **inertial measurement unit (IMU)** is a combined gyroscope and accelerometer. This unit will indicate the complete information about the flight characteristics of the quadrotor. Typically, the unit will measure the acceleration and orientation of the flying craft in all three dimensions.

These sensors allow indoor and outdoor flight. However, all the sensors previously mentioned suffer from slight errors that may accumulate during flight, so caution is necessary while flying in confined spaces.

Quadrotor condition sensors

Many quadrotors have sensors that will indicate information about their condition, including the motor temperature and the percentage of battery charge. This information is relayed by telemetry to the ground-based control device.

ROS, with its message passing capability, is ideally suited for the communication of sensor messages between the quadrotor and the ground-based control device. Various types of ROS sensor messages are listed at `http://wiki.ros.org/sensor_msgs`.

Preparing to fly your quadrotor

Some quadrotors can be dangerous if flown carelessly. Depending on the size, weight, and power of the quadrotor, collisions with property, people, or pets can cause serious damage. At the very least, crashing your quadrotor could damage the craft and end your flying career until you purchase a new one or repair the damaged one.

Although this book is not about flying quadrotors, we believe that some discussion of good flying practice is necessary. This discussion will be particularly helpful to new pilots.

Since this chapter is not about flying the quadrotor, but how ROS is used to control the craft, we will refer you to various websites on the Internet. Searching for *How to fly a quadrotor* or *How to fly a quadcopter* will yield over one million hits. Therefore, it is better to refine the search and specify the type of quadrotor you wish to fly.

Many websites present articles on flying quadrotors. For example, various tutorials are available on the following websites:

- `http://uavcoach.com/`
- `http://uavcoach.com/how-to-fly-a-quadcopter-guide/`

There are also many YouTube videos showing quadrotor or quadcopter flying techniques.

Some of the things that should be considered before and during flight are as follows:

- Testing your quadrotor
- Preflight checklist
- Safety and dangers
- Rules and regulations

Testing your quadrotor

When your new quadrotor first arrives, it is natural to want to begin flying immediately. Our suggestion is to be patient and take time to familiarize yourself with the quadrotor and its flight controller. We found that removing the propellers to test the quadrotor indoors was a good way to understand the craft and its controller without any danger of crashing.

Also, some practice on a simulator such as Hector (described later) will help you understand the flight controls. Remember that the controls will be reversed for direction and pitch control when the quadrotor is flying towards you, as compared to when the craft is flying away from you. A little time using the simulator will improve your flying ability.

Pre-flight checklist

Any good pilot follows a checklist before flight. Some of the basics are as follows:

- Check that the quadrotor is not damaged and that its battery is charged.
- Make sure that the flight controller is disarmed so the quadrotor cannot take off until you are ready.
- Make sure the area for flight is clear of obstacles and people.
- When flying the quadrotor, always be aware of the surroundings and keep the quadrotor in sight. Flying over people or their private property without permission is usually illegal in most countries.
- When flying in a public area, inform the police or the appropriate authorities that flights will take place. Be sure to keep the craft well away from buildings, trees, and people.
- If flying using GPS, be sure the GPS satellite signals are locked on before flying. It could take several minutes for the onboard GPS receiver to get the signals from at least four satellites.

Precautions when flying your quadrotor

When you are learning, start your flights outdoors in light-wind or no-wind conditions. A high wind can cause the quadrotor to fly out of control. Remember that if the battery fails, the quadrotor will not glide but will fall straight down. Keep aware of the battery percentage charge and bring the quadrotor to its landing point when the battery charge is low, below 20 percent to be safe.

Use caution when flying quadrotors

Motors can fail and propellers can break due to a hard landing. Communication between the ground-based control device and the quadrotor can be interrupted or lost. If the motors or propellers are damaged, controlled flight may be impossible. If the battery drains in flight, the quadrotor will fall to the ground unless it has a fail-safe mode that returns the craft home when the battery is low or communication with the quadrotor is lost.

Following the rules and regulations

Quadrotors are considered **drones** and these unmanned aircraft systems are regulated. In the United States, the **Federal Aviation Administration (FAA)** regulates flights and requires the registration of some craft, including quadrotors, based on the weight of the craft. Around the world, the **International Civil Aviation Organization (ICAO)** works with many countries to regulate flights.

The FAA has issued guidelines for flying craft in the general category of *Model Aircraft* with the following guidelines quoted from the website: `https://www.faa.gov/uas/model_aircraft`:

- Fly below 400 feet and remain clear of surrounding obstacles
- Keep the aircraft within a visual line of sight at all times
- Remain well clear of, and do not interfere with, manned aircraft operations
- Don't fly within 5 miles of an airport unless you contact the airport and control tower before flying
- Don't fly near people or stadiums
- Don't fly an aircraft that weighs more than 55 lbs (24.9 kg)
- Don't be careless or reckless with your unmanned aircraft — you could be fined for endangering people or other aircraft

The ICAO website is at `http://www.icao.int/about-icao`.

You can also read the book *Building Multicopter Video Drones*, *Ty Audronis*, *Packt Publishing* (`www.PacktPub.com`). The book contains many useful suggestions and safety tips for flying quadrotors.

Be aware that requirements might change and probably will, so keep up with the latest flying regulations for your quadrotor.

Using ROS with UAVs

The ROS wiki currently contains the following list of ROS quadrotors and quadcopters:

- AscTec Pelican and Hummingbird quadrotors
- Bitcraze Crazyflie
- Erle-Copter
- Navio2

View the list at `http://wiki.ros.org/Robots` in the future for additions to this list and the website `http://www.ros.org/news/robots/uavs/` to get the latest ROS UAV news.

A number of universities have adopted using the AscTec Hummingbird as their ROS UAV of choice. For this book, we present a simulator called Hector Quadrotor and two real quadrotors that use ROS: Crazyflie and Bebop.

Introducing Hector Quadrotor

The hardest part of learning about flying robots is the constant crashing. From learning flight control for the first time, to testing new hardware or flight algorithms, the resulting failures can have a huge cost in terms of broken hardware components. To avoid such costs, a simulated air vehicle designed and developed for ROS is ideal.

A simulated quadrotor UAV for the ROS Gazebo environment has been developed by Team Hector of Technische Universität Darmstadt. This quadrotor, called Hector Quadrotor, is enclosed in the `hector_quadrotor` metapackage. This metapackage contains the URDF description for the quadrotor UAV, its flight controllers, and launch files for running the quadrotor simulation in Gazebo.

Advanced use of the Hector Quadrotor simulation allows the user to record sensor data such as Lidar, depth camera, and so on. The quadrotor simulation can also be used to test flight algorithms and control approaches in simulation.

The `hector_quadrotor` metapackage contains the following key packages:

- `hector_quadrotor_description`: This package provides a URDF model of the Hector Quadrotor UAV and the quadrotor configured with various sensors. Several URDF quadrotor models exist in this package, each configured with specific sensors and controllers.

- `hector_quadrotor_gazebo`: This package contains launch files for executing Gazebo and spawning one or more Hector Quadrotors.

- `hector_quadrotor_gazebo_plugins`: This package contains four UAV specific plugins:

  ○ The simple controller `gazebo_quadrotor_simple_controller` subscribes to a `cmd_vel` topic and calculates the required forces and torques

  ○ A sensor plugin `gazebo_ros_baro` simulates a barometric altimeter

  ○ The plugins `gazebo_quadrotor_propulsion` and `gazebo_quadrotor_aerodynamics` simulate the propulsion, aerodynamics, and drag from messages containing motor voltages and wind vector input

- `hector_quadrotor_controllers`: This package provides a library and a node for controlling a quadrotor using `ros_control`.

- `hector_quadrotor_controller_gazebo`: This package implements the `ros_controlRobotHWSim` interface for the quadrotor controller.

- `hector_quadrotor_model`: This package provides libraries used to model several aspects of quadrotor dynamics.

- `hector_quadrotor_teleop`: This package provides a node and launch files for controlling a quadrotor using a joystick or gamepad.

- `hector_quadrotor_demo`: This package provides sample launch files that run the Gazebo quadrotor simulation and `hector_slam` for indoor and outdoor scenarios.

The entire list of packages for the `hector_quadrotor` metapackage is given in the next section.

Loading Hector Quadrotor

The repository for the `hector_quadrotor` software can be found at: `https://github.com/tu-darmstadt-ros-pkg/hector_quadrotor`.

At the time this chapter is being revised, the `hector_quadrotor` software is in a development release for ROS Kinetic. The instructions for installing this release are provided here, but you should check the GitHub repository identified in the preceding paragraph to determine whether a Debian package has been created. If it has, you can use the `apt-get` command to install it on your system. Otherwise, install the Kinetic development release of `hector_quadrotor` in your catkin workspace using the following commands:

```
$ cd ~/catkin_ws/src
$ wstool init hector https://raw.github.com/tu-darmstadt-ros-pkg/hector_quadrotor/kinetic-devel/tutorials.rosinstall
$ wstool update
```

Prior to performing a `catkin_make` on your workspace, you will need to install the `geographic_msgs` package:

```
$ sudo apt-get install ros-kinetic-geographic-msgs
```

Then proceed with:

```
$ cd ~/catkin_ws
$ catkin_make
```

A large number of ROS packages are downloaded with the `hector_quadrotor` metapackage, including the metapackages for `hector_slam`, `hector_localization`, `hector_gazebo`, and `hector_models`. Within these metapackages, this installation downloads the following packages:

- `hector_components_description`
- `hector_compressed_map_transport`
- `hector_gazebo_plugins`
- `hector_gazebo_thermal_camera`
- `hector_gazebo_worlds`
- `hector_geotiff`
- `hector_geotiff_plugins`
- `hector_imu_attitude_to_tf`
- `hector_imu_tools`
- `hector_map_server`
- `hector_map_tools`
- `hector_mapping`
- `hector_marker_drawing`
- `hector_nav_msgs`
- `hector_pose_estimation`
- `hector_pose_estimation_core`
- `hector_quadrotor_actions`
- `hector_quadrotor_controller_gazebo`
- `hector_quadrotor_controllers`
- `hector_quadrotor_demo`
- `hector_quadrotor_description`
- `hector_quadrotor_gazebo`
- `hector_quadrotor_gazebo_plugins`
- `hector_quadrotor_interface`
- `hector_quadrotor_model`
- `hector_quadrotor_pose_estimation`
- `hector_quadrotor_teleop`
- `hector_sensors_description`
- `hector_sensors_gazebo`
- `hector_slam_launch`
- `hector_trajectory_server`
- `hector_uav_msgs`
- `hector_xacro_tools`
- `message_to_tf`

A number of these packages will be discussed as the Hector Quadrotor simulations are described in the next section.

Launching Hector Quadrotor in Gazebo

Two demonstration tutorials are available to provide simulated applications of the Hector Quadrotor for both outdoor and indoor environments. These simulations are described in the next sections.

Before you begin the Hector Quadrotor simulations, check your ROS Master using the following command in your terminal window:

```
$ echo $ROS_MASTER_URI
```

If this variable is set to localhost or the IP address of your computer, no action is needed. If not, type the following command:

```
$ export ROS_MASTER_URI=http://localhost:11311
```

The preceding command should be typed into every new terminal window that is opened, or it can also be added to your .bashrc file. In the .bashrc file, delete or comment out (with a #) any other commands setting the ROS_MASTER_URI variable.

Flying Hector outdoors

The quadrotor outdoor flight demo software is included as part of the hector_quadrotor metapackage. Start the simulation by typing the following command:

```
$ roslaunch hector_quadrotor_demo outdoor_flight_gazebo.launch
```

This launch file loads a rolling landscape environment into the Gazebo simulation and spawns a model of the Hector Quadrotor configured with a Hokuyo UTM-30LX sensor. An rviz node is also started and configured specifically for the quadrotor outdoor flight. A large number of flight positions and control parameters are initialized and loaded into the Parameter Server.

Note that the quadrotor propulsion model parameters for the quadrotor_propulsion plugin and quadrotor drag model parameters for the quadrotor_aerodynamics plugin are displayed. Then, look for the four **Enabled** messages:

```
Enabled wrench output
Enabled attitude output
Enabled yaw rate output
Enabled thrust output
```

The following screenshots show both the Gazebo and rviz display windows when the Hector outdoor flight simulation is launched:

Hector Quadrotor outdoor Gazebo view

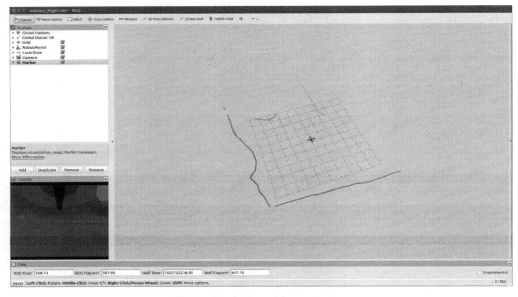

Hector Quadrotor outdoor rviz view

The view from the onboard camera can be seen in the lower-left corner of the rviz window. If you do not see the camera image on your rviz screen, be sure that **Camera** has been added to your **Displays** panel on the left and the checkbox has been checked. If you would like to pilot the quadrotor using the camera, it is best to uncheck the checkboxes for `tf` and `robot_model` because the visualizations sometimes block the view. The quadrotor appears on the ground in the simulation and it is ready for takeoff. Its forward direction is marked by a red mark on its leading motor mount. To fly the quadrotor, you should launch the joystick controller software for the Xbox 360 controller. In a second terminal window, launch the joystick controller software with a launch file from the `hector_quadrotor_teleop` package:

```
$ roslaunch hector_quadrotor_teleop xbox_controller.launch
```

This launch file launches the joy node to process all joystick input from the left stick and right stick on the Xbox 360 controller, as shown in the following figure. The message published by joy node contains the current state of the joystick axes and buttons. The `teleop` node subscribes to these messages and publishes messages on the topic `/command/twist`. These messages provide the velocity and direction for the quadrotor flight.

Several other joystick controllers are currently supported by the ROS `joy` package, including PS3 and Logitech devices. For this launch, the joystick device is accessed as `/dev/input/js0` and is initialized with a deadzone value of 0.050000. Parameters to set the joystick buttons and axes are as follows:

* `/teleop/go_button: 6`
* `/teleop/slow_button: 4`
* `/teleop/stop_button: 2`
* `/teleop/thrust_axis: -3`
* `/teleop/x_axis: 5`
* `/teleop/y_axis: 4`
* `/teleop/yaw_axis: 1`
* `/teleop/z_axis: 2`

These parameters map to the left stick and the right stick controls and buttons on the Xbox 360 controller shown in the following diagram. The directions of the sticks' controls are as follows:

- **Left stick:**
    - ○ Forward (Up) is ascend
    - ○ Backward (Down) is descend
    - ○ Right is rotate clockwise
    - ○ Left is rotate counterclockwise

- **Right stick:**
    - ○ Forward (Up) is fly forward
    - ○ Backward (Down) is fly backward
    - ○ Right is fly right
    - ○ Left is fly left

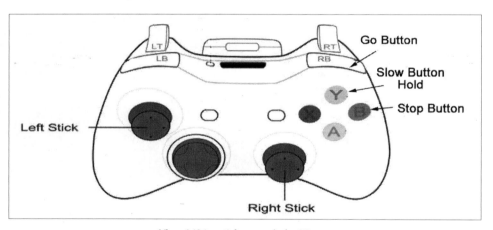

Xbox 360 joystick controls for Hector

To begin your flight, press and release the **Go Button** indicated in the previous figure. Now, use the joystick to fly around the simulated outdoor environment. Pressing and holding the **Slow Button** will cause the quadrotor's speed to decrease to 20 percent.

Pressing the **Stop Button** will cause the simulated quadrotor's motors to stop and the vehicle will drop straight to the ground.

The pilot's view can be seen in the **Camera** image view at the bottom-left of the rviz screen.

Within ROS, a clearer understanding of the interactions between the active nodes and topics can be obtained using the `rqt_graph` tool. The following diagram depicts all currently active nodes (except debug nodes) enclosed in oval shapes. These nodes publish to the topics enclosed in rectangles that are pointed to by arrows:

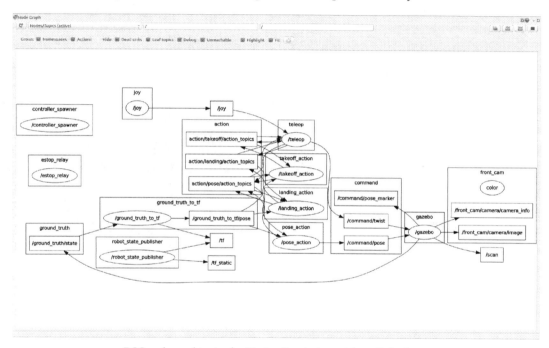

ROS nodes and topics for Hector Quadrotor outdoor flight demo

The command `rostopic list` will provide a long list of the topics currently being published. Other command-line tools such as `rosnode`, `rosmsg`, `rosparam`, and `rosservice` will help gather specific information about Hector Quadrotor's operation.

To understand the orientation of the quadrotor on the screen, use the Gazebo GUI to show the vehicle's tf reference frame. Select `quadrotor` in the **World** panel on the left, and then select the Translation mode on the top **Environment** toolbar (looks like crossed double-headed arrows). This selection will bring up the *red-green-blue* axis for the x-y-z of the tf frame. In the following figure, the x axis is pointing to the left, the y axis is pointing to the right (toward the reader), and the z axis is pointing up:

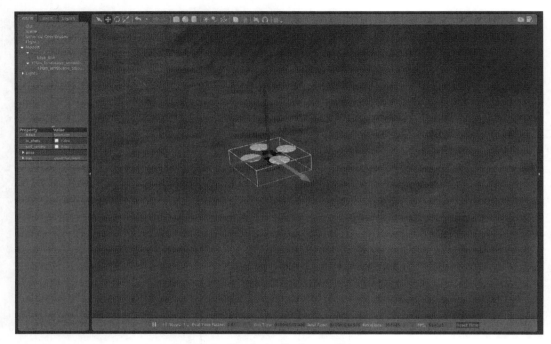

Hector Quadrotor tf reference frame

A YouTube video of a `hector_quadrotor` outdoor scenario demo shows the `hector_quadrotor` in Gazebo operated with a gamepad controller. You can find the video at: `https://www.youtube.com/watch?v=9CGIcc0jeuI`.

Flying Hector indoors

The quadrotor indoor SLAM demo software is included as part of the `hector_quadrotor` metapackage. To launch the simulation, type the following command:

```
$ roslaunch hector_quadrotor_demo indoor_slam_gazebo.launch
```

The following screenshots show both the rviz and Gazebo display windows when the Hector indoor simulation is launched:

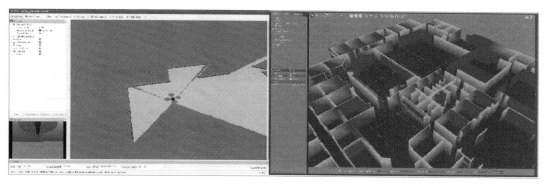

Hector Quadrotor indoor rviz and Gazebo views

If you do not see this image for Gazebo, roll your mouse wheel to zoom out of the image. Then, you will need to rotate the scene to a top-down view in order to find the quadrotor. Click on the icon on the top **Environment** toolbar to **Change the View Angle**, then select the top icon **View** from the top.

The environment was the offices at Willow Garage and Hector starts out on the floor of one of the interior rooms. Just as in the outdoor demo, the `xbox_controller.launch` file from the `hector_quadrotor_teleop` package should be executed:

```
$ roslaunch hector_quadrotor_teleop xbox_controller.launch
```

If the quadrotor becomes embedded in the wall, waiting a few seconds should release it and it should (hopefully) end up in an upright position ready to fly again. If you lose sight of it, zoom out from the Gazebo screen and look from a top-down view. Remember that the Gazebo physics engine is applying minor environment conditions as well. This can create some drifting out of its position.

The rqt graph of the active nodes and topics during the Hector indoor SLAM demo is shown in the following figure. As Hector is flown around the office environment, the `hector_mapping` node will be performing SLAM and creating a map of the environment:

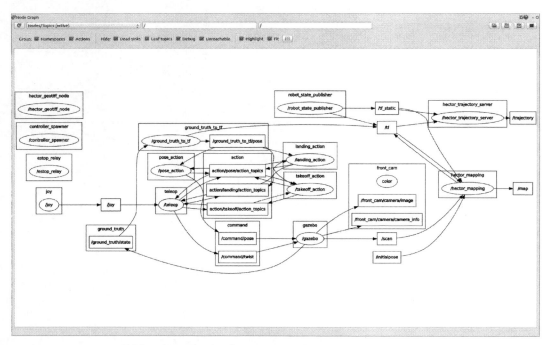

ROS nodes and topics for Hector Quadrotor indoor SLAM demo

The following screenshot shows Hector Quadrotor mapping an interior room of Willow Garage:

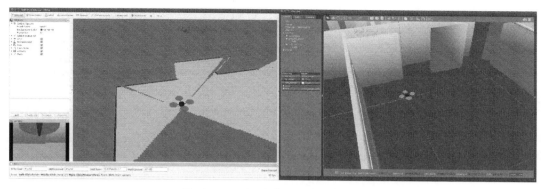

Hector mapping indoors using SLAM

The 3D robot trajectory is tracked by the `hector_trajectory_server` node and can be shown in rviz. The map, along with the trajectory information, can be saved to a GeoTIFF, file with the following command:

```
$ rostopic pub syscommand std_msgs/String "savegeotiff"
```

To find the map, use the `roscd` command:

```
$ roscd hector_geotiff/maps
```

In this directory, there will be two parts of the map, labeled `hector_slam_map`. One file will be a `.tfw` format and the other a `.tif` format. The `.tfw` file is a text file that stores the *X* and *Y* pixel size, rotational information and world coordinates for the map that is stored in the `.tif` file. The `.tif` file contains the TIFF image of the map.

A YouTube video of *hector_quadrotor stack indoor SLAM* (https://www.youtube.com/watch?v=IJbJbcZVY28) demo shows the `hector_quadrotor` in Gazebo operated with a gamepad controller.

Now, we will take a look at real quadrotors. For this chapter, we evaluated the entire spectrum of quadrotors that interface with ROS and were available at the time. At the bottom of the price range, the Crazyflie was an easy pick, due to its small size and the advantage of flying it indoors. The small motors cause the propellers to spin at a high RPM, but the propellers are soft and compliant. Because the vehicle is lightweight, damage to property, people, or the vehicle itself is usually minimal. In addition, replacement parts are inexpensive.

Introducing Crazyflie 2.0

Crazyflie is a quadrotor that is classified as a **micro air vehicle (MAV)**, as it only weighs 27 grams and can fit in your hand. It was developed and is manufactured by Bitcraze AB and comes as a kit—ready to assemble with no soldering required. The designers of Crazyflie wanted to build a small flying electronic board that had minimal mechanical parts. They provide it and support it as an open source development platform, encouraging others to contribute to both Crazyflie hardware and software development. For this book, the Crazyflie 2.0 model was used for testing purposes, but the Crazyflie ROS software indicates that it is compatible with both Crazyflie 1.0 and 2.0 models embedded with stock firmware. The Crazyflie2.0 model is shown in the following figure and is the model referred to in the rest of this chapter:

Crazyflie 2.0

The size of the assembled Crazyflie is 92 mm (3.6 inches) square motor to motor and 29 mm (1.1 inches) high.

The Crazyflie 2.0 system design is based on dual microcontroller architecture, as shown in the following diagram. The STM32F405 **Microcontroller Unit (MCU)** controls the flight of the Crazyflie through power to the motor driver. The STM32 also reads data from the 10-DOF IMU, which includes a three-axis accelerometer, three-axis gyroscope, three-axis magnetometer, and a high precision pressure sensor. It can control telemetry to other components through the expansion port. The other MCU is a Nordic Semiconductor nRF51822. The main tasks of this MCU are to handle the radio communication and the power management for the Crazyflie. Both **Bluetooth Low Energy (BLE)** and **Compressed Real-Time Protocol (CRTP)** are supported by the nRF51. The CRTP mode is compatible with radio communication provided by the Crazyradio. The nRF51 also handles logic from the on/off button and power to the other components in the system:

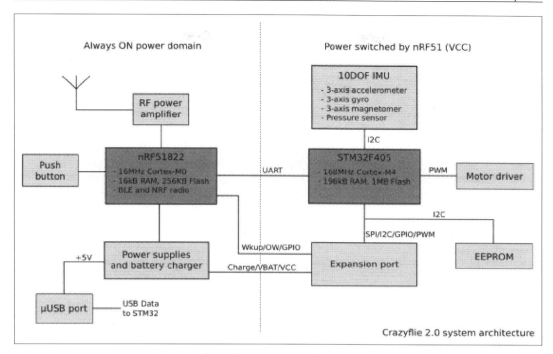

Crazyflie 2.0 system architecture

The Crazyflie is charged through an onboard µUSB port and requires a 40-minute charge cycle for the stock battery. Flight time is up to 7 minutes.

The Crazyflie 2.0 is priced under $200 and is available at www.seeedstudio.com. Its local distributors are listed on the website www.bitcraze.io/distributors.

Bitcraze provides excellent documentation to take you from unpacking your Crazyflie to getting it in the air. Instructions for assembling Crazyflie and getting it ready to fly can be found at https://www.bitcraze.io/getting-started-with-the-crazyflie-2-0/.

For any problems that arise, refer to the support forum at https://forum.bitcraze.io/.

Controlling Crazyflie without ROS

Crazyflie can be controlled through a number of host devices over BLE or a Crazyradio communication channel. A BLE link to Crazyflie limits the flying range to 20 meters. The best communications link, Crazyradio PA, extends the communication range to 1000 meters. Either communication method is supported by the Crazyflie **Python client** (**PC**) software, available for computers running Linux, Windows, or macOS. Bitcraze has also configured its own **virtual machine** (**VM**) that imports into the Oracle VirtualBox to make it easy to start on Crazyflie development projects. For more information on the Bitcraze VM, visit `https://wiki.bitcraze.io/projects:virtualmachine:index`.

For the latest release of the Crazyflie PC, visit `https://github.com/bitcraze/crazyflie-clients-python/releases`.

Instructions for installing the Crazyflie PC can be found at `https://github.com/bitcraze/crazyflie-clients-python`.

The Crazyflie PC can be used to upgrade and flash the Crazyflie firmware over the Crazyradio link. Refer to the following website for instructions: `https://wiki.bitcraze.io/projects:crazyflie2:upgrading:index`.

Application software also exists for controlling the Crazyflie from an Android OS (4.4 or newer) or iOS (7.1 or newer) device. Refer to the appropriate app store for the Crazyflie software:

- For Android users: `https://play.google.com/store/apps/details?id=se.bitcraze.crazyfliecontrol2`.
- For iOS users: `https://itunes.apple.com/us/app/crazyflie-2.0/id946151480?mt=8`.

For Raspberry Pi enthusiasts, check out the client version of software for Raspbian at `https://wiki.bitcraze.io/projects:crazyflie:binaries:raspberrypi#download`.

For user input control, Crazyflie can use any gamepad with a minimum of four analog axes. The primary joystick controllers are the Xbox 360 USB controller, the PS3 USB controller, and the PS4 USB controller. Other controllers can be configured to work with the Crazyflie by modifying the Crazyflie client software.

Communicating using Crazyradio PA

In order to use Crazyflie 2.0 with ROS, a Crazyradio or Crazyradio PA is necessary to provide wireless radio communication with the Crazyflie. The Crazyradio resides on a small circuit board mounted on a USB dongle to interface with a computer, tablet, or smartphone. It has radio amplification to 20 dBm power output and a **Line-of-sight(LOS)** range of greater than 1 kilometer. The design is based on the nRF24LU1+ chip from Nordic Semiconductor, which operates on the 2.4 GHz band of radio communications. It provides 125 radio channels and offers 2 **Megabits per second (Mbps)**, 1Mbps, and 250Kbps communication data rates. Firmware for the Crazyradio is open source and is upgradeable through a bootloader that comes embedded with the hardware.

The following figure shows the Crazyradio PA with its antenna extended. Additional information on the Crazyradio PA can be found at https://www.bitcraze.io/crazyradio-pa.

For the latest stable release of the Crazyradio firmware, go to https://github.com/bitcraze/crazyradio-firmware/releases.

Crazyradio PA

The next sections will focus on using ROS to command and control the flight of the Crazyflie quadrotor. A ROS metapackage for the Crazyflie has been developed by Wolfgang Hoenig, with current information found at his GitHub site: https://github.com/whoenig/crazyflie_ros. His work was partially done as part of his research at the ACTLab at **University of Southern California (USC)**. See the website at: http://act.usc.edu/.

We thank Mr. Hoenig for his generous support in helping us prepare this section.

This software supports both the Crazyflie 1.0 and the Crazyflie 2.0 quadrotors embedded with stock firmware.

Loading Crazyflie ROS software

The Crazyflie ROS software for Crazyflie can be added to the catkin workspace
`catkin_ws` created in *Chapter 1, Getting Started with ROS*, and then used in *Chapter 2, Creating Your First Two-Wheeled ROS Robot (in Simulation)*, for our package
`ros_robotics`. However, we provide instructions here to install the `Crazyflie`
metapackage into a catkin workspace of its own, identified as `crazyflie_ws`. This
workspace will provide you with the chance to examine the existing Crazyflie ROS
packages and be a development space for new software you might wish to create. If
you wish to use the `catkin_ws` workspace for your Crazyflie ROS software, skip to the
step where the command `sudo apt-get update` is issued. (Afterwards, remember to
replace the `crazyflie_ws` name in each of the command lines with `catkin_ws`.)

To create the Crazyflie workspace `crazyflie_ws`, type the following commands:

```
$ mkdir -p ~/crazyflie_ws/src
$ cd ~/crazyflie_ws/src
$ catkin_init_workspace
```

Build and install the Crazyflie workspace:

```
$ cd ~/crazyflie_ws
$ catkin_make
```

Next, source the `setup.bash` file within the Crazyflie workspace to overlay this
workspace on top of the ROS environment for the workstation:

```
$ source ~/crazyflie_ws/devel/setup.bash
```

Remember to add this source command to your `.bashrc` file:

```
$ echo "source ~/crazyflie_ws/devel/setup.bash" >> ~/.bashrc
```

Then:

```
$ source ~/.bashrc
```

Make sure the `ROS_PACKAGE_PATH` environment variable includes the path you just
sourced:

```
$ echo $ROS_PACKAGE_PATH
```

The path `/home/<username>/crazyflie_ws/src` should be displayed as one of the
paths on the screen.

Now that the Crazyflie catkin workspace has been created, update the system information on the newest versions of packages and their dependencies:

```
$ sudo apt-get update
```

Next, move to the Crazyflie workspace source directory and download the software from GitHub:

```
$ cd ~/crazyflie_ws/src
$ git clone https://github.com/whoenig/crazyflie_ros.git
```

Move to the root of the Crazyflie workspace and build the packages:

```
$ cd ~/crazyflie_ws
$ catkin_make
```

These instructions install the latest version of the `Crazyflie` metapackage, which has no dependencies on the Bitcraze Crazyflie SDK.

 Important!
Check your `.bashrc` file to make sure that no `ROS_MASTER_URI` variable is set. If one exists, comment it out with a #.

ROS packages from the `Crazyflie` metapackage are described here:

- `crazyflie_controller`: This package contains a PID controller used during autonomous navigation operations such as hovering and waypoint navigation. It is used with an external motion capture system such as VICON.

- `crazyflie_cpp`: This package contains a C++ library for Crazyflie and for Crazyradio.

- `crazyflie_demo`: This package contains a varied set of launch files and Python scripts to provide the user with sample operations of Crazyflie. Use these files as a starting point to create your own operational setup for Crazyflie. Sample teleoperation modes for hovering, waypoint navigation, and integration to rviz are included.

- `crazyflie_description`: This package provides URDF files and mesh files to create simulation models of the Crazyflie. Both the Crazyflie 1.0 and Crazyflie 2.0 models are supplied.

- `crazyflie_tools`: This package contains helpful tools for Crazyflie. The tool scan is included, which scans for Crazyflie(s) and reports their URI(s).

- `crazyflie_driver`: This package contains two important launch files. The `crazyflie_server.launch` file launches the `crazyflie_server` node. The `crazyflie_server` node communicates with all Crazyflies that have been dynamically added via `crazyflie_add`. The `crazyflie_add.launch` file launches the `crazyflie_add` node to establish communication with a Crazyflie. These operations are explained in more detail in subsequent sections.

Setting up udev rules for Crazyradio

On the computer workstation, Ubuntu uses **udev** to manage system devices and dynamically create and remove device nodes in the `/dev` directory to handle external devices. When the Crazyradio USB dongle is plugged in, udev is notified and special system configuration rules, **udev rules**, link any user-defined device information. These udev rules are stored in a file in the directory `/etc/udev/rules.d`.

The following instructions create rules that will set permission for a user to use the Crazyradio without requiring root privileges.

 The following steps require Superuser (root) or Administrator privileges. If the `sudo` program is not available on your computer, use the following two commands as root:
`$ su –`
`$ apt-get install sudo`

The following commands create the group `plugdev`, to which users can be added who wish to communicate with Crazyflie via the Crazyradio dongle:

`$ sudo group add plugdev`

`$ sudo usermod -a -G plugdev <username>`

Next, the udev rules are created to provide vendor and product identification and user privileges for the Crazyradio and the Crazyflie. Using the command `sudo <editor>` to access your favorite editor, create the file `/etc/udev/rules.d/99-crazyradio.rules`, and within the file, add the following line:

```
SUBSYSTEM=="usb", ATTRS{idVendor}=="1915", ATTRS{idProduct}=="7777",
MODE="0664", GROUP="plugdev"
```

Using `sudo<editor>`, create the file `/etc/udev/rules.d/99-crazyflie.rules` and add the following line:

```
SUBSYSTEM=="usb", ATTRS{idVendor}=="0483", ATTRS{idProduct}=="5740",
MODE="0664", GROUP="plugdev"
```

Restart the computer and prepare to communicate with your Crazyflie!

Pre-flight check

It is advisable to mark the right-front (**M1**) leg of the Crazyflie with something bright. This marking will help you keep track of the forward direction for your Crazyflie. Due to the symmetrical design, it is easy to lose track of the orientation of the Crazyflie.

The Crazyflie should be placed on a stable surface. As you will see, the startup sequence involves spinning the motors and sensor calibration. In the following figure of Crazyflie, identify the on/off power button (near the **M1** leg) and push it on.

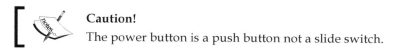

> **Caution!**
> The power button is a push button not a slide switch.

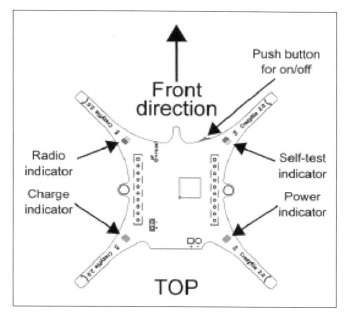

Top view of Crazyflie

After the Crazyflie is powered on, the power-on sequence will spin all four propellers in order. If a propeller does not spin, be sure to check the motor connections. The blue LED lights on the rear of the UAV should be lit to indicate that the power is on. The front-right red LED light should be pulsing at 1 Hz to indicate the vehicle's heartbeat. When Crazyradio communication is established with the Crazyflie, the red and green LED lights on the front-left will be flashing to indicate that communication is being exchanged.

Next, insert the Crazyradio into a USB 2.0 slot on your computer and insert the joystick controller into another USB slot. Check that the joystick knobs are in their center positions so that the throttle is set to zero. You are now ready to start the Crazyflie ROS software.

Flying Crazyflie with teleop

Before flying Crazyflie for the first time, it is recommended to tie the UAV to a heavy object, attaching string to the mounting holes on either side of the **Printed Circuit Board** (**PCB**) body.

> Remember that the Crazyflie can climb to 50 meters when flying at full throttle. This height is dangerous if the battery runs out of power.
>
> The front-right LED will be a steady red light when the battery is low on power. It is advisable to land to prevent damage to the Crazyflie.

Before communicating with your Crazyflie, you need to find the **Uniform Resource Identifier** (**URI**). This URI is associated with the communication protocol of the nRF51 MCU. The format for the URI is as follows:

```
Interface Type:// Interface Id/Interface Channel/Interface Speed
```

For the radio interface, this sequence is as follows:

```
radio://USB dongle number/radio channel number/radio speed
```

The `crazyflie_tools` package provides the program scan to identify all the URIs that are transmitting. Open a terminal window on your computer workstation and enter the following command:

```
$ rosrun crazyflie_tools scan
```

The output will be similar to the following two lines:

```
Configured Dongle with version 0.53
radio://0/80/250K
```

The URI for your Crazyflie may be different. For our Crazyflie, the USB dongle number is `0`, the radio channel is `80`, and the radio speed is `250K`. This means that our communication link is over a 2480 MHz channel.

The package `crazyflie_demo` contains a spectrum of example launch files to use with Crazyflie. Launch files are given for using the Xbox 360 controller or the PS3 controller to teleoperate the Crazyflie. To fly your Crazyflie with an Xbox 360 controller, type the command:

```
$ roslaunch crazyflie_demo teleop_xbox360.launch uri:=<CrazyflieURI>
```

Replace `<CrazyflieURI>` with the URI found from the `scan` command. On the screen, look for the message:

```
SYS: Crazyflie2.0 is up and running!
```

You should see something similar to this:

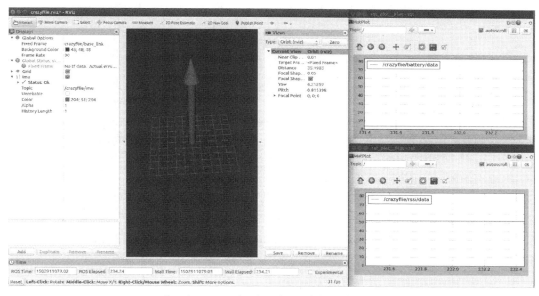

Starting screen for the teleop_xbox360.launch

The window on the left is running rviz and the two `rqt_plot` windows on the right are for battery data and **radio signal strength indicator (RSSI)** data. In rviz, IMU sensor data will be displayed on the grid.

If you are anxious to feel the joystick controls in your hands, proceed to using the left and right stick controls to navigate your Crazyflie. The stick controls are similar to those used for Hector Quadrotor:

- **Left Stick – Forward (Up)**: Throttle provides lift
- **Left Stick – Backward (Down)**: No throttle
- **Left Stick – Right**: Clockwise yaw

- **Left Stick – Left**: Counter clockwise yaw
- **Right Stick – Forward (Up)**: Pitch forward
- **Right Stick – Backward (Down)**: Pitch backward
- **Right Stick – Right**: Roll right
- **Right Stick – Left**: Roll left

You are now ready to use the Xbox 360 joystick to fly your Crazyflie around!

Details of teleop_xbox360.launch

The `teleop_xbox360.launch` file performs a number of operations to launch ROS nodes, pass arguments, and set ROS parameters. The following list highlights the tasks performed:

- The `crazyflie_server.launch` file in the `crazyflie_driver` package is executed. This file launches the node `crazyflie_server`. This server handles communication with the Crazyflie as soon as it is dynamically added by the `crazyflie_add.launch` file.

- The `crazyflie_add.launch` file in the `crazyflie_driver` package is executed. This file launches the node `crazyflie_add` using the URI parameter that is passed into `teleop_xbox360.launch`. Other parameters that are set are as follows:
  ○ `tf_prefix`: This is the `tf` prefix for the Crazyflie frame(s)
  ○ `enable_logging`: This is the flag to log data

- The `joy` node is launched to handle the joystick controller input.

- The `xbox360.launch` file is included to launch the node `quadrotor_teleop` (in the `crazyflie_demo` package) and set the parameters for the joystick controller. These parameters include `x_axis`, `y_axis`, `z_axis`, `yaw_axis`, `x_velocity_max`, `y_velocity_max`, `z_velocity_max`, and `yaw_velocity_max`.

- The `crazyflie_demo_controller` node in the `crazyflie_demo` package is launched via the script `controller.py`.

- The `rviz` node in package rviz is launched and the `crazyflie.rviz` configuration file in the `crazyflie_demo` package launch directory is used to configure rviz.

- Two `rqt_plot` nodes from package `rqt_plot` are launched. One node plots the radio signal strength and the other node plots the battery level.

Take a look at this figure to see some of the relationships between the nodes and topics. The large rectangle marked Crazyflie is the namespace for the enclosed nodes and topics:

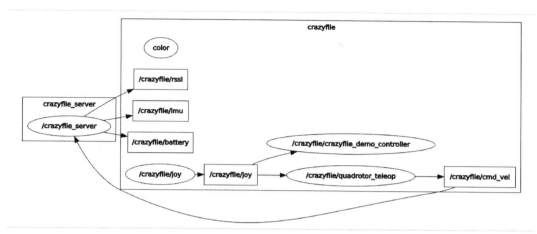

Crazyflie ROS teleop nodes and topics

A number of ROS parameters are initialized at the start of this program. When first flying your Crazyflie, begin with a straightforward push on the Left Stick of the joystick (throttle). The Crazyflie should lift straight up into the air. If the Crazyflie seems unstable, the battery may also be moved forward and back to change the pitch balance. It is recommended to mark the battery position when you get it into the desired spot.

Prior to flying the Crazyflie, using the `rostopic list` command allows us to see the names of the topics that are available. Of primary importance is the `/crazyflie/cmd_vel` topic. This topic is published by the `/crazyflie/quadrotor_teleop` node, and the data fields for this topic are as follows:

- `angular.z`: The yaw rate value is -200 to 200 degrees per second
- `linear.x`: The pitch value is -30 to 30 degrees
- `linear.y`: The roll value is -30 to 30 degrees
- `linear.z`: The thrust value is 10,000 to 60,000 for **pulse-width modulation (PWM)** output

The `crazyflie_server` node publishes sensor data from the Crazyflie as `sensor_msgs`:

- The `imu` topic contains gyroscope and accelerometer data and updates every 10 **milliseconds (ms)**. The covariance matrices and orientation fields are not set.

- The `temperature` topic contains data from the barometer in degrees Celsius. This message is updated every 100 ms.

- The `magnetic_field` topic contains data from the magnetometer and is updated every 100 ms.

- The `pressure` topic contains readings from the pressure sensor in **hectopascals (hPa)** or **millibars (mbar)**. This message is updated every 100 ms.

- The `battery` topic contains readings from the battery in volts and is updated every 100 ms. The stock battery is a 3.7 volt 240 mAh lithium polymer battery.

From this point, feel free to try the `rostopic echo` command with any of the topics listed previously to see the data being passed, especially between the computer and the Crazyflie. The ROS tool rqt can also be used to monitor these topics (**Topic Monitor**) and publish messages (**Message Publisher**) to the Crazyflie.

Flying with a motion capture system

The `crazyflie_demo` package contains launch files to use the Crazyflie with external motion capture systems such as VICON or **Virtual-Reality Peripheral Network (VRPN)**. With an external motion capture system, you can get your Crazyflie to hover at a given location or navigate autonomously to a set of waypoints. For example, to get Crazyflie to hover a meter above its starting location using a VICON system, use the following command:

```
$ roslaunch crazyflie_demo hover_vicon.launch uri:=<CrazyflieURI>
frame:=<CrazyflieTFframe> x:=0 y:=0 z:=1
```

Replace `<CrazyflieURI>` with your Crazyflie's URI and `<CrazyflieTFframe>` is the tf-frame of your Crazyflie. The `hover_vicon.launch` file will automatically run `vicon_bridge`.

Flying multiple Crazyflies

The `crazyflie_demo` package also contains launch files for flying multiple Crazyflies at the same time. To accomplish this, each Crazyflie must have a different address. If Crazyflies are to share communication on the same Crazyradio USB dongle, they should share the same channel and data rate to provide optimum performance. Up to three Crazyflies have been successfully flown over one Crazyradio dongle. Performance degrades as the number of Crazyflies increases due to limitations in bandwidth.

To command and control multiple Crazyflies using the Xbox 360 joystick controller, use the following command:

```
$ roslaunch crazyflie_demo multi_teleop_xbox360.launch
uri1:=radio://0/100/2M/E7E7E7E7E7 uri2:=radio://0/100/2M/E7E7E7E705
```

The URIs used in the `multi_teleop_xbox360.launch` command are left as examples of the duplication of the radio channel and data rate but the difference in the address.

The authors have not performed the commands in these last two sections because, at present, we have only one Crazyflie and no external motion capture system. We have included these examples here to entice you to extend your Crazyflie experience.

Introducing Bebop

The following image shows the Parrot Bebop quadrotor craft, which will be discussed in this section. This quadrotor is a larger quadrotor with more advanced features than the Crazyflie. The Bebop gathers data from onboard sensors such as the three-axes accelerometer, gyroscope, magnetometer, ultrasound sensor and pressure sensor to provide optimal stable control for flight and agile maneuvers. This ability for stable flight allows the pilot to obtain quality video and images with the onboard camera.

Bebop

Parrot is a company, with headquarters in Paris, France, that produces products such as the Bebop quadrotor. As of November 2016, there is now a second version of Bebop: the Bebop 2. The Bebop 2 is described in detail on the Parrot website at `https://www.parrot.com/us/drones/parrot-bebop-2#parrot-bebop-2`. Some differences between the Bebop 1 and Bebop 2 are identified in the following table:

Factors	Bebop 1	Bebop 2
Price	$399.99	$549.99
Battery life	11 minutes	25 minutes
Max horizontal speed	13 m/s	16 m/s
Max climbing speed	2.5 m/s	6 m/s
Signal range	up to 250 m	up to 300 m
GPS	12 satellites max	19 satellites max
Camera	14 megapixel; 180° fisheye	14 megapixel; 180° fisheye (more tilted towards ground)
Video	3-axis full HD 1080p	3-axis full HD 1080p
Frame type	250 mm	290 mm
Overall dimensions	28 x 32 cm	32.8 x 38.2 cm
Propeller size	14 cm	15.2 cm
Weight	400 grams	500 grams
Colors	yellow, red, blue	red, white
Other features		LED tail light

Both versions of Bebop can be controlled by the Parrot Skycontroller or by using smartphones or tablets. Operation of the Skycontroller is described on the following site: `http://blog.parrot.com/2014/12/15/how-to-pilot-skycontroller/`.

Bebop has onboard sensors for autonomous flight through the use of GPS for guidance. The Bebop also has a forward-looking camera for aerial photography. The Wi-Fi communications module of Bebop allows both manual control and control with a ROS package called `bebop_autonomy`. The next section will concentrate on the use of the ROS software to control Bebop.

Important!

Before flying the Bebop or using the ROS interface, visit the Bebop website and download and install the latest firmware version for the Bebop.

The `bebop_autonomy` software is the ROS driver for Parrot Bebop 1 and Bebop 2 quadrotors based on the Parrot ARDrone SDK3 development kit. This driver was developed and is maintained at the Autonomy Lab of Simon Fraser University by Mani Monajjemi. We thank Mr. Monajjemi for his generous assistance in helping us prepare this section.

Loading bebop_autonomy software

The instructions for loading the ROS software and using it for Bebop are well described at:

- `http://bebop-autonomy.readthedocs.org/en/latest/`
- `http://bebop-autonomy.readthedocs.org/en/latest/installation.html`

The features to be incorporated into `bebop_autonomy` and the status of these features can be found in the documentation at `https://media.readthedocs.org/pdf/bebop-autonomy/latest/bebop-autonomy.pdf`. This document covers `bebop_autonomy` versions for Indigo, Jade, and Kinetic.

To load the `bebop_autonomy` software, first get the required Ubuntu packages with the following command:

```
$ sudo apt-get install build-essential python-rosdep python-catkin-tools
```

Update the system information on the newest versions of packages and their dependencies:

```
$ sudo apt-get update
```

Create the Bebop workspace `bebop_ws` and download software from GitHub:

```
$ mkdir -p ~/bebop_ws/src
$ cd ~/bebop_ws
$ catkin init
$ git clone https://github.com/AutonomyLab/bebop_autonomy.git src/bebop_
autonomy
```

Use `rosdep` to install the `bebop_autonomy` package dependencies:

```
$ rosdep update
$ rosdep install --from-paths src -i
```

Then, build the workspace:

```
$ catkin build
```

Once the software is loaded and the files are built, add the following statement in the `.bashrc` file:

```
source ~/bebop_ws/devel/setup.bash
```

Also within the `.bashrc` file, verify that the `ROS_MASTER_URI`, the `ROS_IP`, and the `ROS_HOSTNAME` variables are not set.

Remember, adding the source statement to the `.bashrc` file will apply it to each new terminal window opened.

Also, check your ROS package path with the following command:

```
$ echo $ROS_PACKAGE_PATH
```

The path `/home/<username>/bebop_ws/src` should display as five paths on the screen:

```
/home/<username>/bebop_ws/src/bebop_autonomy/bebop_autonomy
/home/<username>/bebop_ws/src/bebop_autonomy/bebop_description
/home/<username>/bebop_ws/src/bebop_autonomy/bebop_msgs
/home/<username>/bebop_ws/src/bebop_autonomy/bebop_driver
/home/<username>/bebop_ws/src/bebop_autonomy/bebop_tools
```

The software download creates a number of packages that are used to control Bebop. The `bebop_autonomy` package is actually a metapackage with a `package.xml` file that lists four other packages, as follows:

- `bebop_description` which contains the URDF and mesh files
- `bebop_driver` which contains C++ code for the node `bebop_driver_node`
- `bebop_msgs` which contains messages used with Bebop
- `bebop_tools` which contains miscellaneous tools for Bebop

Preparing to fly Bebop

Before flying Bebop, review the Bebop User's Guide available at `http://www.parrot.com/usa/support/parrot-bebop-drone/`.

Read the instructions in that document for the following points:

- Assembling the Bebop quadrotor, charging the battery, and other preliminary matters
- Pay attention to the section on *Preflight Check*, which includes many safety tips
- Study the section on flying, which includes instructions for calibrating the magnetometer of the Bebop

Testing Bebop communications

After a preflight check and clearing the flying area of people and obstructions, power on Bebop and wait for several minutes.

Using the **Systems Settings** tab in the Ubuntu desktop, select **Network** and check your wireless connections to see whether your computer is communicating with Bebop. You should see the Bebop network `BebopDrone-<xxxxxxx>`. The numbers indicate the identification number of your Bebop. The IP address should be `192.168.42.1` for the Bebop as the **Default Route**.

Then, test the communications between the computer workstation and the Bebop by pinging the craft. From a terminal window, issue the ping command to the Bebop and wait for the response:

```
$ ping 192.168.42.1
```

Our output is as follows:

```
PING 192.168.42.1 (192.168.42.1) 56(84) bytes of data.
64 bytes from 192.168.42.1: icmp_seq=1 ttl=64 time=9.41ms
64 bytes from 192.168.42.1: icmp_seq=2 ttl=64 time=5.46ms
```

Flying Bebop using commands

Now, it is time to launch the `bebop_driver` node and use commands to perform a takeoff and landing. Launch Bebop with the following command:

```
$ roslaunch bebop_driver bebop_node.launch
```

Explore the nodes and topics:

```
$ rosnode list
```

The output should be as follows:

```
/bebop/bebop_driver
/bebop/robot_state_publisher
/rosout
```

Then, type the following command:

```
$ rostopic list
```

This will produce a long list, in which the following topics are of interest in getting Bebop to take off and land:

```
/bebop/takeoff
/bebop/land
/bebop/reset
/bebop/autoflight/navigate_home
```

Note that, in both lists, the **namespace (ns)** is `bebop` and the items are listed as `/bebop/<node>` or `/bebop/<topic>`.

Take off

Watch it fly. Bebop goes straight up 1 meter after you execute the following command:

```
$ rostopic pub /bebop/takeoff std_msgs/Empty --once
```

The output should be as follows:

```
publishing and latching message for 3.0 seconds
```

Landing

Bebop will land when you issue this command:

```
$ rostopic pub /bebop/land std_msgs/Empty --once
```

The output is as follows:

```
publishing and latching message for 3.0 seconds
```

There are many other options for the Bebop that are not covered here. Refer to the Bebop website and the instructions for the `bebop_autonomy` software previously listed to explore all of Bebop's functions.

Summary

This chapter featured information about flying robots that are described as quadrotors or quadcopters because of their four propellers. The first few sections of the chapter described quadrotors and their flying characteristics, as well as the sensors that they might have. Sensors such as magnetometers, gyroscopes, and accelerometers were discussed with the aim of explaining how they allow quadrotors to stabilize themselves in the air. Other accessories such as cameras and GPS units were also covered.

The rules for flying safely were presented. These are basically common-sense rules, such as do not fly over people or pets. Government agencies, such as the FAA in the United States, govern the use of airspace and those rules should be followed carefully.

The Hector simulator is excellent, particularly for new pilots of quadrotors, in that a quadrotor can be flown in simulation without any danger of real crashes. Details of downloading the Hector software were covered in this chapter. ROS is used for control and message passing to the simulated quadrotor craft.

Finally, two real quadrotors called Crazyflie and Bebop were described and the ROS software to control them was discussed. The Crazyflie is relatively inexpensive and safe to fly, but it embodies many of the principles of more expensive and sophisticated quadrotors. Enjoy your flights!

In the next chapter, *Chapter 8, Controlling Your Robots with External Devices*, the use of peripheral devices to teleoperate your robot will be considered. Interfacing with joysticks, controller boards, and mobile devices will be handled using standard ROS packages to help you expedite the process of implementing these devices with your robot.

8

Controlling Your Robots with External Devices

In the past few chapters, we have used ROS to control mobile, armed, flying, and simulated robots. The similarities and differences between these robots have been discussed, and we have shown the commonalities that ROS has created between all these robot types. These commonalities are not only in the structure of the software and the communication methods, but also in the simulation environment and the tools used for visualization and analysis.

The influence of ROS goes even further by providing a common interface to control devices external to the robot. These devices include game controllers (gamepads and joystick controllers), mobile devices (smartphones and tablets), and even controller boards (Arduino and Raspberry Pi).

In this chapter, you will learn about the following topics:

- Adding a game controller to a robot
- Using mobile devices to control robot projects
- Interfacing controller boards such as Arduino or Raspberry Pi

Creating a custom ROS game controller interface

If you have played with a joystick with either Baxter or Crazyflie, you may think that the function of certain buttons or joysticks would be better with your own special design. Each type of game controller has one or more joysticks and various buttons or triggers to cause events depending on the game software being used. Here, for the Microsoft Xbox controller, we will do the following:

- Show how to determine the mapping between controller joysticks, buttons, and triggers and the number corresponding to each using a graphical package, jstest-gtk

- Use the terminal command jstest; this will enable you to determine the corresponding numbers of controller joysticks, buttons, and triggers

The following diagram shows the Xbox 360 game controller. Pushing a button changes the output from 0 (off) to 1 (on) on the channel corresponding to the pushed button, which in turn can be read by a program and used to start an application. Moving the stick outputs a numerical value that can be used to control a robot. The joystick movements are described by the axis of the movement; moving the stick up and down defines one axis, and moving the stick to the left and right defines another.

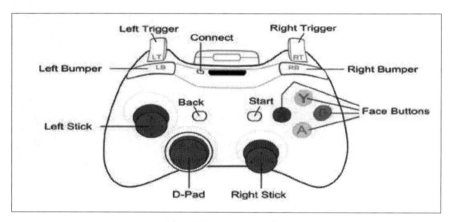

Xbox 360 game controller

Testing a game controller

The graphical program `jstest-gtk` can be used to determine the number of the channel or axis associated with a button or joystick of a game controller. The package `jstest-gtk` is a game controller testing and configuration tool. This package is described at `https://launchpad.net/ubuntu/xenial/+package/jstest-gtk`.

To download and install the package, use the following command:

```
$ sudo apt-get install jstest-gtk
```

Then, plug your game controller into the USB port of your computer. The command to execute the game controller test program is:

```
$ jstest-gtk
```

The following screenshot shows the result with the Xbox 360 controller connected to our computer. As shown, the Microsoft Xbox 360 controller has 8 axes and 11 buttons:

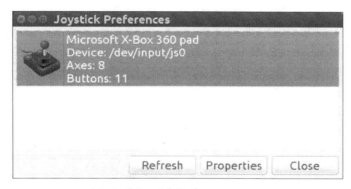

jstest-gtk Joystick Preferences screen

By double-clicking on the name **Microsoft X-Box 360 pad**, a GUI for the axes and buttons of the Xbox 360 controller appears, as shown in the following screenshot:

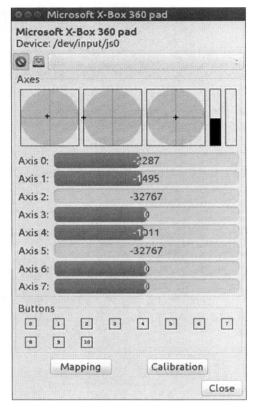

jstest-gtk Xbox screen

As you push a button on the controller, the number of the button will be highlighted in the display. The relative position of a joystick that is moved is shown graphically, and the numerical value associated with the motion is also displayed. More details on this operation are provided at http://manpages.ubuntu.com/manpages/xenial/en/man1/jstest-gtk.1.html.

Alternative test of a game controller

As an alternative to the graphical display of the game controller's properties, terminal commands can be used. First, plug your game controller into a USB port on your computer and then determine the devices connected to the computer by issuing this command:

```
$ ls /dev/input/
```

The output should be similar to the following:

```
by-id     event1    event12   event15   event4    event7    js0       mouse1
by-path   event10   event13   event2    event5    event8    mice
event0    event11   event14   event3    event6    event9    mouse0
```

The game controller will appear as a `js` device in this listing. Note that the system has the game controller named as `js0` in the list. To test the controller and determine the index numbers of the axes and buttons, type the following command:

```
$ jstest /dev/input/js0
```

The output for the Xbox controller should be similar to the following:

```
Driver version is 2.1.0.
Joystick (Microsoft X-Box 360 pad) has 8 axes (X, Y, Z, Rx, Ry, Rz,
Hat0X, Hat0Y)
and 11 buttons (BtnX, BtnY, BtnTL, BtnTR, BtnTR2, BtnSelect, BtnThumbL,
BtnThumbR, ?, ?, ?).
Testing ... (interrupt to exit)
Axes:  0:     0  1:     0  2:     0  3:     0  4:     0  5:     0  6:
0  7:     0 Buttons:  0:off  1:off  2:off  3:off  4:off  5:off  6:off
7:off  8:off  9
```

In this case, the controller is the `Microsoft X-box 360 pad` controller. Experiment with your controller to understand the output when the joystick is moved or a button is pressed. When a button is pressed, the corresponding value changes to `on`. Also, when a joystick is moved horizontally or vertically, the selected axis value will change from its initial value to a new value.

Now, for your controller, you can figure out which buttons or axes you will use for your application. Next, you must consider the type of software or hardware that is to be controlled by the game controller. For ROS, the `/joy` node is used to read the controller output.

A tutorial describing the use of Ubuntu commands is available at `http://wiki.ros.org/joy/Tutorials/ConfiguringALinuxJoystick`.

Using the ROS joy package

ROS has a driver for a generic controller with a joystick. The `joy` package contains the `/joy` node that interfaces a generic Linux joystick to ROS. This node publishes a joy message, which contains the current state of each of the joystick's buttons and axes. Before using the `/joy` node in an application, see whether you have the `joy` package installed by typing this:

```
$ rospack find joy
```

The output should be as follows:

```
/opt/ros/kinetic/share/joy
```

If you do not see the path to the `joy` package, install it with this command:

```
$ sudo apt-get install ros-kinetic-joy
```

Controlling Turtlesim with a custom game controller interface

In this section, an example use of a game controller and the `/joy` node is presented utilizing the following code files:

- The launch file `turtlesim_teleop.launch` that executes three nodes: `/joy`, `turtlesim`, and `turtlesim_joy`.

- A Python program `turtlesim_joy.py` that initiates the `turtlesim_joy` node and allows the joystick to control the movement of the turtle on the screen.

- The program `turtlesim_joy.py` calls another Python program called `move_circle.py` when a button is pushed on the controller.

The Turtlesim simulator was introduced in the *Turtlesim – the first ROS robot simulation* section in *Chapter 1, Getting Started with ROS*. If you wish to create a ROS package for this example, refer to the instructions in the *Creating and building a ROS package* section in *Chapter 2, Creating Your First Two-Wheeled ROS Robot (in Simulation)*. In our case, the files are copied to the `ros_robotics` package created in *Chapter 2, Creating Your First Two-Wheeled ROS Robot (in Simulation)*.

In the `package` directory, the launch file should be copied to a `/launch` directory. The Python code should be copied to a `/src` directory of the package. Make sure the Python scripts are executable by issuing the following command:

```
$ chmod +x <filename>.py
```

Here, `<filename>` is the name of the Python script. Alternatively, type the following:

```
$ chmod +x *.py
```

You can use the preceding command to make all the Python files in the directory executable.

After loading the files into the directories, issue the `catkin_make` command in the catkin workspace directory to link together the ROS files.

The code for the launch file `turtlesim_teleop.launch` is as follows:

```
<?xml version="1.0"?>
<launch>

  <!-- turtlesim and joy node-->
  <node name="turtlesim" pkg="turtlesim" type="turtlesim_node"/>
  <node name="joy" pkg="joy" type="joy_node"/>

  <!-- turtlesim_joy node interfaces Xbox controller to turtlesim -->
  <node name="turtlesim_joy" pkg="ros_robotics"
  type="turtlesim_joy.py" output="screen"/>

</launch>
```

Use the following command to launch the nodes:

```
$ roslaunch ros_robotics turtlesim_teleop.launch
```

You should see output similar to the following (edited):

.

.

```
SUMMARY
========

PARAMETERS
 * /rosdistro: kinetic
 * /rosversion: 1.12.7

NODES
/
  joy (joy/joy_node)
  turtlesim (turtlesim/turtlesim_node)
  turtlesim_joy (ros_robotics/turtlesim_joy.py)

auto-starting new master
process[master]: started with pid [15595]
ROS_MASTER_URI=http://localhost:11311
```

.

The preceding command will launch three ROS nodes as shown in the screen output after the launch file is executed with the `roslaunch` command. You can also check the list of nodes with this command:

```
$ rosnode list
```

The first Python program `turtlesim_joy.py` allows the turtle of Turtlesim to be controlled by the joystick axes `[0]` and `[1]` on the game controller. For the Xbox controller, these axes correspond to the vertical and horizontal left joystick movements, respectively. In addition, pushing the button corresponding to button number `0` will cause another Python program, `move_circle.py`, to drive the turtle in a circle. On the Xbox controller, this is the green button. The code for `turtlesim_joy.py` is as follows:

```
#!/usr/bin/env python

"""

Node converts joystick inputs into commands for Turtlesim
```

```
"""

import rospy
from geometry_msgs.msg import Twist
from sensor_msgs.msg import Joy
from move_circle import move_circle

def joy_listener():

  # start node
  rospy.init_node("turtlesim_joy", anonymous=True)

  # subscribe to joystick messages on topic "joy"
  rospy.Subscriber("joy", Joy, tj_callback, queue_size=1)

  # keep node alive until stopped
  rospy.spin()

# called when joy message is received
def tj_callback(data):

  # start publisher of cmd_vel to control Turtlesim
  pub = rospy.Publisher("turtle1/cmd_vel", Twist, queue_size=1)

  # Create Twist message & add linear x and angular z from left
joystick
  twist = Twist()
  twist.linear.x = data.axes[1]
  twist.angular.z = data.axes[0]

  # record values to log file and screen
  rospy.loginfo("twist.linear: %f ; angular %f", twist.linear.x,
twist.angular.z)

  # process joystick buttons
  if data.buttons[0] == 1:          # green button on xbox controller
      move_circle()

  # publish cmd_vel move command to Turtlesim
  pub.publish(twist)

if __name__ == '__main__':
  try:
      joy_listener()
```

```
        except rospy.ROSInterruptException:
            pass
```

This code initializes the `turtlesim_joy` node and subscribes to the `joy` topic. When a joy message is received, the `tj_callback` function reads the values from `axes[0]` and `axes[1]` and assigns them to a twist message. If the value of `button[0]` is 1, then this button was pressed and the `move_circle` function is called.

The listing of `move_circle.py` is as follows:

```python
#!/usr/bin/env python
"""
Script to move Turtlesim in a circle
"""
import rospy
from geometry_msgs.msg import Twist

def move_circle():

    # Create a publisher which can "talk" to Turtlesim and tell it
    to move
    pub = rospy.Publisher('turtle1/cmd_vel', Twist, queue_size=1)

    # Create a Twist message and add linear x and angular z values
    move_cmd = Twist()
    move_cmd.linear.x = 1.0
    move_cmd.angular.z = 1.0

    # Save current time and set publish rate at 10 Hz
    now = rospy.Time.now()
    rate = rospy.Rate(10)

    # For the next 6 seconds publish cmd_vel move commands to
    Turtlesim
    while rospy.Time.now() < now + rospy.Duration.from_sec(6):
        pub.publish(move_cmd)
        rate.sleep()

if __name__ == '__main__':
    try:
        move_circle()
    except rospy.ROSInterruptException:
        pass
```

When executed, this code will create a twist message and set the `linear.x` and `angular.z` values. As the Python program `turtlesim_joy.py` is executed, you can move the turtle with the joystick. As the selected button is pushed, `move_circle.py` is executed, and the turtle then turns with a linear velocity of 1.0 units/second and an angular velocity of 1 radian/second for 6 seconds. Thus, the turtle moves in a circle. The following screenshot shows the result of one of our experiments with Xbox 360 joystick control of Turtlesim:

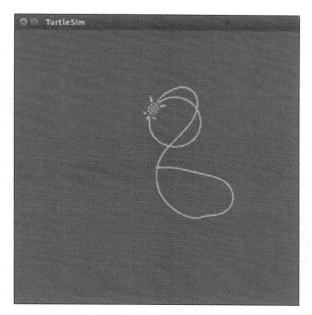

Turtlesim screen

To see the message published by the /joy node, issue this command:

```
$ rostopic echo /joy
```

The results indicate the values of the axes and buttons, as well as other information:

```
header:
  seq: 218
  stamp:
    secs: 1461884528
    nsecs: 370878390
  frame_id: ''
axes: [-0.0, 0.1265602558851242, 0.0, -0.06729009747505188, -0.0, 0.0, 0.0, 0.0]
buttons: [0, 0, 0, 0, 0, 0, 0, 0, 0, 0, 0]
```

Move the stick to start and use *Ctrl + C* to end the output.

To see the nodes and topics, issue the following command:

```
$ rqt_graph
```

This yields the following screenshot:

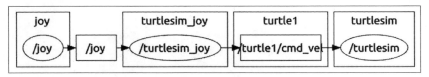

turtlesim_teleop.launch node and topic graph

A tutorial using a C++ program and a launch file for use with a Turtlesim and joystick is available at `http://wiki.ros.org/joy/Tutorials/WritingTeleopNode`.

Creating a custom ROS Android device interface

The **Android** operating system is an open source mobile platform that is widely used on smartphones and tablets. Its design is based on the Linux kernel, and its primary user control interface is via a touchscreen. This user interface consists of touch actions, such as swiping, tapping, or pinching elements on the screen. Tapping a virtual keyboard is one of the methods of entering text input. Various types of game control screens allow user interaction similar to joysticks and pushbuttons. The screen interface typically adjusts from portrait display to landscape based on the orientation in which the device is held. Sensors such as accelerometers, gyroscopes, and proximity sensors are usually available on the mobile device platform and are used by the application software.

To provide this type of interface for the user of a robot, the **ROS Android** metapackage has been developed and made available for use and further development.

The next sections will setup and describe the ROS Android development environment through the use of Android Studio and a **Java Development Kit (JDK)**. We start by downloading this software to become an Android developer using ROS.

Installing Android Studio and tools

There is one non-ROS software package to download in order to become a ROS–Android developer. You will need Android Studio, which is the official **Integrated Development Environment (IDE)** for Android. Android Studio provides all the tools you need to build apps for every type of Android device. Download the Android Studio package as a ZIP file from `http://developer.android.com/sdk/index.html`.

Be sure to load the Linux platform distribution.

It is recommended that you install this package in the `/opt` directory (as `/opt/android-studio`). Next, run the setup script using the following command:

```
$ /opt/android-studio/bin/studio.sh
```

A setup wizard will guide you through the setup process. When prompted to import previous Android Studio settings, you may select **I do not have a previous version of Studio** and click on **OK**. Next you will be prompted for installation instructions, select the **Standard** installation type.

1. The **Android SDK** components will be downloaded as part of the setup process. The location for the Android SDK should be selected as either `/opt/android-sdk` or `/home/<username>/Android/SDK`. We have chosen our location as the second path.

2. When the **Welcome to Android Studio** screen appears, find the **Configure** button at the bottom of the window. From the pop-up menu, select **SDK Manager** and install the Android SDK Platform package(s) for the Android OS running on your devices (tablets and/or phones).

3. If you wish to store your software in GitHub, you may wish to configure this setting. From the **Configure** button on the main screen, select **Settings | Version Control | GitHub**.

4. To create a Desktop icon for Android Studio, use the **Configure** button on the main screen and select **Create Desktop Entry**. A pop-up window will give the option to create a desktop entry for all users. This will require administrator privileges. When visible, be sure to lock the icon to your launcher if you wish to keep it.

Next, execute the following two commands to add Android Studio to your environment variables. If you installed your Android SDK at /opt/android-sdk, modify the first command appropriately:

```
$ echo export ANDROID_HOME=/home/<username>/Android/Sdk >> ~/.bashrc
$ echo export PATH=\${PATH}:${ANDROID_HOME}/tools${ANDROID_HOME}/
platform-tools:/opt/android-studio/bin >> ~/.bashrc
```

For systems that run a 64-bit version of Ubuntu, the following 32-bit libraries will need to be installed using the command in a terminal window:

```
$ sudo apt-get install libc6:i386 libncurses5:i386 libstdc++6:i386
lib32z1 libbz2-1.0:i386
```

With Android Studio installed, the ROS metapackages for rosjava and android are now needed. The installation of these metapackages is described in the upcoming section.

Installing a ROS–Android development environment

The first step in our instructions for creating a ROS–Android development environment is to install the Debian packages rosjava-build-tools and genjava. The rosjava-build-tools package contains simple tools and catkin modules for rosjava development. The genjava package is useful for generating Java Maven artifacts for message definitions that are in your source workspace. To install the rosjava-build-tools and genjava packages, type this command:

```
$ sudo apt-get install ros-kinetic-rosjava-build-tools ros-kinetic-
genjava
```

Next, create a workspace for the core Android libraries:

```
$ mkdir -p ~/android_core
$ wstool init -j4 ~/android_core/src https://raw.github.com/rosjava/
rosjava/kinetic/android_core.rosinstall
$ cd ~/android_core
$ catkin_make
```

Add a source command to this workspace in your .bashrc:

```
$ echo "source ~/android_core/devel/setup.bash" >>.bashrc
```

We continue by overlaying these ready-made android_core libraries onto new workspaces that we will use for Android development. Open a new terminal window and create an empty catkin workspace overlay on top of these files for your Java workspace. Use the following commands:

```
$ mkdir -p ~/myjava
$ wstool init ~/myjava/src
$ cd ~/myjava
$ catkin_make
```

If you have your own Java source code and you wish to use it in this workspace, refer to the instructions at http://wiki.ros.org/rosjava/Tutorials/kinetic/Deb%20Installation.

You can also start from here and create your own rosjava packages. Follow the tutorials at http://wiki.ros.org/rosjava_build_tools/Tutorials/indigo/Creating%20Rosjava%20Packages.

Use the following commands to create an Android workspace, which overlays the rosjava workspace created previously:

```
$ mkdir -p ~/myandroid
$ wstool init ~/myandroid/src
$ source ~/myjava/devel/setup.bash
$ cd ~/myandroid
$ catkin_make
```

Other options for installing the source code for ROS–Android core libraries can be found at http://wiki.ros.org/android/Tutorials/kinetic/Installation%20-%20ROS%20Development%20Environment.

To test your ROS–Android Development Environment, proceed to the instructions for accessing the camera on your Android device, found under the *Testing* section of http://wiki.ros.org/android/Tutorials/kinetic/Installation%20-%20ROS%20Development%20Environment.

Defining terms

Knowing the following terms should help as you learn more about the `rosjava` and `android` development environments:

- **Ant**: An Apache Ant is a Java library and command-line tool used to build Java applications. Developers either build `antlibs` that contain Ant tasks and types, or they have access to numerous ready-made `antlibs`. Apache Ant is a term trademarked by the Apache Software Foundation, which provides support for open source projects.

- **Gradle**: Gradle is an automated build system that works with Ant and Maven to offer a method of declaring a project's configuration by identifying the order of its build tasks. The system can handle large multiproject builds and supports incremental builds for only the portion of a project that is dependent on what has been changed.

- **JAR**: A **Java Archive (JAR)** is the package format that is used to combine Java class files and the metadata to be distributed as a software application or library. JARs are compressed into ZIP file format for archiving purposes.

- **Maven**: As a software project management and compression tool, Maven manages the state of a project's development, including its build, reporting, and documentation aspects. For our purposes, a repository in Maven will be used to hold build artifacts and dependencies for ROS–Android applications. Apache Maven is another open source project of the Apache Software Foundation.

Introducing ROS–Android development

The division between the `/myjava` and `/myandroid` workspaces is important to the development. In the `/myjava` workspace, you can create and build custom `rosjava` message JARs and artifacts. You can also use this space to build and test `rosjava` algorithms for use in your Android applications. To dive into `rosjava` development, refer to the list of tutorials (for ROS Kinetic) at `http://wiki.ros.org/rosjava?distro=kinetic`.

The `/android_core` workspace contains the official ROS `android` stacks, a collection of components and examples that are useful for developing ROS applications on Android.

The following diagram highlights the dependencies between the `rosjava` and `android` libraries:

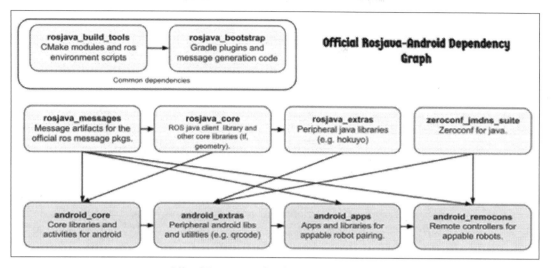

Official Rosjava-Android Dependency Graph

From this point, you are ready to begin with the creation of Android packages using `rosjava` scripts. To begin with, tutorials on creating Android packages and applications are available at `http://wiki.ros.org/rosjava_build_tools/Tutorials/indigo/Creating%20Android%20Packages`.

For a complete list of ROS–Android tutorials, refer to the list of tutorials (for ROS Kinetic) at `http://wiki.ros.org/android?distro=kinetic`.

You can also refer to the book *ROS Robotics Projects* by Lentin Joseph (Packt Publishing, `https://www.packtpub.com/hardware-and-creative/ros-robotics-projects`). *Chapter 8, ROS on MATLAB and Android* in this book provides examples of developing ROS–Android applications.

Creating ROS nodes on Arduino or Raspberry Pi

Arduino and Raspberry Pi are two of the most popular embedded systems on the market today. Sometimes, their names and capabilities are discussed interchangeably, but each platform has its own unique capabilities and usage. In robotics, it is important to know the merits of each of these powerful devices and how each one can be used with ROS to inherit the advantages of ROS.

Rosserial defines the protocol for ROS communication over serial transmission lines to ROS nodes running on microcontrollers or single-board computers. Standard ROS messages are serialized/deserialized in a prescribed format, and topics and services are multiplexed for serial ports or network sockets. For low-level details of this protocol, refer to `http://wiki.ros.org/rosserial/Overview/Protocol`.

In the following section, the capability of `rosserial` is demonstrated in an example program using Arduino and an ultrasonic sensor.

Using Arduino

The Arduino board contains a microcontroller that can process one ROS node at a time. This sequential nature makes it easy to use and understand its processing and communication with external devices, such as motors, sensors, and peripheral devices. Arduino has a set of digital and analog **input/output (I/O)** pins to interface with a wide variety of external sensors and actuators. This simple board can be used to design and build a robot to sense and move about in its environment or to enhance an existing robot with extended capabilities.

Interfacing the Arduino board to an external computer allows you to program the microcontroller using its own Arduino IDE based on the external computer. Programs developed in C in the Arduino IDE are downloaded to the microcontroller over its USB connection using its serial communications interface.

Installing Arduino IDE software

The Arduino IDE allows quick and easy programming of Arduino boards. This open source software can be installed on Windows, macOS, and Linux operating systems. The IDE can generate software for any Arduino board, but check for special instructions for your particular board at `https://www.arduino.cc/en/Guide/HomePage`.

To install the Arduino IDE as Debian packages on your Ubuntu operating system, open a terminal window and enter the following commands:

```
$ sudo apt-get update
$ sudo apt-get install arduino arduino-core
```

If any additional information is needed, refer to `http://playground.arduino.cc/Linux/Debian`.

For installation instructions on how to manually load Arduino, refer to the *Downloading and maintaining manually* section of `http://playground.arduino.cc/Linux/Ubuntu`.

The latest software download can be found at `https://www.arduino.cc/en/Main/Software`.

Arduino offers extensive documentation guides, tutorials, and examples at the following websites:

- `https://www.arduino.cc/en/Guide/Introduction`
- `https://www.arduino.cc/en/Guide/Environment`
- `https://www.arduino.cc/en/Guide/Libraries`
- `https://www.arduino.cc/en/Tutorial/HomePage`

Next, we will install the ROS software for Arduino.

Installing ROS–Arduino software

The `rosserial_arduino` package allows you to implement the ROS communication protocol over Arduino's serial ports. This package helps the software implement ROS messages, access ROS system time, and publish `tf` transforms. Using the `rosserial_arduino` package, an independent ROS node running on your Arduino can publish and subscribe to messages from ROS nodes running on a remote computer.

To load the `rosserial_arduino` package on your computer, use the following installation commands:

```
$ sudo apt-get install ros-kinetic-rosserial-arduino
$ sudo apt-get install ros-kinetic-rosserial
```

The `rosserial` metapackage contains the `rosserial_msgs`, `rosserial_client`, and `rosserial_python` packages. The `rosserial_python` package is used to provide the remote computer serial interface to communicate with the Arduino node.

ROS bindings for Arduino are implemented as an Arduino library within the IDE. This library, `ros_lib`, must be added to the `/libraries` subdirectory within the user's Arduino sketchbook (the code directory). We are using `~/sketchbook` as the directory in which to store our Arduino code (sketches). The subdirectory `/libraries` should already exist, or should be created within your `sketchbook`. Change to this subdirectory with the following command (`<sketchbook>` is the path to your `sketchbook` directory):

```
$ cd <sketchbook>/libraries
```

If the `ros_lib` library already exists, delete it with this command:

```
$ rm -rf ros_lib
```

To generate the `ros_lib` library, type the following command:

```
$ rosrun rosserial_arduino make_libraries.py
```

This command will create a `ros_lib` subdirectory and a number of subdirectories under `ros_lib`. A `ros_lib` subdirectory is a wrapper for ROS messages and services implemented with Arduino data types. The Arduino C/C++ data types are converted by `ros_lib` through the use of special header files. We will use some of these header files in our example with the ultrasound sensor. For now, the subdirectory we are interested in is `/examples`. Type the following commands:

```
$ cd <sketchbook>/libraries/ros_lib/examples/
$ ls
```

Verify that the contents are similar to the following files:

```
ADC        button_example  IrRanger  pubsub         ServoControl  Ultrasound
Blink      Clapper         Logging   ServiceClient  Temperature
BlinkM     HelloWorld      Odom      ServiceServer  TimeTF
```

These files contain examples of the ROS–Arduino code. The examples are used to provide a basic implementation of ROS on Arduino. For example, the `Temperature` code can be used to read the temperature values of a sensor connected to the Arduino board. You can start with the examples and modify them to suit your particular application.

Next, with your Arduino board plugged into the USB port of the computer, start the Arduino IDE with this command:

```
$ arduino
```

The **Arduino Permission Checker** may appear in a pop-up window, stating that **You need to be added to the dialout group**. It is important that you click on the **Add** button and authenticate the selection with a password. An alternative is to enter the following command to assign yourself to the `dialout` group:

```
$ sudo usermod -a -G dialout <username>
```

Administrative privileges are necessary to perform either of these actions.

Check that your screen looks as follows as a result of the `arduino` command:

Arduino sketchbook

Verify that you can access the `ros_lib` examples by navigating the drop-down menus, **File | Examples | ros_lib**, as shown in the following screenshot:

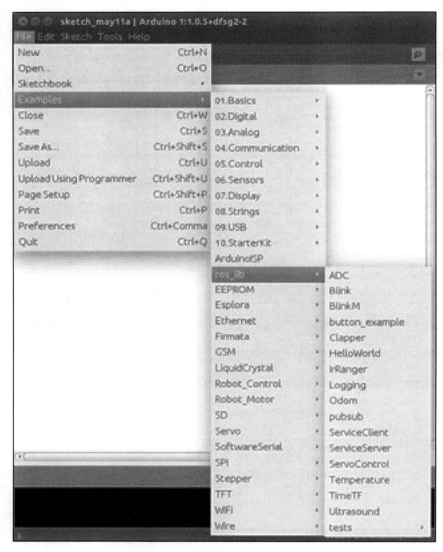

Arduino ros_lib installed

Also, check the serial port connection to the Arduino board. To list the available serial ports on your computer, use the following command:

```
$ ls /dev/tty*
```

From the Arduino IDE drop-down menu, **Tools | Serial Port**, verify the serial port connection. Our Arduino is connected to /dev/ttyACM0, as shown in the following screenshot:

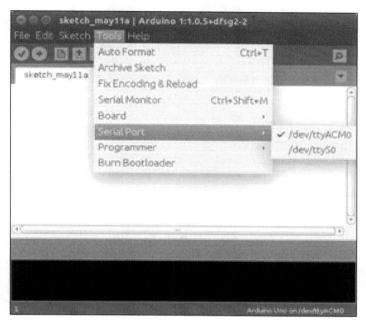

Connecting to a serial port

The ROS wiki presents a series of tutorials related to the rosserial_arduino package. These tutorials are listed and can be accessed from http://wiki.ros.org/rosserial_arduino/Tutorials.

The following example demonstrates the use of a ROS node running on Arduino publishing a sensor_msgs/Range message. This message contains distance data retrieved from an HC-SR04 ultrasonic sensor.

Ultrasonic sensor control using ROS and Arduino

As an example of interfacing a sensor with the Arduino board, we will add an HC-SR04 ultrasonic range sensor. The following screenshot shows the face of the sensor:

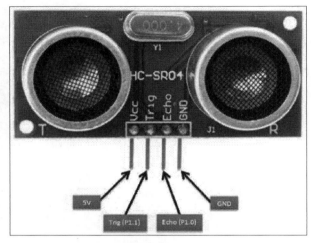

HC-SR04 ultrasonic sensor

In operation, the sensor emits sound pulses well beyond the range of our hearing. If the pulses bounce off an obstacle, the returning sound wave is received by the sensor. Knowing the speed of sound in air as *Velocity*, it is possible to measure the time that the sound takes to reach the obstacle and return to the sensor, since the distance traveled by the sound waves to the object will be:

$$Distance = Velocity * Time/2$$

Time refers to the total time of travel of the sound wave in its two-way trip.

The speed of sound varies with temperature and other factors, but we will use the typical speed of sound in air at 20°C (68°F) to be 343 meters/second (1125.3 feet/second).

To use the sensor with the Arduino board, it is necessary to write code to trigger the sensor to emit the sound and then determine the time of travel of the sound wave. The distance between the sensor and an obstacle is determined from this time, as shown in the previous equation. The range of the HC-SR04 sensor is 2 cm to 400 cm, or from less than 1 inch to 13 ft.

Signals associated with the sensor are shown in the following diagram. The trigger pulse is created by the software as an output from the Arduino board digital pins to the **Trig** pin, shown in the preceding screenshot. The sensor sends out the sonic burst after the trigger pulse has ended. The echo signal on the **Echo** pin of the sensor when HIGH has a width that is proportional to the time the sound signal takes to be emitted and then returned. This signal is connected to a digital input pin of the Arduino board. Software is used to determine the length of the return echo pulse in microseconds. Then, the time in microseconds is converted into distance using the distance formula, as follows:

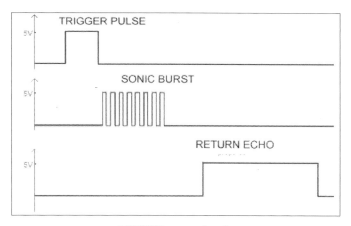

HC-SR04 sensor signals

According to the specifications of the HC-SR04 sensor, the trigger pulse created by the software must be at least 10 microseconds long. The repetition time to measure the distance to an obstacle must be greater than 25 milliseconds to ensure that the trigger pulses do not overlap in time with the return echo pulse. This is a repetition rate of 40 hertz. In the code to follow, the repetition time for the published range is set at 50 milliseconds.

Connecting the Arduino to the HC-SR04 ultrasonic sensor

For our setup, we used an Arduino UNO to interface with the HC-SR04 sensor. The following list describes the connections between the sensor pins and the pins of our Arduino UNO board:

- VCC of the sensor to 5V on the Arduino board for power
- GND of the sensor to GND on the Arduino board for the ground
- Trig input pin of the sensor to digital I/O pin 6 as the output of the Arduino board
- Echo output pin of the sensor to digital I/O pin 5 as the input to the Arduino board

The Arduino UNO is described at `https://www.arduino.cc/en/main/arduinoBoardUno`.

Programming the Arduino to sense distance

An Arduino sketch is provided to interface with the ultrasound sensor and determine the distance values detected by the sensor. The C code for the Arduino should be downloaded and stored in the `<sketchbook>/ultrasound_sr04` directory as an `.ino` file.

> **Downloading the ultrasound_sr04.ino code**
>
> You can download the example code files and other support material for this book from `https://www.packtpub.com/` or at the website: `https://github.com/FairchildC/ROS-Robotics-By-Example-2nd-Edition`.

The following code performs these operations:

- Defines the pins of the Arduino board used for the sensor and outputs the trigger signal when the program runs
- Creates the node to publish range data indicating the distance between the sensor and an object
- Defines the ROS topic `/ultrasound` and causes the range data to be published when the code is run

The code is as follows:

```
/*
 * rosserial Ultrasound Example for HC-SR04
 */

#include <ros.h>
#include <ros/time.h>
#include <sensor_msgs/Range.h>

const int echoPin = 5;   //Echo pin
const int trigPin = 6;   //Trigger pin

const int maxRange = 400.0;   //Maximum range in centimeters
const int minRange = 0.0;     //Minimum range

unsigned long range_timer;    //Used to measure 50 ms interval

// instantiate node handle and publisher for
//  a sensor_msgs/Range message (topic name is /ultrasound)
ros::NodeHandle  nh;
sensor_msgs::Range range_msg;
ros::Publisher pub_range( "ultrasound", &range_msg);

/*
 * getRange() - This function reads the time duration of the echo
 *              and converts it to centimeters.
 */
float getRange(){
    int sample;        //Holds time in microseconds

    // Trigger pin goes low then high for 10 us then low
    //  to initiate the ultrasonic burst
    digitalWrite(trigPin, LOW);
    delayMicroseconds(2);

    digitalWrite(trigPin, HIGH);
    delayMicroseconds(10);
    digitalWrite(trigPin, LOW);

    // read pulse length in microseconds on the Echo pin
    sample = pulseIn(echoPin, HIGH);

    // sample in microseconds converted to centimeters
```

```
        // 343 m/s speed of sound;  time divided by 2
        return sample/58.3;
}

char frameid[] = "/ultrasound";    // global frame id string

void setup()
{
  // initialize the node and message publisher
  nh.initNode();
  nh.advertise(pub_range);

  // fill the description fields in the range_msg
  range_msg.radiation_type = sensor_msgs::Range::ULTRASOUND;
  range_msg.header.frame_id =  frameid;
  range_msg.field_of_view = 0.26;
  range_msg.min_range = minRange;
  range_msg.max_range = maxRange;

  // set the digital I/O pin modes
  pinMode(echoPin, INPUT);
  pinMode(trigPin, OUTPUT);
}

void loop()
{
  // sample the range data from the ultrasound sensor and
  // publish the range value once every 50 milliseconds
  if ( (millis()-range_timer) > 50){
    range_msg.range = getRange();
    range_msg.header.stamp = nh.now();
    pub_range.publish(&range_msg);
    range_timer =  millis() + 50;
  }
  nh.spinOnce();
}
```

Executing the ultrasonic sensor program

To open the Arduino IDE, type the following command:

```
$ arduino
```

From the menu bar, navigate the drop-down menus **File | Sketchbook | ultrasound_sr04** to see the following screen:

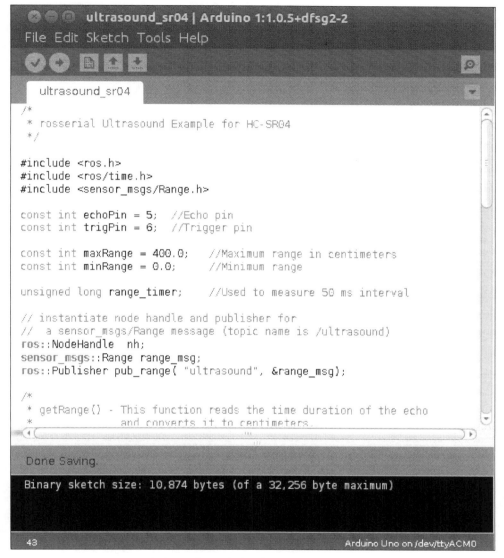

Arduino IDE with the ultrasound_sr04 code

On the toolbar menu, choose the right arrow icon to verify and upload the code to the Arduino board and wait for the **Done uploading** message.

In a second terminal window, start the ROS Master by typing:

```
$ roscore
```

In a third terminal window, execute the `rosserial` program by typing:

```
$ rosrun rosserial_python serial_node.py /dev/<ttyID>
```

Here, `<ttyID>` is the identifier of the serial port you are using.

Our system used `/dev/ttyACM0`, and our output yields the following information:

```
[INFO]  [1505178855.571564]: ROS Serial Python Node
[INFO]  [1505178855.574369]: Connecting to /dev/ttyACM0 at 57600 baud
[INFO]  [1505178857.937858]: Note: publish buffer size is 280 bytes
[INFO]  [1505178857.938173]: Setup publisher on ultrasound [sensor_msgs/
Range]
```

The `rosserial_python` package contains a Python implementation to allow communication between a remote computer and an attached device capable of serial data transfer, such as the Arduino board. The `serial_node.py` script creates the/ `serial_node` node.

The ROS data for distance will be published as **range** data. As the program executes, the range value and other information is published on the `/ultrasound` topic with the `sensor_msgs/Range` message. The message format can be seen by entering the following command in another terminal window:

```
$ rosmsg show sensor_msgs/Range
```

The output shows the message format as follows:

```
uint8 ULTRASOUND=0
uint8 INFRARED=1
std_msgs/Header header
  uint32 seq
  time stamp
  string frame_id
uint8 radiation_type
float32 field_of_view
float32 min_range
float32 max_range
float32 range
```

To see the numerical output of the `/ultrasound` topic, type this:

```
$ rostopic echo /ultrasound
```

The output should look similar to the following:

```
---
header:
  seq: 278
  stamp:
    secs: 1463092078
    nsecs:   3101881
  frame_id: /ultrasound
radiation_type: 0
field_of_view: 0.259999990463
min_range: 0.0
max_range: 400.0
range: 50.0
---
```

In the screen output, we see the information in the message. Note that the `frame_id`, `radiation_type`, `field_of_view` (0.26), `min_range`, and `max_range` variables were defined in the C code, which was shown previously. The range value is in centimeters and the values are published every 50 milliseconds.

To show the topic and range values in a graphical form, type the following command:

```
$ rqt_plot
```

The `rqt_plot` window is shown in the next screenshot. The values will of course depend on your setup and the distance between your sensor and the obstacle:

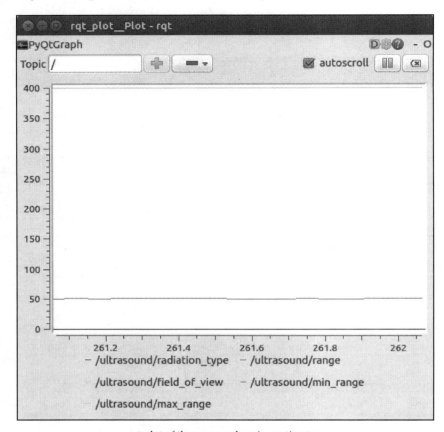

rqt plot of the range values in centimeters

In the screenshot, the range is a constant 50 cm and the `max_range` field is set to 400 cm, as defined in the code. The other values are too small to be seen on the scale.

In our test of the HC-SR04 sensor, we noticed some inaccuracies in the range measurements. As with any sensor like HC-SR04, the system should be calibrated and tested if you wish to ensure the accuracy of the measurement.

Other applications using ROS and Arduino

There are other sensors for ranging as well as for temperature measurement, motor control, and many other applications. A complete list of tutorials for Arduino applications using `rosserial` can be found at `http://wiki.ros.org/rosserial_arduino/Tutorials`.

`rosserial` can also be used to set up wireless communication using `rosserial_xbee` tools in order to create sensor networks using XBee devices and Arduino. More information on this is available at `http://wiki.ros.org/rosserial_xbee`.

Using Raspberry Pi

The Raspberry Pi board is a general-purpose computer that contains a version of the Linux operating system called **Raspbian**. The Pi can process multiple ROS nodes at a time and can take advantage of many features of ROS. It can handle multiple tasks at a time and perform intense processing of images or complex algorithms.

There are several versions of Raspberry Pi available on the market. Each model is based on a Broadcom **system on a chip** (**SOC**) with an ARM processor and a VideoCore **graphics processing unit** (**GPU**). Models vary in the amount of board memory available, and a **Secure Digital** (**SD**) card is used for booting and long-term storage. Boards are available pre-configured with a variety of USB ports, HDMI and composite video output, RJ45 Ethernet, WiFi 802.11n, and Bluetooth communication.

To set up your Raspberry Pi and configure the Raspbian operating system, refer to these websites:

- `https://www.raspberrypi.org/documentation/setup/`
- `https://www.raspberrypi.org/documentation/installation/`

To configure your Raspberry Pi, see the website `https://www.raspberrypi.org/documentation/configuration/`.

To get started learning about Raspbian and interfacing with the general-purpose I/O, camera modules, and communication methods, refer to `https://www.raspberrypi.org/documentation/usage/`.

Technical documentation of the hardware is available at `https://www.raspberrypi.org/documentation/hardware/`.

Installing ROS on the Raspberry Pi

The installation instructions for loading ROS Kinetic onto the Raspberry Pi can be found at `http://wiki.ros.org/ROSberryPi/Installing%20ROS%20Kinetic%20on%20the%20Raspberry%20Pi`.

These instructions are for a source installation of ROS onto a Raspberry Pi with the Raspian version Jessie installed for the operating system. A catkin workspace needs to be created for the source packages, and the ROS–Comm variation is recommended to install basic ROS packages, build tools, and communication libraries. Packages for GUI tools are not downloaded as part of this variation.

The projects you can undertake with the Raspberry Pi and ROS (sometimes called ROSberry Pi) are limitless. You can create programs in either Python or C++. A collection of examples can be found at these websites:

- `http://wiki.ros.org/rosserial_embeddedlinux/Tutorials`
- `http://wiki.ros.org/ROS/Tutorials`
- `http://www.takktile.com/tutorial:raspberrypi-ros`

Summary

This chapter has described ROS interfaces for a number of external devices used for robot control. The advantages of ROS extend to these types of interfaces, as it is evident in the common method and message structure used across similar devices. For game controllers, a custom interface was created using an Xbox 360 controller for the Turtlesim simulation. The buttons and axes for the Xbox 360 controller were mapped so that we could select a button and axes to use for Turtlesim control. A Python script was shown that caused the turtle to move when a joystick was moved or a certain button was pressed.

Android devices can also provide a common ROS interface for controlling robots. We looked at some instructions for installing the software and tools to set up a ROS-Android development environment. We also looked at the key terminology for Android development.

Embedded systems such as the Arduino and Raspberry Pi are often used for controlling robots and interfacing to sensors. ROS nodes can run on these devices and publish messages over topics to nodes on other computers. For serial communication, ROS provides the `rosserial` protocol and metapackage to standardize this interface. Instructions for installing the Arduino–ROS and Raspberry Pi–ROS development environments were presented. Within the Arduino IDE, software was written to create a node and publish a message containing sensor data from an HC-SR04 ultrasound sensor.

In the next chapter, *Flying a Mission with Crazyflie*, we will leverage all of our current ROS knowledge (and then some) to autonomously fly a quadrotor to a specific location. An external camera will be used to coordinate the flight and identify the quadrotor and the location of the target.

9
Flying a Mission with Crazyflie

Robots are fun and sometimes frustrating to program. Quadrotors are particularly difficult to control due to the number of flight factors and the complexity of flight programs required to manage these factors. Quadrotors are currently being tested for surveillance cameras and delivery vehicles for packages and fast food. In this chapter, we will explore the subject of programming quadrotors to fly to specific destinations. This application may be handy for delivering coffee and paperwork around the office. We will begin by using a barebones quadrotor and an inexpensive depth camera to sense the quadrotor's location.

This chapter will highlight the use of ROS communication to coordinate the locations of the quadrotor and the target. A Kinect sensor will be used to visualize the environment and the position of the quadrotor in it to coordinate its landing at a marked location. ROS tf transforms and pose messages will be generated to identify the reference frames and positions of the quadrotor and the target. The transforms enable the control commands to be published to bring the quadrotor to the target location. The navigation, flying, and landing mission implements a spectrum of ROS components — including nodes, topics, messages, services, launch files, tf transforms, rqt, and more — taught in this book.

We will set up this mission scenario between a Crazyflie 2.0, a Kinect for Windows v2 (called Kinect v2 in this chapter), and a target marker acting as the landing position on top of a TurtleBot. The following image shows the arrangement of our setup. Feel free to follow these instructions to prepare an arrangement of the quadrotor, target, and image sensor with the equipment you have available.

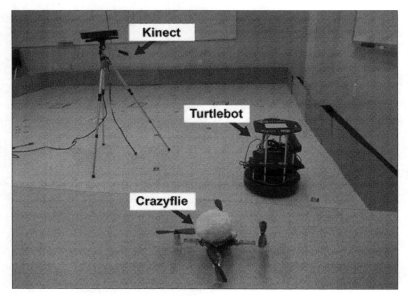

Mission setup

For our mission, Crazyflie will be controlled to hover, fly and land. In this chapter, we will address the following to achieve this mission:

- Detecting the Crazyflie on a Kinect v2 image
- Establishing a tf framework to support the configuration of our camera and robot
- Determining the Cartesian coordinates (x, y, z) of the Crazyflie with respect to the image
- Publishing a tf transform of the coordinates
- Controlling the Crazyflie to hover at its initial location
- Locating a target on the video image, determining its coordinates, and publishing its pose
- Controlling the Crazyflie to takeoff, fly to the target and land

Mission components

The components we will use in this mission include a Crazyflie 2.0 quadrotor, a Crazyradio PA, a Kinect for the Windows v2 sensor, and a workstation computer. *Chapter 7, Making a Robot Fly*, describes the Crazyflie and Crazyradio and their operations. *Chapter 4, Navigating the World with TurtleBot*, is a good introduction to a depth sensor such as the Kinect v2. It is recommended to review these chapters before beginning this mission.

Kinect for Windows v2

Kinect v2 is an infrared time of flight depth sensor that operates at a higher resolution than the Kinect for Xbox 360. The modulated infrared beam measures how long it takes for the light to travel to the object and back, providing a more accurate measurement. This sensor has improved performance in dark rooms and in sunny outdoor conditions. With a horizontal **field of view** (**FOV**) of 70 degrees and a vertical FOV of 60 degrees, the infrared sensor can accurately detect distances ranging from 0.5 to 4.5 meters (20 inches to 14.75 feet) within this FOV. The image resolution for the depth camera is 512 x 424 at a rate of 30 frames per second. The Kinect v2 must be connected to a USB 3.0 port on the workstation computer in order to provide the image data. External electrical power for the Kinect is also required.

Kinect v2 produces a large amount of image data that can overwhelm the workstation computer if it is not equipped with a separate **graphics processing unit** (**GPU**). The ROS packages `libfreenect2` and `iai_kinect2` were developed to interface with Kinect v2 for image-processing applications. The `iai_kinect2` package provides tools for calibrating the sensor and viewing color and depth images from Kinect v2. Kinect images are used with OpenCV tools to process the images for object detection. The *OpenCV and ROS* section provides background information and describes how these two tools are interfaced.

Kinect's color images will be evaluated to locate markers for the Crazyflie and the target positions. These markers will enable the position and altitude of the quadrotor and the target to be determined with respect to the image frame. These positions are not related to real-world coordinates but applied in relation to the sensor's image frame. A ROS tf transform is published to advertise the location of the Crazyflie.

Crazyflie operation

Controlling a quadrotor is the subject of a vast amount of literature. To control Crazyflie, our plan is to follow the same type of control prepared by Wolfgang Hoenig in his success with the `crazyflie` metapackage (`https://github.com/whoenig/crazyflie_ros`). This package was developed as part of his research at the ACT Lab at the University of Southern California (`http://act.usc.edu/`). Within his `crazyflie_controller` package, he created a controller that uses PID control for each of Crazyflie's four dimensions of control: pitch, roll, thrust, and yaw. Our software design mimics this approach but deviates in key areas, as the singular image view of the Kinect requires changes to the control parameters. We also changed the software to Python. A vast amount of testing was required to attain control of a Crazyflie in a hover state. When hover results were acceptable, testing advanced further to add the challenge of flying to the target. Further testing was required to improve flight control.

The controller software uses the difference between the Crazyflie's current position and the goal position (either hover or target) to send correction commands to fly closer to the goal position. This iteration continues every 20 milliseconds with a new position for Crazyflie detected and a new correction computed and sent. This is a closed-loop system that computes the difference between positions, and commands the Crazyflie to fly in the direction of the goal position.

During testing, Crazyflie lived up to its name and would arbitrarily fly to various corners of the room, out of control. Implementing a new ROS node took care of this unwanted behavior. The node `crazyflie_window` was designed to be an observer of Crazyflie's location in the image frame. When Crazyflie's location came too close to the image's edge, a service command was sent to the controller and an appropriate command was published to Crazyflie to fly towards the interior of the image. This implementation resulted in no more flyaway behavior and saved on broken motor mounts.

Mission software structure

The code developed for this mission is contained in the `crazyflie_autonomous` package and divided into four different nodes:

- `crazyflie_detector` in the `detect_crazyflie.py` file
- `target_detector` in the `detect_target.py` file
- `crazyflie_controller` in the `control_crazyflie.py`, `pid.py`, and `crazyflie2.yaml` files
- `crazyflie_window` in the `watcher.py` file

This mission also relies on a portion of Wolfgang Hoenig's `crazyflie` metapackage that was described in *Chapter 7, Making a Robot Fly*. The nodes used are as follows:

- `crazyflie_server` (`crazyflie_server.cpp` from the `crazyflie_driver` package)
- `crazyflie_add` (`crazyflie_add.cpp` from the `crazyflie_driver` package) node runs briefly during Crazyflie startup to set initial parameters for the Crazyflie.
- `joystick_controller` (`controller.py` from the `crazyflie_demo` package)

A third set of nodes is generated by other packages:

- `baselink` (`static_transform_publisher` from the `tf` package)
- `joy` (the `joy` package)
- `kinect2_bridge` (the `iai_kinect2/kinect2_bridge` package) The `kinect2_bridge` works between the Kinect v2 driver (`libfreenect2`) and ROS. Image topics are produced by the `kinect2` node.

The relationship between these nodes is shown in the following node graph:

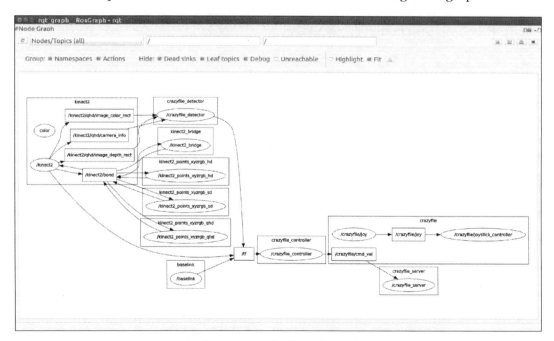

Nodes and topics for Crazyflie mission

All of the code for *Chapter 9*, *Flying a Mission with Crazyflie* is available online at the Packt Publishing website: `http://www.PacktPub.com` or `https://github.com/FairchildC/ROS-Robotics-By-Example-2nd-Edition`. The code is too extensive to include in this chapter. Only important portions of the code are described in the following sections to aid in the learning of the techniques used for this mission.

Python code within a package should be executable. For Python code within your `crazyflie_autonomous/scripts` directory, use the command:
`$ chmod +x *.py`

OpenCV and ROS

In the previous two chapters (*Chapter 4*, *Navigating the World with TurtleBot* and *Chapter 6*, *Wobbling Robot Arms using Joint Control*), we introduced and described a little about the capabilities of OpenCV. Since this mission heavily relies on the interface between ROS and OpenCV, and also on the OpenCV library, we will go into further background details about OpenCV.

OpenCV is a library of powerful computer vision tools for a vast expanse of applications. It was originally developed at Intel by Gary Bradsky in 1999 as a C library. The upgrade to OpenCV 2.0 was released in October 2009 with a C++ interface. Much of this work was done at Willow Garage, headed by Bradsky and Vadim Pisarevsky. It is open source software with a BSD license, and free for both academic and for commercial use. OpenCV is available on multiple operating systems, including Windows, Linux, macOS, Android, iOS, and more. The primary interface for OpenCV is C++, but programming language interfaces exist for Python, C, Java, MATLAB/Octave, and wrappers for C# and Ruby.

The OpenCV library contains more than 2,500 effective and efficient vision algorithms for a wide range of vision-processing and machine learning applications. The fundamental objective is to support real-time vision applications, such as tracking moving objects and detecting and recognizing faces for surveillance. Many other algorithms support object identification, the tracking of human gestures and facial expressions, the production of 3D models of objects, the construction of 3D point clouds from stereo camera data, and the modeling of scenes based on multiple image sources, to name just a few. This extensive library of tools is used throughout the industry and in academia and government as well.

To learn more about OpenCV, visit `http://opencv.org/`. This website provides access to excellent tutorials, documentation on structures and functions, and an API interface for C++, and to a lesser extent Python. ROS Kinetic Kame uses OpenCV version 3 as its default version.

ROS provides the `vision_opencv` stack to integrate the power of the OpenCV library of tools. The wiki website for this interface stack is `http://wiki.ros.org/vision_opencv`.

The OpenCV software and the ROS `vision_opencv` stack were installed when you performed the ROS software install of the `ros-kinetic-desktop-full` configuration in *Chapter 1, Getting Started with ROS*. To install only the OpenCV library with the ROS interface and Python wrapper, use the following command:

```
$ sudo apt-get install ros-kinetic-vision-opencv ros-kinetic-opencv3
```

This `vision_opencv` stack currently provides two packages: `cv_bridge` and `image_geometry`. The `cv_bridge` package is the connection between ROS messages and OpenCV. It provides the conversion of OpenCV images into ROS images and vice versa. The `image_geometry` package contains a powerful library of image processing tools for both Python and C++. Images can be handled with respect to the camera parameters provided in the `CameraInfo` messages. It is also used with camera calibration and image rectification.

For this mission, we will use OpenCV algorithms to analyze the Kinect image and detect the Crazyflie and target within the scene. Using the location of the Crazyflie and target, the Crazyflie will be given commands to fly to the location of the target. This scenario hides the layers of complex computation and understanding required to perform this seemingly simple task.

Loading software for the mission

Part of the software that is needed to perform this cooperative mission has been installed in previous chapters. Refer back to the previous chapters for software that is required to perform this mission:

- The ROS software installation of the `ros-kinetic-desktop-full` configuration is described in the *Installing and launching ROS* section of *Chapter 1, Getting Started with ROS*

- The installation of Crazyflie ROS software is described in the *Loading Crazyflie ROS software* section of *Chapter 7, Making a Robot Fly*

Software for the Kinect v2 to interface with ROS requires the installation of two items: `libfreenect2` and `iai_kinect2`. The following sections provide the details of these installations.

Installing libfreenect2

The `libfreenect2` software provides an open-source driver for Kinect v2. This driver does not support the Kinect for Xbox 360 or Xbox One. Libfreenect2 provides for the image transfer of RGB and depth as well as the combined registration of RGB and depth. **Image registration** aligns the color and depth images for the same scene into one reference image. Kinect v2 firmware updates are not supported in this software.

The installation instructions can be found at `https://github.com/OpenKinect/libfreenect2`. The website lists installation instructions for Windows, macOS, and Linux operating systems. It is important to follow these directions accurately and read all the related troubleshooting information to ensure a successful installation. The instructions provided here are tested for Ubuntu 16.04 and will load the software into the current directory. This installation can be either local to your home directory or system wide if you have `sudo` privileges.

To install the `libfreenect2` software in your home directory, type the following:

```
$ git clone https://github.com/OpenKinect/libfreenect2.git
$ cd ~/libfreenect2
```

A number of build tools are required to be installed as well:

```
$ sudo apt-get install build-essential cmake pkg-config
```

The `libusb` package provides access for the Kinect v2 to the USB device on your operating system. Install `libusb` with the following command:

```
$ sudo apt-get install libusb-1.0-0-dev
```

TurboJPEG provides a high-level open-source API for compressing and decompressing JPEG images in the memory to improve CPU/GPU performance. Install the following packages for TurboJPEG by typing:

```
$ sudo apt-get install libturbojpeg libjpeg-turbo8-dev
```

Open Graphics Library (OpenGL) is an open-source cross-platform API with a variety of functions designed to improve graphics processing performance. To install OpenGL's packages, type the following commands:

```
$ sudo apt-get install libglfw3-dev
```

Some of these packages may already be installed on your system. You will receive a screen message indicating that the latest version of the package is installed.

Additional software packages can be installed to use with libfreenect2, but they are optional:

- **Open Computing Language (OpenCL)** creates a common interface despite the underlying computer system platform. The libfreenect2 software uses OpenCL to perform more effective processing on the system.

  The OpenCL software requires that certain underlying software be installed to ensure that the libfreenect2 driver can operate on your processor. OpenCL dependencies are specific to your computer system's GPU. Refer to the detailed instructions at https://github.com/OpenKinect/libfreenect2.

- Installation instructions for CUDA (used with Nvidia), **Video Acceleration API (VAAP)** (used with Intel), and **Open Natural Interaction (OpenNI2)** are provided at the libfreenect2 website.

Whether or not you install the optional software, the last step will be to build the actual **Protonect** executable using the following commands:

```
$ cd ~/libfreenect2
$ mkdir build
$ cd build
$ cmake .. -DCMAKE_INSTALL_PREFIX=$HOME/freenect2
$ make
$ make install
```

Remember that udev rules are used to manage system devices and create device nodes for the purpose of handling external devices, such as Kinect. Most likely, an udev rule will be required so that you will not need to run Protonect for the Kinect with sudo privileges. For this reason, it is necessary to copy the udev rule from its place in the downloaded software to the /etc/udev/rules.d directory:

```
$ sudo cp ~/libfreenect2/platform/linux/udev/90-kinect2.rules /etc/udev/rules.d
```

Now you are ready to test the operation of your Kinect. Verify that the Kinect v2 device is plugged into power and into the USB 3.0 port of the computer. If your Kinect was plugged in prior to installing the udev rule, unplug and reconnect the sensor.

 Remember that the Kinect v2 can only be used through a USB 3.0 port.

Now run the program using the following command:

```
$ ./libfreenect2/build/bin/Protonect
```

You are successful if a terminal window opens with four camera views. The following screenshot shows our Kinect pointed at Baxter:

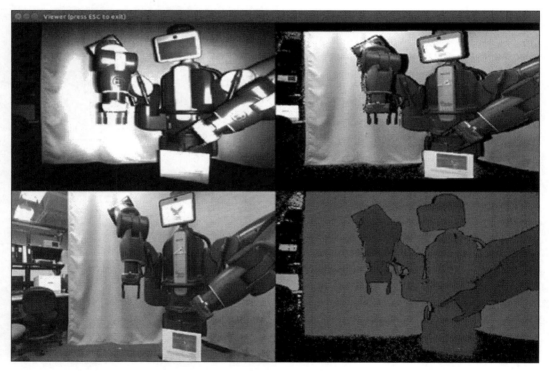

Protonect output

Use *Ctrl* + *C* keys in the terminal window to quit Protonect.

If you are experiencing problems, check the `libfreenect2` software GitHub for the latest master release and installation instructions.

If you experience errors, refer to the FAQ at `https://github.com/OpenKinect/libfreenect2` and the issues at `https://github.com/OpenKinect/libfreenect2/wiki/Troubleshooting`.

 Protonect is a very useful tool when it comes to checking out the operation of your Kinect v2. Anytime the Kinect seems to work improperly, use Protonect to check the operation of the `libfreenect2` driver. The command to do this is:
`$ ./libfreenect2/build/bin/Protonect`

Installing iai_kinect2

The `iai_kinect2` software is a library of functions and tools that provide the ROS interface for Kinect v2. The `libfreenect2` driver is required for using the `iai_kinect2` software library. The `iai_kinect2` package was developed by Thiemo Wiedemeyer of the Institute for Artificial Intelligence at the University of Bremen.

Instructions for the installation of the software can be found at:

`https://github.com/code-iai/iai_kinect2`

For a cooperative mission, you can decide to either add the software to the `crazyflie_ws` workspace or create a new catkin workspace for this software. The authors decided to create a new catkin workspace called `mission_ws` to contain the software for the `iai_kinect2` metapackage and the `crazyflie_autonomous` package developed for this mission.

To install the `iai_kinect2` software, move to your catkin workspace `src` directory and clone the repository:

```
$ cd ~/<your_catkin_ws>/src/
$ git clone https://github.com/code-iai/iai_kinect2.git
```

Next, move into the `iai_kinect2` directory, install the dependencies, and build the executable:

```
$ cd iai_kinect2
$ rosdep install -r --from-paths .
$ cd ~/<your_catkin_ws>
$ catkin_make -DCMAKE_BUILD_TYPE="Release"
```

Notice that running the rosdep command will output an error regarding not being able to locate [kinect2_bridge] and [kinect2_registration]. Disregard this error because these packages are part of the iai_kinect2 metapackage and rosdep is unaware of these packages at this time.

Now it is time to operate the Kinect sensor using the kinect2_bridge launch file. Type the following command:

```
$ roslaunch kinect2_bridge kinect2_bridge.launch
```

At the end of a large amount of screen output, you should see this line:

```
[ INFO] [Kinect2Bridge::main] waiting for clients to connect
```

If you are successful, congratulations! Great work! If not, start your diagnosis by referring to the *kinect2_bridge is not working/crashing, what is wrong?* FAQ and other helpful queries at https://github.com/code-iai/iai_kinect2.

When you receive the waiting for clients to contact message, the next step is to view the output images of kinect2_bridge. To do this, use kinect2_viewer by typing in the following:

```
$ rosrun kinect2_viewer kinect2_viewer
```

The output should be as follows:

```
[ INFO] [main] topic color: /kinect2/qhd/image_color_rect
[ INFO] [main] topic depth: /kinect2/qhd/image_depth_rect
[ INFO] [main] starting receiver...
```

Our screen shows the following image:

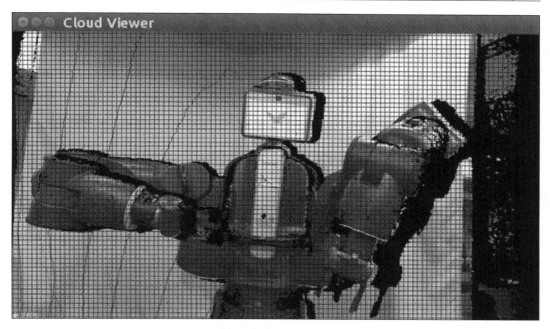

kinect2_viewer output

Use *Ctrl + C* in the terminal window to quit `kinect2_viewer`.

As shown in the preceding screenshot, `kinect2_viewer` has the default settings of **quarter high definition** (**qhd**), `image_color_rect`, and `image_depth_rect`. This Cloud Viewer output is the default viewer. These settings and other options for `kinect2_viewer` will be described in more detail in the following section.

The next section describes the packages that are contained in the `iai_kinect2` metapackage. These packages make the job of interfacing to the Kinect v2 flexible and relatively straightforward. It is extremely important to calibrate your Kinect sensor to align the RGB camera with the **infrared** (**IR**) sensor. This alignment will transform the raw images into a rectified image. The `kinect2_calibration` tool that can be used to perform this calibration and the calibration process is described in the next section.

Using the iai_kinect2 metapackage

The IAI Kinect 2 library provides the following tools for the Kinect v2:

- `kinect2_calibration`: This tool is used to align the Kinect RGB camera with its IR camera and depth measurements. It relies on the functions of the OpenCV library for image and depth processing.

- `kinect2_registration`: This package projects the depth image onto the color image to produce the **depth registration image**. OpenCL or Eigen must be installed for this software to work. It is recommended to use OpenCL to reduce the load on the CPU and obtain the best performance possible.

- `kinect2_bridge`: This package provides the interface between the Kinect v2 driver, `libfreenect2`, and ROS. This real-time process delivers Kinect v2 images at 30 frames per second to the CPU/GPU. The `kinect2_bridge` software is implemented with OpenCL to take advantage of the system's architecture for processing depth registration data.

- `kinect2_viewer`: This viewer provides two types of visualization: a color image overlaid with a depth image or a registered point cloud.

Additional information is provided in later sections.

kinect2_bridge and kinect2_viewer

The `kinect2_bridge` and `kinect2_viewer` provide several options for producing images and point clouds. Three different resolutions are available from the `kinect2_bridge` interface: Full HD (1920 x 1080), quarter Full HD (960 x 540), and raw IR/depth images (512 x 424). Each of these resolutions can produce a number of different images, such as the following:

- `image_color`
- `image_color/compressed`
- `image_color_rect`
- `image_color_rect/compressed`
- `image_depth_rect`
- `image_depth_rect/compressed`
- `image_mono`
- `image_mono/compressed`
- `image_mono_rect`
- `image_mono_rect/compressed`
- `image_ir`

- image_ir/compressed
- image_ir_rect
- image_ir_rect/compressed
- points

The kinect2_bridge software limits the depth range for the sensor between 0.1 and 12.0 meters. For more information on these image topics, refer to the documentation at https://github.com/code-iai/iai_kinect2/tree/master/kinect2_bridge.

The kinect2_viewer has the command-line options to bring up the different resolutions described previously. These modes are as follows:

- hd: for **Full High Definition (Full HD)**
- qhd: for quarter Full HD
- sd: for raw IR/depth images

Visualization options for these modes can be image for a color image overlaid with a depth image, cloud for a registered point cloud, or both to bring up both the visualizations in different windows. An example command is:

```
$ rosrun kinect2_viewer kinect2_viewer sd cloud
```

kinect2_calibration

The kinect2_calibration tool requires the use of a chessboard or circle board pattern to align the color and depth images. A number of patterns are provided in the downloaded iai_kinect2 software, inside the kinect2_calibration/patterns directory. For a detailed description of how the 3D calibration works, refer to the OpenCV website at http://opencv-python-tutroals.readthedocs.io/en/latest/py_tutorials/py_calib3d/py_calibration/py_calibration.html.

The iai_kinect2 calibration instructions can be found at https://github.com/code-iai/iai_kinect2/tree/master/kinect2_calibration.

We used the chess5x7x0.03 pattern to calibrate our Kinect and printed it on plain 8.5 x 11 inch paper. Be sure to check the dimensions of the squares to assure that they are the correct measurement (3 centimeters in our case). Sometimes, printers may change the size of objects on the page. Next, mount your pattern on a flat, moveable surface, assuring that the pattern is smooth and no distortions will be experienced that will corrupt your sensor calibration.

The Kinect should be mounted on a stationary surface and a tripod works well. The Kinect will be positioned in one location for the entire calibration process. Adjust it to align it with a point straight ahead in an open area, in which you will be moving around the calibration chess pattern. The instructions mention the use of a second tripod for mounting the chess pattern, but we found it easier to move the pattern around by hand (using a steady hand). It is important to obtain clear images of the pattern from both the RGB and IR cameras.

If you wish to judge the effects of the calibration process, use the kinect2_bridge and kinect2_viewer software to view and take the initial screenshots of the registered depth images and point cloud images of your scene. When the calibration process is complete, repeat the screenshots and compare the results.

Calibrating your Kinect

First, you will need to make a directory on your computer to hold all of the calibration data that is generated for this process. To do this, type the following:

```
$ mkdir ~/kinect_cal_data
$ cd ~/kinect_cal_data
```

To start the calibration process, set up your Kinect and run:

```
$ roscore
```

In a second terminal window, start kinect2_bridge but pass the parameter for setting a low number of frames per second. This will reduce the CPU/GPU processing load:

```
$ rosrun kinect2_bridge kinect2_bridge _fps_limit:=2
```

Notice as the software runs, similar output should come onto the screen:

```
[Info] [Freenect2Impl] 9 usb devices connected
[Info] [Freenect2Impl] found valid Kinect v2 @2:3 with serial
501493641942
[Info] [Freenect2Impl] found 1 devices
[ INFO] [Kinect2Bridge::initDevice] Kinect2 devices found:
[ INFO] [Kinect2Bridge::initDevice]   0: 501493641942 (selected)
```

Your data will be different, but note the serial number of your Kinect v2 (ours is `501493641942`). When the waiting for clients to connect, text appears on the screen; type the following command:

```
$ rosrun kinect2_calibration kinect2_calibration <type of pattern> record
color
```

Our `<type of pattern>` is the `chess5x7x0.03` pattern. This command will start the process for calibrating the color camera. Notice the output on the screen:

```
[ INFO] [main] Start settings:
Mode: record
Source: color
Board: chess
Dimensions: 5 x 7
Field size: 0.03
Dist. model: 5 coefficients
Topic color: /kinect2/hd/image_mono
Topic ir: /kinect2/sd/image_ir
Topic depth: /kinect2/sd/image_depth
Path: ./
[ INFO] [main] starting recorder...
[ INFO] [Recorder::startRecord] Controls:
[ESC, q] - Exit
[SPACE, s] - Save current frame
[l] - decrease min and max value for IR value range
[h] - increase min and max value for IR value range
[1] - decrease min value for IR value range
[2] - increase min value for IR value range
[3] - decrease max value for IR value range
[4] - increase max value for IR value range
[ INFO] [Recorder::store] storing frame: 0000
```

As the screen instructions indicate, after you have positioned the pattern board in the image frame, hit the spacebar (or *S*) key on the keyboard to take a picture. Be sure that the cursor is focused on the terminal window. Every time you hit the spacebar, a `.png` and `.yaml` file will be created in the current directory (`~/kinect_cal_data`).

The following screenshot shows a rainbow-colored alignment pattern that overlays the camera image when the pattern is acceptable for calibration. If this pattern does not appear, hitting the spacebar will not record the picture. If the complete pattern is not visible in the scene, the rainbow colors will all turn red because part of the board pattern cannot be observed in the image frame:

Calibration alignment pattern

We recommend that you run the following command in another terminal window:

```
$ rosrun kinect2_viewer kinect2_viewer sd image
```

The image viewer will show the image frame for the combined color/depth image. This frame has smaller dimensions than the RGB camera frame in Full HD, and it is important to keep all your calibration images within this frame. If not, the calibration process will try to shrink the depth data into the center of the full RGB frame and your results will be unusable.

Move the pattern from one side of the image to the other, taking pictures from multiple spots. Hold the board at different angles to the camera (tilting the board) as well as rotating it around its center. The rainbow-colored pattern on the screen will be your clue as to when the image can be captured. It is suggested to take pictures of the pattern at varying distances from the camera. Keep in mind that the Kinect's depth sensor range is from 0.5 to 4.5 meters (20 inches to over 14 feet). In total, a set of 100 or more calibration images is suggested for each calibration run.

When you have taken a sufficient number of images, use the *Esc* key (or *Q*) to exit the program. Execute the following command to compute the intrinsic calibration parameters for the color camera:

```
$ rosrun kinect2_calibration kinect2_calibration chess5x7x0.03 calibrate
color
```

Be sure to substitute your type of pattern in the command. Next, begin the process for calibrating the IR camera by typing in this command:

```
$ rosrun kinect2_calibration kinect2_calibration chess5x7x0.03 record ir
```

Follow the same process that you did with the color camera, taking an additional 100 pictures or more. Then, compute the intrinsic calibration parameters for the IR camera using the following command:

```
$ rosrun kinect2_calibration kinect2_calibration chess5x7x0.03 calibrate
ir
```

Now that the color and IR cameras have been calibrated individually, it is time to record images from both the cameras synchronized:

```
$ rosrun kinect2_calibration kinect2_calibration chess5x7x0.03 record
sync
```

Take an additional 100 or more images. The extrinsic calibration parameters are computed with the following command:

```
$ rosrun kinect2_calibration kinect2_calibration chess5x7x0.03 calibrate
sync
```

The following command calibrates depth measurements:

```
$ rosrun kinect2_calibration kinect2_calibration chess5x7x0.03 calibrate
depth
```

At this point, all of the calibration data has been computed and the data must be saved to the appropriate location for use by the kinect2_bridge software. Recall the serial number of your Kinect that you noted earlier from the kinect2_bridge screen output. Create a directory with this serial number under the kinect2_bridge/data directory:

```
$ roscd kinect2_bridge/data
```

```
$ mkdir <Kinect serial #>
```

Copy the following calibration files from ~/kinect_cal_data to the kinect2_bridge/data/<Kinect serial#> directory you just created:

```
$ cp ~/kinect_cal_data/c*.yaml <Kinect serial#>
```

Your `kinect2_bridge/data/<Kinect serial#>` directory should look similar to the following screenshot:

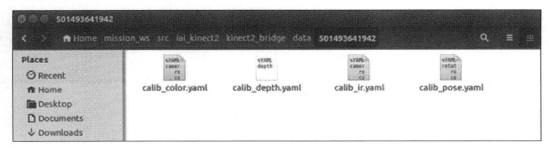

Kinect v2 calibration data files

Running `kinect2_viewer` again should show an alignment of the color and depth images with strong edges at the corners and on the outlines. The `kinect2_bridge` software will automatically check for the Kinect's serial number under the `data` directory and use the calibration data if it exists.

Setting up the mission

For the Kinect, our workstation computer requires us to run Protonect prior to using the `kinect2_bridge` software. If you have trouble launching the `kinect2_bridge` software, use the following command before you begin:

```
$ ./libfreenect2/build/bin/Protonect
```

Verify that Protonect shows color, depth, and IR images and that none of the screens are black. Be aware that Protonect has three optional parameters: `cl` (for OpenCL), `gl` (for OpenGL) or `cpu` (for CPU support). These options can be useful for testing the Kinect v2 operation.

If Protonect has successfully brought up the Kinect image, then press *Ctrl + C* to close this window. The `kinect2_bridge` and `kinect2_viewer` should then work properly until the system is restarted.

Next, we must determine how to identify our robots within the frame of the Kinect image.

Detecting Crazyflie and a target

For our Crazyflie and target location, we have prepared markers to uniquely identify them in our lab environment. For the Crazyflie, we have placed a lightweight green ball on top of its battery and attached it with a sticky mounting tab. For the target, we have placed a pink paper rectangle at the target location. The first step is to find a unique way to identify these markers and find their locations within the Kinect image.

OpenCV offers over 150 color conversion options for processing images. For object tracking, the simplest and recommended method is to convert the **blue-green-red (BGR)** image to **hue-saturation and value (HSV)**. This is an easy and effective method for selecting an object of a desired color. An OpenCV tutorial on object tracking can be found at http://opencv-python-tutroals.readthedocs.io/en/latest/py_tutorials/py_imgproc/py_colorspaces/py_colorspaces.html.

A complete method for object tracking is described in the following sections.

Identifying markers in a color image

The color of these identifiers will be used in our software to pinpoint the location of the quadrotor and the target. First, we must determine the numerical values of the HSV components of their colors. This is done by grabbing an image of the marker with the Kinect and using the **GNU Image Manipulator Program (GIMP)** software on Ubuntu to classify the HSV numbers.

Start by running the `kinect2_bridge` launch file and `kinect2_viewer` in separate terminal windows:

```
$ roslaunch kinect2_bridge kinect2_bridge.launch
$ rosrun kinect2_viewer kinect2_viewer
```

Adjust the Kinect to find an image of your Crazyflie and/or your target on your computer screen. For this exercise, these robots can be in the same view, or you can perform these steps one at a time for each of the markers. Use the *Alt + Print Screen* keys or your favorite screen-capture program to snap a picture of the scene and save it to a file. Click on the Dash tool in the Ubuntu Launcher and type in GIMP to find the GIMP application software.

After starting the GIMP software, open the image and select the following two options from the top menu bar:

- Under the **Tools** options, select **Color Picker** (notice the cursor changes to an eyedropper)
- Under the **Windows** options, select **Toolbox** (or **New Toolbox**)

Move the eyedropper cursor to the center of the identifier (green ball in our case) and click the mouse button. This color will appear in the color rectangle at the bottom of the **Toolbox** window. Click on this colored rectangle and the **Change Foreground Color** window will appear with the color marked with crosshairs in the color image on the left side. On the right side are the hue, saturation, value, red, green, and blue values that correspond to that color. The following screenshot illustrates the results of this process:

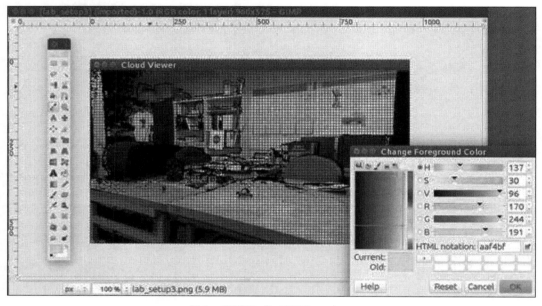

Using GIMP to find HSV numbers

For our green ball, the HSV numbers were H = 137, S = 30, and V = 96, as shown in the previous screenshot. These values apply to the scales for GIMP integer ranges of Hue (0 - 360), Saturation (0 - 100), and Value (0 - 100).

Now we must convert these values to the OpenCV integer ranges of Hue (0 - 179), Saturation (0 - 255), and Value (0 - 255). Therefore, our HSV numbers are computed as follows:

Hue: *137 / 2 ≈ 69*

Saturation: *30 * 255 / 100 ≈ 77*

Value: *96 * 255 / 100 ≈ 245*

Now, to pick range values for the software, we will apply the following rules:

Hue: *use range ± 10*

Saturation: *use range ± 50*

Value: *use range ± 50*

Using these as guidelines, we arrive at the range values for our green ball as follows:

Hue: (59 - 79)

Saturation: (27- 127)

Value: (195- 255)

The HSV numbers for the pink rectangle target were H = 298, S = 28, and V = 96 when the target was directly facing the Kinect. Initially, we chose the following ranges in the code:

Hue: (139 - 159)

Saturation: (21 - 121)

Value: (240 - 255)

We modified these values later as we tested the tracking of these objects in the Kinect image viewer. The Saturation (or whiteness) value ranges from white (0) to full saturated color (100), and the Value (or lightness) ranges from black (0) to the lightest color (100) in GIMP.

Problems with target detection

Tracking the target was especially tricky. As the target was placed in a horizontal position, the light reflecting off the top of the target changed the Saturation and Value components of its HSV. It is extremely important to test the object detection capability from one side of the Kinect image to the other, and for different orientations of the object. Selecting the appropriate range for HSV values is crucial to the success of the mission. For the target, we decreased the lower range of Saturation to improve target detection in our lighting conditions.

Detecting and viewing markers with OpenCV

OpenCV is used to detect these identifiers in the Kinect image, and we use the following code to verify that we have captured the correct identifier for the green ball:

```python
#!/usr/bin/env python
import cv2
import numpy

# read png image and convert the image to HSV
image = cv2.imread("<path>/<png filename>", cv2.IMREAD_COLOR)
hsv = cv2.cvtColor(image, cv2.COLOR_BGR2HSV)

# find green objects in the image
lower_green = numpy.array([68, 42, 182], numpy.uint8)
upper_green = numpy.array([88, 142, 255], numpy.uint8)
mask = cv2.inRange(hsv, lower_green, upper_green)

cv2.imwrite("hsv_mask.png", mask)
```

This code is contained in the `view_mask.py` file. The `kinect2_viewer_green_ball.png` file is provided with the code so that you can duplicate our steps and reproduce a file with the HSV mask of the green ball.

To briefly explain this code, we will examine the lines in relative groupings. First, the packages needed for this code are imported:

```python
#!/usr/bin/env python
import cv2
import numpy
```

The `cv2` package is the OpenCV 3.0 wrapper for Python and provides access to a variety of vision processing functions. The `numpy` package is an extension of Python that handles numerical manipulations for large multidimensional arrays and matrices.

The next section of code handles the reading of the image from a file and processes it for HSV:

```python
image = cv2.imread("<path>/<png filename>", cv2.IMREAD_COLOR)
hsv = cv2.cvtColor(image, cv2.COLOR_BGR2HSV)
```

The first command loads the image from the file using the `cv2.imread` function. The first argument is the image file to be loaded, which can be any image file type. We are using `.png` files. The second argument for `cv2.imread` specifies loading the color image. In OpenCV, the **red-green-blue (RGB)** values are identified in reverse order as BGR. This loaded image is converted from BGR to HSV using the `cv2` function `cvtColor`.

Next, two arrays are created to contain the lower bounds and the upper bounds of the HSV values for the green ball. The values in these arrays were identified and calculated in the previous section, *Identifying markers in a color image*. These arrays are used to find pixels in the image that fit within those bounds:

```
# find green objects in the image
lower_green = numpy.array([68, 42, 182], numpy.uint8)
upper_green = numpy.array([88, 142, 255], numpy.uint8)
mask = cv2.inRange(hsv, lower_green, upper_green)

cv2.imwrite("hsv_mask.png", mask)
```

A numpy array is created with unsigned integer values for the lower bounds of H, S, and V. A second array is created to contain the upper bounds for these elements. The `cv2` function `inRange` compares each pixel of the image to determine whether it falls within these bounds. If it does, a white pixel is placed in the mask image; otherwise, a black pixel is placed in the image. The last command `imwrite` stores the binary image to the `hsv_mask.png` file. The following screenshot shows the resulting HSV mask image of the green ball:

HSV mask image of green ball

This code is implemented in the `detect_crazyflie.py` and `detect_target.py` scripts described in the next sections.

Using Kinect and OpenCV

Using Kinect to locate the position of the Crazyflie provides only a (pixel) location relative to the image frame of the Kinect. Relating this location to the world coordinate frame cannot be accurately accomplished.

Advanced camera systems, such as the VICON motion capture system, provide the object location in world coordinates. In a VICON system, it is possible to establish Crazyflie's position as (0, 0, 0) in *x*, *y*, and *z* and relate the movement in terms of meters. If you have this type of system available, check out Wolfgang Hoenig's ROS Crazyflie code at `http://wiki.ros.org/crazyflie`. The `crazyflie_controller` package provides simple navigation to goal using VICON. The `crazyflie_demo` package contains sample scripts and launch files to perform teleoperation, hovering, and waypoint navigation. The controller within our `crazyflie_autonomous` package was created based on concepts used in Mr. Hoenig's packages.

For our mission, the Python script `detect_crazyflie.py` creates the `crazyflie_detector` node to handle the process of identifying the location of the Crazyflie within the Kinect image frame and the publishing of its location. This node subscribes to three topics published by the `kinect2` node, specifying the `qhd` resolution (960 x 540). The code for subscribing to these topics is as follows:

```
rospy.wait_for_message('/kinect2/qhd/camera_info', CameraInfo)

rospy.Subscriber('/kinect2/qhd/camera_info', CameraInfo, self.camera_data, queue_size=1)
rospy.Subscriber('/kinect2/qhd/image_color_rect', Image, self.image_callback, queue_size=1)
rospy.Subscriber('/kinect2/qhd/image_depth_rect', Image, self.depth_callback, queue_size=1)
```

The `rospy` call to `wait_for_message` will ensure that the `kinect2` node is publishing topics. Then, the `crazyflie_detector` node will subscribe to the three topics: `camera_info`, `image_color_rect`, and `image_depth_rect`. The `/kinect2/qhd/camera_info` topic will contain a `sensor_msgs/CameraInfo` message that is processed by the callback function `camera_data`. The `camera_data` function will extract the camera height and width fields from the `CameraInfo` message and set the parameters on the Parameter Server for `camera_height` and `camera_width`. For the `qhd` resolution, these parameters are 540 and 960, respectively.

The `/kinect2/qhd/image_color_rect` and `/kinect2/qhd/image_depth_rect` topics subscribe to `sensor_msgs/Image` messages. For the rectified color `Image` message, the function `image_callback` is called to handle image processing. The rectified depth `Image` message is processed by the `depth_callback` function. The message queue size is limited to one, so that only the latest `Image` message will be processed.

The `image_callback` function processes the color image similar to the object detection method described in the *Detecting and viewing markers with OpenCV* section. The green objects in the image are detected, and a binary mask image is created. The `cv2.morphologyEx` function is called to first dilate and then erode the image with an 11 x 11 kernel. This process removes the small pixels within the white objects and the surrounding black background. More than one white object may be present in the binary image. The next step is to find all the objects and order them by size. The `cv2` function `findContours` finds all the pixels within the contour objects in the binary image. A hierarchy of nested contours is created. A check is made to assure that there is at least one contour in this hierarchy, then the area of each of the contours is calculated. The largest contour area is selected as the green ball on top of Crazyflie.

Since we know that this object is round, the `cv2` function `minEnclosingCircle` is used to find the object's center and radius. The horizontal center of the object is saved as `cf_u`, and the vertical center is saved as `cf_v`. The object center and radius values are used by the `cv2.circle` function to draw a blue circle outline around the object in the original color `Image` message. This image message is then displayed in a terminal window using the `cv2.imshow` function.

We verified the operation of this code using the following commands:

```
$ roslaunch kinect2_bridge kinect2_bridge.launch
$ python detect_crazyflie.py
```

The resulting image is shown in the following screenshot:

Crazyflie detected

When a `/kinect2/qhd/image_depth_rect` topic arrives, the `depth_callback` function will be called to process this `sensor_msgs/Image` message. For this rectified depth `Image` message, the `cf_u` and `cf_v` values will be used as the pixel coordinates to access the depth value `cf_d`, at the center of the circle. Sometimes, an erroneous value is returned for the depth at this location. If the depth value returned is zero, the last depth value will be reused.

Next, the `update_cf_transform` function is called to publish the tf transform of Crazyflie. The `cf_u`, `cf_v`, and `cf_d` values are passed to this function to be used as the *x*, *y*, and *z* values of Crazyflie's transform. A `tf.TransformBroadcaster` object is created to publish transforms from the `crazyflie_detector` node. The `update_cf_tranform` function uses the `sendTransform` function (from the `tf` package) so that the transform broadcaster can publish a transform for the Crazyflie relative to the Kinect. Details of this transform are described in the next section.

How to track Crazyflie

Using ROS tf transforms to identify the location of the Crazyflie in an image frame is a variation of the concept of ROS tf. Typically, tf transforms relate the coordinate frame of a robot's component to the rest of its system and the environment (world) in which it is operating. The tf transform keeps all the robot's coordinate frames in a tree-like structure that relates them to the world environment. In addition, these coordinate frames are tracked by tf with relation to time. The tf transform provides functions to transform from one coordinate frame to any other frame in the tf structure at a desired point in time. For more information on this implementation of tf, refer to the *Understanding tf* section in *Chapter 6, Wobbling Arms Using Joint Control*.

For our mission, Crazyflie's tf transforms are limited to operations within the 2D image plane of the Kinect's color image, and the third dimension of depth from the Kinect's depth image. Crazyflie's position, with respect to the image's horizontal position *u* and its vertical position *v*, is used to identify its location with respect to the color image frame. Its 3D position can be completed by accessing the depth value from the depth frame for the (*v*, *u*) location. These values are used as the *x*, *y*, *z* of Crazyflie's translation fields for the transform message. The rotation fields are fixed with values to change the orientation of Crazyflie from the Kinect's camera orientation.

For the **Kinect coordinate frame**, the x axis is horizontal from the upper-left corner of the camera image to the right, the y axis is vertical from this same corner downward, and the z axis is from the front face of the camera out to the scene. The Kinect coordinate frame is represented in the following rviz image, using the convention of x (red), y (green), and z (blue). The position of this coordinate frame is at the origin of the Kinect and does not represent the location on the image frame:

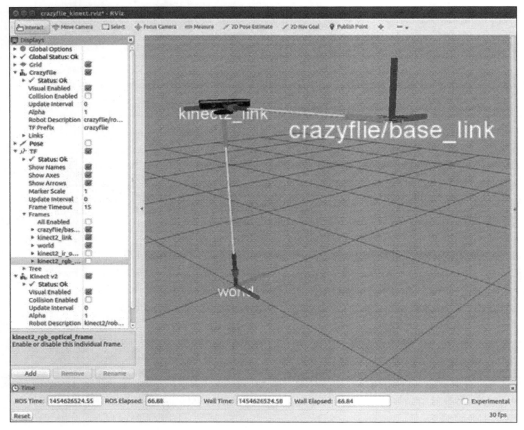

tf coordinate frames in rviz

For Crazyflie, a rotation of this Kinect coordinate frame must be made to adhere to the ROS conventional orientation of x forward, y left, and z up, standardized in REP 103 *Coordinate Frame Conventions*. Therefore, for rotation fields in Crazyflie's tf transform, values are fixed to the set of Euler angles:

- Roll of $-\pi/2$
- Pitch of 0
- Yaw of $-\pi$

These values are used to compute a quaternion with the `tf.transformations.quaternion_from_euler` function. The transform pose is published using the `sendTransform` function (from the `tf` package) as a transform from the `kinect2_ir_optical_frame` to the `crazyflie/baselink`. The `kinect2_ir_optical_frame` is the parent frame of `crazyflie/baselink`. A diagram of the tf frames broadcast for this mission is shown as follows:

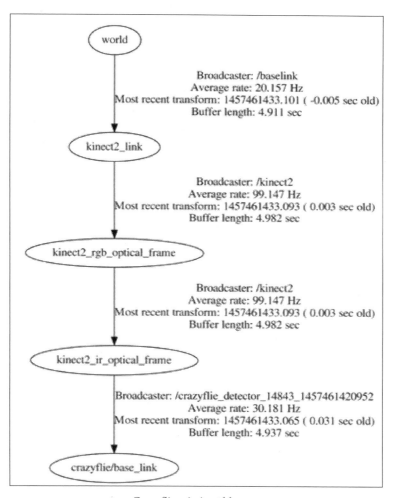

Crazyflie mission tf frames

To implement yaw control of Crazyflie, additional markers could be added to Crazyflie's structure to determine its yaw position around its vertical z axis. We have selected not to implement yaw control at this time, but plan to control Crazyflie in x, y, and z, placing the quadrotor so that its x axis aligns parallel to the Kinect's -x axis. The value for yaw control will be set to `0`.

How to control Crazyflie

As you have seen throughout this book, the `cmd_vel` topic (the `geometry_msgs/Twist` message) is the common control method for ROS robots, whether driving on the ground or flying in the air. For TurtleBot, `mobile_base_commands/velocity` and `cmd_vel_mux/input/navi` are used to move around the base. For Crazyflie, the `crazyflie/cmd_vel` topic is published to control the flight of the quadrotor.

Within the `crazyflie_autonomous` package, the `crazyflie_controller` node (`control_crazyflie.py`) determines the Crazyflie's control state and publishes the `crazyflie/cmd_vel` topic. To launch the `crazyflie_controller` node, the `control_crazyflie.launch` file is used. This launch file also launches the `crazyflie_window` node that observes the Crazyflie and takes action when it flies near the edge of the Kinect image frame. The function of this node is described in the subsequent section, using an observer mode.

Crazyflie control states

The `crazyflie_controller` node has five states of flight control: **idle**, **takeoff**, **hover**, **flight**, and **land**. The private variable `_cf_state` is used to indicate the current control state. Regardless of the control state, the `cmd_vel` topic is published at a rate of 50 hertz (20 milliseconds). This rate is obtained as the frequency parameter from the Parameter Server and can be changed by either adding this parameter and a new value to the `crazyflie_controller` node in the `control_crazyflie.launch` file, or using the `rosparam set` command in the terminal window command line. The main launch file for this mission is `hover_kinectv2.launch`.

With respect to the state of control, the fields for the `cmd_vel` topic (the `geometry_msgs/Twist` message) are assigned linear velocity values of x, y, and z, and the angular velocity values are left at zero. Recall from *Chapter 7*, *Making a Robot Fly*, that the data fields for the Crazyflie `cmd_vel` topic are as follows:

- `linear.x`: The pitch value is from -30 to 30 degrees
- `linear.y`: The roll value is from -30 to 30 degrees
- `linear.z`: The thrust value is from 10,000 to 60,000 (for **pulse-width modulation** (**PWM**) output)
- `angular.z`: This field is not currently used by the `crazyflie_controller` node

The contents of these data fields and the operation of the control states are described in detail throughout the following sections.

Using ROS services to control takeoff and land

The control states of takeoff and land are activated using ROS service calls. Within the crazyflie_controller node, two ROS services are created with callback functions to be invoked by a client when a request for the service is sent. The services for /crazyflie/land and /crazyflie/takeoff are created by the following statements in control_crazyflie.py:

```
s1 = rospy.Service("/crazyflie/land", Empty, self._Land)
s2 = rospy.Service("/crazyflie/takeoff", Empty, self._Takeoff)
```

Note that the /crazyflie namespace has been appended to these services to identify that they are specific for the quadrotor. Land and Takeoff are private callback functions that handle the service requests.

These services are of the type Empty, one of the service types provided by the ROS std_srvs package. The std_srvs package contains common service patterns for signals to a ROS node. The Empty service definition contains no actual data, but is used only to cause the execution of a function.

For the land service, the following function is executed:

```
def _Land(self, req):
    rospy.loginfo("Landing requested!")
    self._cf_state = 'land'
    return ()
```

When the /crazyflie/land service is requested, the loginfo function writes a log message to stdout (the terminal window) and to the /rosout topic. The message also appears in the ~/.ros/log file for the crazyflie_controller node. The next statement changes the Crazyflie control state to land. An Empty service response message is returned to the client node.

The takeoff service is handled by a function similar to _Land. It also writes a log message and changes the Crazyflie control state to takeoff. An Empty service response is sent back to the client node.

Activating takeoff and land

The services of takeoff and land can be activated using the Xbox 360 joystick controller. The `hover_kinectv2.launch` file launches the node for `joystick_controller`, which contains requests for Crazyflie takeoff, land, and emergency. These service requests are activated by pressing the blue (takeoff), green (land), or red (emergency) buttons on the Xbox 360 controller. The emergency service request is handled by the `crazyflie_server` node (`crazyflie_server.cpp` in the `crazyflie/crazyflie_driver` package). The code for the `joystick_controller` node is found in `controller.py` in the `crazyflie/crazyflie_demo` package.

What makes takeoff and land work?

The flight controls for takeoff and land are part of the state-based logic of the iteration function of `control_crazyflie.py`. When `_cf_state` is idle, the linear velocity values of x, y, and z (pitch, roll, and thrust, respectively) are set to `0.0`. The thrust variable is also set to `0.0`. The location of the Crazyflie received as a transform is saved in the `takeoff_position` variable. This `takeoff_position` variable is used during the `takeoff` control state.

When the `_cf_state` control state is takeoff, the `cmd_vel` linear velocity values of x and y are set to `0.0`. The vertical value y of the `takeoff_position` variable (`takeoff_position[1]`) is used to compute an upper takeoff height of 25 pixels in y, above its takeoff y value. When Crazyflie's position in the Kinect's image frame has achieved that height, the `_cf_state` control state will transition to flight. If the value of the `thrust` variable exceeds 50,000, this condition will also transition the `_cf_state` from `takeoff` to `flight`.

During takeoff, the value of the `cmd_vel` linear z velocity (thrust) is incremented by 10,000 multiplied by a delta time `dt` and a fudge factor `ff`. The delta time is computed as the time between the last iteration cycle and the present iteration cycle, which is typically 0.02 seconds (based on 50 hertz). The fudge factor is an easy way to vary the amount of thrust increase applied. When the value of the thrust reaches 36,000, the increments of the additional thrust decrease by approximately one-third to slow the ascent of the Crazyflie.

When the upper takeoff height is achieved, or the thrust is greater than 50,000, the previous error and time values for the PID controllers are reset to zero. The initial integral value for the z PID controller is set to the following:

(current thrust value - 1500) / (ki for the z PID controller)

Success messages are sent to the log file and the `/rosout` topic to indicate takeoff is achieved. Info messages are also sent to log the data being published in the `cmd_vel` messages.

Using PID control for hover and flight

The control states of hover and flight utilize the PID class constructor, attributes, and methods from `pid.py`, and data from `crazyflie2.yaml`. There are three PID objects created to provide proportional, integral, and derivative control for Crazyflie's linear x, y, and z (pitch, roll, and thrust) values. The `crazyflie_controller` node instantiates a separate flight PID controller for X, Y, and Z, as shown in the following statements:

```
from pid import PID      # for PID class, attributes and methods

# object instances of type PID with initial attributes assigned
self.m_pidX = PID(rospy.get_param("~PIDs/X/kp"),
                  rospy.get_param("~PIDs/X/kd"),
                  rospy.get_param("~PIDs/X/ki"),
                  rospy.get_param("~PIDs/X/minOutput"),
                  rospy.get_param("~PIDs/X/maxOutput"),
                  rospy.get_param("~PIDs/X/integratorMin"),
                  rospy.get_param("~PIDs/X/integratorMax"))
self.m_pidY = PID(rospy.get_param("~PIDs/Y/kp"),
                  rospy.get_param("~PIDs/Y/kd"),
                  rospy.get_param("~PIDs/Y/ki"),
                  rospy.get_param("~PIDs/Y/minOutput"),
                  rospy.get_param("~PIDs/Y/maxOutput"),
                  rospy.get_param("~PIDs/Y/integratorMin"),
                  rospy.get_param("~PIDs/Y/integratorMax"))
self.m_pidZ = PID(rospy.get_param("~PIDs/Z/kp"),
                  rospy.get_param("~PIDs/Z/kd"),
                  rospy.get_param("~PIDs/Z/ki"),
                  rospy.get_param("~PIDs/Z/minOutput"),
                  rospy.get_param("~PIDs/Z/maxOutput"),
                  rospy.get_param("~PIDs/Z/integratorMin"),
                  rospy.get_param("~PIDs/Z/integratorMax"))
self.m_pidYaw = PID(rospy.get_param("~PIDs/Yaw/kp"),
                    rospy.get_param("~PIDs/Yaw/kd"),
                    rospy.get_param("~PIDs/Yaw/ki"),
                    rospy.get_param("~PIDs/Yaw/minOutput"),
                    rospy.get_param("~PIDs/Yaw/maxOutput"),
                    rospy.get_param("~PIDs/Yaw/integratorMin"),
                    rospy.get_param("~PIDs/Yaw/integratorMax"))
```

A PID controller is also created for yaw control but is not used at this time. The values of the parameters kp, kd, ki, minOutput, maxOutput, integratorMin, and integratorMax are loaded from the crazyflie2.yaml file as part of the control_crazyflie.launch process. This arrangement of loading the parameters from the YAML file has made it quick and easy to change parameters while testing flight control.

The PID class has several methods to perform operations for the PID controller object instance. A method to reset the controller is provided by the reset method. This method sets the m_integral and m_previousError values to zero and the m_previousTime to the current time. The setIntegral method sets the m_integral value to a value passed to the function. The third method update performs the PID calculations between the current location and the target location, as shown in the following statements:

```
def update (self, value, targetValue):

  time = float(rospy.Time.to_sec(rospy.Time.now()))
  dt = time - self.m_previousTime

  error = targetValue - value
  self.m_integral += error * dt
  self.m_integral = max(min(self.m_integral, self.m_integratorMax),
self.m_integratorMin)

  p = self.m_kp * error
  d = 0
  if dt > 0:
    d = self.m_kd * (error - self.m_previousError)/dt
  i = self.m_ki * self.m_integral

  output = p + d + i

  self.m_previousError = error
  self.m_previousTime = time

  return max(min(output, self.m_maxOutput), self.m_minOutput)
```

Note that rospy.loginfo statements have been removed to enhance clarity.

In the `update` method, the current time in seconds is determined by a call to the `rospy` routines, `Time.now` and `Time_to_sec`. The variable `dt` is set to the number of seconds elapsed between the last call to the controller and the current time. The difference between `value` and `targetValue` is stored as the variable `error`. This error value is multiplied by `m_kp` to obtain the proportional variable `p`. The difference in this error value and the last error value is calculated and divided by the delta time `dt`. This value is multiplied by `m_kd` to find the derivative term `d`. The last term, the integral `i`, is calculated as the value of `m_ki` times `m_integral`. The three terms `p`, `i`, and `d` are added to compute the `output` variable. This variable is compared to the `m_minOutput` and `m_maxOutput` values to determine whether it falls within this range. If it does, then the value of `output` is returned. Otherwise, if the `output` value is larger than `m_maxOutput`, `m_maxOutput` is returned. If it is less than `m_minOutput`, `m_minOutput` is returned.

Using an observer node

Throughout the testing phase for this mission, Crazyflie exhibited some erratic behavior. Due to the modular nature of ROS, we decided to implement an observer node that would keep track of the location of Crazyflie. The `crazyflie_window` node (in `watcher.py`) listens to the tf transforms, publishing the location of Crazyflie. In a loop that runs at 10 times a second, the following statements are executed:

```
if listener.frameExists(camera_frame) and listener.
frameExists(crazyflie_frame):
  t = listener.getLatestCommonTime(camera_frame, crazyflie_frame)
  trans, rotate = listener.lookupTransform(camera_frame,
  crazyflie_frame, t)
```

This code checks the transforms that are buffered by the listener for the existence of a transform between `crazyflie/baselink` and `kinect2_ir_optical_frame`. When this specific transform is found, the data fields for translational and rotational data are extracted into the `trans` and `rotate` variables. The `trans` variable contains the location in the *x*, *y*, and *z* of the Crazyflie. This location is compared to the edge of the Kinect image:

```
if (trans[0] < 100) or (trans[0] > (camera_width - 100)) or (trans[1]
< 20) or (trans[1] > (camera_height - 20)):

  # Crazyflie is going outside the frame
  rospy.loginfo("Crazyflie outside of window %f %f %f",
              trans[0], trans[1], trans[2])
  rospy.loginfo("Landing requested")
```

```
# wait until land service is available, then create handle for it
rospy.wait_for_service('/crazyflie/land')
try:
    _land = rospy.ServiceProxy('/crazyflie/land', Empty)
    _land()
except rospy.ServiceException, e:
    rospy.loginfo("Service call failed: %s", e)
```

If the position of Crazyflie is within 100 pixels of the left or right edge of the image frame, or within 20 pixels of the upper or lower edge, a service request is made for Crazyflie to land. A private local `proxy` `_land` is used to make the service call with an `Empty` service request. The land service request is handled by the `crazyflie_controller` node as described in the previous section, *Using ROS services to control takeoff and land.*

Messages are sent to the log file and the `/rosout` topic to identify the location of the Crazyflie that caused the `crazyflie_window` node to send the service request. These messages are important when determining the events of Crazyflie's flight. The Kinect's depth data `trans[2]` is too erratic to use for this monitoring instance.

The next sections describe how the Crazyflie operates when the `_cf_state` variable is set to `flight`. The Crazyflie will either hover in place or fly to a target depending on whether any `target_pose` messages have been received.

Flying Crazyflie

Now we are finally ready to fly our mission. Making Crazyflie fly to a target requires that the quadrotor be controllable to hover in place. Once this task is successful, the next step is to fly to a stationary target. We will introduce the steps to accomplish these tasks in the next sections.

Hovering in place

The first step to control Crazyflie's flight is the ability to demonstrate control of the quadrotor hovering in one location. To start the process, use the launch command:

```
$ roslaunch crazyflie_autonomous hover_kinectv2.launch
```

Then, turn on Crazyflie and let it run through its startup routine. When it is complete, type the following in a second terminal window:

```
$ roslaunch crazyflie_autonomous control_crazyflie.launch
```

The hover mission can be started by pushing the Takeoff (blue) button on the Xbox 360 controller. After Crazyflie has achieved takeoff, the quadrotor will begin to receive cmd_vel (geometry_msgs/Twist) messages telling it to stay in its same location with respect to the Kinect image frame. Crazyflie will try to maintain this location until the Land (green) button on the controller is pressed. If Crazyflie drifts to the edge of the Kinect image, a land service request will be generated by the crazyflie_window node to (hopefully) safely land the quadrotor.

What makes hover work?

As described in the *What makes takeoff and land work?* section of this chapter, the _cf_state variable changes from takeoff to flight when one of the two takeoff conditions is met. These conditions are that the Crazyflie's position in *y* changes by 25 pixels or that the thrust value is over 50,000. When one of these conditions is met, the initial values for the PID controllers are reset, and the initial integral variable for the z PID controller is set.

The initial check in flight mode is to determine whether the target flag has been set to True. This flag is set by the _update_target_pose function if a target pose (geometry_msgs/PoseStamped) message has been received. If this message has not been received, then the target flag is False and _cf_state is set to hover. The current x, y, and z position of Crazyflie is captured as the three element list hover_position.

As described in the *Using Kinect and OpenCV* section of this chapter, the crazyflie_detector node publishes the Crazyflie's tf transform as its x, y, and z position in the Kinect image frame. The crazyflie_controller node calls the _getTransform function every 20 milliseconds to get this transform and uses it for processing both flight and hover control.

In hover mode, the PID controllers are used to calculate the linear values of x, y, and z for the cmd_vel message. Crazyflie's (x, y, z) position in the Kinect frame is altered so that the direction of control corresponds to Crazyflie's coordinate frame (*x* forward, *y* left, and *z* up). First, the value of Crazyflie's location in its *x* axis needs to increase as it flies to the left in the image. The value in its *z* axis needs to increase as Crazyflie flies up in the image. For Crazyflie's *y* axis, the values need to decrease as it flies closer to the Kinect camera. The following lines of code show the remapping of Crazyflie's positions (current and hover) in the camera frame to Crazyflie's coordinate axes:

```
# camera -x position
self.fly.linear.x = self.m_pidX.update(
                        (self.camera_width - cf_trans[0]),
                        (self.camera_width -
                         self.hover_position[0]))
```

```
# camera -z position
if cf_trans[2] == 0.0:
  self.fly.linear.y = self.m_pidY.update(self.hover_position[2],
                                          self.last_depth)
else:
  self.fly.linear.y = self.m_pidY.update(self.hover_position[2],
                                          cf_trans[2])
  self.last_depth = cf_trans[2]

# camera -y position
self.fly.linear.z = self.m_pidZ.update(
                        (self.camera_height - cf_trans[1]),
                        (self.camera_height -
                         self.hover_position[1]))
```

Note that `rospy.loginfo` statements have been removed to enhance clarity.

The `m_pidX.update` method is called to calculate the correction needed in x to maintain the hover position. The *x* position values for both current and hover are subtracted from the camera image width to achieve the correct difference. The value returned is used as the `cmd_vel linear.x` (pitch) control.

The camera's z position (depth) maps to the *y* axis control for Crazyflie. Sometimes, Kinect publishes bad depth values for Crazyflie's current position. For this case, the z (depth) value is checked for a zero value. If a zero value is found, the last good depth value is used. The `m_pidY.update` method is called to handle these z (depth) values, and the resulting value is assigned to the `cmd_vel linear.y` (roll) control.

The Kinect y position corresponds to the *z* axis control for Crazyflie. The camera height value is used to make the current location and the hover location values increase as Crazyflie moves closer to the top of the image frame. The `m_pidZ.update` method is called to process the y values and provides the resulting `cmd_vel linear.z` (thrust) control.

Now we will look at how the Crazyflie is automatically controlled as it flies to a target.

Flying to a stationary target

Each step in this mission builds on the previous step. To get Crazyflie to fly to a particular location, a separate node was created and named `target_detector` to handle the operation of locating the target and publishing its location. The code for this node is contained in the `detect_target.py` script in the `crazyflie_autonomous` package. To perform this phase of the mission, begin by typing the following launch command:

```
$ roslaunch crazyflie_autonomous hover_kinectv2.launch
```

Then turn on Crazyflie and let it run through its startup routine. When it is complete, start the `crazyflie_controller` node by typing the following into a second terminal window:

```
$ roslaunch crazyflie_autonomous control_crazyflie.launch
```

Then, in a third window, execute the following command to start the `target_detector` node:

```
$ rosrun crazyflie_autonomous detect_target.py
```

The `target_detector` node will begin to transmit messages containing the location of the target marker with respect to the Kinect image frame.

Begin the mission by pushing the Takeoff button on the joystick controller. After Crazyflie has achieved takeoff, the quadrotor will begin to receive `cmd_vel` (`geometry_msgs/Twist`) messages to fly towards the target marker. Since the target is stationary, the location message is only published at 1 hertz. The quadrotor will hover above the target until the Land button on the joystick controller is pressed.

The following image shows our mission setup. The Crazyflie is positioned on the table with a blue circle around its ball marker, and the pink target (on top of TurtleBot in the lower left corner of the screenshot) has a red rectangle around it:

Crazyflie and target positions located

Using the software described in this chapter, Crazyflie was able to take off from a position, hover, and then fly and land at a second position identified by a target marker.

The next section elaborates on the target detection method.

What makes target detection work?

The `target_detector` node works similar to the `crazyflie_detector` node. The node subscribes to the `Image` messages from the Kinect specifying the `qhd` quality. Images of both `image_color_rect` and `image_depth_rect` are requested. When a color image (`image_color_rect`) is received, the callback function `image_callback` will use the same object detection techniques described for the Crazyflie to find the target within the Kinect color image frame. The u and v pixel coordinates of the center of the target are saved by this function. These pixel coordinates are used by the callback function `depth_callback` for the depth image (`image_depth_rect`) to access the depth value at that location.

These values of u, v, and depth are used as x, y, and z respectively by the `update_target_pose` function. This function assigns these values to a `PoseStamped` message and publishes the message.

When `_cf_state` changes to flight from takeoff, the target flag is checked to determine whether a target `PoseStamped` message has been received. If the target flag is true, the target message has been received and `_cf_state` will stay in flight mode. The x, y, and z PID controllers are used to calculate the control values for the `cmd_vel` message. Similar to the processing described for hover, the Crazyflie's location in the Kinect image frame must be changed to correspond to the direction of control for the Crazyflie's coordinate frame. The previous section *What makes hover work?* describes this remapping of Crazyflie's position in the camera frame to its coordinate axes. The following lines of code show this remapping:

```
# camera -x position
self.fly.linear.x = self.m_pidX.update(
                        (self.camera_width - cf_trans[0]),
                        (self.camera_width -
                         self.target_position.pose.position.x))

# camera -z position
self.fly.linear.y = self.m_pidY.update(cf_trans[2],
                        self.target_position.pose.position.z)

# camera -y position
self.fly.linear.z = self.m_pidZ.update(
                        (self.camera_height - cf_trans[1]),
                        (self.camera_height -
                         self.target_position.pose.position.y + 25))
```

The `update` methods of the `m_pidX`, `m_pidY`, and `m_pidZ` object instances are used to obtain the values for the `cmd_vel` message, as explained in the previous section. The difference is the hover values have been replaced by the `PoseStamped` position values of the target coordinates.

Learned lessons

This chapter would not be complete without documenting a few of the lessons we have learned along the way and would like to pass on to you. These are as follows:

- **Weight is important**: Even for a 27 gram quadrotor, the position of the battery, the weight, and the position of a lightweight ball make a big difference to the pitch and roll control of the Crazyflie.

- **PID parameters are hard to select**: Testing and changing parameters for the PID control of a quadrotor is a never-ending cycle. If you can get the weight and balance problem mentioned previously fixed, you have a chance at establishing more stable PID control parameters.

- **Don't fly in a cluttered environment**: Sometimes problems are created because the camera detects erroneous things in the environment, and this fluctuation in data can wreak havoc on your mission.

Logging messages with rosout and rospy

The use of logging messages was critical to the development of this mission. ROS provides a number of ways to gain insight into the output of nodes through publishing information and debugging messages to `rosout`. These messages can be viewed while processes are active with `rqt_console` or via `stdout` (a terminal window). Messages can also be examined afterwards through log files written for each ROS node under the `~/.ros` directory.

There are several levels of logging messages that can be written to `rosout`. These levels include the following:

- `DEBUG`: For information needed when the system is not working, but should not be seen when the system is working correctly
- `INFO`: For information useful to the user
- `WARN`: To caution the user regarding less than optimal results
- `ERROR`: To warn the user of a serious condition
- `FATAL`: To warn the user of an unrecoverable condition

The use of `rospy.loginfo` and `rospy.debug` messages have been scattered throughout the code developed for this mission. We encourage the use of these logging methods as you adapt this software for your purposes.

Now, we wrap up this adventure!

Summary

The aim of this chapter was to stretch your knowledge of ROS by implementing an advanced practical experience to identify and highlight some of the ROS advantages. A ROS system of nodes was created to visualize the environment in which a Crazyflie quadrotor was seen and controlled. The Kinect for Windows v2 depth camera was used to visualize this environment, and ROS nodes handled the detection of markers on the Crazyflie and the target. The location of the Crazyflie was identified in Cartesian coordinates (x, y, z), with the x and y values referring to the quadrotor's position in the image frame and z referring to its distance from the camera. These coordinates were converted into a tf transform and published. The target location was published in a message by a separate ROS node.

The advantage of ROS layers of tf and message passing leaves lower-level details to be handled by another dedicated node. The tf transform for the Crazyflie was used by a controller node to apply PID control to Crazyflie's flight. This controller node implemented a state machine to control the Crazyflie based on its state of flight. These states included idle, takeoff, hover, flight, and land. PID controllers were implemented to determine the control command based on the position errors for hover and flight to the target. Crazyflie control commands included pitch, roll, and thrust components to accomplish the feat of hovering or navigating the quadrotor accurately to a target location.

The next chapter, *Chapter 10, Controlling Baxter with MATLAB©*, will introduce the MATLAB Robotics System Toolbox. The Robotics System Toolbox enables MATLAB to communicate with ROS robots giving the user the advantage of MATLAB tools for image processing, path planning, motor control and more. Baxter will be added to MATLAB and controlled with ROS commands through the Robotics System Toolbox.

10
Controlling Baxter with MATLAB©

In *Chapter 6, Wobbling Robot Arms Using Joint Control*, Baxter the two-armed robot was described. The purpose of this final chapter is to spark your imagination by presenting control of Baxter using the MathWorks© MATLAB **Robotics System Toolbox**. The MathWorks corporation produces the popular MATLAB software that is widely used in industry and academia. In addition to the MATLAB software for mathematical operations and visualization, modules called **add-ons** can be added to the software.

The Robotics System Toolbox add-on considered in this chapter allows us to use MATLAB scripts using ROS commands to control robots. For users of MATLAB, this capability opens up new possibilities to design and implement sophisticated robotic programs for applications.

In this chapter, we will introduce the following:

- Installing the MATLAB Robotics System Toolbox
- Using MATLAB and ROS with the Robotics System Toolbox
- Controlling Baxter with the Robotics System Toolbox

References for MATLAB software and the Robotics System Toolbox can be found at the following websites:

```
https://www.mathworks.com/
```

```
https://www.mathworks.com/products/robotics.html
```

Installing the MATLAB Robotics System Toolbox

Versions of MATLAB and its add-on toolboxes are updated as often as twice a year. For example, the version for our Linux operating systems is using MATLAB R2017b and version 1.5 of the Robotics System Toolbox. To add the toolbox, visit the following website:

```
https://www.mathworks.com/help/robotics/ug/install-robotics-system-
toolbox-support-packages.html?s_tid=srchtitle
```

After MATLAB is installed and running, do the following to load the Robotics System Toolbox:

- Go the **Home** tab of MATLAB and the **Environment** section
- Click **Add-Ons** on the menu and choose **Get Add-Ons** from the dropdown menu

There appears a screen with a number of possible add-ons including the Robotics System Toolbox. If you have paid for the toolbox, simply choose it and download it.

MATLAB and the toolboxes are not open source. They must be purchased from the MathWorks corporation. In some cases, trial versions or reduced price student versions of the software are available.

Check the MATLAB and Robotics System Toolbox versions

In the MATLAB Command window, type the following command:

```
>> ver
```

Then, check from the output the version of MATLAB that is present and the toolboxes that are installed.

View the Robotics System Toolbox commands for ROS

In the MATLAB Command window, type the following command:

```
>> help robotics
```

This allows you to see the version of the toolbox and a list of the ROS commands and other commands useful for robotics.

Clicking on **View Examples** in the Command window brings up a window showing the Robotics System Toolbox examples, including several using a real TurtleBot and TurtleBot in simulation using Gazebo.

For a shortened version with just ROS commands, type the following in the command window:

```
>> help robotics.ROS
```

Using MATLAB Robotics System Toolbox and Baxter Simulator

In these next sections, we will explore using MATLAB to publish and subscribe to the Baxter Simulator and control some primary functions of his arms and grippers.

Installing Baxter messages in MATLAB

Baxter has a unique set of ROS messages that are used to communicate with a real Baxter and Baxter Simulator in Gazebo. MATLAB requires that these custom Baxter message and service definitions be processed into ROS custom messages understood by MATLAB.

Locate the ROS packages for Baxter on your computer. If you followed the installation instructions in *Chapter 6*, *Wobbling Robot Arms Using Joint Control*, these packages will be located in your Baxter workspace, `~/baxter_ws`.

In the MATLAB command window, type the following command:

```
>> rosgenmsg('~/baxter_ws/src/baxter_common')
```

This is the location of Baxter's message files. If your Baxter workspace is in another location, use the absolute path name to the `baxter_common` package.

For our computer, Baxter's packages were placed with the system files at `/opt/baxter_ws/src/baxter_common`. Be aware that the following screen text and screenshots reflect this location instead of `~/baxter_ws/src/baxter_common`.

You may see a warning message like the one following, but the process should still be able to build the MATLAB message files.

```
Warning: The folder /opt/baxter_ws/src/baxter_common/.git does not
contain a valid ROS package, because the 'package.xml' file is missing.
Create the 'package.xml' file in this folder.
```

The following message should appear on the screen to show that all of Baxter's packages have been searched for message files:

```
Building custom message files for the following packages:

baxter_common

baxter_core_msgs

baxter_description

baxter_maintenance_msgs

rethink_ee_description
```

After additional screen output, the following instructions will appear:

```
To use the custom messages, follow these steps:
1. Edit javaclasspath.txt, add the following file locations as new lines,
and save the file:

/opt/baxter_ws/src/baxter_common/matlab_gen/jar/baxter_common-1.2.0.jar

/opt/baxter_ws/src/baxter_common/matlab_gen/jar/baxter_core_msgs-
1.2.0.jar

/opt/baxter_ws/src/baxter_common/matlab_gen/jar/baxter_description-
1.2.0.jar

/opt/baxter_ws/src/baxter_common/matlab_gen/jar/baxter_maintenance_msgs-
1.2.0.jar

/opt/baxter_ws/src/baxter_common/matlab_gen/jar/rethink_ee_description-
1.2.0.jar

2. Add the custom message folder to the MATLAB path by executing:

addpath('/opt/baxter_ws/src/baxter_common/matlab_gen/msggen')

savepath

3. Restart MATLAB and verify that you can use the custom messages.

Type rosmsg list and ensure that the output contains the generated custom
message types.
```

To follow these instructions, click on the link in the screen instructions preceding, on the word **javaclasspath.txt**. Cut and paste the five /opt/baxter_ws/src/baxter_common... lines from instruction 1 to the javaclasspath.txt file but add the <before> tag on the first line. The <before> token at the front of the JAR file will tell MATLAB to use this file, instead on any built-in messages. Our javaclasspath.txt is shown in the following screenshot. Be sure your file contains the absolute path names to your .jar files:

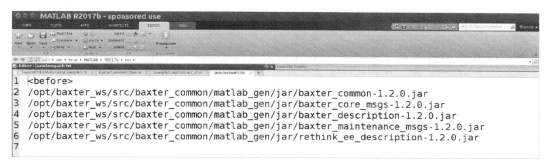

Contents of jarclasspath.txt file

As described in instruction 2, cut and paste the addpath and savepath commands into MATLAB's command window. After these commands have executed, restart MATLAB and these new ROS Baxter messages should be available in MATLAB. Type the command rosmsg list to verify that Baxter's messages have been added to the entire list of ROS messages in MATLAB.

Running Baxter Simulator and MATLAB

To start Baxter Simulator, open a terminal window and go to the baxter_ws workspace; then, run the Baxter shell script with the sim parameter specified:

```
$ cd ~/baxter_ws
$ ./baxter.sh sim
```

> **Important**:
>
> Check the ROS environment variables with the following command:
>
> `$ env | grep ROS`
>
> Within the output screen text, look for the following result:
>
> `ROS_MASTER_URI=http://localhost:11311`
>
> `ROS_IP= <your workstation's IP address>`
>
> Alternatively, it may show the following output:
>
> `ROS_HOSTNAME=<your workstation's hostname>or "localhost"`
>
> The `ROS_HOSTNAME` field need not be present.
>
> If the `ROS_IP` or `ROS_HOSTNAME` environment variable does not match the IP address of your workstation, type `exit` to stop communication with the simulated Baxter. Then, edit the `baxter.sh` script to change the `your_ip` variable (near line 26) to the current IP address of your workstation or change the `your_hostname` variable (near line 28) to `localhost`. Save and exit the `baxter.sh` script.
>
> To continue, repeat the preceding steps for a final check.

Next, call the `roslaunch` command to start the simulation:

`$ roslaunch baxter_gazebo baxter_world.launch`

These are the same commands used in *Chapter 6, Wobbling Robot Arms Using Joint Control*. You should see Baxter appear on the Gazebo screen with its **BaxterIO** window open to show the navigator buttons and cuff buttons.

Now, MATLAB should be started from the icon or command line. After it is up and running you should have screens similar to the following screenshot:

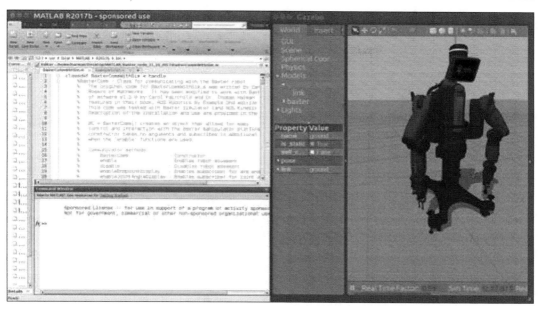

MATLAB and Baxter Simulator running

All of the code for *Chapter 10, Controlling Baxter with MATLAB©*, is available online at the Packt Publishing website at http://www.PacktPub.com, or from GitHub at https://github.com/FairchildC/ROS-Robotics-By-Example-2nd-Edition. Download the .m files from the Chapter10_code to a location on your computer.

These MATLAB .m files were originally written by Carlos Santacruz-Rosero of MathWorks. Carlos developed the MATLAB classdef of BaxterCommWithSim to have Baxter to play checkers with a human opponent (2014). The code has been modified to work with Baxter's latest version of software v1.2.0 by this book's authors for use in this chapter.

After you have downloaded the code to your computer, locate the .m files for the Chapter10_code. These files include:

- BaxterCommWithSim.m
- ExampleScript.m
- armUpdateTimerForRobot.m
- armUpdateTimerForSim.m

Add the path to these files using the **Set Path** menu option on the MATLAB **HOME** menu bar. Now you are ready to start communicating with and moving Baxter.

Troubleshooting tip

When running the `BaxterCommWithSim` functions in MATLAB, infrequently errors may appear on the screen. At this point, it is best to shutdown both MALAB and Gazebo and restart from the instructions above in *Running Baxter Simulator and MATLAB*.

Making Baxter move

The `ExampleScript.m` file can be used as an example of the functions possible with the `BaxterCommWithSim` class as defined in the `BaxterCommWithSim.m` file. These functions are explained in the order they appear in `ExampleScrip.m`:

```
rosshutdown;
```

The `rosshutdown` command is issued as the first command in the script to assure that MATLAB is disconnected from any ROS network and that the global node and the ROS Master are not running.

```
rosinit;
```

The `rosinit` command starts the global ROS node and connects to the ROS Master running on `localhost` and port `11311`. This communication will be with the ROS Master started by Baxter Simulator on Gazebo, as it should already be up and running.

```
bc = BaxterCommWithSim(true);
```

This command instantiates a class for communicating with the Baxter robot in the Gazebo simulation. The `BaxterCommWithSim` class provides data structures and methods to support enabling Baxter and moving Baxter's head, arms and grippers. The object `bc` is created as an instance of `BaxterCommWithSim` to allow the use of these data structures and methods.

```
enable(bc);
```

The `enable` command enables the Baxter robot to move. The robot must be put in an enabled state before any movement commands will move Baxter's joints.

```
handles.bc = bc;
timer1 = timer('TimerFcn',{@armUpdateTimerForSim,handles},'Period',0.1,
'ExecutionMode','fixedSpacing');
start(timer1);
```

These three commands start a timer to periodically send Baxter's joint commands. The timer object `timer1` is created and specifies a callback the function `armUpdateTimerForSim` with a handle to the `bc` object. This `armUpdateTimeForSim` function calls the function `updateArms` passing the handle to the `bc` object indicating that both arms should be updated. The `updateArms` function will publish `ArmCmdLeftMsg` and `ArmCmdRightMsg` messages to set the positions of each of the joints on both of Baxter's left and right arms. The publication of these messages is performed periodically at 10 Hz.

In the following commands, the commands to control the arms and grippers have a value that is passed as an argument that indicates whether the left, right, or both arm(s) or gripper(s) should be activated. These values correspond to the selections:

- `1` = left
- `2` = right
- `3` = both

```
untuck(bc, 3);
```

This `untuck` command sets the fields in the `ArmCmdLeftMsg` and `ArmCmdRightMsg` messages specifying the arm joint positions for Baxter's untuck position.

```
calibrateGrip(bc, 3);
```

This `calibrateGrip` command calibrates both of Baxter's grippers. The grippers must be calibrated before use.

```
grip(bc, 2);
```

This `grip` command closes Baxter's right (2) gripper. The `GripRightMsg` message is set with the position `0.0` which is the gripper closed position.

```
release(bc, 2);
```

This `release` command opens Baxter's right (2) gripper. The `GripRightMsg` message is set with the position 100.0 which is the gripper open position.

```
panHead(bc, 1.0);
panHead(bc, 0.0, 0.2);
```

These `panHead` commands are used to move Baxter's head to a set angular position. The first command moves the head to a `1.0` radian (57 degrees) position to Baxter's left side. The second command moves the head to the `0.0` radian position which is straight ahead facing forward. The second argument in this command sets the speed to `0.2` which is slow. The speed setting is a percentage that ranges from `0.0` to `1.0`.

```
pose_Y(bc);
```

The `pose_Y` command is an example of a function that moves Baxter's arms to a specific pose. This function sets each of the joint positions in both the right and left arms to create a pose for Baxter where his arms form the letter Y. The following screenshot shows Baxter in a Y pose:

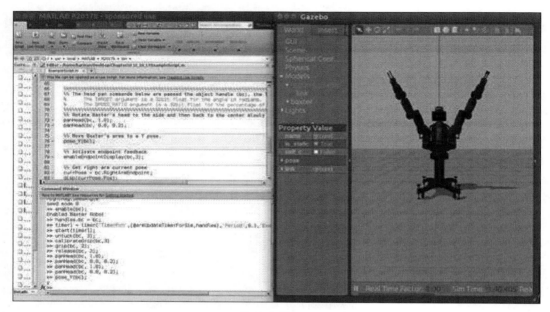

Baxter's Y pose

```
enableEndpointDisplay(bc,3);
```

The `enableEndpointDisplay` command enables the display of endpoint information for both (3) of Baxter's arms.

```
currPose = bc.RightArmEndpoint;
```

```
disp(currPose.Pos);
```

```
disp(currPose.Orientation);
```

The variable `currPose` is set to the current `endpoint_state` information of Baxter's right arm. The `disp` function is called to print the information on the endpoint position and orientation to the screen as shown in the following screenshot:

```
Command Window
New to MATLAB? See resources for Getting Started.                                    ×
  >> enableEndpointDisplay(bc,3);
  >> disp(currPose.Pos);
     ROS Point message with properties:

        MessageType: 'geometry_msgs/Point'
                  X: 0.5901
                  Y: -0.7851
                  Z: 1.3047

     Use showdetails to show the contents of the message

  >> disp(currPose.Orientation);
     ROS Quaternion message with properties:

        MessageType: 'geometry_msgs/Quaternion'
                  X: 0.1078
                  Y: 0.2602
                  Z: -0.3672
                  W: 0.8865

     Use showdetails to show the contents of the message
fx >>
```

Display of Baxter's endpoint position and orientation

```
untuck(bc, 3);
```

The `untuck` command resets both (3) of Baxter's arms into the untuck position.

```
tuck(bc, 3);
```

The `tuck` command sets both (3) of Baxter's arms to the tuck configuration that is used for storing Baxter.

```
disable(bc);
```

The `disable` command disables Baxter's movement. No movement commands will move Baxter's joints until an `enable` command is issued.

```
stop(timer1);
```
```
delete(timer1);
```

The `stop` command will stop the `timer1` timer from incrementing and the `delete` command will delete `timer1`.

```
rosshutdown;
```

The `rosshutdown` command shuts down the global node and the ROS Master, if it is running. MATLAB will no longer be connected to the Baxter Simulator in Gazebo.

Summary

In this chapter, we introduced MATLAB and the Robotics System Toolbox and described how to install the toolbox. The toolbox connects MATLAB software and the Robot Operating System.

Baxter the robot simulator, introduced in *Chapter 6, Wobbling Robot Arms Using Joint Control*, was used with MATLAB to control the simulated Baxter in Gazebo. Before the simulator could connect with Baxter, it was necessary to install a unique set of ROS messages used to communicate with Baxter as described in the section *Installing Baxter messages in MATLAB*.

Once the messages are installed, Baxter's limbs can be moved with the Robotics System Toolbox commands and the .m files listed in the section *Running Baxter Simulator and MATLAB*. These files are found on the book's website.

For more information about the Robotics System Toolbox, see the excellent webinar *Developing Robotics Applications with MATLAB, Simulink, and Robotics System Toolbox* by *Carlos Santacruz-Rosero* of MathWorks at the website:

```
https://www.mathworks.com/videos/developing-robotics-applications-
with-matlab-simulink-and-robotics-system-toolbox-108696.html?elqsid=1
510619981837&potential_use=Education
```

Now, it is time to consider other aspects of ROS that will extend your learning to the more advanced features that ROS provides. There are a number of additional books and web resources available on ROS. ROS has an extensive community of users that develop, use, and support the open source software that we all access. We hope that you enjoy becoming a part of this community. We have enjoyed providing you with a glimpse into some of the many aspects and advantages of ROS.

Index

Symbols

3D sensors
  ASUS 149-151, 159, 160
  camera software structure 161
  comparison 147
  Hitachi-LG LDS 157, 158
  Intel RealSense 153-156, 160
  Kinect 159
  Microsoft Kinect 147, 148
  obstacle avoidance drawbacks 158
  PrimeSense 159, 160
  PrimeSense Carmine 152
  reference 147
  software, installing 158
  terms, defining 161
  testing, in standalone mode 162
3D vision systems 146

A

adaptive monte carlo localization (amcl) 146
add-ons 433
Android 366
Android packages
  references 371
Ant 370
application programming interface (API) 241
application-specific integrated circuit (ASIC) 153
Arduino
  references 372
Arduino applications, using rosserial
  references 386

arm control modes, Baxter
  joint position control 247
  joint torque control 248
  joint velocity control 248
  raw joint position control 248
  reference 282
arm sensors, Baxter
  references 250
articulated robot arm
  controlling, in Gazebo 220
  controlling, with ROS command line 229-231
  controlling, with rqt 232-234
  controls, adding to Xacro 225
  fixing 222, 223
  rqt, exploring 234
  viewing, in Gazebo 223, 224
articulated robot arm URDF
  building, with Xacro 203
  namespace, specifying 203
  Xacro property tag, using 204, 207
ASUS 149, 151, 159

B

banking 314
base coordinate system 246
Baxter
  about 238, 240
  arm sensors 249
  Baxter arm 243, 244
  Baxter Simulator 242
  bend joints 244, 245
  controlling 294
  control modes, for arm 247
  coordinate frame 246, 247

pose 273
PrimeSense 159
PrimeSense Carmine 152
Printed Circuit Board (PCB) 342
proportional-integral-derivative (pid) 227
PS3 joystick controller
  reference 268
pulse-width modulation (PWM) 345
pulse-width modulation (PWM) output 420
puppet response, Baxter
  reference 297
Python client (PC) 336
Python script
  used, for navigating waypoints
    with map 186
  writing, to control TurtleBot 2 101, 102

Q

quadrotors
  about 312
  bluetooth 317
  characteristics 313
  communications 317
  components 316
  flight, precautions 320
  flight, preparation 319
  flying 314-316
  GPS 317
  pitch, defining 313, 314
  pre-flight checklist 320
  Radio Frequency (RF) 318
  references 313, 317, 319
  roll, defining 313, 314
  rules and regulations 321
  sensors, adding 317
  testing 319
  Wi-Fi 317
  yaw, defining 313, 314
quadrotor sensors
  accelerometer 318
  altimeter 318
  barometer 318
  condition sensors 318
  gyroscope 318
  inertial measurement unit (IMU) 318
quaternion 85

R

Radio Frequency (RF) 318
radio signal strength indicator (RSSI) 343
range data 384
Raspberry Pi
  ROS, installing 387
  reference 388
  reference, for loading ROS Kinetic 387
  using 387
Raspbian 387
red, green, and blue (rgb) color
  about 25
  reference link 25
Registered DepthCloud 161
Registered PointCloud 161
remote computer
  network addresses 91
  network connection, troubleshooting 94
  networking 90, 135, 136
  network setup 92, 136
  networks types 90
  TurtleBot 2 system, testing 94, 95
REP
  about 103
  reference 247
Rethink Robotics
  references 241
robot chassis
  creating 43, 44
Robotics System Toolbox
  about 433
  commands, viewing for ROS 435
  installing 434
  reference 434
  using 435
  versions, checking 434
robot model
  moving 73, 74
  tweaking 72
Robot Operating System (ROS)
  about 1
  benefits 2
  controlling 3
  environment, setup 8
  functions 2
  installing 5

76663727R00270

Made in the USA
San Bernardino, CA
14 May 2018